# Institutional Origins of Isla

Muslim countries experience wide variation in levels of Islamist political mobilization, including such political activities as protest, voting, and violence. *Institutional Origins of Islamist Political Mobilization* provides a theory of the institutional origins of Islamist politics, focusing on the development of religious common knowledge, religious entrepreneurship, and coordinating focal points as critical to the success of Islamist activism. Examining Islamist politics in more than fifty countries over four decades, the book illustrates that Islamist political activism varies a great deal, appearing in specific types of institutional contexts. Detailed case studies of Turkey, Algeria, and Senegal demonstrate how diverse contexts yield different types of Islamist politics across the Muslim world.

QUINN MECHAM is Assistant Professor of Political Science at Brigham Young University. His research focuses on political Islam, identity politics, civil conflict, electoral behavior, and democratic development. He is co-editor (with Julie Chernov Hwang) of *Islamist Parties and the Normalization of Muslim Politics* (2014) and is the author of numerous scholarly articles focusing on topics including opposition in authoritarian regimes, Islamist electoral behaviour, and protest movements. He has taught at Middlebury College and George Washington University. He was an Academy Scholar at Harvard University and served as Franklin Fellow on the policy planning staff of the U.S. Department of State.

# Institutional Origins of Islamist Political Mobilization

QUINN MECHAM
*Brigham Young University*

CAMBRIDGE
UNIVERSITY PRESS

CAMBRIDGE
UNIVERSITY PRESS

One Liberty Plaza, 20th Floor, New York NY 10006, USA

Cambridge University Press is part of the University of Cambridge.

It furthers the University's mission by disseminating knowledge in the pursuit of education, learning and research at the highest international levels of excellence.

www.cambridge.org
Information on this title: www.cambridge.org/9781107041912



First published 2017

Printed in the United Kingdom by Clays, St Ives plc

*A catalog record for this publication is available from the British Library*

*Library of Congress Cataloging-in-Publication Data*
NAMES: Mecham, Quinn, author.
TITLE: Institutional origins of Islamist political mobilization / Quinn Mecham.
DESCRIPTION: New York, NY : Cambridge University Press, 2017.
IDENTIFIERS: LCCN 2016042163| ISBN 9781107041912 (hardback) | ISBN 9781107615106 (paperback)
SUBJECTS: LCSH: Political participation–Islamic countries. | Islam and politics–Islamic countries. | Islamic countries–Politics and government.
CLASSIFICATION: LCC JQ1852.A91 M43 2017 | DDC 323/.042091767–dc23
LC record available at https://lccn.loc.gov/2016042163

ISBN 978-1-107-04191-2 Hardback
ISBN 978-1-107-61510-6 Paperback

# Contents

# Figures

# Tables

# Acknowledgments

A great number of people have contributed their time and ideas to this project, far more than I can name individually. They include scholars and mentors such as David Abernethy, Larry Diamond, David Laitin, Jim Fearon, Doug McAdam, Abdulkader Sinno, David Patel, Eva Bellin, Jorge Dominguez, and many, many others. I am grateful to a number of great research assistants over the years, including but not limited to Ted Ellsworth, James Fallon, Abe Katz, Ronan McGee, Toral Patel, Will Van Heuvelen, Justin Curtis, Emily Schild, Joshua Balleck, and Nick Hafen. Many organizations provided advice, opportunities, and sometimes habitat that made it possible for me to complete the research for this study, and to them I owe a great deal of thanks. They include the Center for International Security and Cooperation at Stanford University; the Harvard Academy for International and Area Studies; the U.S. Fulbright Commission in Ankara, Turkey; the West African Research Center in Dakar, Senegal; Bilkent University in Ankara, Turkey; the Turkish Economic and Social Studies Foundation (TESEV); the Institut du Monde Arabe in Paris, France; the Institute for Middle East Studies at George Washington University; Middlebury College; and Brigham Young University. Most of all, I am grateful to my parents for their inspiration and support, and to my wife Maren, for sharing in the process, travels, blunders, and all.

## Abbreviations

| | |
|---|---|
| AIS | Armé Islamique du Salut, Algeria |
| AKP/PJD | Adalet ve Kalkınma Partisi (Justice and Development Party), Turkey |
| AMUPI | Association Malienne pour l'Unité et le Progrès de l'Islam, Mali |
| ANAP | Motherland Party, Turkey |
| APR | Alliance for the Republic, Senegal |
| BDS | Bloc Démocratique Sénégalais, Senegal |
| CERID | Centre d'Etudes et de Recherches "Islam et Développement," Senegal |
| CHP | Cumhuriyet Halk Partisi (Republican People's Party), Turkey |
| CIRCOFS | Comité Islamique pour la Reforme du Code de la Famille au Sénégal, Senegal |
| DP | Demokrat Partisi (Democratic Party), Turkey |
| DYP | True Path, Turkey |
| FAIS | Fédération des Associations Islamiques au Sénégal |
| FFS | Front des Forces Socialistes, Algeria |
| FIS | Front Islamique du Salut, Algeria |
| FJP | Freedom and Justice Party, Egypt |
| FLN | Front de Libération Nationale, Algeria |
| FSD | Front pour le Socialisme at la Démocratie – Sewe Sa Dek (Save your Country), Senegal |
| GIA | Groupes Islamique Armée, Algeria |
| GSPC | Groupe Salafiste pour la Prédication et le Combat, Algeria |
| HADEP | Kurdish People's Democratic Party. Turkey |
| HAMAS | Islamic Resistance Movement, Palestine |
| IBDA-C | Islamic Front of Fighters of the Great East, Turkey |
| MIA | Mouvement Islamique d'Algérie, Algeria |

| | |
|---|---|
| MIA | Movement Islamique Armée, Algeria |
| MHP | Milliyetçi Hareket Partisi (National Action Party), Turkey |
| MSP | Mouvement de la Société pour la Paix (Movement for a Peaceful Society), Algeria |
| MUSIAD | Müstakil Sanayici ve İşadamları Derneği, Turkey |
| NOP | National Order Party, Turkey |
| NSP | National Salvation Party, Turkey |
| PKK | Kurdistan Worker's Party, Turkey |
| PDS | Parti Démocratique Sénégalaise, Senegal |
| PSS | Parti de la Solidarité Sénégalaise, Senegal |
| RND | Rassemblement National Démocratique, Algeria |
| RNS | Rassemblement pour le Salut National, Senegal |
| RPP | Cumhuriyet Halk Partisi (Republican People's Party), Turkey (see CHP) |
| SP | Saadet Partisi (Felicity Party), Turkey |
| TUSIAD | Türk Sanayicileri ve İşadamları Derneği (Turkish Industrialists' and Businessmen's Assocation), Turkey |
| UCM | Union Culturelle Musulmane, Senegal |
| UPS | Union Progressiste Sénégalaise, Senegal |

# Introduction

On 12 June 1990, voters cast their ballots in local polls that were to inaugurate a new era of democratic participation in Algeria. The Algerian one-party state led by the Front de Libération Nationale (FLN) had come under severe strain, leading some in the party to support democratic participation as a measure to alleviate popular demands on the state. When the votes were tallied, the state party was shocked and dismayed at the news. The historical vanguard of Algerian nationalism, the FLN, received only 28 percent of the total vote, while an immature, recently recognized party highlighting its Islamic credentials had almost doubled the state party's returns with over 54 percent. The new Front Islamique du Salut (FIS) reveled in the magnitude of the challenge it had brought against "le pouvoir," highlighting its moral leadership as a key source of popular strength. Although the state portrayed the local elections as of minor consequence, the first round of National Assembly elections the following year demonstrated that the Islamists again captured the popular imagination along with half (47%) of the popular vote.[1] At this point the Islamist challenge to the state became transparently clear to the Algerian military, which stepped in to abort the second round of voting and to dissolve the FIS by force.

A remarkably similar story occurred in Egypt two decades later. After the Egyptian military ousted long-standing president Hosni Mubarak in the context of mass popular protest on 11 February 2011, Islamists took the lead in filling the political void as the country prepared for free democratic elections. The Egyptian Muslim Brotherhood encouraged its supporters to vote for its new Freedom and Justice Party (FJP), leading the FJP to win both parliamentary elections in January 2012 and presidential elections in June of that year. Mohammed Morsi, formerly a Muslim Brotherhood-affiliated MP in the Egyptian assembly, became the first democratically elected president of Egypt. Other Islamist political parties, such as the Salafi-oriented al-Nour (Light) Party, also performed surprisingly well in the context of free elections, outperforming all of the Islamists' more secular political competitors. As in Algeria, however, the Islamists' electoral triumphs were short-lived. The new Islamist-dominated parliament was dissolved by court order within six months after its election, and the military ousted President Morsi in the context of widespread social mobilization and increasing conflict in July 2013.

The electoral victories of the Algerian Islamists and the decision to move against them militarily defined Algerian politics throughout the 1990s. Mass electoral mobilization by the Islamist party quickly turned into mass demonstrations against the state. As political demonstrations by the FIS were forcefully repressed, demonstrations themselves became increasingly violent. The conflict deepened as it progressed; groups of Islamists began to actively mobilize as revolutionaries using guerrilla tactics. Before 1990, Islamists were at the margins of Algerian politics; by the mid-1990s they were embedded in a horrific civil war that would claim over 100,000 lives by the decade's end.

After President Morsi's ouster in Egypt in 2013, the Egyptian military and state security services also moved aggressively against the Muslim Brotherhood as an organization, jailing as many of the organization's leadership as they could find, as well as massacring large numbers of Brotherhood protesters in an infamous incident in Cairo's Raba'a Square. Despite having won both parliamentary and presidential elections, the state moved against the Brotherhood by confiscating its assets and declaring it a terrorist organization, making membership in this long-vibrant social organization a violation of Egyptian law. By early 2015, both former President Mohammed Morsi and the leader of the Egyptian Muslim Brotherhood, Mohammed Badie, had been sentenced by Egyptian courts to death. Violence in Egypt increased, and although the Brotherhood formally maintained its rejection of political violence, violence by a number of self-proclaimed Islamist groups occurred across Egypt.

The tragic story of Algerian politics in the 1990s, as well as that of Egyptian politics in the wake of the Arab uprisings of 2010–2011, highlights several puzzles regarding mobilization by religious actors in the Muslim world. First, why did these countries experience such a dramatic rise in Islamist mobilization compared with previous decades? In other words, why did rapid political mobilization revolve around a Muslim identity and an "Islamic" agenda when other issues had previously defined politics?

Second, why did mass Islamist mobilization occur in Algeria and Egypt, while it did not occur to the same degree in neighboring countries? In many respects, Tunisia and Morocco share a similar history, culture, and demography with Algeria, yet there was no dramatic electoral, protest, or violent manifestation of Islamist mobilization in these countries that compared with what happened in Algeria. Only recently has electoral mobilization for Islamist parties occurred in these countries.[2] Similarly, while the Muslim Brotherhood claimed dominant electoral victories in Egypt, it lost the founding free election in neighboring Libya in July 2012. Countries on North Africa's southern border (Mauritania, Mali, Niger, Chad) are dominantly Muslim, yet they have historically experienced far less political mobilization by religious actors than their northern neighbors. Why?

Finally, what causes Islamist actors to shift the type of political mobilization that they support (from voting to protest to violence)? Very little Islamist violence occurred in Algeria before 1992. Within a few years tens of thousands of Islamist, military, and civilian deaths had occurred. The extent to which Islamist violence will continue to spread through Egypt is unknown, but attacks by both Islamist actors and state security services increased substantially in the wake of President Morsi's ouster. What are the conditions under which an act of voting for an Islamist party is transformed into an act of violence on behalf of an Islamist movement?

Although each of these questions highlights a prominent puzzle in the Algerian and Egyptian cases, they are also central puzzles in explaining variation in Islamist mobilization throughout the Muslim world. Today, a number of countries with large Muslim populations hold competitive elections in which parties that brand themselves as the "Islamic choice" compete with other types of parties. Elections in Tunisia and Morocco brought Islamist parties to power in 2011 and 2012. Iraq has been led by Islamist political parties since free elections began in 2005. As early as the 1970s, parties articulating a religious frame of reference have competed in Turkey, with varying degrees of success. By the mid-1990s, the Islamically oriented Welfare (Refah) party had risen from obscurity to become the largest party in parliament, producing an "Islamist" prime minister in a country with an explicitly secular constitution. One of its successors, the Justice and Development Party (AKP), has dominated Turkish elections since 2002. Likewise, the 2002 elections in Pakistan demonstrated the dramatic political rise of an Islamist electoral coalition led by the Jamaat-i-Islami, which had seen only limited success in previous elections. Islamist parties in Malaysia and Indonesia have also competed with variable degrees of success over the course of iterated elections, beginning as far back as the 1950s in Malaysia and the 1970s in Indonesia.

In addition to experience with Islamist political parties, different regions of the world have also seen wide variation in their experience with Islamist protest and Islamist violence. The post-Soviet republics of Central Asia vary dramatically in the extent to which they have experienced Islamist mobilization in the political arena since independence in the 1990s. Islamist actors played a central role in Tajikistan's first years of independence, figuring prominently in an anti-Communist electoral coalition in 1991 and leading a revolutionary challenge against Tajikistan's Communist leadership. The violent challenge rapidly evolved into a civil war that killed about 50,000 between June 1992 and January 1993.[3] On a smaller scale, Islamists have also proven a significant challenge to the government of Uzbekistan. Uzbek Islamic activists, grouped under the banner of the cross-national Islamic Renaissance Party, are considered a major security threat, which the government has confronted through violent repression and mass arrests. In contrast with Tajikistan and Uzbekistan, other Central Asian countries (Kazakhstan, Kyrgystan, Turkmenistan) have had much less mobilization for Islamist political causes. This is the case in both the strongly repressive state of Turkmenistan and the comparatively more open country of Kyrgystan.

West African states with large Muslim populations saw little formal Islamist mobilization in the twentieth century compared with Arab Muslim states, demonstrating significant differences in mobilization across regions. Even within West Africa, countries with similar religious compositions have quite different experiences with religious mobilization. The protests and violence that accompanied debates over Islamic law in Northern Nigeria, and which led to the subsequent rise of the fiercely militant Islamist Boko Haram movement, are largely absent in neighboring states that also have northern Muslim populations. Despite prominent discussion of the role of Islamic law after Nigerian independence, mobilization in support of Islamic law was muted or absent for decades. Why did it reemerge in the 1990s, and why has support for Islamist militancy in Nigeria increased in recent years? By contrast, why has dominantly Muslim Senegal avoided Islamist violence, and also seen virtually no electoral mobilization on behalf of Islamist political parties?

Similar questions can be raised about variations in Islamist militancy (militancy is defined here simply as the use of political violence) in the Middle East. Why has the organization that calls itself the "Islamic State" been so successful at mobilizing militants on behalf of a violent, state-building jihad in Iraq in Syria, while its influence remains neglible in most areas of the Middle East? Why did a dominantly peaceful, non-Islamist opposition in Syria in 2011 transition to an almost entirely Islamist set of militant actors fighting the Syrian regime beginning in 2012? Likewise, why did Islamist militancy spread after the overthrow of Muammar Qaddafi in Libya, while it has remained more muted in neighboring Tunisia and Algeria?

The puzzling comparative variation in cases such as those highlighted here is the product of a combination of factors with qualities that are unique to the history of each case. One of the purposes of this study is to highlight the diversity of contexts and types of religious and political mobilization that occur across the Muslim world. While highlighting the range and diversity of Islamic political behavior, this study also seeks to systematically measure variations in Islamist mobilization across a wide range of countries and regions. This is done with two purposes: first, to provide an accurate description of the range of religious–political (Islamist) mobilization outcomes across the Muslim world; and second, to provide a foundation for building theory about the sources of Islamist political mobilization more generally.

## THE FRAMEWORK OF THIS STUDY

This study attempts to explain variation in Islamist mobilization by trying to answer two broad questions. First, what factors best account for varying levels and types of Islamist political mobilization across countries? Second, what factors best account for varying levels and types of Islamist political mobilization in the same country over time? In answering these questions, I seek to examine competing theories of Islamist mobilization and provide a new, institutional theory that I believe captures a significant portion of this variation, though certainly not all of it. Although one study cannot comprehensively evaluate the claims made by a wide range of competing theories, the aim here is to assess observable implications of competing claims through comparative analysis. In the process, a theoretical perspective is presented that seeks both to integrate previous theoretical arguments and to challenge arguments that receive little support across a range of cases.

The study utilizes comparative analysis on two levels. The first level takes a broad look at a defined population of relevant cases. The cases under consideration consist of all global polities whose self-defined domestic Muslim population is at least 25 percent of the polity's total population. A cutoff of 25 percent was selected to avoid including countries in which Muslim populations do not have a realistic hope of obtaining a significant measure of state power.[4] This yields 57 polities for analysis, 55 of which are currently in the global system.[5] In the large number of countries with Muslim populations less than 25 percent of the total, any Islamic mobilization is largely mobilization either for minority rights or for secession. These objectives are here considered theoretically distinct from mobilization to gain state power, as they include mobilization around a narrower set of policy concerns and a general lack of interest in building broad coalitions or mobilizing large sections of society on behalf of their interests. Countries with proportionately small Muslim populations were thus excluded in order to avoid distorting the results for the largely Muslim countries that are the central interest of the study. The remaining population of 57 polities is examined through both statistical and comparative historical analysis to yield general patterns of Islamist mobilization across space and time.

The second level of analysis uses largely qualitative research methods to closely examine three particular cases of interest: the experiences of Algeria, Turkey, and Senegal. The cases were chosen for the following theoretical reasons. First, they demonstrate a range of variation across the dependent outcome of Islamist political mobilization. Broadly speaking, Algeria in the late 1980s and 1990s represents a case of very high Islamist mobilization, Turkey in the 1970s to early 2000s represents a case of moderate levels of mobilization, and Senegal represents a case of low Islamist mobilization throughout the period since independence. The chosen cases should therefore provide evidence supporting the range of possible outcomes. Second, the cases exhibit considerable variation on possible explanatory variables highlighted both in existing theories and in the institutional theory presented here. These include differing levels of economic development, ethnic and linguistic backgrounds, colonial experiences, Islamic historical experiences, types of Islamic institutions, levels of urbanization, levels of political openness, types of political institutions, and levels of government stability. Third, despite this variance, these three cases share several important commonalities that serve as control variables and keep the comparison from being too loose to make causal inferences. Notably, all the cases have dominantly Muslim populations, have extensive ties to the non-Muslim West, have traditions of state secularism, and have had experience with electoral politics.

Finally, out of several possible cases that might fit these criteria, Algeria, Turkey, and Senegal each has distinct attributes that provide particular leverage on the research question. In Algeria, the level and success of Islamist political activity rose rapidly in a short period of time, and came to dominate Algerian politics throughout the 1990s. Algeria has arguably witnessed both the highest level of electoral support for Islamist parties (in the early 1990s) and the largest number of deaths in political violence by explicitly Islamist actors in the modern period, at least prior to the Syrian civil war (2012–present).[6] Additionally, Algeria in the 1990s provides some insight into the conditions under which electoral mobilization can be transformed into mass protest and long-term political violence.

Turkey represents a mid-range case, where Islamist mobilization (primarily electoral mobilization) has been present for decades and has shown significant variation in levels of political success. Turkey is the most enduring case in the Muslim world of Islamist actors actively participating in democratic politics. Likewise, it demonstrates better long-term variation in Islamist electoral success than any other case. Turkey also has historically had a unique regional divide in electoral support for Islamically oriented political parties, falling very roughly between its Eastern and Western regions, which allows for greater control in assessing the determinants of Islamist support. The Turkey chapter in this project is the richest chapter in data presentation and in discussion of an Islamist political party tradition that endured from the 1970s to the early 2000s. After 2002, Islamist electoral politics shifted in interesting ways, both diluting and consolidating the impact of Islamist actors.

In contrast to Algeria and Turkey, Senegal represents a case with comparatively low levels of Islamist political mobilization. Sub-Saharan Africa is a regional outlier in which Islamist mobilization has played a relatively minor part in politics, with a few notable exceptions. Senegal, however, has comparatively strong Islamic institutions and a civil society largely dominated by Muslim brotherhoods. Among sub-Saharan countries,[7] one might expect that Senegal would be most likely to have experienced Islamist mobilization in politics, and yet it has not done so to a significant degree. Senegal therefore provides some insight into sub-Saharan cases and other countries with low formal Islamist mobilization.

Data collected both across the larger population of Muslim countries and in the individual case studies in the period from 1970 to 2010 demonstrate the diversity of historical experience with Islamist mobilization. This diversity is manifest in the type of mobilization that occurs as well as in the levels of mobilization over time. Comparison across the cases highlights patterns of mobilization in the past four decades that enable us to assess many prominent (if overly general) theories of Islamist mobilization, including religious, structural, incentive-based, grievance-based, and social movement theories.

The core argument of this study is that three explanatory factors are individually necessary and jointly sufficient to account for the majority of Islamist political mobilization in Muslim countries during the four decades from 1970 through 2010. The factors are the development of *Islamic common knowledge* through the social penetration of Islamic religious institutions, *opportunities for religious entrepreneurship* due to a misalignment of institutional incentives between "religious entrepreneurs" and the state, and the creation of *public focal points* at the state level, which channel religious common knowledge into collective action. These factors generally are found in three separate types of institutions: the development of common knowledge is achieved through *diffuse Islamic institutions*, incentives are generated at the level of *hierarchical Islamic organizations*, and focal points are created by the *state*. This theory seeks only to explain the dominant form of Islamist mobilization, which is domestic mobilization by Islamist oppositions. It does not account for all mobilization and provides less leverage in explaining either transnational Islamist movements (such as Hizb al-Tahrir or al-Qa'eda) or mobilization directly generated by Islamist governments (as in Iran or the Sudan).

The theory suggests a process by which religious (and/or political) entrepreneurs make decisions regarding whether or not to politicize Islam in a context of religious common knowledge about symbolic meaning and appropriate behavior. Their efforts to politicize Islam achieve success when they are not effectively policed by religious elites and when they coincide with focal state events that can channel political protest into an Islamist framework.

Religious common knowledge is more likely to lead to Islamist mobilization in contexts where it extends deeper into a potential constituency and centers around appropriate communal behavior. This kind of Islamic common knowledge can be exploited by political entrepreneurs promoting a vision of sacred authority that includes engagement with the state. Political entrepreneurs claiming sacred authority have opportunities to politicize Islamic common knowledge under conditions of fragmented religious and political competition, and when they cannot be effectively policed by religious superiors. By contrast, Islamist actors that have access to state rent in the form of subsidies, economic agreements, or employment have low incentives to politicize Islam.

Political and religious entrepreneurs who make the decision to politicize Islam depend upon events at the level of the state that frame their activities and serve as focal points for substantial protest mobilization. Prominent focal events include crises of confidence in the state that contrast with Islamic conceptions of justice, piety, order, and communal protection. Under conditions of certain state crises, protest can be effectively channeled into Islamist organizations. Alternatively, events that signal new policies of political openness, such as founding elections, may also serve to channel protest into an Islamist framework. Through this process, Islamic norms are introduced in support of political arguments. The incorporation of religious common knowledge into political communication lowers the costs of collective action, which is subsequently coordinated through focal public events at the state level.

These processes depend on individual incentives interacting with shifting institutional arrangements that build Islamic common knowledge, opportunities for religious entrepreneurship, and public focal points for collective action. When these conditions are simultaneously present, it is likely to lead to mass Islamist political mobilization.

The study proceeds as follows. Chapter 1 starts by engaging with the difficult conceptual terrain of political Islam, discussing the key theoretical assumptions of the study, and defining the core dependent variable: *Islamist political mobilization*. It then turns to a brief overview of some of the foundational scholarship on political mobilization and existing categories of arguments about the sources of specifically *Islamist* political mobilization. This is followed by Chapter 2, which builds an original theoretical framework for understanding variation in Islamist political mobilization, detailing the aforementioned hypotheses about the role of rational incentives for mobilization in an institutional context.

Chapter 3 presents the range of cases in which the argument is considered to hold. A descriptive account of Islamist mobilization across the Muslim world is outlined, with general observations regarding the prevalent forms of mobilization and variations in the amount of mobilization across regions. Statistical and comparative historical analyses are used to identify broad patterns in mobilization outcomes and their correlates. The implications of an institutional theory and its alternatives are then evaluated within this broad cross-national context.

Chapter 4 examines the possible sources for low mobilization in certain regions, and particularly in sub-Saharan Africa, by looking in detail at the case of Senegal. Although Senegal has strong Islamic social institutions, it has historically had very low levels of Islamist political mobilization. The chapter discusses the reasons and incentives for a historical alliance between Islamic brotherhoods and the state, the effects of a social structure fragmented by brotherhood allegiances, and the characteristics of Sufi Islamic organization that create disincentives for traditional Islamist mobilization. The emergence of an urban Senegalese Islamist movement in the 1990s is discussed, highlighting the reasons for its limited impact on Senegalese politics. The chapter also provides a brief comparison of Senegal with Mali in this context.

Chapter 5 examines variation in Islamist mobilization across space and time by assessing the history of Islamist electoral mobilization in Turkey. Although similar to Senegal in the secular foundations of its independence movement, Turkey has had moderately high levels of Islamist mobilization, primarily in the context of electoral politics. The chapter addresses this puzzle, introducing the role of political Islam in the Turkish context through discussion of a series of Islamically oriented political parties from 1970 to 2002. Variation in Islamic and social institutions and historical alienation from the central state are noted as potential explanatory factors for regional variation in Turkish support for Islamist parties over time. Long-term growth in national support for Islamist parties is explained by looking at the diffusion of Islamic education and media, increasing entrepreneurial use of Islamic symbols, and the fragmentation of the Turkish party system. Short-term variation in support for Islamist parties is explained through a discussion of multiple public crises of order and justice and the impact of Islamist participation in national government.

Chapter 6 describes the rapid rise of Islamist mobilization in Algeria during the late 1980s and early 1990s within the context of domestic Islamic institutional growth during earlier periods. It describes the institutional context supporting religious entrepreneurship during French occupation, the war of independence, and the late 1980s, arguing that a large-scale crisis of state confidence combined with significant political liberalization in the early 1990s created the context for Islam to become highly politicized in a short period. It discusses how rapid growth in Islamic institutions parallel to the state provided an effective institutional framework from which political entrepreneurs could quickly define a new dominant political cleavage in Algeria. The chapter shows how repression of Islamist actors in the early 1990s further intensified the religious–secular cleavage by failing to allow other protest outlets against the state and transformed Islamist mobilization from voting to violence.

Chapter 7 summarizes the core arguments of the project and highlights remaining theoretical caveats and questions. These include questions about distinctive aspects of Islamist mobilization, questions about the role of common knowledge and in-group policing, and speculation on what may lead to low levels of Islamist mobilization more generally. Several implications of the argument are highlighted in conclusion.

An Epilogue, which discusses patterns of Islamist mobilization in the Arab world following the Arab uprisings of 2010–2012, is provided at the end of the volume. The Epilogue looks briefly at why Islamists were late to enter into the revolutionary fray in countries such as Tunisia and Egypt, how they entered, and their varying fortunes in the wake of engagement with the state. The dramatic Islamist electoral successes in Tunisia, Egypt, and Morocco during 2011–2012 are examined, as are the subsequent patterns of state repression and emerging trends in Islamist violence.

## REFERENCES

Capisani, Giampaolo R. 2000. *The Handbook of Central Asia: A Comprehensive Survey of the New Republics*. London: I. B. Tauris.

Fontaine, Jacques. 1990. "Les elections locales Algériennes du 12 Juin 1990: approche statistique et géographique." *Maghreb-Machrek* 129 (July–September): 12–140.

Sutton, Keith and Ahmed Aghrout. 1992. "Multiparty Elections in Algeria: Problems and Prospects." *Bulletin of Francophone Africa* 2 (Autumn): 76–77.

Sutton, Keith, Ahmed Aghrout, and Salah Zaimche. 1992. "Political Changes in Algeria: an Emerging Electoral Geography." *Maghreb Review* 17/1/2: 3–27.

Willis, Michael 1996. *The Islamist Challenge in Algeria: A Political History*. New York: New York University Press.

1

# Islam and Political Mobilization

## WHAT IS ISLAMIST POLITICAL MOBILIZATION?

The core phenomenon of interest in this study is broadly termed "Islamist political mobilization," and encompasses a significant range of both actors and political behaviors. Over time, scholars of political Islam have used a number of terms to discuss this phenomenon, including "Islamic fundamentalism" (Piscatori 1991, Tibi 1998), "Islamic activism" (Wiktorowicz 2001), and "religious nationalism" (Juergensmeyer 1993). Each has different connotations. The use of "Islamic fundamentalism" implies a particular religious perspective centered on religious fundamentals that may include scripture, ritual, or the life of the prophet Muhammed.[1] "Islamic activism" implies a focus on collective action, often in the form of a social movement. "Religious nationalism" implies the use of religion in the production of national political identities. While Islamic fundamentalism and Islamic activism may not involve political claims, religious nationalism does. As a concept, however, religious nationalism does not imply particular Islamic claims.

A preferable term for most purposes is "political Islam," which narrows the scope of the previous terms to the intersection of Islam and politics. It implies that Islam has aspects that are not political, but includes the wide range of political activities, symbols, or beliefs that are characteristic of Islamic actors. The term "political Islam" has been used by scholars to cover a range of topics, including Muslim conceptions of democracy, political mobilization, terrorism, gender policy, civil society, and revolution (Roy 1994, Beinin and Stork 1997a, Kepel 2002). "Muslim politics" serves as a prominent alternative with essentially similar connotations (Eickelman and Piscatori 1996).

The concept under examination in this study is found at the intersection of Islam and politics, but is narrower than the encompassing category of "political Islam." Islamist political mobilization as used here focuses specifically on political action designed to engage the state. Political mobilization includes activities that seek to affect state policy or to influence the balance of state power. These activities are performed by actors who view their actions as an outcome of their identity as Muslims. Their actions are "Islamist" in the sense that they pursue a self-defined Islamic religious agenda through engagement with the state. Many studies of political Islam beginning in the early 2000s have utilized a similar concept, focusing on the mobilization aspect of Muslim politics (White 2002, Wickham 2002, Hafez 2003, Wiktorowicz 2003, Clark 2004).

The concept of Islamist political mobilization encompasses a wide range of "Islamic" political behaviors and beliefs. The term "Islamist" is used here instead of "Islamic" because of the predominantly religious connotations usually associated with the latter adjective. By contrast, "Islamist" implies a range of religious–political behaviors that may not be defined as Islamic by the traditional arbiters of Islam, such as the clerical class (*'ulema*). Rather, "Islamist" behaviors are essentially self-defined by the Islamist actor as religiously motivated and appropriate under his or her vision of Islam. "Islamist" is not used here to refer to a particular class of Islamic belief or a particular category of Islamic activist as it is by some authors, but instead encompasses the range of beliefs and actors that choose to define themselves by their Islamic identity.

Distinctions are often made between types of Islamists according to either their belief system or their political strategies. Most often, authors who distinguish between types of Islamism conflate ideology and strategy, categorizing Islamists as either "moderate" or "radical" (Moussalli 1999). A group's ideology (type of claims) is thus seen as predictive of strategy (how those claims are made). Other authors use ideological signifiers such as Wahhabi, Salafi, Sufi, or Shi'i to doctrinally delineate types of Islamic groups.

For the purpose of this study, Islamic groups are distinguished along two general criteria. The first distinction is the social sphere with which the group's ideology is dominantly engaged. Does the group focus its attention and resources on promoting individual belief and personal improvement, on developing communal religious norms, or on making claims about state behavior? This ideological distinction has little to do with religious doctrine and much more to do with beliefs about the roles and responsibilities of certain classes of actors.[2] For example, many Sufi brotherhoods focus primarily on aiding believers in a personal journey to communion with the divine. Although this is generally done within the context of a spiritual community, the ideological focus is on personal improvement. Other types of organizations have primarily communal objectives, such as proselytizing under the divine prescription for Islamic call (*da'wa*), providing welfare or civic services, enforcing communal religious norms, or even punishing non-Muslim groups (Christians, Jews, pagans) for perceived offenses against Islam. A third type of organization has a dominant objective of engagement with the state. This is done in an effort to change state policy, capture aspects of state policy formation, or even wholly capture or create state power. A wide range of Islamist organizations seek to engage the state, from political parties that have limited claims, to militias, secretive militant cells, or even revolutionary armies.

A second distinction used in this study is primarily one of organizational strategy. Given a dominant social and political system, does the Islamic group pursue its ideology within the framework of the system, or does it move beyond the accepted rules of the system to achieve its goals? Groups that choose to work within the rules of the dominant system are labeled "accommodative," while groups that choose to work outside the dominant social and political norms and use political violence (including violent enforcement of Islamist norms) are labeled "militant." A typology of Islamic movements using these criteria and highlighting a diverse sample of groups is outlined in Table 1.1.

Although one group (or set of groups) may fit into one category at a given time, it may subsequently move to another. Islamic groups may rapidly shift their strategy from accommodative to militant, or vice versa, as the political situation or balance of power changes. As the case of Algeria demonstrates, a political party (the Front Islamique du Salut, FIS) can rapidly change into a protest or revolutionary group under certain circumstances. Although ideologies are usually slower to change, group ideology on the dimension outlined here may also be malleable. Sufi brotherhoods, for example, may shift their primary ideological focus away from the individual to engagement with broader communal or state issues, as they have done at times in the Sudan or in Turkey. Likewise, political parties may retreat into an organization that focuses on communal or individual piety if political parties are banned or repressed, as has been the case with Egyptian Islamist groups at times in their history.

This study focuses primarily on groups that are actively politically engaged with the state. Explicitly political groups are found most commonly in the bottom row of Table 1.1, but groups with a dominantly communal or individualist ideology may engage in political mobilization when the central religious interests of the community or individual are impacted by the state.

TABLE 1.1 *Typology of Islamic Movements*

| | | Strategy | |
|---|---|---|---|
| | | Accommodative | Militant |
| Ideology | Individualist | Sufi brotherhoods | |
| | Communal | Civic/welfare organizations | Ethno-Muslim militias; norm enforcement squads |
| | Statist | Political parties | Revolutionaries |

Under these circumstances, the group may use its dominant ideology to create an innovative rationale for engaging the state. This rationale may recede after the state's threat to the movement's purpose recedes. Alternatively, it may become embedded in the organization's ideology and ultimately serve to make the group more "statist" in its orientation. The majority of organizations and movements of interest in this study, however, are explicitly political organizations that deliberately and repeatedly mobilize in order to change state policy or to capture state power.

As a total population, these explicitly political groups are far outnumbered by Islamic groups with individualist or communal ideologies throughout the Islamic world. While extraordinarily important to religious and social life in most Muslim societies, these primarily apolitical groups are not the central interest here. Militant groups with primarily individualist and communal ideologies are relatively rare, due to both the apolitical goals of these groups and the state's interest in controlling militancy. When the state confronts militant groups with an individualist or communal purpose, they are likewise forced to confront the state. This process tends to produce an ideological shift in which militant groups increasingly interact with the state, becoming more explicitly political in their ideology over time.

Political *mobilization* is here conceptualized as a category with several distinct manifestations. In countries with free and open elections, Islamist political mobilization often takes the form of campaigning and voting for political parties with an Islamist agenda. Those agendas are diverse in their religious claims and political prescriptions, but united in their direct engagement with state policy and their use of accommodative strategies to gain participation rights within the existing political system. In countries with closed political systems, accommodative strategies are often crowded out or confined to attempts at elite influence through such mechanisms as petitions by religious authorities.

In systems with few avenues for political participation, militant strategies of mobilization are more common and are sometimes accompanied by aggressive statist ideologies that advocate the purging or violent overthrow of regimes (Hafez 2003). Organizations may mobilize to pursue political violence in the form of direct attacks against the state and military, in the form of symbolic attacks on prominent individuals, or in the form of indiscriminate attacks against civilians in an attempt to gain recognition and instill fear. Political violence in these forms may also occur in open societies, usually perpetrated by groups with little backing in formal political channels or by groups with visions of rapid, dramatic political change.

In both open and relatively closed political systems, mobilization may also take a third path, which involves public activism in the form of street demonstrations that express approval or disapproval of state policy. The less protest is supported or protected by a political system, the greater the potential personal cost to those who engage in public protest. Protests in closed systems often lead

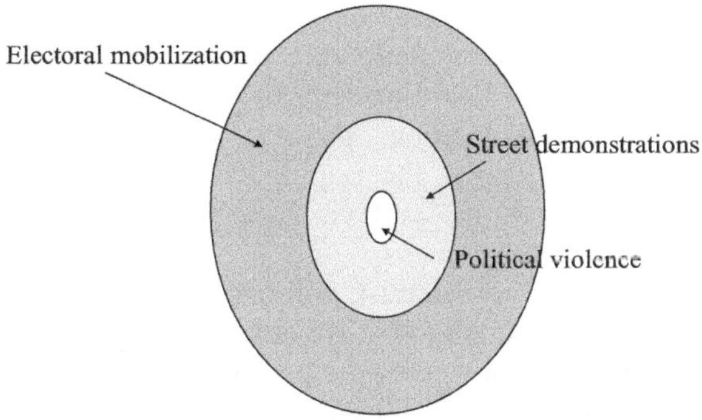


FIGURE 1.1 Spheres of mobilization.

to violent clashes between protesters and the military, as well as significant prison time for organizers of the event. Demonstrators in comparatively open systems are less likely to bear these personal costs, but the costs of participating in public protest are nevertheless higher than the costs of voting for a legal political party.

Voting for Islamically oriented political parties, participation in street demonstrations related to religious policy issues, and actions of political violence on behalf of a self-defined Islamist agenda are the core manifestations of mobilization as used in this study. Although these activities have distinctive characteristics that make them analytically different forms of political mobilization, the subsequent discussion makes an assumption regarding the relationship of these forms of mobilization to one another. The assumption is twofold: (a) actors engaged in Islamist political violence are a smaller set (and potential subset) of those actors engaged in Islamist demonstrations and (b) actors engaged in Islamist demonstrations are a smaller set (and potential subset) of those actors who may vote for Islamically oriented parties. This assumption is portrayed in Figure 1.1.

In most cases, this "inclusiveness" assumption is empirically accurate, although in some cases it may not be. For example, some militant Islamists in a country with elections may refrain from voting for Islamist parties if they are ideologically opposed to elections or view the party leaders as traitors who have betrayed their ideology in order to pursue an accommodative strategy with the government. However, the logic behind the inclusiveness assumption is that all actors who engage in some form of Islamist political mobilization do so to enable state policies that are more reflective of their Islamic vision than the status quo. They may pursue different strategies, but these strategies are all designed to enable pro-Islamic policy change.

What distinguishes actors engaged in different forms of mobilization is the personal cost that they are willing to pay to engage in the activity. The personal cost that an actor is willing to pay is often correlated with the depth of his or her ideological commitment. The perceived personal costs of demonstrating are considered to be higher than those for voting, while the perceived personal costs of engaging in political violence are treated as higher than those for demonstrating. Although there are exceptions to the inclusiveness assumption in some contexts, Islamist voting, protest, and violence are related to one another empirically. Across the population of cases used in the study, Islamist voting, demonstrations, and violence are each positively correlated with one another.[3]

Several other indicators of Islamist political mobilization are tangentially referenced in the study, although these are less reliable indicators of the underlying mobilization phenomenon than the previous indicators of voting behavior, demonstrations, and violence. These other indicators include the number of Islamist political organizations, the number of alleged Islamists arrested by the state, and political petitions or elite pressure on the state to modify its religious policy.[4]

A final issue of interest, which varies significantly across countries and time periods, is the relative importance of political Islam in defining the political cleavages of a system. The relevance of political Islam to the central political cleavages in a system is here termed "cleavage salience." The cleavage salience of political Islam is positively correlated with expressions of Islamist political mobilization across the population of countries in this study, but is not correlated in every case. For example, high Islamist mobilization in Algeria in the 1990s paralleled the dominant political division between the military/ruling party and Islamist parties/militias. By contrast, high Islamist mobilization by Hezbollah in Lebanon during the Israeli occupation of Southern Lebanon in the 1980s did not reflect the compounding cleavages of region, class, and religious identity that provided justification for extended civil conflict involving many parties.[5]

In the majority of countries examined with moderate levels of Islamist mobilization, religion is a significant factor in the country's political cleavage structure. In cases with high levels of Islamist mobilization, religious policy often served to create the dominant political cleavage. Levels of Islamist mobilization generally both affect cleavage salience and are affected by it, making it difficult to establish whether religious-political cleavages cause Islamist mobilization or are caused by it. In this study, cleavage salience is treated as a correlate of mobilization rather than an explanatory factor. In some cases, however, high levels of mobilization may occur despite the fact that religion is not a significant cleavage in the political system. Islamist mobilization as it is defined here may also be absent in cases where religion is prominent in the polity's political cleavage structure, as in historical periods of Lebanese politics.

## THEORIES OF MOBILIZATION

Sources of mobilization have been theorized in general terms by looking at a variety of different phenomena. Studies of collective action in analyses of revolution, nationalism, social movements, political parties, ethnic politics, and democratization all make assumptions or claims about the sources of political mobilization. Four general theoretical perspectives on the sources of mobilization are briefly discussed here. They are differentiated from one another both by the central unit of analysis and by the theorized factors that drive mobilization.[6] Theories of mobilization are often based in analyses of revolutionary or protest mobilization, although theories of radical parties make similar types of claims.[7] The four perspectives are here classified as structuralist, incentive-based, grievance-based, and social movement theories.

Structuralist perspectives on mobilization have figured prominently in theories of revolution and are characterized by a focus on broad historical and institutional changes that either facilitate or drive mobilization. Marxist-oriented theories of mobilization by social class serve as classic examples of a structuralist perspective. Early structuralist perspectives by modernization theorists argued that political institutions serve a functional purpose in addressing social needs. When the needs of society change such that existing political and social structures become unrepresentative of the social system in which they operate, existing institutions fail to fulfill their functional purpose. The political and social system becomes "disequilibrated" and ripe for revolutionary change (Huntington 1968, Johnson 1982). Revolutionary political mobilization occurs at the point when political and social structures fail to adequately process the demands of changing societies.

Skocpol (1979) provides a paradigmatic structural argument about the sources of social revolution. She argues that mass social revolutions, as a rare but consequential type of political mobilization, are the result of large-scale structural changes. These changes occur, most notably, as the result of internal state weakness in the form of fiscal and military crises, pressure on states from other countries abroad, and agrarian sociopolitical structures that facilitate widespread peasant revolts against landlords (154). Social revolutions are thus a product of a particular pattern of both state and societal institutions that interact under high pressure from exogenous factors in the international system.

Other structural theories of mobilization also focus on the state and social conditions, examining the roles of such variables as social class and state repression.[8] Agrarian structures that facilitate peasant support, combined with institutional weaknesses of the state, figure prominently into explanations of guerilla mobilization in Latin America, for example (Wickham-Crowley 1992). Likewise, the structure of the state and its repressive ability are central explanatory variables for structural theorists looking at violent forms of mobilization. Moderate levels of state repression have been found to increase levels of political violence in a wide variety of cases (Muller 1985, Weede 1987). Violent political rebellion is theorized to be the highest when the state's ability to coerce its opponents is equivalent to its opponents' ability to challenge the state (Gurr 1970:237).

An alternative to structural theories includes explanations that center on the individual's decision to participate in political mobilization. From the perspective of these theories, macro units of analysis, such as those at state level, are less helpful than an examination of motivations at the level of the participant. Individualist accounts have strikingly different perspectives on the dominant motivations for political mobilization, however. Two prominent visions of individual motivations include economic theories of incentive-driven mobilization and psychological theories of grievance-driven mobilization.

Incentive-based theories of mobilization start with a common assumption that mobilization is costly to the participant and thus difficult to sustain. Further, most of the benefits of political mobilization (with the exception of directly capturing power) are distributed across the population, not just to the participants. Because participation is personally costly and the benefits are a public, collective good, individuals always have an incentive to defect from opportunities to mobilize. Incentive-based explanations thus tell a compelling story to explain the lack of mobilization in many instances where political interests would be directly served by collective action.

For incentive-based mobilization theorists, potential participants in a movement will not mobilize if the perceived personal costs of mobilization are higher than the perceived personal benefit that accrues from the activity. In some situations, the costs of participation may be relatively low compared with the potential rewards that come as the result of mobilization. In most cases, however, the perceived benefits of the mobilization attempt are both unclear and diffuse, while personal costs for participation are considerable. Potential participants may therefore require personal benefits beyond the expected outcome of mobilization if they are to participate.

Olson's (1965) classic formulation of the logic of collective action asserts that potential participants must perceive either positive or negative personal incentives to participate. Many of these incentives may precede the outcome of the collective action. Positive incentives may be financial, or promises of increased status; negative incentives may be financial, loss of status, punishment, or ostracism from the group. The structure and size of groups affects incentives and is therefore crucial to generating mobilization. Small groups are more likely to mobilize due to positive incentives in situations where benefits can be allocated to participants. Where this is not the case, small groups with structured information networks can nevertheless monitor and punish non-participants better than large groups.

Organizations can incent individuals to participate if they can create benefits that accrue only to participants in the organization. Participant-specific benefits may include rights to the organization's financial resources, human capital, knowledge base, or reputation. Incentives in the form of basic welfare services serve as a common benefit for participation in political organizations that draw on marginal populations (Popkin 1979, Akinci 1999).

In incentive-based theories, therefore, potential individual participants make strategic choices to maximize their expected benefit after costs. The sum of a series of innumerable individual choices determines the overall macrobehavior (Schelling 1978). Individual choice is admittedly a choice made in the context of largely structural constraints (Berejikian 1992), but the outcome is less the product of structural constraints than shifting perceptions of the costs and benefits of participation. Changing patterns of information about costs and benefits of mobilization are crucial to a potential participant's choice. Mass collective action therefore has the potential to occur very rapidly and unexpectedly in the context of changing structural constraints that convey new information about the potential costs of mobilization (Kuran 1991, Lohmann 1994).

An alternative set of individualist theories views mobilization as the result of grievance, with a particular interest in the psychological effects of grievances. Early scholars focused primarily on socioeconomic grievances, particularly poverty and its correlates. Likewise, economic and social discrimination against groups is seen as a prominent source of mobilization. Grievance-based theories of mobilization examine the sources of discontent cited by mobilizing actors and then look for psychological mechanisms that channel discontent into action.

Aggressive mobilization is seen by some early scholars of mobilization to be the natural outcome of frustration that results from unsatisfied expectations (Feierabend and Feierabend 1966, Berkowitz 1968). A prominent theory highlights relative deprivation as the dominant cause of mobilization and revolution (Davies 1962, Gurr 1970). Relative deprivation theory distinguishes between deprivation and psychological expectations about deprivation and opportunity. Since mobilization does not occur under most conditions of deprivation, the theory asserts that mobilization and rebellion occur only when perceptions about deprivation change. Violent mobilization is expected when increasingly positive expectations about the future are shattered, creating psychological discomfort that is assuaged through mobilization.

Psychological grievances can be generated through broad structural changes that directly impact individual expectations. Demographic changes, such as rapidly expanding populations, can create strains on resources that prevent individuals from realizing economic aspirations (Goldstone 1993, 1997). When population growth outpaces economic growth, new generations may find that they cannot attain the socioeconomic status of their parents, creating a feeling of relative deprivation. Additionally, rapid population growth may lead to rapid urbanization in search of employment, which in turn may lead to significant disappointment when opportunities do not materialize. Some studies have focused on political sources of grievance, as well (Walton 1984, Dudley and Miller 1998). Political sources of grievance that lead to feelings of relative deprivation include the introduction of repression or political discrimination, unfulfilled promises of political liberalization, efforts to undermine the integrity of elections, or the cancellation of electoral results.

Responding to claims made by structural, incentive-based, and grievance-based explanations of mobilization, a fourth set of scholars has generated hypotheses in a prominent contemporary tradition of claims loosely grouped together under the banner of "social movement theory." Social movement theory is less a theory of what drives mobilization than an affiliated group of classifications and hypotheses relevant to the study of mobilization. What unifies the social movement tradition is a focus on several key components of mobilization from which hypotheses are generated.

Early social movement theory resembled both structural and grievance-based explanations by articulating a process in which psychological discomfort leads to political mobilization. Structural strains, such as population growth, industrialization, rapid urbanization, or economic collapse, create discomfort among affected sectors of the population, who then feel alienated from existing social and political systems. This sense of alienation drives membership in social movements, which promise a renewed sense of personal efficacy in the face of change (Smelser 1962).[9]

By the 1970s and early 1980s, social movement theorists began responding to these arguments by framing more explicitly institutional and political approaches to collective action. Scholars began to treat social movements in their organizational context, focusing on resources available to movement organizations. These organizations have the dual task of creating more resources and mobilizing existing resources behind a social or political agenda. Theorists began to look explicitly at what resources different organizations possess, how they expanded those resources, and how they mobilized them around a common cause (Oberschall 1972, Tilly 1978). Questions such as these formed the basis for what came to be known as "resource mobilization theory" (Jenkins 1983, McCarthy and Zald 1987). Incarnations of the theory posit that organizations have access to both formal and informal resources and that access to those resources is crucial for mobilization. Formal resources may include finances, capital, and leadership. Informal resources include access to a variety of social networks that can be activated for recruitment or mobilization purposes. Informal networks are often more resilient sources of mobilization than formal institutions because they are networks that serve the ordinary purposes of social life and are thus difficult for the state to target.

In addition to a focus on resources, organization, and mobilizing structures, social movement theorists have focused on political opportunities as a central determinant of mobilization. Political opportunities encompass a wide range of phenomena, but typically have a temporal component. Where opportunities were previously absent, new events provide social movements with chances to mobilize. The "window" of opportunity is often open for a limited time and therefore is theorized to have some predictive power regarding the timing of mobilization. Because "opportunity" is such a broad concept, social movement theorists have difficulty specifying *a priori* what events will become opportunities. Nevertheless, opportunities are theorized as a change that reduces the perceived costs of mobilization. This may be in the form of public decisions by the state to no longer repress a movement, for example (Tilly 1978). Tarrow (1998:71) argues that opportunities are common "when institutional access opens, rifts appear within elites, allies become available, and state capacity for repression declines." In contrast to resource mobilization theory, political opportunity theorists emphasize changes exogenous to the mobilizing group.[10] Opportunity theories are often better at predicting the onset of mobilization or conflict than grievance theories, as grievances can build up for long periods of time without collective action surrounding them.[11]

A final focus of contemporary social movement theory is on how organizations frame their ideology in order to mobilize most effectively. Frames are sometimes thought of as "ideological" frames or "cultural" frames and refer to how organizations publicly interpret the meaning of events and the meaning of a participant's mobilization (Snow et al. 1986, Snow and Benford 1992). Interpretive frames both draw on the background of a movement's potential constituency and produce a vision of how the world looks and why it looks that way. Framing is the process of rhetorically constructing the meaning of mobilization in order to recruit and justify collective action. The rhetorical process of framing involves highlighting the extent of a problem and the appropriateness of an organization's solution (Snow and Benford 1988). The chosen frame also seeks to persuade the potential participant of the virtue of joining the movement. A related argument posits that the opportunities for mobilization are bounded by "repertoires of contention," repertoires that are both culturally determined and affected by the movement's prior history of activity (Tarrow 1998).

Although social movement theorists have clearly demonstrated that framing is a central activity of mobilizing organizations, as it is for most political actors, how frames may *cause* political mobilization is less clear. Each mobilizing actor and situation has unique contextual properties that serve to infuse frames with meaning that may not have resonance across mobilizing events or issues. The social movement tradition has eloquently shown that both resource mobilization and political opportunities affect the potential for and timing of mobilization. However, social movement theorists have had much more difficulty specifying precisely which aspects of mobilizing structures or which types of political opportunities matter most, and most often. Further work in the tradition has not narrowed the theory's claims, but rather has focused on expanding social movement theory into a dynamic model with further descriptive mechanisms of the mobilization process (McAdam, Tarrow, and Tilly 2001).

## THEORIES OF ISLAMIST POLITICAL MOBILIZATION

Theories of Islamist political mobilization borrow from the theoretical perspectives on mobilization more generally. Although the prolific research on Islamic political activism has been much more descriptive than theoretical in its content, both implicit and explicit theoretical claims regarding the sources of Islamist mobilization have been made from diverse sources. Claims made by theorists of Islamic activism reflect the diverse perspectives of many academic fields engaged in Islamic studies, generating distinct arguments based in religious, cultural, historical, sociological, and political perspectives. These arguments reflect the structural, incentive-based, grievance-based, and social movement perspectives common to broader theoretical arguments regarding mobilization. In addition, theorists of Islamism have made unique cultural and religious arguments about sources of mobilization.

Theorists of Islamism from within Islamist movements make a common argument that situates the origins of mobilization in religion itself. This perspective does not have a direct parallel in more general theories of mobilization, although arguments have been made about the mobilizing effects of certain communal or cultural bonds (Anderson 1983, Connor 1994). From the perspective of many Islamist actors, political mobilization is the natural response of a sincere believer who lives in a world in which states fail to adhere to Islamic norms. Foundational Islamist theorists such as Hasan al-Banna or Sayyid Abu'l-A'la Mawdudi eloquently argued that political action is the natural response of the believing Muslim who understands the potential of the Islamic community (*'umma*) (Euben and Zaman 2009).[12] This argument asserts that Islam is inherently a politicized religion, and thus it is natural for believers to behave as political activists. Al-Affendi, for example, argues that the proper research question is not what accounts for Islamic activism but "why is it necessary to remind Muslims to abide by the faith they profess?" He continues: "We should not be asking why Muslims want to live as Muslims, but what reasons prevented them from doing so before" (1991:1). More recently, the head of the Islamic State group in Iraq, Abu Bakr al-Baghdadi, has argued that all Muslims are obligated to join in the creation of the Islamic State, and that fighting on its behalf is obligatory for the faithful.[13]

Political and religious scholars have long made arguments about political Islam by examining Islam as a religion and looking for political characteristics of Islamic thought (Darif 1992, 2000, Sara 1994, Abd al-Karim 1995). Islamist mobilization is often assumed to occur as a natural result of sincere religious reflection on the nature and purpose of the Islamic community. Non-Muslim scholars have also been partial to this explanation, viewing Islam as inherently political and distinct from Western secular ideologies. Islamist revolt has been seen as a natural outcome of the religion's contact with modern secular ideology (Juergensmeyer 1993). Some argue that Islam is essentially a religion of protest, because it is the supreme underlying value system against with all earthly inadequacies are judged (Waardenburg 2002:378–79). Islamist mobilization is therefore, at base, motivated by Islam itself more than by any exogenous factors (Murphy 2002:75–76). Cultural and religious explanations are thus distinguished by a view of Islamist mobilization as a proactive rather than as a reactive force.

Structural perspectives on Islamist political mobilization, by contrast, see large-scale social and political changes as the driving forces behind the Islamic "resurgence" from the 1970s onward. Some scholars prioritize colonialism and Western imperial projects as early catalysts for social change that had wide-ranging and long-standing effects on the potential for Islamic activism. Macro-historical events such as Western imperialism in the Muslim world are seen as creating both the appropriate conditions and motivations for long-term Islamist mobilization. Such contact with the West created an identity crisis and sense of failure in the Muslim world that could be ameliorated by creating "indigenous" Muslim political institutions (Lewis 1964, Burke 1988, Esposito 1998, Shadid 2002).

Additional structural pressures affected the Muslim world in the twentieth century as modern technologies and Western secular ideologies further penetrated newly independent states. Some have theorized that incorporation into the global capitalist economy and the pursuit of European-style state-building projects created a cultural and institutional response from Muslim societies that found its voice in newly assertive religious movements. Processes of economic and cultural globalization in the latter half of the twentieth century engendered a cultural backlash that became particularly prominent by the late 1970s (Lewis 1990, Juergensmeyer 1993, Burgat and Dowell 1993, Keddie 1994, Tibi 1998). By this period, the claims of early modernization theory that societies would become increasingly secular as they became more "modernized" appeared resoundingly false. Some scholars subsequently reversed the predictions of modernization theory by claiming that modernization was actually the driving force behind Islamist mobilization (Lawrence 1989, Lewis 1990). Others argued that although an initial expansion of Islamist mobilization occurred as traditional Islam came into increased contact with the West, Islamism would subsequently decline in the wake of modern secularism (Tibi 1990, Hunter 1998). Despite the high profile of Islamist movements in recent years, some prominent scholars asserted that this decline actually had begun by the end of the twentieth century (Roy 1994, Kepel 2002).

Other structural changes in the global system have been held responsible for generating Islamic activism. Economic development in the Persian Gulf states through the exploitation of petroleum resources altered the balance of power between "Islam and the West," making conservative Islamic actors more assertive in challenging Western interests (Pipes 1983). Additionally, the fall of the Soviet Union severely weakened leftist challengers in Muslim countries, creating an oppositional vacuum that Islamist groups were best poised to fill.

International events that affected the global positions of Arab and Muslim countries also served as catalysts for Islamist mobilization. A series of perceived defeats and ignominies, often centered around the persistence and power of Israel to displace and embarrass its Arab neighbors, created a climate of Muslim solidarity and protest. Arab defeats at the hands of Israel, particularly in 1967, and a later decision by Anwar Sadat of Egypt to recognize the Israeli state are seen as events that generated Muslim anger and protest directed at Muslims' governments (Owen 1992, Hiro 2002). The Soviet invasion of Afghanistan is likewise seen as a driving force for Islamic collective action. Additionally, the Western-led war against Iraq in 1991 was followed by protests in a variety of Muslim countries and contributed to Islamist mobilization (Piscatori 1991). Subsequent Western interventions in Afghanistan (2001) and Iraq (2003) are also seen to drive Islamist political mobilization in the Arab world. In contrast to these interventions, the success of the Iranian revolution in 1979 was seen to have a positive demonstration effect for Islamists throughout the Muslim world, acting as the inspiration for a significant wave of mobilization (Wright 1985).

Structural perspectives make two general claims about the effects of the state on Islamist mobilization. The first is that state failure, and particularly the failure of secular, Western-oriented states within the Muslim world, created disillusionment with what are seen to be imported political institutions. Structural crises within these states led political activists to promote an alternative path of indigenous, religious political development (Dekmejian 1980, 1995, Voll 1994, Faksh 1997). The second claim is that the authoritarian character of Muslim regimes leads to mobilization. Scholars cite differing mechanisms linking authoritarianism to Islamist activism. Authoritarian regimes may support a state secularizing project in which Muslims feel that they are prevented from performing their religious obligations. Enforcement of the secular vision thus threatens potential religious activists (Roberts 1988, Deeb 1996, Moaddel 2002a). Alternatively, authoritarian regimes may actively repress Islamists, forcing Islamic activists to directly confront the state in order to preserve their interests. In addition to creating more Islamist mobilization, active repression may force Islamists into a militant strategy and thus may engender more Islamist political violence (Keddie 1988, Kepel 1993, Halliday 1996). Mohammed Hafez (2003), for example, argues that patterns of indiscriminate and reactive repression are most likely to explain "why Muslims rebel." Finally, authoritarianism may simply close potential outlets for formal opposition, leading opposition activists to work out of informal civil and religious institutions that cannot be completely controlled by the state (Wiktorowicz 2001, Wickham 2002).

Structural perspectives therefore highlight both macro-historical changes and the effects of macro-institutions such as the state. Macro-historical changes such as colonialism, modernization, and globalization may produce social transformations leading to Islamist versions of class conflict (Lubeck 1988, Nasr 1997), create identity crises, and generate cultural revival. Macro-historical events such as the Arab defeat of 1967, the Iranian revolution of 1979, or the collapse of the Soviet Union in 1990 are also seen as driving factors. The Islamist resurgence is thus seen as a natural response to a series of structural "traumas" (Ferro 2002). International events such as the Soviet invasion of Afghanistan, which became the cradle of radical Islamist jihadism, create new networks, resources, and opportunities for Islamist mobilization (Hegghammer 2010). The state is also held responsible for mobilization as a response to state failure, state secularist policies, repression, and the lack of formal protest outlets under authoritarian regimes.

Other broad structural theories that may credibly help to explain the degree of Islamist mobilization include neighborhood demonstration effects and the degree of domestic political competition. Neighborhood demonstration effects refer to the idea that Islamist mobilization can be "contagious" from one country to another and spread through role modeling to opposition actors who have not yet used Islamist frameworks for mobilization. Likewise, Islamists in different countries have different sets of political competitors, such as leftist organizations or tribal networks, which may vary in strength and have the potential to crowd out opportunities for Islamists to be successful.

Though less prominent than structural theories of Islamist activism, some scholars focus on individual incentives for mobilizing within an Islamist framework. Although incentive-based theories are most successful in explaining why mobilization does not occur (Islamists are co-opted or heavily repressed), they are also used to explain positive outcomes in a variety of cases. Incentive-based theories focus largely on economic incentives for supporting Islamic movements, devoting less attention to possible negative sanctions for not mobilizing. Because in many contexts the costs for personal participation are high (from state repression) and the personal benefits are diffuse or low (with little resultant change), theorists have had difficulty constructing incentive-based arguments that hold where mobilization is costly. In some contexts, however, scholars argue that economic incentives generate support for Islamist movements.

Economic incentives may play a role at both the level of the Islamic organization and the level of the individual. Organizations may have access to financial resources from abroad, particularly from states that sponsor international Islamic activities such as Saudi Arabia and Iran. In diverse contexts, Saudi Arabia, Iran, and other countries have devoted considerable monetary resources to building Islamist movements beyond their borders. The availability of these resources generates financial incentives for Islamic organizations to mobilize both religiously and politically (Pipes 1983, Roy 1994, Weaver 2000, Ferro 2002, Kepel 2002). Funding may also be provided by states to domestic Islamic groups and interests. This occurred in the 1970s and 1980s in states such as Egypt and Turkey as regimes courted the Islamists to counter what they perceived as the dominant threat coming from the left. Saudi Arabia's historical patterns of funding international Islamist networks have also had broad effect (Hegghammer 2010).

Financial resources give Islamic organizations the ability to provide economic incentives for individual participation in their activities. In some cases, Islamist organizations have gained control of prominent financial channels, as they did by creating a dominant system of Islamist finance in the Sudan (Medani 1997). Other benefits of participation in Islamist movements may include access to Islamic welfare services, schools, scholarships, and elite networks (Akinci 1999). Some scholars thus argue that if membership in Islamist organizations provides access to new opportunities or capital, Islamist mobilization may simply be the outcome of short-term individual self-interest. Islamists may be interested in buying votes or paying off demonstrators by providing services or "grants."

Once inside an Islamist organization, particularly one that uses militant strategies, there may be strong disincentives for leaving the group or for failing to fulfill one's assigned role. Some Islamist groups actively use a strategy of branding organizations or individuals as "infidels," and assign consequences to such a designation (Kepel 1993). Although this strategy is applied primarily to political opponents, variations of branding may also be applied to individuals within the group who defect from the group's norms. This strategy has been deliberately applied by the Islamic State group in Iraq and Syria, for example, to maintain the allegiance of foreign fighters who join its ranks. Enforcement of group norms within an Islamic group may therefore provide incentives for participation among members. Such a strategy may also be applied to civilian populations in an effort to generate at least passive support for Islamist activities (Kalyvas 1999).

In contrast to incentive-based explanations, grievance-based theories of individual mobilization view participation in Islamist activities as a result of intense personal dissatisfaction. Often personal grievances are linked to structural changes, particularly population growth, urbanization, and economic downturns. Economic grievances, including poverty and unemployment, are common explanations for the appeal of Islamist groups who channel these grievances into a framework of economic injustice. Frustration is channeled into Islamist oppositions both because a retreat to religious identity provides psychological comfort in a changing world and also because Islamists prove an effective channel of protest against secular governments.

Most of the Muslim world witnessed dramatic population growth in the latter half of the twentieth century, a pattern that has continued in many countries in the last decade. This demographic explosion has led to an oversupply of labor in rural economic sectors and a subsequent large-scale migration into cities. Urban migrants bring expectations of employment and opportunity with them into the cities, while distancing themselves from traditional social structures and sources of identity. Some grievance-based theories assert that social dislocation, combined with economic hardship and disappointment, leads to feelings of disorientation and frustration that make urban migrants particularly open to Islamist appeals (Kepel 1993). Islamism is appealing to this population group because it grounds the migrant in traditional values while framing disappointment within normative claims about justice.

Urban migrants are likewise exposed to the material benefits and inequalities associated with development. Many received much more education than the generation before them but had few promising avenues of employment.

Scholars who have studied the backgrounds of Islamic militants in Egypt, for example, found that they often shared a common social background. Many were unemployed but educated young men coming from families that recently immigrated to urban centers (Ibrahim 1980, Kepel 1993).[14] Some argue that these background characteristics demonstrate how social change leads to feelings of relative deprivation. Unemployment and inflation in a context of rapid modernization lead individuals to join Islamist movements both as a psychological retreat and as a form of social protest (Munson 1986, Eickelman and Piscatori 1996, Hefner and Horavitch 1997, Tessler 1997, Kepel 2002).

Other types of grievances may be channeled into Islamist mobilization as well. Political grievances such as restrictions on religious actors, general state repression, or interference in elections are often cited. Grievances that result from attacks on the autonomy of the clerical establishment are prominent in explanations of the Iranian revolution (Akhavi 1980, Halliday 1996). The cancellation of the Algerian elections (1991) was followed shortly by large-scale Islamist protests and later by violence (Hafez 2003). Political grievances resulting from the Soviet invasion of Afghanistan were cited by multiple competing militias of Islamist *mujahideen*. The subsequent fighting and chaos in Afghanistan created widespread political grievances that helped the Taliban to rapidly mobilize in most of the country during the 1990s (Rashid 2000).

Grievance-based explanations are challenged by an increasing number of theorists working from the perspective of social movement theory. Like social movement theorists who have long examined political movements in the West, those who seek to explain Islamist political mobilization focus on three broad factors: resource mobilization, political opportunities, and the cultural frames in which mobilization occurs.

Scholars who focus on resource mobilization in Islamist movements examine the types of organizations that work to motivate Islamist action, the methods that they use, and networks that they draw upon to build support (Wiktorowicz 2004a). The theoretical assumptions behind studies of resource mobilization are (a) the more resources an organization has available, and (b) the more effective the organization is at utilizing those resources, the more mobilization will result. Some religious institutions have established networks of economic resources that they build up through alliances with business interests, such as the alliance of the *baazaris* and the clerical establishment in Iran, or the alliance of the Turkish Welfare party with a Muslim businessmen's association (MÜSIAD). Many of the resources most important to Islamist organizations are social and cultural, rather than economic, however.

Islamist organizations can often draw upon dense social networks, religious trust, and religious institutions in an effort to promote their political agenda (Owen 1992, Eickelman and Piscatori 1996, Hefner and Horvatich 1997, Wiktorowicz 2004a). While mosques have a primary religious purpose, they also may serve as a means of political communication for Islamists and a base for protest. Islamic non-governmental organizations, professional associations, and student associations all have their primary purpose outside of politics, but their networks can be drawn upon for recruitment and communication (Fahmy 1998, Wickham 2002). Islamists utilize even more informal networks, such as kinship networks or social clubs, under conditions of authoritarianism or strict state monitoring of political behavior (Wiktorowicz 2001, Wickham 2002).

Social movement theorists view political (and other) opportunities as central to understanding the conditions under which these resources become effectively mobilized. Political opportunities relevant to Islamist mobilization may take the form of state weakness, political liberalization, the appearance of new coalition partners, an opponent's political defeat, and others. For political opportunities to be taken advantage of, an Islamist organization must exhibit some degree of doctrinal or strategic flexibility in order to place the organization in increasingly advantageous positions as the political climate changes. Strategic behavior under conditions of political opportunity has been noted looking at cases such as those of Hamas in Palestine, Hizbullah in Lebanon, the FIS in Algeria, and the Muslim Brotherhood in Jordan, among others (Roberts 1996, Kalyvas 1999, Robinson 2004). Democratic transitions or state collapse provide dynamic situations in which Islamist groups find new opportunities to rapidly mobilize (Esposito and Voll 1996, Vergès 1997, Rashid 2000, Hafez 2003).

Social movement theorists also find a wealth of evidence that "cultural framing" plays a central role in Islamist mobilization. Islamists draw upon a rich backdrop of Islamic history, scripture, and symbolic language to frame their battles and justify their political behavior to potential recruits. For some scholars, Muslim politics is largely defined by an ongoing contest over the nature and control of "sacred authority" (Eickelman and Piscatori 1996). Because sacred authority confers power, many aspire to attain it. This often leaves the contest over sacred authority highly fragmented among competing frames that are offered up by the state and the clerical establishment, as well as accommodative and militant Islamists.

The use of Islamic language and symbolism as a mobilizing tool has long been noted (Lewis 1991, Owen 1992, Hefner and Horvatich 1997). Likewise, ideological frameworks for viewing the state and other actors help determine both the appeal of Islamist groups and the range of strategies that they employ (Vergès 1997, Wickham 2002). Wiktorowicz (2005) argues, for example, that militant Islamists frame their action within a discourse of jihad, bounded by interpretations of religious texts, but designed for particular political purposes. Common elements of militant Islamic frames include claims that state leaders are infidels (*kafirun*), block Islamic preaching (*da'wa*), are equivalent to foreign occupying powers, and must be removed as a defensive measure. Although scholars who highlight cultural and religious framing in the mobilization process assert its central importance in giving meaning to Islamist activities, much about the mobilizing effects of different types of frames remains unspecified.

## ASSESSMENT

The comparative approach used in this study casts doubt on religious or cultural theories that assert that Islamist political mobilization is a direct result of high levels of religious belief. Although patterns of religious belief change only slowly, mobilization of Islamic sentiment for political purposes can change rapidly within a given religious context. Additionally, some of the most avowedly religious Muslim societies manifest comparatively low levels of Islamist mobilization over time.

Some of the macro-structural theories discussed here likewise receive little support, while others remain difficult to assess both because of low theoretical specification and because of data limitations. This study shows little evidence that globalization produces Islamist mobilization or that Islamism is a direct correlate of authoritarian state policies. Other structural variables such as the rise of Arab oil; the fall of the Soviet Union; or the overall impact of international events in Israel, Afghanistan, and Iran are more difficult to assess. Potential indicators of "modernization" and of state "failure" receive mixed support in this study. The study does suggest that demonstration effects and variations in competitor strength are likely to impact the overall degree of Islamist mobilization over time. Indeed, this study reveals broad patterns of multiple countries experiencing a rise in Islamist mobilization during similar periods. Although the strength of domestic competition is not addressed across all countries in this study because of measurement obstacles, there is some evidence in the case studies in subsequent chapters that Islamist groups tend to do better when their competitors are divided and scattered. The design of this study is unable to fully capture the extent of these competitive influences over time and space, however.

Incentive-based theories that focus on economic incentives for mobilization are promising in some respects, but do not accurately reflect the motivations of the majority of individuals who mobilize for the Islamist cause. Most voters for Islamist parties never receive economic rewards for so voting; most Islamists who participate in street demonstrations or in political violence face potentially high personal costs for participation but only ambiguous, diffuse, or nonexistent economic rewards. It is clear that in some cases the provision of welfare services, finance, or other opportunities increases the appeal of Islamist groups, but it is not clear in most cases how this economic appeal is transformed into mobilization. Tracing the impact of Iranian or Saudi funding on mobilization is difficult except in select cases (such as the Lebanese Hizbullah), but mobilization clearly occurs in many areas without significant financial support from abroad.

Many grievance-based explanations for mobilization have come under attack in the broader scholarship on mobilization and social movements but remain prominent in theories of political Islam. This study supports the general critique of many grievance-based theories, finding little support for common claims that poverty, rapid demographic growth, urbanization, unemployment, or inequality lead to Islamist mobilization. Political grievances, however, appear to have a more significant impact. These may include state attacks on the autonomy of religious actors, government interference with the political process, state crisis, or the breakdown of civil order. Specific forms of state repression and state crisis do appear to affect the prospects for mobilization and figure prominently in the theory articulated in Chapter 2.

The processes of mobilization highlighted by social movement theorists such as resource mobilization, exploitation of political opportunities, and cultural framing are each present in the cases examined in this study. Highlighting these relevant processes, however, does not entail creation of a robust theory of why Islamist mobilization occurs in some contexts and not in others. For example, the types of resources that matter, the types of political opportunities that get exploited, and the types of frames that induce mobilization are all under-specified in the scholarship. The resources, opportunities, and frames in a particular context or case may be possible to assess, but the most recent social movement work on political Islam has difficulty specifying both the relative impact of these variables and a comparative framework for these factors across cases.

This study seeks to borrow from the insights and intuitions of social movement theorists while attempting to go considerably farther in specifying the sources of mobilization across diverse contexts. Some elements of structural, incentive-based, and grievance-based theories are also incorporated into the theoretical framework for the study. The result is an *institutional theory* with rationalist foundations that attempts to explain Islamist mobilization both across type of mobilization and across case. Explanatory factors are broadly construed to accommodate a variety of possible contexts. At the same time, the boundaries of those variables are defined as precisely as possible to generate observable implications that can be used to test the theory.

The institutional theoretical perspective presented in Chapter 2 is therefore the result of substantial compromises between generality and specificity in formulating the explanatory argument. It focuses on the interaction between diffuse Islamic institutions that generate Islamic common knowledge, hierarchical Islamic institutions that create variation in opportunities for Islamist political entrepreneurship, and shifts at the state level that provide political focal points for mass action.

## REFERENCES


Abd al-Karim, Khalil. 1995. *Al-Islam been al-Dawla al-Diniyya wa al-Dawla al-Madaniyya*. Cairo: Sina.

Akhavi, Shahrough. 1980. *Religion and Politics in Contemporary Iran*. Albany: State University of New York Press.

Akinci, Uğur. 1999. "The Welfare Party's Municipal Track Record: Evaluating Islamist Municipal Activism in Turkey." *Middle East Journal* 53/1 (Winter): 75–94.

Al-Affendi, Abdelwahab. 1991. *Turabi's Revolution: Islam and Power in Sudan*. London: Grey Seal.
Al-Baghdadi, Abu Bakr. 2015. "Al-Furqan media."
Anderson, Benedict. 1983. *Imagined Communities*. New York: Verso.
Ansari, Hamied N. 1984. "The Islamic Militants in Egyptian Politics." *International Journal of Middle East Studies* 16/1 (March): 123–144.
Beinin, Joel and Joe Stork. 1997a. "On the Modernity, Historical Specificity, and International Context of Political Islam." In Beinin and Stork, *Political Islam*. Berkeley, CA: University of California Press.
eds. 1997b. *Political Islam*. Berkeley: University of California Press.
Berejikian, Jeffrey. 1992. "Revolutionary Collective Action and the Agent-Structure Problem." *American Political Science Review* 86/3 (September): 647–657.
Berkowitz, Leonard. 1968. "The Study of Urban Violence: Some Implications of Laboratory Studies of Frustration and Aggression." In Louis H. Masotti and Don R. Bowen, eds. *Riots and Rebellion: Civil Violence in the Urban Community*. New York: Sage.
Betz, Hans-Georg and Stefan Immerfall, eds. 1998. *New Politics of the Right: Neo-Populist Parties and Movements in Established Democracies*. New York: Palgrave.
Burgat, François and William Dowell. 1993. *The Islamic Movement in North Africa*. Austin: University of Texas Center for Middle Eastern Studies.
Burke, Edmund III. 1988. "Islam and Social Movements: Methodological Reflections." In Burke and Lapidus, *Islam, Politics, and Social Movements*.
Burke, Edmund III and Ira M. Lapidus, eds. 1988. *Islam, Politics, and Social Movements*. Berkeley: University of California Press.
Clancy-Smith, Julia. 1988. "Saints, Mahdis, and Arms: Religion and Resistance in Nineteenth-Century North Africa." In Burke and Lapidus, *Islam, Politics, and Social Movements*. Berkeley, CA: University of California Press.
Clark, Janine. 2004. *Islam, Charity, and Activism: Middle Class Networks and Social Welfare in Egypt, Jordan, and Yemen*. Indiana University Press: Bloomington, IN.
Collier, Paul, Anke Hoeffler, and Nicholas Sambanis. 2005. "The Collier-Hoeffler Model of Civil War Onset and the Case Study Project Research Design." In Paul Collier and Nicholas Sambanis, eds. *Understanding Civil War: Evidence and Analysis, Vol. 1*. Washington, DC: World Bank.
Connor, Walker. 1994. *Ethnonationalism: The Quest for Understanding*. Princeton: Princeton University Press.
Darif, Mohammed. 1992. *Al-Islam al-Siyasi fi al-Watan al-'Arabi*. Rabat: al-Ma'arif al-Jadida.
2000. *Al-Din wa al-Siyasah fi al-Maghrib*. Casablanca: al-Najah al-Jadida.
Davies, James C. 1962. "Toward a Theory of Revolution." *American Sociological Review* 6/1 (February): 5–19.
Deeb, Mary Jane. 1996. "Islam and the State in Algeria and Morocco: A Dialectical Model." In Ruedy, *Islamism and Secularism in North Africa*. New York, NY: St. Martin's Press.
Dekmejian, R. Hrair. 1980. "The Anatomy of Islamic Revival: Legitimacy Crisis, Ethnic Conflict, and the Search for Islamic Alternatives." *Middle East Journal* 34:1.
1995. *Islam in Revolution: Fundamentalism in the Arab World*, 2nd ed. Syracuse, NY: Syracuse University Press.
Dudley, Ryan and Ross A. Miller. 1998. "Group Rebellion in the 1980s." *Journal of Conflict Resolution* 42/1 (February): 77–96.

Eickelman, Dale and James Piscatori. 1996. *Muslim Politics*. Princeton, NJ: Princeton University Press.

Esposito, John L. 1988. *Islam and Politics*, 4th ed. Syracuse, NY: Syracuse University Press.

Esposito, John L. and John O. Voll. 1996. *Islam and Democracy*. Oxford: Oxford University Press.

Euben, Roxanne L. and Muhammad Qasim Zaman, eds. 2009. *Princeton Readings in Islamist Thought: Texts and Contexts from al-Banna to Bin Laden*. Princeton, NJ: Princeton University Press.

Fahmy, Ninette S. 1998. "The Performance of the Muslim Brotherhood in the Egyptian Syndicates: An Alternative Formula for Reform?" *Middle East Journal* 52/4 (Autumn): 551–562.

Faksh, Mahmud A. 1997. *The Future of Islam in the Middle East*. Westport, CT: Praeger.

Feierabend, Ivo K. and Rosalind L. Feierabend. 1966. "Aggressive Behaviors Within Polities, 1948–1962: A Cross-National Study." *Journal of Conflict Resolution* 10/3 (September): 249–271.

Ferro, Marc. 2002. *Le Choc de L'Islam*. Paris: Odile Jacob.

Foran, John, ed. 1997. *Theorizing Revolutions: New Approaches across the Disciplines*. London: Routledge.

Goldstone, Jack A. 1993. *Revolution and Rebellion in the Early Modern World*. Berkeley: University of California Press.

1997. "Population Growth and Revolutionary Crisis." In Foran, *Theorizing Revolutions*.

Gurr, Ted Robert. 1970. *Why Men Rebel*. Princeton, NJ: Princeton University Press.

Hafez, Mohammed M. 2003. *Why Muslims Rebel: Repression and Resistance in the Islamic World*. Boulder, CO: Lynne Rienner.

Halliday, Fred. 1996. *Islam and the Myth of Confrontation: Religion and Politics in the Middle East*. London: I.B. Tauris.

Hefner, Robert W. and Patricia Horvatich, eds. 1997. *Islam in an Era of Nation-States: Politics and Religious Renewal in Muslim South-East Asia*. Honolulu: University of Hawaii Press.

Hegghammer, Thomas. 2010. *Jihad in Saudi Arabia: Violence and Pan-Islamism since 1979*. Cambridge: Cambridge University Press.

Hiro, Dilip. 2002. *War Without End: The Rise of Islamist Terrorism and Global Response*. London: Routledge.

Hunter, Shireen T. 1998. *The Future of Islam and the West: Clash of Civilizations or Peaceful Coexistence?* Westport, CT: Praeger.

Huntington, Samuel H. 1968. *Political Order in Changing Societies*. New Haven, CT: Yale University Press.

Ibrahim, SE. 1980. "Anatomy of Egypt's Militant Islamist Groups: Methodological Note and Preliminary Findings." *International Journal of Middle East Studies* 12/4: 423–453.

Jenkins, J. Craig. 1983. "Resource Mobilization Theory and the Study of Social Movements." *Annual Review of Sociology* 9: 527–53.

Johnson, Chalmers. 1982. *Revolutionary Change*. 2nd ed. Stanford, CA: Stanford University Press.

Juergensmeyer, Mark. 1993. *The New Cold War? Religious Nationalism Confronts the Secular State*. Berkeley, CA: University of California Press.

Kalyvas, Stathis N. 1999. "Wanton and Senseless? The Logic of Massacres in Algeria." *Rationality and Society* 11/3: 243–85.

Keddie, Nikki R. 1988. "Iranian Revolutions in Comparative Perspective." In Burke and Lapidus, *Islam, Politics, and Social Movements*. Berkeley, CA: University of California Press.

1994. "The Revolt of Islam, 1700 to 1993: Comparative Considerations and Relations to Imperialism." *Comparative Studies in Society and History* 36/3 (July): 463–87.

Kepel, Gilles. 1993. *Muslim Extremism in Egypt: The Prophet and Pharaoh*. Berkeley, CA: University of California Press.

2002. *Jihad: The Trail of Political Islam*. Cambridge, MA: Harvard University Press.

Kitschelt, Herbert P. 1986. "Political Opportunity Structures and Political Protest: Anti-Nuclear Movements in Four Democracies." *British Journal of Political Science* 16: 57–85.

1997. *The Radical Right in Western Europe: A Comparative Analysis*. Ann Arbor: University of Michigan Press.

Kuran, Timur. 1991. "Now out of Never: The Element of Surprise in the East European Revolution of 1989." *World Politics* 44/1: 7–48.

Lapidus, Ira M. 1988. "Islamic Political Movements: Patterns of Historical Change." In Burke and Lapidus, *Islam, Politics, and Social Movements*. Berkeley, CA: University of California Press.

Lawrence, Bruce. 1989. *Defenders of God*. New York: Harper & Row.

Lewis, Bernard. 1964. *The Middle East and the West*. Bloomington: Indiana University Press.

1990. "The Roots of Muslim Rage." *The Atlantic Monthly* 266/3: 47–60.

1991. *The Political Language of Islam*. Chicago, IL: University of Chicago Press.

Lohmann, Susan. 1994. "Dynamics of Informational Cascades: The Monday Demonstrations in Leipzig, East Germany 1989–91." *World Politics* 47/1: 42–101.

Lubeck, Paul. 1988. "Islamic Political Movements in Northern Nigeria: The Problem of Class Analysis." In Burke and Lapidus, *Islam, Politics, and Social Movements*. Berkeley, CA: University of California Press.

McAdam, Doug. 1982. *Political Process and the Development of Black Insurgency, 1930–1970*. Chicago, IL: University of Chicago Press.

McAdam, Doug, John D. McCarthy, and Mayer N. Zald, eds. 1996. *Comparative Perspectives on Social Movements: Political Opportunities, Mobilizing Structures, and Cultural Framings*. Cambridge: Cambridge University Press.

McAdam, Doug, Sidney Tarrow, and Charles Tilly. 2001. *Dynamics of Contention*. Cambridge: Cambridge University Press.

McCarthy, John D. and Mayer N. Zald. 1987. "Resource Mobilization and Social Movements: A Partial Theory." In Mayer N. Zald and John D. McCarthy, eds. *Social Movements in an Organizational Society*. New Brunswick, NJ: Transaction.

Medani, Khalid. 1997. "Funding Fundamentalism: The Political Economy of an Islamist State." In Beinin and Stork, *Political Islam*. Berkeley, CA: University of California Press.

Moaddel, Mansoor. 2002a. *Jordanian Exceptionalism: A Comparative Analysis of State–Religion Relationships in Egypt, Iran, Jordan, and Syria*. New York: Palgrave.

2002b. "The Study of Islamic Culture and Politics: An Overview and Assessment." *Annual Review of Sociology* 28:359–86.

Moussalli, Ahmad S. 1999. *Moderate and Radical Islamic Fundamentalism: The Quest for Modernity, Legitimacy, and the Islamic State*. Gainesville: University Press of Florida.

Muller, Edward N. 1985. "Income Inequality, Regime Repressiveness, and Political Violence." *American Sociological Review* 50: 47–61.

Munson, Henry Jr. 1986. "The Social Base of Islamic Militancy in Morocco." *Middle East Journal* 40/2 (Spring): 267–284.

Munson, Ziad. 2002. "Islamic Mobilization: Social Movement Theory and the Egyptian Muslim Brotherhood." *The Sociological Quarterly* 42/4 (Fall): 487–510.

Murphy, Caryle. 2002. *Passion for Islam: Shaping the Modern Middle East: The Egyptian Experience*. New York: Scribner.

Nasr, Salim. 1997. "Roots of the Shi'i Movement in Lebanon." In Beinin and Stork, *Political Islam*. Berkeley, CA: University of California Press.

Oberschall, Anthony. 1972. *Social Conflict and Social Movements*. Englewood Cliffs, NJ: Prentice Hall.

Olson, Mancur. 1965. *The Logic of Collective Action: Public Goods and the Theory of Groups*. Cambridge, MA: Harvard University Press.

Owen, Roger. 1992. *State, Power and Politics in the Making of the Modern Middle East*. London: Routledge.

Pipes, Daniel. 1983. *In the Path of God: Islam and Political Power*. New York: Basic Books.

Piscatori, James, ed. 1991. *Islamic Fundamentalisms and the Gulf Crisis*. Chicago, IL: American Academy of Arts and Sciences.

Pope, Nicole and Hugh Pope. 1997. *Turkey Unveiled: A History of Modern Turkey*. New York: Overlook.

Popkin, Samuel L. 1979. *The Rational Peasant: The Political Economy of Rural Society in Vietnam*. Berkeley: University of California Press.

Rashid, Ahmed. 2000. *Taliban*. New Haven, CT: Yale University Press.

Roberts, Hugh. 1988. "Radical Islamism and the Dilemma of Algerian Nationalism: The Embattled Arians of Algiers." *Third World Quarterly* 10/2: 556–589.

1996. "Doctrinaire Economics and Political Opportunism in the Strategy of Algerian Islamism." In John Ruedy, *Islamism and Secularism in North Africa*. Berkeley, CA: University of California Press.

Robinson, Glenn E. 2004. "Hamas as a Social Movement." In Quintan Wiktorowicz, ed. *Islamic Activism: A Social Movement Theory Approach*. Bloomington: Indiana University Press.

Roy, Olivier. 1994. *The Failure of Political Islam*. Cambridge, MA: Harvard University Press.

Ruedy, John, ed. 1996. *Islamism and Secularism in North Africa*. Washington, DC: Georgetown University Center for Contemporary Arab Studies.

Sara, Faiz. 1994. *Dirasat fi al-Islam al-Siyasi*. Damascus: Dar Mashraq-Maghrib.

Schelling, Thomas C. 1978. *Micromotives and Macrobehavior*. New York: W. W. Norton.

Shadid, Anthony. 2002. *Legacy of the Prophet: Despots, Democrats, and the New Politics of Islam*. Boulder, CO: Westview.

Skocpol, Theda. 1979. *States and Social Revolutions*. Cambridge: Cambridge University Press.

Smelser, Neil J. 1962. *Theory of Collective Behavior*. New York: Free Press.

Snow, David A. and Robert D. Benford. 1988. "Ideology, Frame Resonance, and Participant Mobilization." In Bert Klandermans, Haspeter Kriesi, and Sidney Tarrow, eds. *From Structure to Action: Comparing Movement Participation Across Cultures*. Greenwich, CT: JAI Press.

1992. "Master Frames and Cycles of Protest." In Aldon Morris and Carol McClurg Mueller, eds. *Frontiers in Social Movement Theory*. New Haven, CT: Yale University Press.

Snow, David A., E. Burke Rochford Jr., Steven K. Wordon, and Robert D. Benford. 1986. "Frame Alignment Processes, Micromobilization, and Movement Participation." *American Sociological Review* 51: 464–481.

Tarrow, Sidney. 1998. *Power in Movement: Social Movements and Contentious Politics*. 2nd ed. Cambridge: Cambridge University Press.

Tessler, Mark. 1997. "The Origins of Popular Support for Islamist Movements: A Political Economy Analysis." In John P. Entelis, ed. *Islam, Democracy, and the State in North Africa*. Bloomington: Indiana University Press.

Tibi, Bassam. 1990. *Islam and the Cultural Accommodation of Social Change*. Boulder, CO: Westview.

1998. *The Challenge of Fundamentalism: Political Islam and the New World Disorder*. Berkeley: University of California Press.

Tilly, Charles. 1978. *From Mobilization to Revolution*. Reading, MA: Addison-Wesley.

Vergès, Meriem. 1997. "Genesis of a Mobilization: The Young Activists of Algeria's Islamic Salvation Front." In Beinin and Stork, *Political Islam*. Berkeley, CA: University of California Press.

Voll, John Obert. 1994. *Islam: Continuity and Change in the Modern World*, 2nd ed. Syracuse, NY: Syracuse University Press.

Waardenburg, Jacques. 2002. *Islam: Historical, Social, and Political Perspectives*. Berlin: Walter de Gruyter.

Walton, John. 1984. *Reluctant Rebels*. New York: Columbia University Press.

Weaver, Mary Anne. 2000. *A Portrait of Egypt: A Journey through the World of Militant Islam*. New York: Farrar, Strauss, and Giroux.

Weede, Erich. 1987. "Some New Evidence on Correlates of Political Violence: Income Inequality, Regime Repressiveness, and Economic Development." *European Sociological Review* 3: 97–108.

White, Jenny B. 2002. *Islamist Mobilization in Turkey: A Study of Vernacular Politics*. Seattle: University of Washington Press.

Wickham, Carrie Rosefsky. 2002. *Mobilizing Islam: Religion, Activism, and Political Change in Egypt*. New York: Columbia University Press.

Wickham-Crowley, Timothy P. 1992. *Guerillas and Revolution in Latin America: A Comparative Study of Insurgents and Regimes since 1956*. Princeton, NJ: Princeton University Press.

1997. "Structural Theories of Revolutions." In Foran, *Theorizing Revolutions*. New York, NY: Routledge.

Wiktorowicz, Quintan. 2001. *The Management of Islamic Activism: Salafis, the Muslim Brotherhood, and State Power in Jordan*. Albany, NY: State University of New York Press.

2003. "Explaining Cycles of Islamist Violence: Preliminary Thoughts on Frames and Muslim Rebellion in the Middle East 1990–1999." (working paper)

Wictorowicz, Quintan. 2004a. "Introduction: Islamic Activism and Social Movement Theory." In Wiktorowicz, *Islamic Activism: A Social Movement Theory Approach*. Bloomington, IN: Indiana University Press.

ed. 2004b. *Islamic Activism: A Social Movement Theory Approach*. Indiana University Press.

2005. "A Geneology of Radical Islam." *Studies in Conflict and Terrorism* 28/2: 75–97.

Wright, Robin. 1985. *Sacred Rage: The Wrath of Militant Islam*. New York: Touchstone.

2

# From the Sacred to the State

## *A Theory of Islamist Mobilization*

This chapter presents a basic theory of Islamist political mobilization that seeks to explain why Islamist mobilization occurs in some contexts and not in others. This theoretical perspective is referenced throughout the remainder of the study and is assessed in subsequent chapters through both data analysis and the investigation of critical country case studies from the data set.[1] The theory presented is not intended to depict observed processes of mobilization, nor to represent how Islamist mobilization works in all cases. Rather, it is an abstract representation of key actors, decisions, and causal variables designed to highlight the contexts in which mobilization may be expected and the reasons these contexts matter.

The theory presented is distinct from the range of theories presented by other scholars that have been summarized in Chapter 1. At the same time, however, it is indebted to several of these theoretical perspectives, drawing upon important elements both from politically oriented perspectives and from the more established body of social movement theory. In addition, the institutional story presented here has distinctly rational foundations, and as such owes much in terms of language and concepts to many theories based in rational assumptions of human behavior.

While the micro-foundations of the theory are based in rationalist assumptions about individual behavior, the causal weight of the theory is found in much more "macro" variables that are institutional in nature. As such, the theory is a macro-theory that suggests large-scale variables are the causative factors that lead to broad collective action and mobilization outcomes over time. These macro-variables are all institutional arrangements that are complex and often historically rooted, but which may also change or be changed. Some of these institutional arrangements may change rapidly, while others are dynamic only over the longer term of many years or even decades. As noted by Acemoglu and Robinson (2012), institutional development is often the result of "critical junctures" that put a polity on the path to either virtuous or vicious circles of prosperity and failure. In this case, institutional junctures may lead to political Islam becoming either a dominant political cleavage or only a tangential one.

The theory focuses on providing an explanation for Islamist political mobilization as defined in Chapter 1. This type of mobilization includes attempts by self-defined Islamist actors to align state policy with perceived Islamic principles or to capture a portion of state power. In practical terms, this includes the political behaviors of voting for Islamically oriented parties, participating in Islamist-sponsored street demonstrations, or committing political violence on behalf of self-defined Islamist causes. These manifestations of Islamist mobilization capture the large majority of public activities associated with political Islam.

A number of important expressions of political Islam are not explained by the theory, however. These include human rights or tolerance campaigns by small Muslim minorities (e.g., headscarf campaigns in France), international terrorism directed at global targets (e.g., attacks on Western institutions from abroad), or Islamist mobilization directed by the state (e.g., official Islamic rallies in Iran). While the sources of these activities may have some relationship to the causal variables suggested here, different social mechanisms are likely at play in each of these cases and they require different types of explanations.

I argue in this chapter that significant levels of Islamist political mobilization are most likely to occur when three general conditions are present: first, Islamic institutions (such as mosques, religious schools, and Islamic media) are active participants in social life and create joint expectations through common knowledge; second, the incentives of religious leaders are poorly aligned with the incentives of the state and/or religious leaders have little hierarchical control; and third, public focal points at the level of the state (such as certain types of governmental crisis or rapid political liberalization) are present to collectively channel and focus common expectations. All of these conditions are important for successful mobilization, and the presence of only one or two of these conditions is not sufficient. The three conditions are individually necessary and jointly sufficient to generate Islamist mobilization. The three conditions must each be present to some degree for successful mobilization because of the central role that each plays in the mobilization process discussed in the following.

The remainder of this chapter serves to outline and discuss the theoretical claims as well as offer hypotheses regarding the underlying mechanisms that make mass Islamist mobilization possible. This is done first through a discussion of the micro-foundations of the theory, focusing on key actors and assumptions that drive mobilization at the level of the individual. These actors and assumptions are then combined to outline an abstract story of the mobilization process. The bulk of the chapter focuses on how these mobilizing actors are dependent on institutional contexts, with a description of how institutional arrangements lead to mobilization outcomes. This is done first through a discussion of the institutional relationships between religious entrepreneurs, religious elites, and the state. This is followed by a discussion of the role of Islamic institutions in generating common cultural expectations and channels for political communication. A presentation of the role of the state in creating both costs for mobilization and focal points around which those costs can be lowered concludes the discussion.

## KEY ACTORS AND ASSUMPTIONS

I present here in abstract form the key actors and assumptions that serve as the micro-foundations of the broader theory. These foundations are theoretical rather than empirical descriptions and are not directly tested in this study at the level of the individual actor.[2] They are presented in an effort to establish the reasoning behind the deductive claims of the theory, as well as to provide a record of assumptions that may be evaluated and challenged within specific empirical contexts. Many of the assumptions presented here regarding an actor's preferences and choices reflect rational behavior and motivations of self-interest. These assumptions represent theoretical abstractions that collectively underlie the logic of the theory and provide the theory with observable implications. They are occasionally violated in Islamic and other religious contexts in which self-sacrifice may at times be preferred over traditional conceptions of self-interest. The motivations of the suicide bomber, for example, do not reflect standard conceptions of self-interest. Nevertheless, assuming that actors are self-interested is a useful theoretical tool that supports predictions of most observed mobilization outcomes.

The foundational actor in this story is the individual Muslim, who will potentially mobilize in support of Islamist causes. The decision of individuals to mobilize is considered the immediate precedent of observed mobilization, and is the key outcome that leads to observations of mass mobilization.[3] Mass Islamist mobilization is simply the collective manifestation of many individual mobilization decisions. Potentially mobilizing individuals include all Muslims who have broadly construed Islamic preferences. An individual's preference may range from a vague preference for a religious and moral society to a stronger and more specific preference for elements of Islamic governance, state-guaranteed Islamic resources, and/or Islamist political leaders.

The religious-political preferences of individual Muslim citizens are diverse, and may be arrayed on a spectrum ranging from a complete separation of Islam and politics to a fully Islamic state. Even as individual preferences regarding the amount of Islam in politics differ, so does the intensity of that preference. The intensity and type of preference are not necessarily correlated. For example, an individual may weakly prefer a strong Islamic state, but another may strongly prefer Islam and politics to be separated, or vice versa. Figure 2.1 provides a graphic representation of the array of individual Islamist

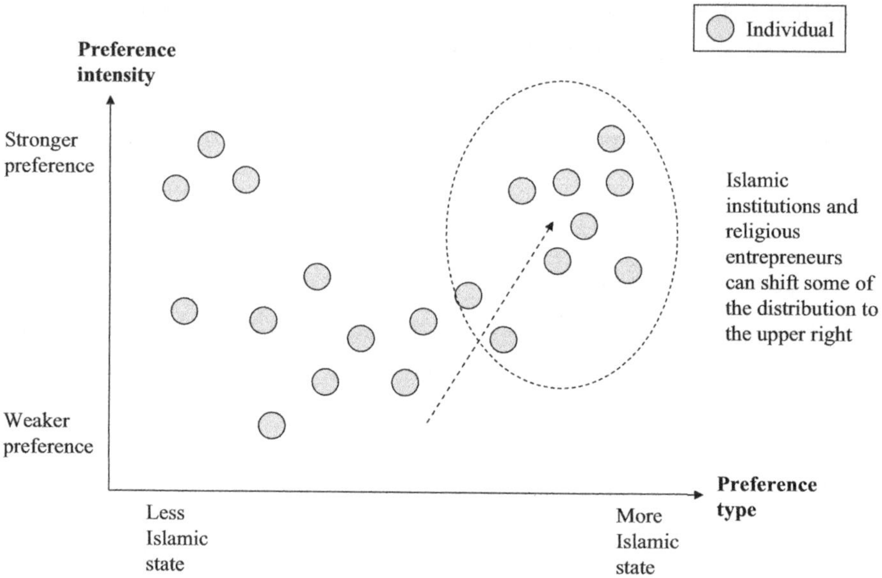


FIGURE 2.1 Islamist preferences vary both in type and in intensity.

preferences in a hypothetical society. The placement of individuals on this matrix differs in different types of Muslim societies.

At any one moment, the array of individual preferences on this matrix is static, but over time individual preferences are malleable and will change. Preferences, both type and intensity, are here assumed to change as the result of three interactions.[4] These three interactions are, first, participation in Islamic associations or social institutions (including group worship, religious education, membership in other Islamic social groups, and consumption of religious media); second, responding to motivating calls from self-styled religious leaders (here called "religious entrepreneurs" and "religious elites"); and third, reacting to the political behavior of Islamist (or Islamic religious) leaders. I assume here that participation in Islamic institutions and public calls from "religious entrepreneurs" increase both the preference for political Islam and the intensity of that preference. I also assume that a reaction to the political behavior of Islamist leaders can shift preferences (and intensities) in any direction depending on perceptions of the behavior – but that at times reactions to the political involvement of Islamist leaders will shift preferences (and intensities) away from political Islam.

In addition to individuals having a range of preferences for political Islam, I assume that individuals are concerned about the personal costs of mobilization. While these costs may or may not be high enough to prevent any one individual from mobilizing, I assume that over a distribution of individuals, lower personal costs make more individuals likely to mobilize. An individual with a strong preference for an Islamic state is willing to pay a higher personal cost to mobilize than an individual with a weak preference for an Islamic state. Intensity of preference is correlated with the costs an individual is willing to accept to mobilize on behalf of that preference. Thus in a context of high personal cost (through state repression, for example), only the few individuals with intense preferences will mobilize. As the cost is lowered (through the collapse of the military, for example), individuals with less intense preferences will mobilize alongside them, thus increasing the amount of observed mobilization. This follows the logic of "tipping point" or "cascade" models (Kuran 1991, Lohmann 1994).

I also assume that individual costs of mobilization are lower when large numbers of individuals are mobilizing than when only small numbers are mobilizing. This is primarily because under conditions of limited repressive capacity, the costs of repression are spread across the larger group. In cases where repression is not a major issue, other costs may come into play. In competitive elections, for example, the larger the group voting for an Islamist party, the more likely that party is to gain seats in parliament, and the less likely the individual is to suffer the cost of a "wasted" vote. In other words, individuals will vote strategically. The individual costs for mobilization also tend to be lower in large groups because of lower individual costs to organize and communicate,[5] as well as lower reputational costs (i.e., not having to defend one's actions before as many non-mobilizers).[6]

Expectations about whether others will mobilize are therefore centrally important to decision of the individual. The individual knows his/her preferences and receives some personal value from mobilizing on behalf of those preferences, but the value received from a successful policy change (or from the capture of power) as well as the personal cost for mobilizing are unknown. The individual must form expectations about whether others will mobilize in order to estimate both the personal costs of mobilization and the possibility of the mobilization being successful. Expectations that others will also mobilize increase the individual's willingness to mobilize on behalf of an Islamist cause, assuming Islamist preferences.

After the Muslim individual, the second actor in the theory is what I will call the "religious entrepreneur." Religious entrepreneurs are individuals who are interested in mobilizing others on behalf of Islamist causes. Given the political nature of Islamist mobilization, the religious entrepreneur is, in fact, a political-religious entrepreneur in that he or she tries to mobilize others politically within a religious framework. The religious entrepreneur may thus have a background either in politics or in religion, but is called a religious entrepreneur for the purposes of the theory.

Religious entrepreneurs are not always motivated exclusively by religious causes, but may be motivated by strong political interests such as opposition to the regime or a desire for power. They can be distinguished from other "opposition figures," however, because they promote policy change in the direction of self-defined "Islamic" religious interests. While many religious entrepreneurs emerge directly out of Islamic social circles, the boundaries of the category are not necessarily stable in the long term. For example, a Marxist fighting the dominant regime in the 1970s and 1980s could re-emerge as a religious entrepreneur after the dissolution of prominent leftist movements in the 1990s. This conversion to a platform of religious opposition may or may not be motivated directly by religious sentiment, but is nevertheless characterized by direct calls for change in religious policy and appeals to religious sentiments opposed to current state practice.

I assume that there is always a reservoir of potential religious entrepreneurs in a Muslim society. Status as an important religious figure is not a prerequisite to being a religious entrepreneur, although recognized religious status may make a difference in how successful the entrepreneur is at motivating others. The motivations of the entrepreneur are not of particular theoretical interest; they may be either religious or career-oriented without affecting the theory's predictions. In practice, religious entrepreneurs come from a wide variety of backgrounds and often articulate a stricter or more radical version of Islam than the Islamic clerical leadership (*'ulema*). In many cases religious entrepreneurs are students, engineers, businessmen, intellectuals, politicians, mystics, or theologians.[7]

I assume that religious entrepreneurs make a decision about whether to try to mobilize others, and that they will attempt to mobilize others when two conditions are met: (1) they believe that their interests diverge from the interests of the state; and (2) they believe that others will join them. The first condition reflects assumptions that the entrepreneur has different preferences from those of the state and also that challenging the state has lower costs for those without state ties. The second condition reflects an expectation of both greater gain (through a better chance of success) and less personal cost (through the wider distribution of costs) of mobilization.

The third actor is a group that I call the "religious elite." The religious elite are often clerical leaders (*'ulema, mullahs, ayatollahs*), but may also be mystics (*sheikhs, sufi marabouts*), prominent intellectuals, heads of state religious institutions, or established Islamist political leaders. Members of the religious elite might also be religious entrepreneurs, but the religious elite and religious entrepreneurs are often distinct. What usually distinguishes the religious elite from religious entrepreneurs is prominent religious status and an authority over Islamic matters that is recognized by a wide (if domestic) audience. The religious elite do not have to be Islamic scholars, and an entrepreneur may become a member of the religious elite over time, by building sufficient reputation and establishing a widely recognized institutional base.

I assume that the religious elite are always interested in promoting Islamic interests, but that they may or may not be "Islamist" in the sense that they promote political Islam. The religious elite may have ties to the state, often through official state recognition of their status, through the distribution of state resources, or even through direct participation in government. Some members of the religious elite may also be employed by the state, and are thus tied to the state through direct financial or reputational interest. For example, Islamic scholars in the preeminent Islamic university in Egypt, al-Azhar, are state employees who are paid by the state and who often make Islamic pronouncements on behalf of the state. There may be some tension between the interests of Islamic elites at al-Azhar and the state, but the university most often acts as an agent of state interests, a complaint among many Islamists who see the state as restricting the autonomy of senior scholars. Religious elites do not have to have only material motivations, and indeed many care more about religious issues than they do about financial compensation, but they can become embedded in institutional arrangements that effectively align their interests with state interests.

I also assume that because of their prominent Islamic status, the religious elite have some ability to influence the behavior of religious entrepreneurs and individual Muslim citizens. They may influence individual citizens through Islamic sermons, Islamic legal opinions (*fatwas*), or generic religious appeals. They may influence entrepreneurs through these same mechanisms, as well as through direct personal communication, particularly if the entrepreneur is part of a hierarchical organization directed by the religious elite. A prominent contemporary example of a member of the transnational religious elite is the Egyptian scholar Yusuf al-Qaradawi, whose program "Shari'a and Life" on Qatari satellite network al-Jazeera reaches many millions across the Muslim world. Other members of the religious elite are bounded to more domestic audiences.

The final principal actor is the state. While states usually have very diverse components, and these components do not always agree or act in the same ways, I assume here a unified state at the top levels of power. I also assume that state actors are primarily interested in maintaining power. Additionally, they usually have a preference for the policy status quo.[8] Therefore, the state views challenges by mobilizing Islamist actors hoping to gain political power or change the status quo as threatening. However, state actors also have an interest in maximizing their support from the population. They will not relinquish power in order to gain additional support for the population, but they may be willing to trade off their interest in the policy status quo with their interest in maximizing their support from the population.

State actors also have some capabilities. First, they have the ability to set state policy toward Islam. The state can either choose to align a state policy with Islamic interests, or it can choose to move existing policy further away from Islamic interests. State policy may become more aligned with Islamic interests through activities such as channeling resources to Islamic institutions, introducing elements of Islamic law into the legal system, or designating the state as an "Islamic state." State policy may move away from Islamic interests through such activities as restricting the behavior of religious organizations, eliminating Islamic elements from the constitution, or removing resources from Islamic institutions.

Additionally, I assume that the state has the ability to make Islamist mobilization costly for participants. This can be done through state repression, such as setting restrictions on gathering, eliminating state benefits, and dispensing jail terms or even death sentences to Islamist actors. The state may also create communication obstacles for coordination, popularize reputational costs for mobilizing, or provide the Islamists' competitors with competitive advantages. I assume that the state will always set some cost for mobilization, and that it does so strategically. Costs articulated by the state may or may not be viewed as credible, as the state may not have the will or ability to exact those costs in all cases.

## THE MOBILIZATION PROCESS

Given these assumptions and key actors (individuals, religious entrepreneurs, religious elite, and the state), how does mobilization take place? We can start by thinking about mobilization as a series of individual decisions that begin with religious entrepreneurs who make a decision about whether or not to try to politicize Islam. The process ends with many simultaneous decisions by individual Muslim citizens about whether or not to mobilize for an Islamist cause. The social interactions and combination of choices that lead to mobilization decisions by individuals are here called the mobilization process. The level and type of mobilization at the end of the process is called the mobilization outcome. While the mobilization process described here is in reality embedded within a larger group of social processes and may not have a discrete beginning or ending, for theoretical purposes I here consider the process to have both a beginning and an end point with a measurable outcome. I suggest a stylized sequence of actions within the mobilization process described in the following. Note that there is a logic to this sequence, but that the sequencing of actions is not critical to the success of the mobilization process. In practice, each element of this mobilization process is happening to some degree and at least at some level simultaneously, although each actor in the theory is observing others prior to making his or her own decisions.

The process begins with religious entrepreneurs. As noted, potential religious entrepreneurs are always present; they start the mobilization process if they try to mobilize others around an Islamic cause. They will only try to mobilize others, however, if they believe it is in their self-interest and if they believe that they have some chance of attracting others to the cause. Religious entrepreneurs therefore must assess their personal positions before attempting to mobilize others. Because mobilizing may be understood as a threat to the state, which prefers the status quo, the entrepreneur may choose not to mobilize if he or she is linked to the state. In this case, either the entrepreneur shares interests with the state and has little incentive to change the status quo, or the personal costs of mobilization may be too high due to economic dependence on state resources. In these contexts, potential religious entrepreneurs remain dormant because it is not in their self-interest to mobilize.

Even if religious entrepreneurs have interests different from those of the state, they must assess whether or not trying to mobilize others is worth the anticipated costs. It is considered worthwhile if many others will join in mobilization, and not considered worthwhile if others are unlikely to follow. Others will not follow if the dominant majority of individual Muslim citizens have different religious preferences from the entrepreneur, if more prominent religious elites will effectively discourage others from following the entrepreneur, or if the individual costs of mobilization (due to repression or communication barriers) appear too high. Under these conditions, potential religious entrepreneurs are less likely to try to mobilize others because they recognize that the chances of success are low. On the other hand, if the entrepreneur believes that he or she represents religious preferences more broadly, that he or she will not be outflanked by prominent religious elites, and that the individual costs of mobilization will be acceptable, the entrepreneur then calls for mobilization.

The first stage in the process, therefore, determines whether or not entrepreneurs actively call for Islamist mobilization. While there are many potential Islamist entrepreneurs in a given society, there are also many reasons entrepreneurs may not attempt to mobilize. If the entrepreneurial class is embedded in the state, either influencing state policy toward Islam or as a recipient of state patronage resources, there will be few entrepreneurs who see it in their self-interest to call for mobilization. In this case, the mobilization process does not begin. Even if entrepreneurs have different interests from those of the state, they must make a calculation about whether or not others will follow a call for mobilization. In a social context of weak Islamist preferences, little religious tolerance for entrepreneurship, or high levels of repression, entrepreneurs are likely to decide that attempts at mobilization will have little chance for success. In this case, even independent entrepreneurs who wish to challenge a secular state will not begin the mobilization process.

Religious entrepreneurs are a very loose class of individuals, however. They differ from one another not only in background and preferences, but also in their assessments of the social context and in their tolerance for risk. It makes sense, therefore, to conceive of entrepreneurs as a collection of individuals who are more or less likely to call for mobilization in a given context, rather than as a class that will or will not collectively mobilize. In most contexts we would thus expect to see some attempts at religious entrepreneurship because individual entrepreneurs have different interests from one another and will make different assessments of the likelihood that others will follow. The more prominent the entrepreneur, however, the more likely he or she is to be sensitive to the personal costs of mobilizing and to make accurate assessments of the likelihood that others will follow. We may thus anticipate that in difficult mobilization contexts, less prominent entrepreneurs will be more likely to call for mobilization. Less prominent entrepreneurs are also more likely to fail in their attempts to mobilize others, however, because they are less well-known.[9]

If a religious entrepreneur calls on others to mobilize around an Islamist cause, this starts the mobilization process. The next stage of the process involves an interaction between the religious entrepreneur and the class of religious elites. In contrast to the loose class of potential religious entrepreneurs, the religious elite are a well-defined and publicly acknowledged group with religious status. They share many interests and often act as a more coherent class. Most often this is as the official clerical (*'ulema*) class, although it may include prominent Sufi sheikhs, Islamic intellectuals, or established Islamist political figures.

The religious elite make a decision about how to respond to the religious entrepreneur's call for mobilization. Specifically, they choose whether or not to police the entrepreneur's attempted mobilization.[10] By "police," I mean to act in such a way as to punish or constrain the entrepreneur in order to stop the mobilization process. This might be done by asking the entrepreneur to stop mobilizing, by publicly attacking the religious credentials of the entrepreneur, or by appealing to the public not to follow the entrepreneur's call. Because the entrepreneur threatens the state by challenging the status quo, the religious elite will attempt to police the entrepreneur when their interests are tied to the interests of the state.

The religious elite may share the state's interests either because they have a preferred position in setting state policy toward Islam or because they receive state patronage resources (as individuals or for Islamic institutions under their control). In contrast to the interests of the broader class of potential religious entrepreneurs, the interests of the religious elite are often collective interests. Additionally, the religious elite have significant social status and control over Islamic or political institutions that can be leveraged to punish or undermine the efforts of religious colleagues.

Although the religious elite will attempt to police entrepreneurial attempts when the elite's interests are aligned with those of the state, those policing attempts will not always be successful. If the religious elite are relatively disconnected from their broader Muslim constituency and if they have little control over Islamic institutions, then their policing efforts may fail. Because religious entrepreneurs often emerge outside of the religious elite, they may not be particularly responsive to the elite's concerns unless they are part of a religious hierarchy through which the elite can exercise influence.

If the religious elite have some control over hierarchical religious structures of which the entrepreneur is a part, then the in-group policing activity is likely to succeed. These structures may include networks of *imams* (mosque prayer leaders), brotherhoods (often Sufi), religious schools, or other Islamic organizations including broad Islamic movements. The elite may threaten to expel members from Islamic institutions or even charge the member with apostasy. Additionally, the religious elite may exercise special influence over hierarchical structures that are not explicitly religious in nature. For example, religious elites may attempt policing through family or clan networks by pressuring prominent family leaders into controlling entrepreneurial attempts by less prominent family members.

Two questions thus frame this second stage of the mobilization process. First, do the religious elite attempt to police the entrepreneur? Second, if so, does the attempt at in-group policing succeed or fail? The answer to the first question depends upon the relationship of the Islamic elite to the state. The answer to the second question depends upon the nature of Islamic hierarchy of which the elite and entrepreneurs are a part. If a policing attempt is made and it is successful, the mobilization process stops before the Muslim public becomes mobilized. If either a policing attempt is not made or the policing attempt fails due to poor hierarchical control, then the mobilization process continues. The process begins to move beyond the realm of the sacred and into the realm of the state.

The third stage involves the response of state actors to the attempt at Islamist mobilization. If the mobilization is not effectively policed within the Islamic community itself, then the state must decide how it will choose to police the attempt. It does so by articulating a cost for individuals who choose to mobilize. This cost may be stated explicitly or it may be implied by state actions against early mobilizers.[11] Because the mobilization challenges the status quo, there will always be some cost associated with individual mobilization. This cost may range from individual costs in coordinating a common platform and obtaining access to the relevant state authorities with whom to present the platform all the way to harsh repression that includes the threat of death. In most cases, the cost of mobilization includes both difficulties in coordination and some level of political repression for openly challenging state policy.

While the state prefers the status quo, we have also assumed that the state prefers to be popular with its constituency as long as it can guarantee the continuation of its power. Therefore, articulating costs of repression toward individuals who mobilize involves tradeoffs that may make the state hesitant to repress. The state strategically sets the cost of mobilization in such a way that it hopes will limit the threat of policy change without excessively antagonizing its constituency. In an attempt to minimize both the amount of policy change and popular anger, the state tries to articulate costs for individual mobilization just above the threshold for participation. It may do this either through setting similar costs for all participants or by heavily repressing a small group while letting others off with little cost, thus distributing the costs unequally but creating a demonstration effect.

Although the state tries to set these costs strategically, there are reasons this may fail to prevent mobilization. First, the state may have poor information about the distribution of preferences and/or the coordination costs of individuals. For example, the state might misjudge the shape of social preferences on Islam (as distributed along the axes in Figure 2.1) and set costs that are below the threshold for mass participation. In another type of information error, the state overestimates the coordination costs that individuals face, and threatens only limited state repression that falls below the threshold for participation.[12]

Second, the costs for mobilization articulated by the state may not be viewed as credible by potential mobilizers. This may be either because the state lacks the capacity to enforce those costs or because the threatened costs for mobilization would risk the regime's leaders' primary goal of maintaining power. In a case of questionable state capacity, the state may simply have few repressive resources at its disposal that would make the threat of costs unenforceable in the face of mass mobilization. Even if the state has the functional capacity to carry out its threat, however, transmitting costs onto the population inevitably creates strains within the state. These strains could expose divisions within the government, risking state unity and ultimately its ability to maintain power. Enforcement of the threat of high costs may not be possible without antagonizing key constituencies of the state and potentially undermining its support base. In either of these situations, the ability of the governing regime to maintain control of the state is reduced. Enforcing costs through repression may create risks that the state is unwilling to bear, and thus the costs for mobilization articulated by the state are not credible.

The fourth and final stage in the mobilization process is that of individual Muslim citizens deciding whether to mobilize around the cause of the Islamist entrepreneur. Individuals choose to mobilize based on the balance between their policy preferences and an assessment of the expected personal costs that they will bear by mobilizing on behalf of those preferences. Policy preferences are correlated with the extent of individual association with Islamic institutions and are distributed across society with some individuals having both more Islamic and more intense preferences than others. Given similar anticipated costs, these individuals will mobilize earlier than others who have less Islamic and less intense preferences.

Assuming a wide distribution of preferences, individual expectations of mobilization costs become crucial in determining the mobilization outcome. To assess the potential costs, individuals take into consideration both the difficulties of coordination and the credibility of the state threat. Expected costs in both of these areas are high when the number of individuals mobilizing is low, but they decline as the number of individuals mobilizing becomes larger.[13] This is because both the requisite effort for coordination and the distribution of repressive capacity is spread among a larger number of individuals. The costs to the state in carrying out its threat to repress will also become harder for the state to bear as the number of participants increases. While the repressive capacity of the state may rise as the number of mobilizing individuals grows larger, the ability to repress cannot grow as fast as the number of participants, thus lowering the overall costs borne by the individual as more people mobilize.

Individual expectations of the behavior of others are thus crucial in generating an assessment of the personal costs of mobilizing. When others will mobilize, each individual is more likely to mobilize as well. An accurate assessment of when others will mobilize is more likely when individuals have common knowledge about each other's preferences and share focal points around which coordination is likely. Public events may help provide focal points around which common knowledge of Islamic norms is activated. Both a common language of symbolic reference and established institutional communication channels can lower the costs of communicating expectations and provide individuals with more accurate information about the potential behavior of others.

To summarize, the Islamist mobilization process outlined here is a four-step process. First, religious entrepreneurs make a decision about whether or not to attempt to mobilize others around a politicized version of Islam. Second, the religious elite may attempt to police the entrepreneurial effort and may either succeed or fail. Third, if the entrepreneur continues with his or her efforts, the state articulates a cost for individual mobilization. Fourth, individual Muslim citizens make decisions about whether or not to mobilize around the entrepreneur, which leads to a collective mobilization outcome. Mobilization can fail at any one of these four stages, and thus the right conditions must be present for each of them to be activated successfully. In practice, the state or religious elites can act preemptively against religious entrepreneurs, or religious entrepreneurs could act without fully assessing the anticipated responses, but it is helpful here to think through the calculations made by each actor in sequence.

Figure 2.2 provides a graphic representation of the key actors and interactions in the process. The actors are represented within different shapes, with

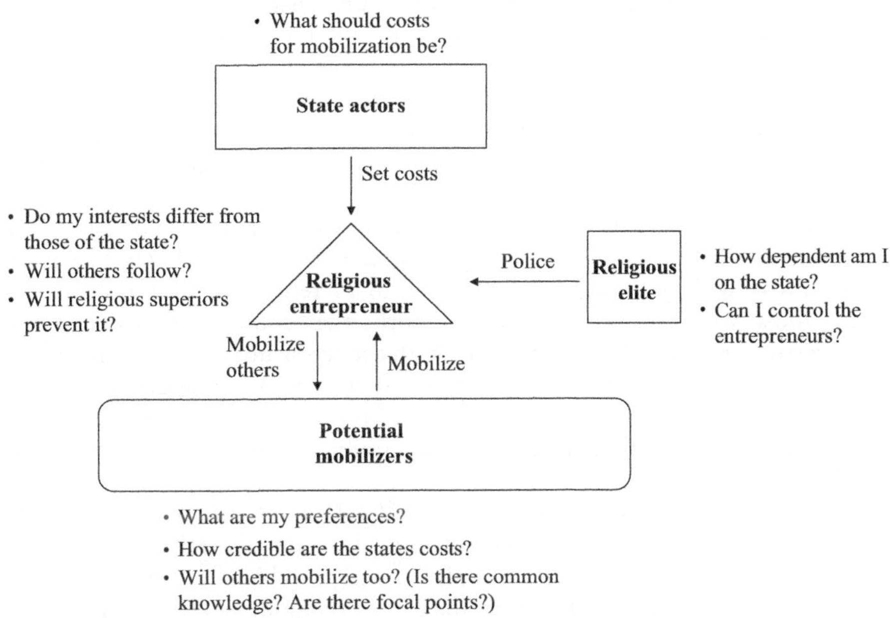


FIGURE 2.2 Key actors and decisions in Islamist mobilization.

the religious entrepreneur in the middle as the center of several interactions. The arrows represent the actions taken and the direction of the action. The bulleted questions next to the actors represent key questions that help the actors determine the action they will take.

While the mobilization process is driven by individual decisions and calculations of interest, the weight of the theory rests with institutional contexts that enable or constrain those decisions. Although it may be very difficult to observe decision-making in process, particularly among the mass of potentially mobilizing individuals, institutional structures and relationships between the actors can be observed. Indeed, the theory presented here is a macro-theory because it hypothesizes about the effects of structural contexts on mobilization outcomes. What follows in the remainder of this chapter is an application of institutional variables and institutional relationships to this mobilization process.

## STRUCTURAL FOUNDATIONS OF RELIGIOUS ENTREPRENEURSHIP

The emergence of religious entrepreneurs is the first step in the mobilization process, without which Islamist mobilization would not begin. What are the conditions that make the emergence of religious entrepreneurs more likely? To answer this question it is helpful to return to the previous assumption that potential entrepreneurs are always present and will find personal reasons to politicize Islam unless there are disincentives or constraints against doing so. The relevant question, therefore, is why would religious entrepreneurs fail to emerge in a given context? I here highlight some structural reasons religious entrepreneurs may fail to emerge or to attract attention. If these structural arrangements inhibit religious entrepreneurship, then we should expect that alternative structural arrangements would make the emergence of entrepreneurs seeking to politicize Islam more likely.

While, in principle, every individual Muslim citizen could become a religious entrepreneur, I assume that religious entrepreneurs are more likely to emerge among those with a background of activism in religion and/or politics and among those with established social networks that could be activated. These characteristics provide the entrepreneur with the requisite confidence and social resources to attempt to mobilize others in Islamist terms. The group of likely religious entrepreneurs is thus smaller than Muslim society as a whole and may share other characteristics, such as similar family, social class, or employment backgrounds.

The incentives of this group of potential religious entrepreneurs may be either similar or dissimilar to the incentives of the state. The relevant incentives are often economic ones, but they can also extend into broader expectations for the future such as the role of the state, the role of religion, and the incorporation of society into political decision-making. To the extent that potential religious entrepreneurs share the incentives of the state, they will have little interest in entrepreneurship that challenges the political status quo.[14]

There are several institutional contexts in which potential religious entrepreneurs share the incentives of the state. Potential entrepreneurs may be the recipients of state resources as part of a patronage network in which the state distributes large oil or export revenues. They could also be incorporated into the state through employment in the state bureaucracy, with strong incentives to support the state in order to sustain their families or obtain promotion. State policy toward Islam may be aligned with the preferences of potential religious entrepreneurs, or potential entrepreneurs may receive preferential treatment under the existing regime. To the extent that potential entrepreneurs are well-incorporated into the state and identify with it they are more likely to share the incentives of the state. This in turn leads to low incentives to challenge the state through Islamist mobilization.

By contrast, potential entrepreneurs who are not well-incorporated into the state are more likely to have incentives to challenge it. They may be poorly incorporated because they are deliberately excluded from patronage networks, they may be underrepresented in the state bureaucracy, they may be from remote regions, or they may be discriminated against based on their class, sect, or ethnicity. Potential entrepreneurs who are poorly integrated into the state are also more likely to have some autonomy from the state, which makes it easier to initiate a challenge. Autonomy often corresponds to the possession of an independent resource base, which may serve as an early source of social and/or economic capital for an Islamist challenge.

While measuring the level of a social group's incorporation into the state can be difficult, it is easier to observe a change in incorporation over time. For example, a loss of state patronage may be associated with an economic downturn, leaving fewer individuals with economic ties to the state. Potential entrepreneurs could be dismissed from state or military employment; government support for Islamic programs or education could be removed. The state's relationship with Islamic activists can also change from one of active support or cooperation to one of targeted repression. Under these circumstances it is clear that the interests and incentives of potential entrepreneurs become less aligned with those of the state than they were previously. This makes the emergence of Islamist entrepreneurship more likely.

Even if the relationship between the state and society is conducive to the emergence of entrepreneurs, however, entrepreneurs might be effectively policed by the Islamic elite. If they are prevented from mobilizing within their own religious institutions, the call for Islamist mobilization may never be heard by the broader public. In this context, the process of "in-group policing" refers to one in which the religious elite, who strategically cooperate with state interests, prevent defections from that cooperative equilibrium by religious entrepreneurs. The religious elite use their authority within the Islamic institutional framework to prevent religious entrepreneurs from challenging the state. In-group policing is often desirable for the religious elite because they receive resources through their cooperation with the state, and a challenge from religious entrepreneurs may put these resources at risk. If in-group policing is successful, the resulting equilibrium is a non-politicized outcome because the relationship between the Islamic elite and the state remains at the status quo.

This process resembles an "in-group policing equilibrium," as applied to models of intraethnic cooperation, in that Islamic co-religionists effectively prevent defections by Islamic religious entrepreneurs who want to challenge the state before the state has a chance to repress them. It differs from previous ethnic cooperation models in that it is applied within one religious community rather than between ethnic groups, and that defection is defined by a religious challenge to state authority rather than by interethnic violence.[15]

The religious elite that serve to police the activities of Islamist entrepreneurs have recognized status in the religious community. They may have advanced theological training (and thus recognized authority over Qur'anic interpretation) as well as a knowledge of Islamic law. In the dominant Sunni Muslim tradition, these individuals are broadly known as *'ulema* (the learned ones) and comprise something of a clerical class. In the Shi'ite tradition the clerical class is even more hierarchical in providing authoritative guidance for the community, with top clerical leadership (e.g., *marjas* or *ayatollahs*) taking on a public role in community decision-making. In areas with a strong mystical Sufi tradition, Sufi sheikhs (or *marabouts*) serve as a religious elite with significant in-group policing capability. In both Shi'a and Sufi contexts, therefore, more rigid in-group hierarchies are likely to make in-group policing more effective, on average.

The potential for alignment of incentives between religious entrepreneurs and the state also applies to the relationship of the religious elite and the state, but it is easier to observe. The religious elite is a smaller class of individuals whose relationship with the state is often more publicly apparent. In many Muslim countries, members of the Islamic elite are incorporated directly into the state through employment and the distribution of state resources. They might occupy official positions that oversee mosque construction, Islamic schools, the employment of prayer leaders (*imams*), or courts that rule on issues of Islamic law (shari'a courts). They may be employed to provide religious legitimacy for the state and to help craft state policy toward Islam and other religions. Even when they are not directly incorporated into the state, the state may provide them with preferential treatment and defer to them on some religious or social issues. Alternatively, the religious elite may be poorly incorporated into the state. This may be the result either of exclusion by a secular-minded state or of a decision by the elite themselves, who wish to maintain autonomy and would prefer not to be associated with an unpopular regime.

For the religious elite whose incentives are aligned with those of the state, religious entrepreneurship is viewed as a challenge to their existing position and they will attempt to police the entrepreneur. Their attempt at in-group policing will be successful when two conditions exist: (1) when the religious elite control hierarchical institutional structures of which the entrepreneur is a part, and (2) when Islamic institutions are not highly fragmented.

A hierarchical religious institution is one in which leadership rights are highly structured and participants lower in the hierarchy are expected to defer to the senior leadership on substantive matters. Power in the hierarchical institution is invested at the top, and participants who violate the wishes of senior leadership are subject to sanction or expulsion. Islamic institutions vary in the extent of their hierarchical control both across the type of institution and across context. For example, Islamic legal institutions often have more rigid hierarchies of control than do Qur'anic schools or religious media outlets. Likewise, control of mosques and Islamic schooling is highly regulated and institutionalized in some countries but is controlled at a community level in others. Some Islamic movements have very hierarchical control structures, and the leaders of those movements may also serve as elites who police the behavior of their members.

Note that there are significant differences in the institutional hierarchies across Sunni and Shi'a Islam, in general terms. Shi'a Islam, with its focus on the importance of following a scholarly source of emulation (*marja*), tends to have more rigid religious hierarchies, at least within the structure of an individual *marja*'s following. Historically, many Shi'a scholarly communities have also been better at preserving their own sources of revenue (as from religious endowments) than Sunni communities, which can give them more independence from the state than hierarchies of Sunni elites. This does not discount the very real possibility that substantial variation in elite hierarchies and elite independence exists within both Shi'a and Sunni religious communities (such as among Sufi vs. non-Sufi groups in both traditions).

The number of Islamic organizations in a country is also highly variable. In some contexts the Islamic movement has been relatively unified in one or a dominant few organizations (such as in Iran, Saudi Arabia, Malaysia, or Turkey). In other contexts, there has been extensive fragmentation of the Islamic movement, with a wide variety of organizations that vary based on ideology and on their target constituency (such as in Afghanistan, Algeria, Lebanon, or Egypt). Fragmentation is important in determining the potential for in-group policing because in a fragmented context religious entrepreneurs may defect to other organizations if they are sanctioned by the one to which they belong. Fragmentation lowers both the costs of being policed and the capacity of the policing organization to control its members. In a context of only a few dominant Islamic groups, on the other hand, coordination over sanctioning the member is considerably easier. Additionally, if the entrepreneur is forced to leave the dominant organization, it also deprives him or her of a potentially large constituency of the organization's members. Fragmentation of the Islamist movement thus enables religious entrepreneurship. Note, however, that if the large number of organizations leads to emphasis on different aspects of Islam (such as Shi'a vs. Sunni groups), it may be hard for members of one group to join another; the fragmentation may also hinder the development of shared Islamic expectations in the broader Islamic community.

Fragmentation therefore does not always provide the opportunity for defection to other groups. Institutions, religious or otherwise, that are demarcated along family or ethnic lines are very difficult to join if one does not have the correct heredity. Some Islamic institutions may have tribal or family membership preferences that make it difficult to join from outside the family.[16] Hereditary organizations can also be policed relatively easily, and may be informally used by the religious elite to sanction religious entrepreneurs. Patrimonial social structures are particularly capable of in-group policing and can be used by religious elites to sanction entrepreneurs, who may be seen as putting the whole family at risk by their activities.

In summary, there are several institutional contexts in which the emergence of Islamist entrepreneurs is likely. They are more likely to emerge when potential entrepreneurs have different incentives from those of the state because they are poorly incorporated into state networks for decision-making and resource distribution. This is easiest to observe when the state changes its patterns of patronage or political incorporation. A contraction in state patronage toward religious actors or the increased repression of Islamic institutions can increase the distance between the incentives of the state and those of potential entrepreneurs. Likewise, if the religious elite are poorly incorporated into the state or if they are fragmented and have little hierarchical control of Islamic institutions, the entrepreneurs are not likely to be successfully policed by religious associates.

Some institutional relationships also make the emergence of religious entrepreneurs much more difficult. If potential entrepreneurs are generally incorporated into the state through employment or through the allocation of state resources, they will have little incentive to mobilize in Islamist terms. If they have a role in shaping state policy toward Islam or if the state aligns itself with Islamic interests, the distance between the incentives of potential entrepreneurs and the state will be small. The religious elite are especially prone to incorporation into state resource networks, and will actively try to police any entrepreneurship that threatens that relationship. In-group policing by religious elites will prevent religious entrepreneurship when elites control hierarchical religious institutions and maintain sufficient unity to prevent defection from one Islamic organization to another.

## INSTITUTIONAL SOURCES OF ISLAMIC PREFERENCES AND EXPECTATIONS

Once religious entrepreneurs emerge and issue the call to mobilize, why do individuals follow? Why would they want to follow, and how might they coordinate their efforts? Part of the answer to these questions lies in the role of Islamic institutions that shape individual preferences and create common expectations about the behavior of others. Islamic institutions influence not only their members' religious beliefs, but also their beliefs about whether others will mobilize in any given context.

The types of Islamic institutions that shape preferences and collective expectations differ somewhat across Islamic contexts, but they almost always include the mosque, Islamic schools, social and welfare organizations, and usually some form of Islamic media.

Mosques typically adhere to one of two models, that of the small neighborhood center for worship (*masjid*), or that of the large public mosque designed to accommodate Friday prayer services for a larger quarter (*jami'*). Both types of mosques have one or more *imams* to lead prayer services and provide for the general management of the facility. Mosques may be either privately run or state-controlled, depending on the context, and the struggle for control over mosques is typically a central issue in the relationship between Islam and the state. The *masjid* provides a context for local religious leadership, communication, and coordination. The larger *jami'* usually has a broader, if less closely knit, constituency. The Friday prayers and sermons that take place there aggregate neighborhoods and provide a forum for enhancing personal networks and discussing public issues. Friday sermons have historically referenced the role of the state within the Muslim community, and changes in the types of references made in an *imam*'s sermon can serve as an important signaling device regarding the current perspective of religious leaders on state activities.

Islamic schools can be very different types of institutions depending on the context, but may be thought of as either *madrasas* for Islamically oriented basic schooling, Qur'anic schools that focus on memorization of scriptural text, or clerical training schools that provide a more advanced curriculum of Islamic theology and practice. At times Islam may be incorporated into official state schooling through a standardized religious curriculum. Islamic schools play a different role than do mosques because they provide smaller, and often less self-selected, groups with a more extensive repertoire of Islamic language, symbols, and worldviews. Despite the differences in types of schooling, a strong emphasis on memorizing texts (from the Qur'an) dominates most Islamic schools, creating a measure of standardization even under conditions of diverse administration. The more pervasive and the more standardized the Islamic schooling, the larger is the social group that shares this Islamic identity and canon of Islamic references.[17]

As an extension of the mosque and of the Islamic school, social organizations and Islamic media outlets often emerge. Social organizations usually place significant focus on the temporal welfare of members, supported by the Islamic mandate of charitable donations (*zakat*). They may also be organized around a proselytizing mission (*da'wa*), calling upon others to strengthen their Muslim identity and religious commitment, thus extending the spiritual boundaries of the Muslim community *('umma)*. An Islamic intellectual class usually develops out of the more advanced theological training schools, which publishes religious treatises and may create Islamic media organizations. If the media restrictions of the state do not prevent it, a popular Islamic media of recorded sermons, newspapers, pamphlets, radio, television, and internet broadcasts can develop. With the advent of social media, Islamic groups have readily taken to communication websites such as Facebook and Twitter to advertise their positions on issues and spread information instantaneously.

Collectively, these Islamic institutions can have a far reach and may represent the dominant forums of community participation for a devout Muslim individual. They have three important roles in the mobilization theory presented here. First, they can shape individual *preferences* on the role of Islam in politics. Second, they create a shared canon of symbolic *references* and meaning that enables the development of Islamic "common knowledge" among those who share that canon. Third, they create channels for rapid interpersonal *communication*. The first of these roles increases the amount of personal benefit individuals anticipate from mobilizing. The second and third roles serve to lower the anticipated individual costs of mobilization.

Islamic institutions specifically help shape individual preferences about the relationship between Islam and the state. They can do so because individual preferences on this issue are difficult to derive internally and are highly conditioned on an understanding of the meaning of Islam. For example, while one may derive an internal preference for food or literature based on personal experience with the pleasure it brings, the preference for an Islamic state is dependent upon an external belief that this is the proper institutional arrangement. This external belief may come from religious sources or actors, potentially including religious entrepreneurs. Even in contexts in which individuals have had some exposure to an "Islamic state," the preference is less directly experiential and more an abstract preference dependent upon a belief system. Because Islamist preferences are tied to the development of a worldview and are not experiential by nature, they are likely to be shaped through association with institutional religious authorities and confirmed through the collective acknowledgement of those preferences by participants.

While there is no universal agreement among Islamic scholars around whether or not an Islamic state is appropriate or what the characteristics of an Islamic state should be, the common sources of instruction in Islamic schools and other institutions enable the politicization of Islam. Much of the Qur'an and other sacred texts such as the Hadith (traditions of the prophet Muhammed) refer to an Islamic community with state-like characteristics; the daily governance of that community is both a political and religious affair. Likewise, the traditions of Islamic law codified in the early Middle Ages envisage an Islamic political community and a highly articulated legal system that continues to be referenced in many public religious institutions, as well as by Islamist groups (Feldman 2012). Islamic institutions therefore communicate a vision of the true Islamic community that shapes individual preferences for governance and is often at odds with government policy in Muslim countries.[18]

In addition to shaping preferences, Islamic institutions can help create a shared canon of symbolic references that build common knowledge. These references fall into at least three main categories: (1) historical, referring to social evolution through illustrative periods in Islamic history; (2) moral, referring to norms of appropriate personal behavior; and (3) relational, referring to appropriate relationships between the individual, God, and others. A mention of the "rightly guided caliphs" (*rashidun*) or of Imam Ali in the Shi'i tradition, for example, conjures up a range of historical events that create contemporary meaning through contrast between early Islamic governance and the subsequent Shi'a breakaway from mainstream Islam. Likewise, a mention of an act as religiously forbidden or a description of others as "people of the book" (*'ahl al-kitab*) provides structure to the norms of appropriateness and categorization of individuals that echo with meaning far beyond the original reference.

Collective exposure to this canon of symbolic references can create common knowledge of those references. Common knowledge is defined not just as knowledge shared by individuals, but *knowledge that each individual also knows is shared among the whole group* (Geanakopolos 1992, Chwe 1998). In other words, it is collective knowledge about the kinds of information and symbolic reference points to which others have access. Common knowledge is not to be confused with close personal relationships or dense social networks, although close friends may have much knowledge in common. Rather, it performs a function not entirely unlike the role of "weak ties" in Granovetter's formulation, in which general acquaintances with others (or in this case with *what others know*) serve as the bridge between localized dense social networks and thus make widespread collective action possible.[19] Common knowledge serves to bridge the gaps between networks of personal relationships by building shared expectations that span across narrow patterns of social communication, and can thus support collective action across groups whose members do not know one another. This is because these groups share similar expectations about how others will act due to common religious or cultural understanding.

Note that common knowledge in the sense of shared cultural understanding is not explicitly required for collective action in some popular models of mobilization, such as in Lohmann's "cascades of mobilization."[20] Prior to the fall of East Germany, for example, social information appeared quite fragmented. Indeed, what common knowledge existed was due to a shared historical experience in living under the rules of a police state. One could suspect that others were as frustrated and demoralized living in the police state as oneself, but widespread confirmation of discontent was absent due to the limitations on communication. Common knowledge of the sanctions present under such a regime likely acted to prevent collective action because of a shared understanding of the high personal costs of challenging the state.

Nevertheless, common knowledge in such a repressive context became rapidly relevant during the initial Leipzig demonstrations documented by Lohmann. The suspected collective feeling of discontent became clear through the "informational cascade" brought on by the series of public demonstrations. Common knowledge of individual preferences had been diluted or destroyed in the German Democratic Republic, but this could change quite rapidly given the focal demonstrations that rapidly publicized suspected discontent.

For a practical and universal example of how common knowledge is created and used, consider the potential for cultural common knowledge gained through film. Even though my favorite movie line may be filled with meaning for me, I am unlikely to reference it in conversation unless I know that my conversation partner has also seen the film. If I know that she has seen the film, then referencing the line may deliver significant meaning with great economy of language because of the broader context and story implied by it. Even if we have both seen the film, however, unless we know that the other has seen it the reference will remain unutilized.[21] Common knowledge requires knowing what others know.[22]

Like two conversationalists who have seen the same film, participants in Islamic institutions share great meaning through a collective knowledge of the symbolic canon. What makes this knowledge common knowledge is group participation in obtaining it. In this regard, a shared Islamic educational background and attendance at Friday sermons are particularly important. Standardized Islamic education enables common knowledge in a way that diverse loci for learning do not. The standardization of the text (the Qur'an) facilitates common knowledge even in a poorly institutionalized educational system, but educational priorities may still be quite different among different groups. If, for example, multiple hierarchical sects or brotherhoods autonomously establish distinct Islamic education, we may expect that there would be extensive common knowledge within the sect, but only limited common knowledge across them. Attendance at a large Friday prayer service can create common knowledge among participants who are able to recognize that they are part of a broader community of others who are receiving the same information. Common knowledge is a general social construct that occurs both within and without Islamic contexts, but within the in-group context, the particularities of that set of common knowledge and the knowledge that others share those same peculiarities is important to creating the potential for collective action.

Common knowledge is important because it allows for the rapid communication of meaning and because it creates shared expectations of what others will do. Communicating why something is necessary or how it is to be done can take much effort unless the parties share similar reference points. It creates shared expectations because not only do I know what my inclination is in a given context, but I also know that others know what my inclination is, and they know that I know what their inclination is also.

For a non-Islamic example of mobilization, consider the popular gatherings that took place after the string of World Cup football victories in Turkey, when the author was resident in the country. The mobilization in this case was manifest in raucous public victory parties and creative displays of the Turkish flag. The uninitiated celebrant, such as myself, knew not where to gather, nor that one should bring a flag, nor that it would be impossible to drive through the jam-packed streets to meet an interview contact. On the other hand, to those with common knowledge of how important the victory historically was, mass gathering in specific locales with proper accoutrements and the implicit cancellation of all other work or social obligations appeared to be a spontaneous response that required no explicit or external coordination. Common knowledge shaped both the meaning of the event and the expectation of how others would behave to great effect.

For an Islamic example, consider the mass pilgrimages of Shi'a in Southern Iraq shortly after the fall of Saddam's regime in 2003. To the observer that did not share in the common knowledge of the Iraqi Shi'a community, the sudden assembly of millions at Shi'ite holy sites that had seen no mass pilgrimages for a long period was puzzling if not astonishing. For those who shared in the collective meaning of the pilgrimage, however, the fall of Saddam's regime activated the common expectation that the long-suppressed event would recur and would be an event one should not miss.

Other examples of Islamic common knowledge supportive of collective action include access to a historical mythology of the early Islamic caliphate, as well as a basic understanding of the hierarchy of permitted actions under Islamic law (al-ahkam), including obligatory (*fard*) or forbidden (*haram*) actions. A knowledge of what is mandatory or forbidden in Islam often extends into the realm of common knowledge, in which I also know that others know that those acts are either mandatory or forbidden. When a group that shares this common knowledge collectively witnesses the performance of an action forbidden in Islam, coordination around an appropriate response to that action becomes much easier than if that common knowledge were not present. In its most brutal form, this can support the spontaneous collective punishment of an individual caught in an adulterous act, or more commonly, a collective refusal to eat in public during the month of Ramadan. A shared historical mythology of the early Islamic caliphate has likewise been critical to many attempts by Islamists to mobilize others on behalf of the creation of an Islamic state, including the 2014 attempt by the group calling itself the "Islamic State" in Iraq and Syria to rally large numbers of foreign supporters to rapidly build a new system of governance based on "Islamic" assumptions. This assumed shared belief in a version of Islamic history helped to resolve significant coordination challenges among those with diverse national backgrounds.

Islamic institutions also support mobilization through more formal channels that enable rapid communication because of their organizational structure. The mosque creates a community of individuals that regularly associate with one another and have frequent communication. Direct communication to a large group is possible at least every Friday during the sermon (*khutba*). As one Shi'ite cleric campaigning for political office in Iraq in 2004 stated when asked about the difficulty of obtaining media access: "Our television is the Friday prayer; this is better anyway. Governments can regulate what goes on television, but only God controls what is said in Friday prayer."[23]

Islamic schooling is often administered through a hierarchical structure that can communicate information rapidly to students. Islamic social and welfare organizations generally have a well-ordered, "cell-like" or "cadre" structure that provide leaders with the ability to communicate to diverse populations. The Islamic media are also efficient communicators within their constituency and can disseminate a range of explicit or implied messages to the Muslim public. These everyday religious institutions are typically flexible enough to accommodate a range of information outside the strictly religious, thus also serving a function of social and sometimes political organization.

The reason that the development of Islamic common knowledge and institutional channels for communication matter for mobilization is that they lower the mobilization costs for individuals. Assuming a wide distribution of individual preferences for Islamist policy, lower costs for mobilization will lead to a larger number of individuals mobilizing. Islamic institutions lower the costs of mobilization both by increasing the ease of communication and by creating common knowledge that leads to collective expectations.

Communication in support of collective action is intrinsically costly, regardless of the political context.[24] Even in a context of free media and open political dialogue, sending a message to many people takes significant amounts of time, and often money. Yet, communication is crucial to any collective endeavor. It is necessary not only to shape logistical expectations (e.g., everyone meet at Tahrir Square at 2 PM on Friday) but also to provide reason and meaning for mobilization (e.g., if we don't meet, the government will view its behavior on this matter as acceptable). Islamic institutions can effectively lower mobilization costs in both regards; such institutions were particularly crucial at solving collective action problems before technologies of texting and social media made this process easier for individuals to access. These institutions provide easy channels for logistical communication because the institutions already exist for other, religious, purposes, and because they often have authoritative status among a broad constituency. By investing particular events or actions with religious meaning, Islamic institutions can communicate a much richer account of the need for mobilization than alternative voices can do relying on logical persuasion only.[25]

By generating Islamic common knowledge, religious institutions also shape expectations of others' reactions and behavior in a given context. If I want to mobilize but am unsure whether others will mobilize or not, I may not mobilize because the costs of being the one individual who mobilizes may be too high. For example, I may be shot, be imprisoned, or simply suffer reputational costs for standing out awkwardly in a crowd. If I want to mobilize and believe that others will mobilize as well, then I will perceive my individual costs as lower. If the state chooses to repress those mobilizing, the costs of repression will be spread across a broader group of participants, lowering the costs to any one individual. Even without repression, participation within a large group will create lower reputational costs (because so many others are also doing it) and will lower the likelihood of a wasted effort.

In summary, the Islamic institutions described here play three important roles in Islamist mobilization. First, they help shape preferences for Islamist policies. While they are not strictly exogenous to those preferences (after all, those with Islamist preferences may express this through active support of Islamic institutions), they can play an independent role in creating individual preferences. This is most clear in the case of Islamic education where children are taught prior to establishing personal preferences, but also applies to adults in other institutions whose *a priori* preferences on abstract Islamist ideology are, at best, amorphous. As Islamic preferences change over time, they may also impact the potential for the emergence of religious entrepreneurs that are inspired by and build on these preferences. A trajectory of changing preferences may therefore impact the ability of other actors in this theoretical story to emerge and be successful.

Second, Islamic institutions help create common knowledge about those preferences. The act of participation in Islamic institutions is often a public one and reveals one's preferences to others. Additionally, an individual's participation over time exposes him or her to a canon of symbolic references, historical context, and the believer's worldview. To the extent that this referential canon is held collectively in a given community, that community possesses Islamic common knowledge that shapes expectations about others' beliefs and preferred responses to events. Expectations of others' preferences with respect to mobilization lower the expected individual cost for mobilization. Expectations of others' preferences also affect the calculations of religious entrepreneurs, who assess those preferences in determining their likelihood of leading a successful mobilization effort.

Third, Islamic institutions lower the individual costs of more formal communication by facilitating the coordination of mobilization through existing, widespread, and authoritative institutions. This can be done efficiently through hierarchical channels and networks that have been previously established through participation in a religious community. It can also be done in the context of large Islamic events and rituals (such as the Friday sermon or celebrations during a mass pilgrimage).

Although Islamic institutions facilitate the efforts of the religious entrepreneur by shaping preferences and creating common knowledge, this is not enough to enable mass Islamist mobilization. The common knowledge generated through Islamic institutions will remain largely dormant unless there are focal points around which to coordinate shared expectations. Institutional contexts that enable the emergence of religious entrepreneurs and build common knowledge together create the *potential* for Islamist mobilization. The timing and extent of that mobilization, however, are dependent upon a third institutional element – state focal points for public coordination.

## THE ROLE OF STATE FOCAL POINTS

Many have cited the importance of a shared religious language, symbolism, and culture as a constitutive element of political Islam (Eickelman and Piscatori 1996). While this symbolic language may be an essential component, the impact of religious symbolism becomes activated in politics only when it is juxtaposed against an external political context. Cruise O'Brien uses a theatrical metaphor to describe the interaction between religion and politics. For him, the presentation of religious symbolism within a political context is a show, a show that "will only work when players and the audience share a vocabulary, a common set of values and symbols, the elements of a culture with something religious at the core."[26] He notes, however, that this show may have little impact unless there is something that helps to turn the audience's attention toward the show. I argue here that specific types of public state events can effectively turn the attention of the audience (potentially mobilizing individuals) toward the show (entrepreneurial attempts to activate Islamic common knowledge).

One of the inherent difficulties with activating common knowledge is that its component parts are many and diverse. It is therefore difficult to know which part of common knowledge should or will be activated at any point. Likewise, for common knowledge to play a role in coordinating mobilization, the same parts of common knowledge must be activated within a community at approximately the same time. The time frame in which one expects others to act on their preferences is potentially as important as knowing what those preferences are. Even though I know what others know and that we all know that we know it (in general terms), if I am to act I need to know what part of that common knowledge we are acting upon and when we are doing it. Only then would I expect that collective mobilization will result in lower individual costs.

The catalyst that helps individuals coordinate on both a selected portion of their common knowledge and the timing of mobilization is a public state event that serves as a focal point. Following its use in game theory, I use the term "focal point" to designate the locus of anticipated coordination among several acceptable coordinated outcomes. Specific types of public events at the state level may serve to activate common knowledge by directing attention to one particular area of common knowledge at one particular time. In addition, the public nature of these events builds further common knowledge by including the event in the canon of what is collectively known. When juxtaposed against the backdrop of collective Islamic references, the event may take on religious meaning and become framed as part of Islamic common knowledge.

Common knowledge makes focal points possible, on the one hand, because it creates the collective potential for coordination around selected areas of shared expectations or preferences. On the other hand, focal points as conceptualized here must emerge from an external stimulus to target coordination activities. I hypothesize that this external stimulus comes most often in the form of a public state event. These focal state events both narrow the arena for coordination of Islamist actions and focus attention on a shared expectation both *publicly* and *simultaneously*. Focal state events sometimes take the form of a "signal" from the state, although this signal is often unintentional. At base, focal state events signal both the narrow issue area and timing around which to coordinate collective action.[27]

For example, imagine a scenario in which many individuals with a shared background in Islamic morality and conceptions of social justice exist in a political community. They may not know each other individually, but they do know that others with similar Islamic preferences and religious backgrounds exist within that community. Although the political community in which they live is far from their Islamic ideal on a range of issues, coordinating across all relevant issues to push for political change is very difficult and does not occur.

Now imagine that through some investigative journalism it becomes public knowledge that the political leader of this community has siphoned off public donations to Islamic state charities and has spent this money shopping for his mistress in Europe. This creates a scandal that focuses the Islamic common knowledge in this community around two issues, those of Islamic conceptions of justice and morality. Because the scandal comes to light to the public as a single event, it also focuses individual Muslims around these issues simultaneously, with everyone knowing that others are focusing on the same issues at the same time. This external event thus serves as a focal point, drawing the attention of individuals simultaneously to the same issues, creating expectations that others will respond and thus significantly lowering the costs of mobilization. In a context where religious entrepreneurs are available to specify the logistical means for mobilization, lower costs for individual mobilization increase the likelihood that Islamist mobilization will occur. Even though the individual preferences on Islamic issues of justice and morality have not changed, the scandal changed the status quo by lowering the individual costs for expressing those preferences.

While this is a stylized example, there are several generic types of public focal points that occur in the Muslim world that may serve to activate Islamic common knowledge and lower individual mobilization costs. I focus here on two types of public state events that have institutional foundations: (1) internal state crisis and (2) rapid political liberalization. Note that for focal points to play a role in Islamist mobilization, they do not need to explicitly be "Islamic" focal points, such as a public act of immorality. While the type of focal point may have particular resonance because of its association with Islamic common knowledge, often more generic focal points can activate common knowledge, which then becomes channeled into collective action through Islamic channels because Islamic common knowledge sets up the possibility of a localized communal response to a broader political or social challenge.

Specific types of state crisis, in particular, may serve as focal points around which Islamist mobilization may occur. While political crisis in some form is present in most parts of the Muslim world across multiple periods, some types of crisis more effectively serve as focal points than do others. Some types of state crisis have origins that are external to the state, such as international conflict, regional economic collapse, or natural disasters. Internal crises, by contrast, are based in difficulties within state institutions and leadership choices, and provide more effective catalysts for Islamist mobilization. Likewise, some crises are both amorphous and extended, based in a prolonged political malaise rather than in distinct public events. The gradual, extended crisis is less effective at lowering the costs of coordination than the event-based crisis and therefore is less likely to serve as a focal point for mobilization. Internal, public, event-based crises will therefore be the focus here.

Some of these crises, however, can be more resonant in an Islamic context than are others. In particular, political crises of *order* and/or *justice* can be easily framed against commonly shared Islamic notions of both of these concepts. Historical emphasis in the Islamic tradition on the importance of order and social justice among believers has created significant cultural resources that can be deployed to juxtapose the Islamic conception of these two notions against the political backdrop of state events. The divine importance of an orderly community of believers can be contrasted against a chaotic or paralyzed government, while the command for just rulers can be contrasted against government greed, corruption, and nepotism. Examples of internal state crises of order and justice that can be observed exogenous to Islamist mobilization include government collapse, leadership turnover (especially unexpected turnover), civil violence, sudden inflation, or corruption scandals.

Islam also has much symbolic language that can be leveraged on the issue of personal morality, particularly on leadership piety, the role of women, and the boundaries between men and women outside of the family. These issues of morality are often more personal than institutional, however, and may be difficult to accurately assess prior to observing mobilization outcomes.

Internal state crises of order and justice lower the costs of mobilization by focusing collective norms of acceptable political behavior around specific events and thus coordinating expectations of how to react to those events. In addition, they may lower the expected costs of mobilizing by reducing the credibility of the state's threat to impose costs on mobilization. If the state is in the middle of a crisis of order – a public division in the government, for example – the state may have lower repressive capacity and/or less unity over whether repression should take place. This serves to cast doubt on the willingness or ability of the state to repress if the individual chooses to mobilize. Crises of justice may also call into question the state's willingness or ability to repress all mobilizing individuals equally, leaving some to doubt whether or not the state's threat applies to them.

A second, distinct, type of focal state event that enables Islamist mobilization is *rapid political liberalization* from an authoritarian regime. In many ways this is a more formalized focal point than that of internal state crisis. The purpose of the mobilization during a period of political liberalization is less ambiguous, usually focusing on obtaining votes and positions in the government. As elections are held, the timing for electoral mobilization becomes readily apparent and is well publicized independent of Islamist efforts. If there are structured rules to campaigning and political organization under the new regime, these can also serve to facilitate the coordination of Islamist activities.

Transition from authoritarianism also signals to individuals that the state is less willing to impose independent costs on mobilization than it was previously, lowering the expected personal cost of mobilizing on behalf of an Islamist cause. By moving from a more authoritarian regime to a more liberal regime, the state decreases its capacity to repress because the transition changes expectations both within the state and without about the acceptability of political repression. Although Islamist *electoral* mobilization is more likely to take place under a politically liberal regime, other forms of mobilization such as street demonstrations and political violence may potentially also increase due to the lower anticipated costs from repression.

The sudden change from an unpopular authoritarian regime to a relatively liberal political regime creates opportunities for Islamist entrepreneurs to contrast their Islamic political vision with the old regime, which is fresh on the minds of individuals. It also opens up new prospects for redefining the terms of governance and changing the nature of state–society relations. Shared Islamic understanding of divine sovereignty (*hakimiyya*) and historical characteristics of Islamic governance provide a number of elements with which entrepreneurs may craft an Islamist vision of the state (although these visions can be diverse). Coordination around this holistic vision is facilitated by the collective expectation of a focal point (transition from the old regime) for the political redefinition of the state.

For political liberalization to most effectively coordinate Islamist efforts, however, it needs to be rapid. There are three reasons for this. First, a rapid transition effectively allows for a juxtaposition of the Islamist political vision with the unpopular legacies of the authoritarian regime while those legacies are still present in individual memory. Second, a rapid transition may help frame Islamist political solutions as distinct from more worldly political solutions and give them a millenarian character. If Islamists have had no previous experience in politics, then their characteristic vision of divine sovereignty and Islam as the answer to all social problems (as reflected in the popular Islamist phrase "Islam is the Solution") may be viewed as standing apart from normal politics. By contrast, if in the course of a lengthy political liberalization Islamists are gradually incorporated and seen in the role of political actors, the idealistic character of a comprehensive Islamic political solution may be lost.

The third reason a rapid transition facilitates Islamist mobilization is that a fast move from an authoritarian regime to a system of competitive politics typically finds competing organizations poorly developed. Development of political parties with effective ties to a social constituency often takes a long period of time, so a rapid transition to a party system may leave liberal competitors with little public status or institutional support base.[28] This was readily observed in the aftermath of the 2011 Egyptian revolution, for example, as the fragmented liberal revolutionaries scrambled (and failed) to build institutional capacity in time for elections. By contrast, Islamists often have ready access to religious institutions and may be able to draw on reservoirs of religious authority, particularly if they can incorporate religious elites into the cause. They can exploit existing cultural resources and Islamic common knowledge, as well as access existing social institutions for networking and communication. Liberal or even socialist competitors may need to build their own institutional base and common knowledge, which takes a significant amount of time. Rapidity in transition, therefore, gives Islamists a competitive advantage over entrepreneurs using alternative frameworks for mobilization.

To summarize, mass Islamist mobilization is not simply the result of religious entrepreneurship in a dense Islamic institutional environment. To activate the religious common knowledge and communication networks that such an institutional context provides, public state events may serve as focal points. These focal points help coordinate individuals around aspects of their shared common knowledge and around the timing of mobilization. This serves to lower the inherent costs of coordination for individuals with a preference to mobilize around an Islamist cause. The focal points that the theory predicts will most effectively enable Islamist mobilization are discrete public events at the level of the state. These include internal state crises of order and justice, as well as rapid political liberalization. In addition to lowering the coordination costs of individuals, these state events may also reduce the credibility of state threats and strengthen Islamists vis-à-vis alternative mobilizing entrepreneurs.

## CONCLUSION

The institutional theory of Islamist political mobilization presented here attempts to account for observed variation in the level and timing of popular mobilization on behalf of Islamist causes. While this mobilization may manifest itself in diverse forms, including voting for Islamist political parties, street demonstrations, and political violence, the enabling institutional contexts cited here are general enough to support these diverse manifestations.

The theory posits four categories of actors who make decisions that influence mobilization outcomes. These include religious entrepreneurs, religious elites, the state, and individual Muslim citizens. The mobilization process begins with religious entrepreneurs who decide whether or not to try to mobilize others around an Islamist cause. If they attempt to mobilize others, they face potential obstacles. First, the Islamic elite may attempt to stop the mobilization through in-group policing. If the religious elite can successfully persuade the entrepreneur to stop the process, or alienate him sufficiently from his intended audience, then the mobilization process stops. If the mobilization process continues, it is then addressed by the state. The state articulates costs that individuals will bear by mobilizing around the entrepreneur. Individuals then make decisions about whether or not to mobilize by weighing the anticipated personal costs against the benefit they receive from mobilizing on behalf of their preferences. The collective result of individual mobilization decisions is the observed mobilization outcome.

Several institutional contexts are individually necessary and jointly sufficient for the mobilization process to yield significant levels of Islamist mobilization. I theorize that the stronger each of the supportive institutional contexts is in a given country and time period, the more likely it is that Islamist mobilization will reach high levels. These institutional contexts collectively shape Islamist preferences and affect the anticipated individual cost of mobilization. As these institutional factors cause the individual costs of mobilization to decline, more individuals will mobilize for Islamist causes.

The first institutional context is one that supports a climate of religious entrepreneurship. Entrepreneurship is likely when potential entrepreneurs are poorly incorporated into the state and when the religious elite cannot control entrepreneurs through hierarchical religious or social institutions. In contexts where either the religious elite or potential entrepreneurs are heavily dependent upon state patronage and where the elite have hierarchical control over Islamic activities, religious entrepreneurship is difficult and the mobilization process may not begin.

The second institutional context occurs when there is dense penetration of Islamic institutions across Muslim society, especially institutions that build individual knowledge of symbolic Islamic references and language. Islamic institutions can shape religious preferences, which generate more interest in Islamist causes. Institutions such as Islamic schools, mosques, media, and welfare organizations also create Islamic common knowledge among participants that helps to shape expectations about the behavior of others. This common knowledge can lower expected costs of individual mobilization, making a decision to mobilize more likely. In addition, Islamic institutions may provide structured channels for rapid communication of formal or informal political messages to a broad audience.

The final institutional context is one in which public events at the level of the state provide focal points around which Islamic common knowledge becomes activated. Internal state crises, especially crises of order or justice, help to channel Islamic expectations around appropriate responses to state activities and therefore lower the expected individual costs for mobilization. Likewise,

| | | | |
|---|---|---|---|
| **Context** | Entrepreneurial climate | Extensive Islamic institutions | State focal points |
| **Supporting factors** | • Poor state incorporation of religious and political activists<br>• Poor state incorporation of religious elite<br>• Independent Islamic resource base<br>• Little religious hierarchy<br>• Large number of Islamic organizations | • Large percentage educated through Islamic institutions<br>• Dense networks of independent mosques, especially Friday mosques<br>• Widespread independent Islamic media<br>• Multiple Islamic social and welfare organizations | • Internal state crises of order (e.g., government breakdown, leadership turnover)<br>• Internal state crises of justice (e.g., corruption scandals, election cancellation)<br>• Rapid political liberalization from an authoritarian regime |

FIGURE 2.3 Institutional contexts that enable Islamist mobilization.

rapid political liberalization can serve as a focal point for channeling Islamic expectations. Both of these types of focal point also lower the credibility of the threat of repression and may provide Islamist movements with competitive advantages against political competitors.

A summary of the key structural contexts of the theory and some institutional factors that contribute to those contexts is presented in Figure 2.3.

The theory presented here echoes some of the contributions made in other scholarship on mobilization highlighted in Chapter 1. In particular, the theory reflects some recent developments in social movement theory as well as rationalist models of political behavior. It differs from most treatments using social movement theory or rationalist models in several respects, however. First, while supported by a rationalist perspective on individual decision-making, the causal focus of the theory lies in institutional contexts and not with individual actors. Individual decisions are what make the institutions relevant to mobilization outcomes, but the change in institutional context is what is predictive of a change in outcome. Second, while much of social movement theory provides a descriptive assessment of how mobilization takes place, the theory here attempts to provide an explicitly causal vision of the determinative factors for mobilization. In doing so, the theory specifies institutional contexts in which mobilization should take place if the theory is correct, and should not take place if the theory is incorrect. Third, very broad concepts in social movement theory such as "cultural frameworks" or "political opportunities" are here given narrower and more explicitly institutional specifications; other aspects of social movement theory, such as network analysis, are not directly employed.[29]

Finally, the theory presented is intended to explain only a specific category of mobilization, namely Islamist political mobilization. While further abstraction of the theory may lead to broader application among other religious or social groups in different contexts, several aspects of the theory presented here are specific to Islamic contexts. In particular, the patterns of interaction between religious elites and entrepreneurs, the prevalent types of religious institutions, the nature and content of religious common knowledge, and the capacity for reacting to specific state focal points should be understood against an Islamic historical backdrop.

## REFERENCES


Acemoglu, Daron and James Robinson. 2012. *Why Nations Fail: The Origins of Power, Prosperity, and Poverty*. New York: Crown Business.

Anderson, Benedict. 1991. *Imagined Communities: Reflections on the Origins and Spread of Nationalism*. Revised edition. London: Verso.

Brenner, Louis. 2001. *Controlling Knowledge: Religion, Power and Schooling in a West African Muslim Society*. Bloomington, IN: Indiana University Press.

Chwe, Michael Suk-Young. 1998. "Culture, Circles, and Commercials: Publicity, Common Knowledge, and Social Coordination." *Rationality and Society* 10: 47–75.

2001. *Rational Ritual: Culture, Coordination, and Common Knowledge*. Princeton, NJ: Princeton University Press.

Cruise O'Brien, Donal B. 2003. *Symbolic Confrontations: Muslims Imagining the State in Africa*. London: Hurst & Company.

Debray, Régis. 2000. *Transmitting Culture*. Translated by Eric Rauth. New York: Columbia University Press.

Eckholm, Erik. 2005. "Ally of Militant Cleric is on the Stump in Sadr City." *New York Times*, 5 January.

Eckstein, Harry. 1975. "Case Study and Theory in Political Science." In Fred Greenstein and Nelson Polsby, eds., *Handbook of Political Science*, Vol. 7, Strategies of Inquiry: 79–137. Reading, MA: Addison-Wesley.

Eickelman, Dale F. and James Piscatori. 1996. *Muslim Politics*. Princeton, NJ: Princeton University Press.

Fearon, James and David D. Laitin. 1996. "Explaining Interethnic Cooperation." *American Political Science Review* 90/4 (December): 715–735.

Feldman, Noah. 2012. *The Rise and Fall of the Islamic State*. Princeton, NJ: Princeton University Press.

Geanakopolos, John. 1992. "Common Knowledge." *Journal of Economic Perspectives* 6: 53–82.

Granovetter, Mark. 1973. "The Strength of Weak Ties." *American Journal of Sociology* 78/6 (May): 1360–1380.

Hashmi, Sohail H., ed. 2002. *Islamic Political Ethics: Civil Society, Pluralism, and Conflict*. Princeton, NJ: Princeton University Press.

King, Gary, Robert Keohane, and Sidney Verba. 1994. *Designing Social Inquiry: Scientific Inference in Qualitative Research*. Princeton, NJ: Princeton University Press.

Kuran, Timur. 1991. "Now Out of Never: The Element of Surprise in the East European Revolution of 1989." *World Politics* 44/1: 7–48.

Laitin, David D. 1998. *Identity in Formation: The Russian-Speaking Populations in the Near Abroad*. Ithaca, NY: Cornell University Press.

Lewis, Bernard. 1988. *The Political Language of Islam*. Chicago, IL: University of Chicago Press.

Lohmann, Susanne. 1993. "A Signaling Model of Informative and Manipulative Political Action." *American Political Science Review* 87/2: 319–333.

1994. "The Dynamics of Informational Cascades: The Monday Demonstrations in Leipzig, East Germany, 1989–91" *World Politics* 47: 42–101.

McAdam, Doug, Sidney Tarrow, and Charles Tilly. 2001. *Dynamics of Contention*. Cambridge: Cambridge University Press.

Nyang, Sulayman. 2002. "Religion and the Maintenance of Boundaries: An Islamic View." In Hashmi, Sohail H., ed. *Islamic Political Ethics: Civil Society, Pluralism, and Conflict*. Princeton, NJ: Princeton University Press.

Olson, Mancur. 1965. *The Logic of Collective Action: Public Goods and the Theory of Groups*. Cambridge, MA: Harvard University Press.

Ray, William. 2001. *The Logic of Culture: Authority and Identity in the Modern Era*. Oxford: Blackwell.

Wickham, Carrie Rosefsky. 2002. *Mobilizing Islam: Religion, Activism, and Political Change in Egypt*. New York: Columbia University Press.

# 3

# A Political Geography of the Sacred

## *Variation in Islamist Political Mobilization across Space and Time*

The Muslim world's remarkable diversity is reflected in the type and extent of Islamist political mobilization in Muslim countries. This chapter examines the diversity in mobilization across the broader Muslim world from 1970 to 2010. It does so by looking at voting behavior, protest mobilization, and political violence for self-defined Islamist causes in fifty-seven polities (including fifty-five currently in the global system). These polities comprise the population of countries in which at least 25 percent of the population may be identified as Muslim.[1] As noted in Chapter 1, this cutoff point is used to isolate the population of countries in which Muslims have sufficient demographic standing to potentially pursue state power as an identity group.

Although this list of polities[2] comprises countries across a broad range of geographies, they are grouped here for reference as belonging to distinct regions. The list of polities with Muslim populations over 25 percent are grouped according to region and presented in Table 3.1. In some cases regional boundaries are not distinct or may be controversial. The regional groupings used here are for reference purposes only.

This chapter outlines broad patterns in religious mobilization across these countries and regions during the past three decades. It does so first by highlighting patterns in mobilization across space, focusing on histories of Islamist violence, Islamist protests, and voting for Islamist political parties. Potential methods of aggregating these forms of mobilization into general indicators of Islamist mobilization are discussed and used to highlight broadly spatial patterns in mobilization. The discussion then turns to temporal patterns of mobilization across the range of countries, examining differences in mobilization across the four decades under consideration. Temporal patterns are used to assess potential linkages in the origins of mobilization across individual cases and contexts. This is done by examining comparative changes in violence, protests, voting behavior, and aggregate mobilization indicators over time.

TABLE 3.1 *Polities with Muslim Population >25 Percent*

| **Europe** | **North Africa** | **Sub-Saharan Africa** |
|---|---|---|
| • Albania | • Algeria | • Burkina Faso |
| • Kosovo | • Egypt | • Chad |
| • Bosnia-Herzegovina | • Libya | • Comoros |
| **Asia** | • Morocco | • Cote d'Ivoire |
| • Bangladesh | • Tunisia | • Djibouti |
| • Brunei | **Arab Levant and Gulf** | • Eritrea |
| • Indonesia | • Bahrain | • Ethiopia |
| • Malaysia | • Iraq | • Gambia |
| • Maldives | • Jordan | • Guinea |
| • Pakistan | • Kuwait | • Guinea-Bissau |
| **Central Asia** | • Lebanon | • Kenya |
| • Afghanistan | • North Yemen | • Mali |
| • Azerbaijan | • Palestine | • Mauritania |
| • Iran | • Oman | • Niger |
| • Kazakhstan | • Qatar | • Nigeria |
| • Kyrgyzstan | • South Yemen | • Senegal |
| • Tajikistan | • Saudi Arabia | • Sierra Leone |
| • Turkey | • Syria | • Somalia |
| • Turkmenistan | • United Arab Emirates | • Sudan |
| • Uzbekistan | • Yemen | • Tanzania |

Time-series data on the cases in the population are then used to assess a number of theories of Islamist mobilization outlined in Chapters 1 and 2. Implications of theories developed in case-specific contexts are tested for correlation with mobilization outcomes across the Muslim world. As some of the implications of the theories outlined in Chapters 1 and 2 are difficult to directly test due to data limitations, suggestive proxies are used to examine the potential for various theoretical claims in a comparative context. While many theoretical claims about the sources of Islamist mobilization outlined in Chapter 1 receive little support across the range of cases, implications of the institutional theory outlined in Chapter 2 appear generally consistent with the larger data. The results of the statistical analysis are presented at the end of the book in the Appendices.

## PATTERNS OF MOBILIZATION ACROSS SPACE

The central indicators of Islamist mobilization used in this study are Islamist political violence, street demonstrations by Islamist actors, and electoral mobilization by Islamist political parties. Which countries and regions of the world have been most affected by these forms of mobilization since 1970?

TABLE 3.2 *Geography of Islamist Violence 1970–2010**

| > 50,000 | 1,000–9,999 | 10–99 |
|---|---|---|
| Afghanistan | Indonesia | Chad |
| Iraq | Palestine | Morocco |
| Algeria | Syria | Tunisia |
| | Turkey | Kyrgyzstan |
| **10,000–49,999** | | Sudan |
| Tajikistan | **100–999** | Mauritania |
| Iran | Saudi Arabia | Tunisia |
| Lebanon | Egypt | Libya |
| Nigeria | Uzbekistan | Ethiopia |
| Pakistan | Bangladesh | Kosovo |
| Somalia | Yemen | Malaysia |
| | Eritrea | Kuwait |
| | Jordan | Kenya |
| | Mali | Bosnia |
| | | Tanzania |

* Numbers of deaths are rough approximations only. Deaths from Islamist-oriented violence are often a subset of deaths resulting from larger conflicts

A geography of Islamist violence reveals several countries that have witnessed Islamist violence on a large scale, several that have witnessed moderate levels of violence, and a large number of countries that have seen some Islamist violence but relatively few deaths as a result. Affected countries from between 1970 and 2010 are listed in groups in Table 3.2. Total number of deaths per country should be treated only as a rough approximation as it is difficult to ascertain both accurate numbers of dead and the amount of total violence that has a specifically Islamist-driven component. Data are collected in the period up until 1 January 2010. In the period from 2010 to the time of writing, Syria's numbers rose significantly. The number of deaths caused by Islamist actors also increased to a lesser degree in Nigeria, Egypt, Mali, Libya, and Tunisia.

Several observations should be made. First, total levels of Islamist violence are dominated by the multiple conflicts in Afghanistan from 1979 onward, and then subsequently by high levels of violence in Algeria and in Iraq. The long Afghan wars between the Soviet-backed government and *mujahideen* fighters, between tribal groupings of *mujahideen*, and ultimately between the Taliban and their opponents exacted an enormous toll on Afghanistan, with considerably more than one million deaths as a result. These wars were actively promoted by self-defined Islamic freedom fighters and brought in outside combatants from across the Muslim world, particularly from Arab countries. The conflicts also had a strong tribal and regional character, however, and much of the Islamic symbolism prominent in the Afghan conflicts overlaid divisions along ethnic and clan lines. The levels of violence in

Afghanistan over the last four decades are considerably beyond those in any other Islamist-related conflict.

Second, there are a number other countries that saw large-scale episodes of Islamist political violence. Some of these episodes are embedded in larger conflicts, but fit the study's definition of Islamist political mobilization. Three of these countries experienced Islamist violence in the course of civil war. In Algeria, the civil war of the 1990s was dominated by attacks and counter-attacks between the military-dominated government and Islamist rebel groups. Iraq's Islamist violence, particularly between 2003 and 2010, was particularly high as it was the dominant area of al-Qa'eda operations during this period. Total numbers of violent deaths in Iraq since 2003 vary widely, but those tied to Islamist violence are in the tens of thousands and potentially over 100,000 over this period. Tajikistan and Lebanon also experienced civil wars in which Islamist actors played an important role. In Tajikistan, Islamists with some links to Afghanistan initially united with liberal opposition against the government in civil war and later sustained the conflict through guerrilla warfare. In Lebanon, civil war from 1975 to 1990 claimed over 100,000 lives. Most of the violence in the Lebanese wars was not directly related to Islamist political mobilization, although a component of the Muslim opposition (most notably Hezbollah) launched many attacks as part of a self-defined Islamist agenda. Violence in Iran during the late 1970s and early 1980s was less the product of a civil war than the product of a revolution in which the clerical establishment secured control of the state. In Nigeria, multiple episodes of violence from the late 1970s onward have a distinctly communal character that colors controversies over Islamic law and tensions between the north and the south. In the twenty-first century, these tensions fed a brutal Islamist insurgency known as Boko Haram. In the last decade, the ongoing violent conflict over Somalia's failed state also became increasingly Islamist in character. The Islamic Courts Union of Somalia, and later the offshoot militia al-Shabaab, began to redefine the Somali civil conflict as one of Islamists versus others, beginning in the middle of the decade.

Third, of the countries that have seen medium-scale losses due to Islamist violence, three have seen Islamist claims within the context of broader civil violence, while violence in the others may more accurately be characterized as the result of insurgency. Indonesia, Pakistan, and Turkey have all witnessed moderate degrees of civil violence in which Islamist actors have been implicated. In Indonesia, much of the violence has been between Muslim and Christian communities; there have also been dramatic instances of indiscrimate Islamist violence, such as the Bali bombings of 2002 and 2005. Similarly, much of the Islamist violence in Pakistan has occurred between divergent sects within the Muslim faith. These episodes often have a political component as groups seek to define or enforce political demands for land or orthodox behavior. Civil violence in Turkey during the late 1970s and early 1980s was less communal and more ideological in its nature, with radical Islamists targeting prominent leftists. Islamist assassinations of prominent secular officials in Turkey continued through the 1990s. Islamist groups in the Arab polities of Syria, Palestine, Saudi Arabia, Egypt, and Yemen have led significant insurgencies against their governing officials. Long before Syria's current civil war that includes multiple Islamist groups, a large Islamist rebellion in Syria was brutally crushed (1982), as were numerous insurgency activities in Saudi Arabia. Islamist groups in Palestine and Egypt have led longer, relatively low-scale insurgencies against the Israeli and Egyptian governments, respectively. These groups led sporadic attacks that have nevertheless been sustained over considerable periods. Islamist insurgency has also occurred in Uzbekistan, Mali, and Bangladesh.

Fourth, Islamist violence affected approximately two-thirds of the total countries in the study during the four decades from 1970. Low-scale Islamist violence has emerged in a wide variety of countries, in four regions of the world, under very diverse circumstances. Low-scale violence sometimes occurs in the broader context of communal clashes, but is more often related to isolated incidents of violence by fringe militant Islamist groups. Polities with very little or no Islamist violence throughout the period are found largely in sub-Saharan Africa, parts of Central Asia, Muslim Europe, and the Arab Gulf.

Patterns of Islamist protest provide a useful comparison with this geography of Islamist violence. How does the geography of Islamist street demonstrations compare? The extent of total Islamist-oriented protest is measured in three ways: the number of five-year periods in which Islamist protest occurs since 1970, the scale of the protest (number of participants), and the intensity of the protest.[3] The polities that have been affected by significant levels of Islamist protest since 1970 are presented in Table 3.3 using an ordinal score that combines multiple indicators of protest strength.

Several observations should be noted. First, significant Islamist demonstrations occur in a little more than half of the polities that make up the population of the study. This is a similar proportion to the number of polities affected by Islamist violence. However, large-scale Islamist protests have been present in many more countries than has large-scale Islamist violence. This observation is consistent with an assumption that political protest should be more common than political violence because it carries a lower personal cost for participants.

Second, the polities affected by Islamist protest are a diverse crowd, representing all regions of the study, although they occur comparatively less often in sub-Saharan Africa and post-Communist countries.[4] Although Arab countries represent less than 40 percent of the countries in the total population of cases, they are over-represented among countries that have large- and medium-scale protest histories, comprising more than half of this group. Prior to the year 2000, Arab countries were considerably more likely to have experienced significant Islamist protest than countries from outside the Arab world. The Asian countries in the population also have histories of considerable Islamist protest.

TABLE 3.3 *Geography of Islamist Protest 1970–2010**

| | | | | | |
|---|---|---|---|---|---|
| **Large-scale demonstrations** | | | | | |
| Afghanistan | 6 | Iraq | 6 | Syria | 6 |
| Algeria | 6 | Lebanon | 6 | Tunisia | 6 |
| Bangladesh | 6 | Nigeria | 6 | Yemen | 6 |
| Egypt | 6 | Pakistan | 6 | Bahrain | 5 |
| Indonesia | 6 | Palestine | 6 | Kenya | 5 |
| Iran | 6 | Somalia | 6 | Libya | 5 |
| **Medium-scale demonstrations** | | | | | |
| Azerbaijan | 4 | Tanzania | 4 | Maldives | 3 |
| Kuwait | 4 | Turkey | 4 | Niger | 3 |
| Mauritania | 4 | Uzbekistan | 4 | Oman | 3 |
| Morocco | 4 | Bosnia | 3 | Sudan | 3 |
| Saudi Arabia | 4 | Jordan | 3 | Tajikistan | 3 |
| **Small-scale demonstrations** | | | | | |
| Kyrgyzstan | 2 | Chad | 0 | Guinea-Bissau | 0 |
| Malaysia | 2 | Comoros | 0 | Kazakhstan | 0 |
| Mali | 2 | Cote d'Ivoire | 0 | Kosovo | 0 |
| Qatar | 2 | Djibouti | 0 | North Yemen | 0 |
| Albania | 1 | Eritrea | 0 | Sierra Leone | 0 |
| Brunei | 1 | Ethiopia | 0 | South Yemen | 0 |
| Senegal | 1 | Gambia | 0 | Turkmenistan | 0 |
| Burkina Faso | 0 | Guinea | 0 | UAE | 0 |

* Ordinal score based on estimates of temporal distribution, number of participants, and the occurrence of violent clashes.

Third, large, middle-income countries tend to have higher levels of Islamist protest than small countries; they also have more protest on average than countries at the top or bottom of the economic development scale. Countries affected by significant Islamist protest (high or medium scale) often have mid-range human development scores (HDI from 0.6 to 0.8) and an annual GDP per capita ranging from $2,500 to $7,500 (in 2010 figures). There are certainly some notable exceptions, including Nigeria, Tanzania, and Yemen, which are very poor countries, and Pakistan and Bangladesh, which are poorer than the average. Saudi Arabia and Bahrain, both of which have protest histories, have higher-than-average GDP levels due to their petroleum production, but lower GDP per capita than most other Gulf oil producers. Similarities in levels of human development may reflect similarities in the degree to which these countries have undergone economic and social transformations in recent decades. It is interesting to note that many of the countries with the highest levels of Islamist protest have also experienced significant political changes, often in the form of liberal experimentation, or re-experimentation in recent decades. Despite this political dynamism, however, average levels of political freedom across the three decades are not significantly correlated with

TABLE 3.4 *Average Freedom House Score 1970–2010**

| | | | | | |
|---|---|---|---|---|---|
| **Moderately free** | | | | | |
| Turkey | 3.2 | Bangladesh | 3.8 | Malaysia | 3.8 |
| Senegal | 3.7 | Gambia | 3.8 | | |
| **Less free** | | | | | |
| Morocco | 4.6 | Kyrgyzstan | 4.9 | Lebanon | 5.1 |
| Indonesia | 4.7 | Pakistan | 4.9 | Jordan | 5.1 |
| Mali | 4.7 | Sierra Leone | 4.9 | Maldives | 5.2 |
| Comoros | 4.7 | Nigeria | 5.0 | Yemen | 5.2 |
| Kuwait | 4.8 | Kosovo | 5.0 | Tanzania | 5.3 |
| Djibouti | 4.8 | Guinea-Bissau | 5.0 | | |
| **Least free** | | | | | |
| Egypt | 5.5 | Cote d'Ivoire | 6.0 | Eritrea | 6.4 |
| Niger | 5.5 | Algeria | 6.0 | Syria | 6.5 |
| Bahrain | 5.7 | Kenya | 6.0 | Palestine | N/A |
| UAE | 5.7 | Tajikistan | 6.1 | Guinea | 6.5 |
| Iran | 5.7 | Oman | 6.1 | Saudi Arabia | 6.6 |
| Ethiopia | 5.8 | Mauritania | 6.2 | Libya | 6.7 |
| Tunisia | 5.9 | Afghanistan | 6.2 | Iraq | 6.7 |
| Azerbaijan | 5.9 | Sudan | 6.3 | Somalia | 6.8 |
| Kazakhstan | 5.9 | Brunei | 6.3 | Uzbekistan | 6.9 |
| Qatar | 5.9 | Chad | 6.4 | Turkmenistan | 6.9 |

* Average score for political liberties, 1970–2009.

protest outcomes, indicating that more liberal political systems are not more prone to Islamist protest.[5]

What about patterns of electoral mobilization on behalf of Islamist political parties? Voting in free elections is, on balance, a rare event across the Muslim world in most of the four decades under consideration. Of the countries that held any credible elections at all, some held only one or two elections before tightening restrictions on political behavior. Others have held elections under a system of considerable constraint regarding who may compete and what outcomes are considered acceptable to the governing regime. Table 3.4 demonstrates both the lack of political freedom across the Muslim world and geographical variations in political freedom over time. Note that the Freedom House scores range from 1 (most free) to 7 (least free) and that the scores presented here are a country's average score from 1970 through 2009.[6] These scores are an average across four decades and are not necessarily representative of the current situation in each country.

Very few completely transparent and open elections have occurred in these countries, although the number of countries holding somewhat credible elections has increased over the last decade. Despite the broad trends of authoritarianism, a considerable number of elections have occurred that are free enough to allow for significant variation in the electoral outcome. Although not all possible players may be allowed to compete, and there are often restrictions on the type of political platform parties may have, democratic political competition has occurred in a range of settings and time periods. Elections judged sufficiently free to generate a credible outcome through competition among the most relevant political actors are included in the electoral data presented in the following. Voting outcomes are coded as Islamist political mobilization when votes are cast for parties that promote an Islamically oriented vision of state policy in their campaigns. Often the votes are cast for one party that is publicly seen as the Islamic choice. In other instances, several parties may try to distinguish themselves by their Islamic message (as in Pakistan or Indonesia). In this case, all votes for Islamically oriented parties are included in the total presented. Differences in ideology between the Islamic parties may vary significantly, but they are not reflected in these data. In competitive no-party systems where independents are clearly aligned with a conservative Islamic platform (e.g., Iran, Kuwait), votes for these candidates are also included.

Table 3.5 highlights countries in which Islamically oriented parties and movements won votes in electoral competition prior to 2010. The numbers are the average percentage votes for Islamically oriented parties per period in

TABLE 3.5 *Geography of Islamist Voting 1970–2010*

| **Large-scale electoral mobilization** | | | |
|---|---|---|---|
| Country | % Votes* | Algeria | 48 |
| Bahrain | 75** | Bangladesh | 46 |
| Sudan[1] | 75 | Palestine | 45 |
| Iran[2] | 67 | Mauritania | 43** |
| Iraq | 65 | Kuwait | 51 |
| Malaysia | 51 | Afghanistan | 39 |
| Turkey | 51 | Indonesia | 37 |
| Pakistan | 50 | Yemen | 23 |
| **Medium-scale electoral mobilization** | | | |
| Country | % Votes* | Jordan | 15 |
| Egypt | 19** | Morocco | 13 |
| Tunisia | 17 | Lebanon | 11** |
| **Small-scale electoral mobilization** | | | |
| Country | % Votes* | Maldives | 1 |
| Tajikistan | 8 | Senegal | 1 |

* Average vote for Islamically oriented parties per period in which a reasonably free election is held. Some countries have only one free election on which this number is based, while for other countries the number is the highest achieved success during the time period.

** Percentage of seats won, not vote percent.

[1] Election in the North only

[2] Based on Conservative Alliance performance

which there is a reasonably free election. The voting percentages are not directly comparable, as some are the result of only one election, and others an average of multiple elections across time. The numbers are also sensitive to the inclusion or exclusion of parties with a moderately Islamic agenda and should therefore be treated as rough approximations only. Note that in the years immediately after 2010, Islamist parties considerably outperformed their previous average in competitive elections in Egypt, Tunisia, and Morocco.

About 40 percent of the countries in the study experienced some degree of voting for Islamically oriented parties. These countries comprise the majority of the total number of countries in which reasonably credible voting has taken place since 1970. In some countries credible national elections occurred only once in the study period or were infrequent (Sudan, Maldives). In others, there were iterated elections over a sustained period of time, including in countries such as Turkey, Malaysia, Indonesia, Pakistan, and Bangladesh. In a large portion of countries in Table 3.5, including countries such as Kuwait, Jordan, Yemen, Iran, and Morocco, elections were held in constrained democratic systems in which voting outcomes may have been considerably altered by regime constraints.

Countries in which Islamist voting has occurred are dominantly found in Asia, Turkey, and the Arab world. By contrast, Muslim countries in Europe and in sub-Saharan Africa have held credible elections, but Islamically oriented political parties have not participated actively in the electoral process. While some degree of liberalization has occurred in all majority Muslim regions, Islamically oriented political parties have only arisen in some of these regions.

It is also interesting to note that most countries that have seen large- and medium-scale Islamist electoral mobilization have developed comparatively moderate Islamist movements. These movements may be considered moderate in the sense that they choose to work within the existing political system rather than openly challenging it. While this is often the case because liberalizing regimes do not allow anti-systemic parties to compete, Islamist groups may also find that they cannot achieve widespread electoral success among their potential constituency without articulating a message that appeals to a wide range of voters.

How are spatial patterns of Islamist violence, protest, and voting related to one another? It may not be intuitively clear whether these activities should be found together or in different contexts. Voting and street demonstrations might be found in countries with greater political liberalism, for example, while violence could be confined to areas where no other outlets are available. On the other hand, if the causal forces behind different types of Islamist mobilization are similar, we may expect to see multiple manifestations of Islamist mobilization in the same space and at the same time.

In fact, all three manifestations are positively correlated with each other across the range of data. Islamist violence and street demonstrations are particularly correlated in the first several decades of the study, occurring largely in the same places over time. In the decade after 2000, more elections took place and correlation between Islamist demonstrations and Islamist voting increased. The correlation between protest and violence can be noted by comparing Tables 3.2 and 3.3. Protest and violence are also positively correlated with Islamist voting, although to a lesser extent.[7] Other data associated with Islamist mobilization, such as data on arrests of Islamists and the number of political Islamic groups in a country, are also positively correlated with the central indicators and with each other across the data. Confirmation of the related nature of these diverse activities is also obtained through factor analysis. Performing factor analysis on the aforementioned indicators of Islamist political mobilization yields one dominant "factor" to which these different forms of data are related. While the analysis itself does not specify the nature of that connection, it is hypothesized here that these multiple activities reflect an underlying movement of Islamist mobilization.[8] This combined factor that incorporates patterns of Islamist voting, protest, and violence is used as one possible dependent variable to measure Islamist mobilization.

It is important to note that the substantial correlation between Islamist protest, violence, and electoral behavior is clear when one examines large periods of time in a given geography (as in the five-year periods examined in the large-n portion of this study). It does not imply that the same actors are involved in all three activities, nor that they are correlated in shorter temporal periods. For example, it is not uncommon for Islamist protest to dominate in one six-month period, followed by government repression of those protests, which is then followed by a shift to Islamist violence. Likewise, voting for Islamists in elections is usually a discrete, time-bound event that may not overlap with periods of Islamist violence. What is striking in the data, however, is that when one broadens the time period to a block of several years, multiple forms of Islamist mobilization are likely to be either present or absent together. I theorize that this can best be explained by the presence of an underlying set of Islamist actors who may disagree on ideology and strategy, and therefore will respond to different institutional opportunities in different ways, but who nevertheless seek to use their preferred strategies and opportunities during similar time periods and can build on each others' motivations and discourse.

For the purposes of this study, the underlying phenomenon of Islamist political mobilization is measured in two ways. The first is by taking statistical values from the dominant factor that emerges after performing factor analysis on the multiple types of mobilizing activities for which data were collected. The second is by summing relative values of violence, demonstrations, and voting, and dividing the total by the total possible value in that country.[9] In order to capture the intensity of the mobilization, this value is then multiplied by the highest ordinal score the country received in any given activity. Ordinal values are obtained by individually scaling absolute values of violence, demonstrations, and voting on a 0–6 scale that encompasses the range of existing values.[10] While this method of approximating overall mobilization levels has some clear drawbacks, it is useful as an alternative method to compare with mobilization scores derived from factor analysis.

The result is two different orderings of countries in the population based on their average levels of Islamist political mobilization. These two methods of calculating total Islamist mobilization differ in the weight they give to different aspects of mobilization, but are very highly correlated.[11] Both the factor method and the ordinal method are based on violence, demonstrations, and voting data, and give considerable weight to diversity in forms of mobilization when making the final calculation. Factor scores are the principal way in which combined patterns of Islamist mobilization are measured in what follows. The factor scores for each country for the period 1970–2010 are presented in Table 3.6.

Figure 3.1 presents a map of the study's countries coded for the factor scores found in Table 3.6. All current polities included in the study are named and those with significant levels of Islamist mobilization are shaded accordingly.

Overall patterns of Islamist mobilization in the last four decades yield some interesting observations. With a couple of notable exceptions, the countries that experienced the most Islamist mobilization were large countries in the middle range of income among the countries of the study. Countries with small populations have considerably less mobilization on average. Very poor countries likewise have less mobilization on average. However, most of the poorest are found in sub-Saharan Africa, which is a regional outlier. Europe and sub-Saharan Africa have generally low levels of Islamist mobilization, while the Arab world, Iran, and South Asia have generally high levels. Post-Soviet countries in Central Asia have low levels of mobilization, with the exception of Tajikistan and Uzbekistan.

When we examine patterns of overall mobilization only in the decade 2000–2010, we see that these historical patterns largely hold, but with significant increases in mobilization in four countries: Afghanistan, Pakistan, Iraq, and Somalia. Increases in Afghanistan and Pakistan correspond with a decade-long conflict between the Taliban and both Western and domestic military forces. Iraq since 2003 saw very high levels of violent and non-violent Islamist mobilization in the wake of the overthrow of Saddam Hussein's regime. The sudden rise in Islamist mobilization in Somalia during the last decade makes it a relative outlier in sub-Saharan Africa.

## PATTERNS OF MOBILIZATION ACROSS TIME

How have levels of Islamist mobilization changed across time? When has mobilization increased and when has it declined? While Islamist mobilization occurred in a variety of historical contexts prior to 1970, the early 1970s are notable for having low levels of Islamist mobilization. Mobilization on behalf

TABLE 3.6 *Factor Scores of Islamist Mobilization by Country 1970–2010*

| | | | | | | | |
|---|---|---|---|---|---|---|---|
| **1st Quintile*** | | | | | | | |
| Algeria | 2.54 | Afghanistan | 2.47 | Bangladesh | 2.23 | Yemen | 2.09 |
| Iran | 2.54 | Indonesia | 2.47 | Egypt | 2.18 | | |
| Iraq | 2.54 | Palestine | 2.38 | Nigeria | 2.13 | | |
| Pakistan | 2.54 | Lebanon | 2.26 | Somalia | 2.13 | | |
| **2nd Quintile** | | | | | | | |
| Turkey | 1.98 | Tunisia | 1.87 | Saudi Arabia | 1.57 | Bahrain | 1.57 |
| Syria | 1.97 | Tajikistan | 1.66 | Uzbekistan | 1.57 | Jordan | 1.56 |
| **3rd Quintile** | | | | | | | |
| Kuwait | 1.52 | Sudan | 1.48 | Kenya | 1.31 | Malaysia | 1.12 |
| Mauritania | 1.52 | Morocco | 1.47 | Libya | 1.16 | Mali | 1.02 |
| **4th Quintile** | | | | | | | |
| Azerbaijan | 0.96 | Kyrgyzstan | 0.86 | Maldives | 0.67 | | |
| Tanzania | 0.96 | Niger | 0.76 | Eritrea | 0.62 | | |
| Bosnia | 0.91 | Oman | 0.76 | Qatar | 0.55 | | |
| **5th Quintile** | | | | | | | |
| Chad | 0.46 | Kosovo | 0.15 | Guinea-Bissau | 0.00 | Turkmenistan | 0.00 |
| Albania | 0.35 | Burkina Faso | 0.00 | Kazakhstan | 0.00 | UAE | 0.00 |
| Ethiopia | 0.31 | Djibouti | 0.00 | North Yemen | 0.00 | Comoros | 0.00 |
| Senegal | 0.27 | Gambia | 0.00 | Sierra Leone | 0.00 | Cote d'Ivoire | 0.00 |
| Brunei | 0.20 | Guinea | 0.00 | South Yemen | 0.00 | | |

* Signifies those countries with a score in the top fifth of the score range.

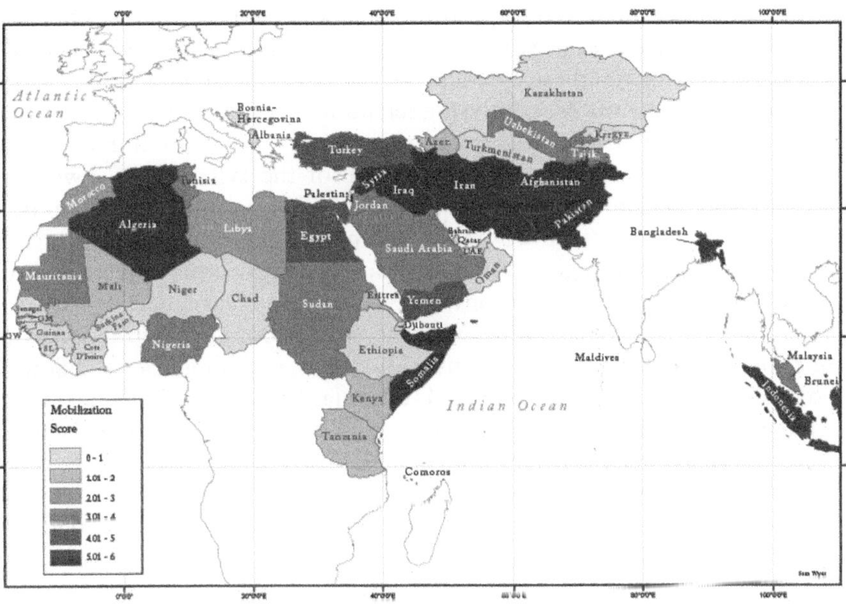


FIGURE 3.1 Islamist political mobilization, 1970–2010.

of other causes, such as Marxism or Arab nationalism, was prominent during this time period, but political action on behalf of an Islamist agenda was not widespread in 1970.[12] This changed significantly in subsequent periods. Temporal changes in overall levels of violence, demonstrations, and electoral behavior are discussed briefly in the following.

As noted previously, overall levels of Islamist violence are strongly affected by the enormously destructive civil conflicts in Afghanistan from the late 1970s onward. Partly due to the high levels of violence in Afghanistan, the total amount of Islamist violence in the countries of the study increases throughout the 1970s and 1980s, falling during the 1990s as the number of casualties in Afghanistan declines, and then rising again in the 2000s. In the Muslim world beyond Afghanistan, levels of Islamist violence increase from 1970 to the mid-1980s, at which point they decline. In the early 1990s, however, levels of violence dramatically rise again and gradually decline throughout the decade. The rise in violence in the 1990s may be attributed, in large part, to the emergence of violent conflicts in Algeria and Tajikistan. In the 2000s, violence spikes in Iraq and Somalia, with comparably high levels of Islamist violence also affecting Afghanistan, Pakistan, Lebanon, Palestine, Algeria, and Nigeria.

While total levels of Islamist violence are highest in the 1980s and early 1990s, the number of countries affected by Islamist violence increases steadily throughout the period until the late 1990s. At this point the number of countries affected doubles. In the period 1995–1999, twenty-five polities (47% of the total) experience at least ten deaths as a result of Islamist violence. With the exception of Algeria, these conflicts are not large-scale conflicts, but they are remarkably widespread. A slightly higher number of countries sees low-level Islamist violence in the period after 2000, with more than thirty countries affected by Islamist violence over the course of the last decade. Two major temporal trends in violence are thus apparent. First, an increasing number of countries are affected over time, with the number rising dramatically in the late 1990s. Second, the average amount of Islamist violence per affected country declines from the early 1990s onward. Islamist violence declines in many countries in the decade beginning with the year 2000, although it spikes in a number of countries that had previously low levels, including Iraq and Somalia, and to a lesser extent in Bahrain and Mauritania. Violence continued to be high in Afghanistan throughout this period. In the period after 2010, which is discussed in more detail in the Epilogue, Islamist violence spikes in Syria and rises significantly in Iraq and Nigeria.

The temporal data on Islamist demonstrations reflects similar trends. The amount of Islamist protest rose from the early 1970s to the late 1970s, with eight countries affected by notable Islamist protests from 1975 to 1979. Protests during this period were generally large in scope and often resulted in violent clashes with state security agents. This was the case, most notably, in Iran. The overall amount of Islamist protest across cases held relatively steady in the 1980s, then jumped considerably in the 1990s. Islamist demonstrations then continued to rise, reaching their highest levels in the last decade of the 2000s.

Islamist demonstrations occurred in an increasing number of countries over time, affecting a total of fourteen polities in the late 1990s. This is double the number of polities that experienced Islamist protests two decades earlier. On average, however, the protests that occurred in the late 1980s and 1990s were somewhat smaller in scope and less violent in outcome than those that occurred in the previous decade. These trends may reflect a degree of increased political openness in some Muslim countries during the 1990s, although many notable protests of the late 1990s occurred in closed political systems, such as Egypt, Algeria, and Iraq. Trends in Islamist protest parallel trends in Islamist violence in that the number of countries affected grows over time, but the average intensity of mobilization events declines. In the decade beginning with the year 2000, Islamist protest increased substantially. In the period 2005–2009, thirty-eight countries experienced notable Islamist protests, which is again more than double the number of countries affected in the late 1990s. Not all Islamist protests were as dramatic as many of the 1990s, but they were much more widespread, marking a considerable departure in the extent of Islamist mobilization compared with previous decades.

Voting for Islamically oriented parties has taken place in considerably fewer countries than has Islamist violence or demonstrations. Opportunities for Islamists to contest elections were not present in the majority of countries included in this study during the period prior to 2010, and therefore much of the electoral data are conditioned upon the openness of regimes. Nevertheless, similar trends over time regarding proliferation and scope can be seen.

Some degree of credible Islamist voting took place in the 1970s in four countries: Malaysia, Pakistan, Bangladesh, and Turkey. Despite a collapse in democratic opportunities in the early 1980s, the late 1980s saw voting continue in Malaysia, Pakistan, and Turkey, along with democratic experiments in two other countries in which Islamically oriented candidates polled very well: the Sudan (1986)[13] and Jordan (1989)[14]. By the early 1990s, Malaysia, Pakistan, and Turkey had been rejoined by Bangladesh as countries with continued experience in Islamist democratic competition. The Sudan's democratic experiment waned with increasing restrictions on political freedom. Jordan's continued, although with tactical refinements imposed by the monarchy to restrict the electoral potential of Jordanian Islamists.[15]

New democratic experiments in the Arab world in the early 1990s, however, brought more Islamists into electoral competition in Algeria (1990/91), Kuwait (1992),[16] and Yemen (1993)[17]. While the Algerian elections were subsequently canceled and the political system became increasingly closed, some substantive competition continued in the Kuwaiti and Yemeni systems through the 1990s. Two further openings in the late 1990s subsequently brought Islamically oriented parties into electoral competition in Morocco (1997) and Indonesia (1999).[18] By the close of the century, Islamists were actively competing in reasonably credible elections in nine countries. After the year 2000, however, voting for Islamist parties expanded considerably, with fifteen countries seeing Islamist parties meaningfully compete in the electoral arena from 2000 to 2004. This subsequently expanded to twenty countries, or more than 35 percent of the countries in this study, which saw Islamists compete in elections during the period 2005–2009. Countries that saw new Islamist electoral competition include places such as Iraq, which began a transition to electoral politics; Afghanistan; Mauritania; and a number of additional sub-Saharan African countries.

In the late 1980s, therefore, Islamist electoral competition began to slowly affect an increasing number of countries, making the overall levels of Islamist electoral mobilization in the 1990s considerably higher than in any previous period. Despite the comparatively large electoral mobilization of the 1990s, the average percentage of votes won by Islamists per country began to decline toward the end of the 1990s. This appears to be the combined result of gradual electoral losses by some longstanding Islamist parties and the limited introduction of Islamist competition in new countries. As more countries experienced Islamist electoral competition, the average level of electoral success across all cases in which Islamists competed shows some decline. Indeed, in the decade of the 2000s, more countries than ever before were seeing Islamist parties compete in elections, but the average percentage of votes for those parties did not increase in most cases.

The decade of the 2000s saw significant differences in Islamist mobilization when compared with the previous period, for a variety of reasons. The attacks on the United States on 11 September 2001 and the subsequent reaction of the United States and broader international community in Afghanistan, Iraq, and beyond put into motion important changes throughout the Muslim world that helped to catalyze the spread of political Islam throughout the region during the 2000s. Islamic political mobilization from 2000 to 2009 significantly increased with respect to the number of affected countries along each of the three measured dependent variables – Islamist electoral success, Islamist demonstrations, and Islamist political violence.

Looking at specific countries, Somalia, Iraq, Mauritania, and Bahrain experienced the greatest increase in Islamic mobilization with their maximum ordinal values increasing by 5.42, 4.75, 4.00, and 3.67, respectively (see Table 3.7 below). Five countries – Tunisia, Bangladesh, Afghanistan, Turkey, and Malaysia – experienced increases between 2.00 and 3.00 whereas eleven countries (including Kenya) saw increases between 1.00 and 1.94. Further, the remaining fourteen countries saw increases below 1.00. In any case, states from all regions of the Muslim world (from the Middle East to Africa to Southeast Asia) experienced significant increases in Islamic political mobilization.

A visual summary of temporal changes in the spread of Islamist mobilization from 1970 to 2009 is provided in Figure 3.2.

Note that for Islamist violence, demonstrations, and voting, the number of countries affected has dramatically risen throughout the period, with a sharp rise in the later 1990s. The rise in violence and demonstrations is particularly notable in the parallel growth of these two activities over time across the broad set of countries. A brief decline in Islamist voting occurred in the late 1970s and early 1980s, but in general Islamist political mobilization has become a much more widespread phenomenon over time. Each of the forms of mobilization particularly proliferated in the 1990s.

Total levels of Islamist mobilization also generally increased over time. Partly as a result of decline in the Afghan conflict, total Islamist violence dropped in the 1990s, but the total levels of Islamist demonstrations and electoral mobilization increased during this period. Outside Afghanistan, violence levels also increased in the early 1990s, then subsequently declined. The increase in total levels of mobilization has not kept pace with the proliferation of Islamist activities to new contexts, as the average intensity of Islamist political mobilization has remained relatively stable. Since the 1990s, average levels of mobilization per country affected have been declining, with the exception of voting, which has increased in the decade of the 2000s. Indeed, Islamist violence dropped from the 1990s to the 2000s, while Islamist voting saw a comparable rise. Islamist violence rose again, however, in the period from 2010 to 2015.

TABLE 3.7 *Change in Ordinal Mobilization Score between the Periods 1970–1999 and 2000–2009 by Country*

| | Max ordinal score | | | | | | |
|---|---|---|---|---|---|---|---|
| | 1970–1999 | 2000–2009 | Difference | | 1970–1999 | 2000–2009 | Difference |
| Somalia | 0.08 | 6.00 | 5.92 | Niger | 0.33 | 0.67 | 0.33 |
| Iraq | 1.25 | 6.00 | 4.75 | Ethiopia | 0.06 | 0.22 | 0.17 |
| Mauritania | 0.00 | 4.00 | 4.00 | Albania | 0.00 | 0.11 | 0.11 |
| Bahrain | 0.33 | 4.00 | 3.67 | Brunei | 0.00 | 0.08 | 0.08 |
| Bangladesh | 1.78 | 4.67 | 2.89 | Kosovo | – | 0.06 | 0.06 |
| Tunisia | 1.17 | 4.00 | 2.83 | Iran | 5.33 | 5.33 | 0.00 |
| Afghanistan | 3.00 | 5.67 | 2.67 | Burkina Faso | 0.00 | 0.00 | 0.00 |
| Turkey | 2.44 | 4.67 | 2.22 | Comoros | 0.00 | 0.00 | 0.00 |
| Malaysia | 1.00 | 3.00 | 2.00 | Cote d'Ivoire | 0.00 | 0.00 | 0.00 |
| Kenya | – | 1.94 | 1.94 | Djibouti | 0.00 | 0.00 | 0.00 |
| Uzbekistan | 0.75 | 2.67 | 1.92 | Gambia | 0.00 | 0.00 | 0.00 |
| Yemen | 2.78 | 4.67 | 1.89 | Guinea | 0.00 | 0.00 | 0.00 |
| Lebanon | 2.50 | 4.33 | 1.83 | Guinea-Bissau | 0.00 | 0.00 | 0.00 |
| Libya | 0.50 | 2.08 | 1.58 | Jordan | 2.22 | 2.22 | 0.00 |
| Mali | 0.00 | 1.33 | 1.33 | Kazakhstan | 0.00 | 0.00 | 0.00 |
| Pakistan | 4.67 | 6.00 | 1.33 | North Yemen | 0.00 | – | 0.00 |
| Morocco | 1.00 | 2.22 | 1.22 | Sierra Leone | 0.00 | 0.00 | 0.00 |
| Azerbaijan | 0.00 | 1.11 | 1.11 | South Yemen | 0.00 | – | 0.00 |
| Kuwait | 3.00 | 4.00 | 1.00 | Turkmenistan | 0.00 | 0.00 | 0.00 |
| Oman | 0.00 | 1.00 | 1.00 | UAE | 0.00 | 0.00 | 0.00 |
| Nigeria | 2.78 | 3.67 | 0.89 | Eritrea | 0.33 | 0.33 | 0.00 |
| Bosnia | 0.00 | 0.83 | 0.83 | Saudi Arabia | 2.33 | 2.33 | 0.00 |
| Palestine | 5.00 | 5.67 | 0.67 | Senegal | 0.11 | 0.00 | −0.11 |
| Maldives | 0.00 | 0.67 | 0.67 | Tanzania | 1.11 | 0.22 | −0.89 |
| Chad | 0.00 | 0.50 | 0.50 | Egypt | 5.50 | 4.33 | −1.17 |
| Qatar | 0.00 | 0.50 | 0.50 | Algeria | 6.00 | 4.67 | −1.33 |
| Kyrgyzstan | 0.06 | 0.44 | 0.39 | Syria | 3.75 | 2.33 | −1.42 |
| Indonesia | 5.33 | 5.67 | 0.33 | | | | |

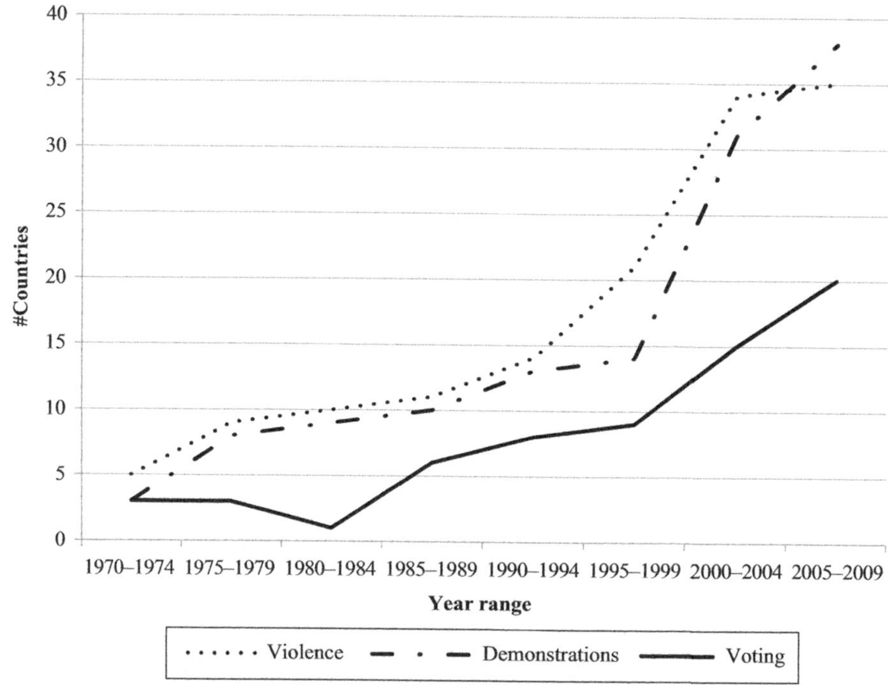


FIGURE 3.2 Number of countries with Islamist political mobilization 1970–2009.

## CORRELATES OF ISLAMIST MOBILIZATION

The data presented provide numerous opportunities to evaluate hypotheses about the sources of Islamist mobilization presented in Chapters 1 and 2. While many theoretical claims cannot effectively be tested across the range of cases due to data limitations or the lack of quantifiable indicators, initial evaluation of some claims is possible through the use of cross-national proxy indicators. Correlates of Islamist mobilization across the range of cases are determined as the result of statistical analysis and are described in the following.[19] Many of the relationships described in the text are presented in the statistical models included in the Appendix.

Some religious theories suggest that the greater the number of Muslim believers in a given society, the higher the overall level of Islamist political mobilization will be. Likewise, some argue that different varieties of Islam are more prone to political mobilization than others. For example, some have hypothesized that Shi'a populations are more prone to political action than others, while Muslims in the Sufi tradition are less politicized.

While no broad cross-national data provide the opportunity to test for a correlation between belief and Islamist political activism across the countries of the data set, there appears to be some correlation between the percentage

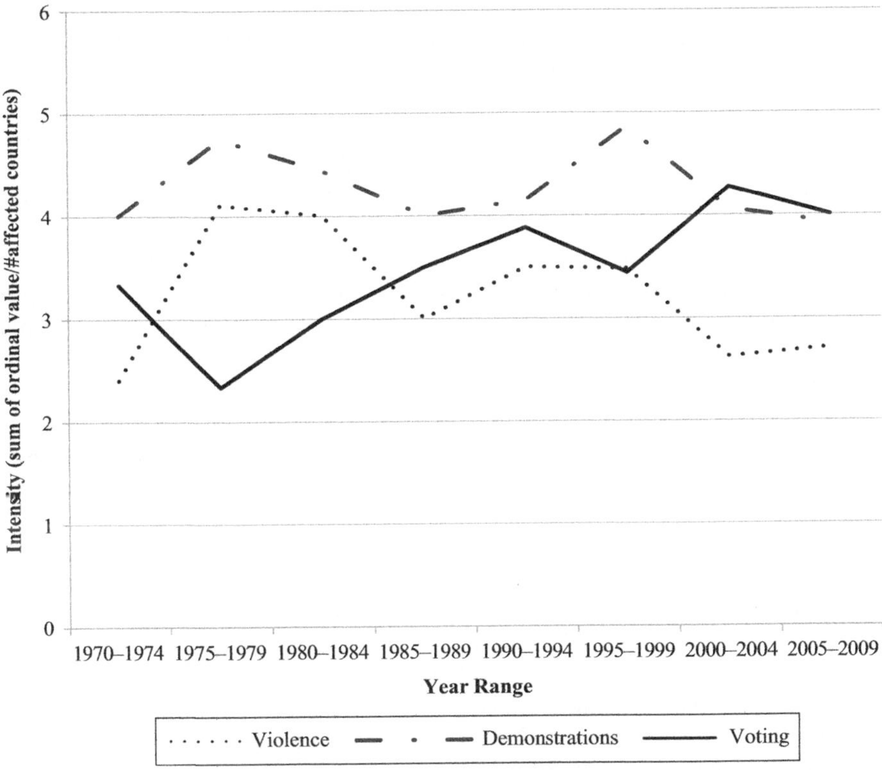


FIGURE 3.3 Average intensity of Islamist political mobilization, 1970–2010.

Muslim population of a given polity and its experience with Islamist political mobilization. West African states with comparatively small Muslim populations have less Islamist mobilization on average, which drives much of this correlation. However, this relationship does not persist in other cases or when control variables are taken into account. The countries of the Arabian Peninsula, for example, all have dominantly Muslim populations, but many have had very little Islamist mobilization. Despite prominent political activism by some Shi'i religious leaders (i.e., in Iran, Lebanon, Iraq), there likewise appears to be an uncertain relationship between Islamist mobilization and the percentage of the Muslim population that is Shi'a. A number of countries with comparatively large Shi'a populations (Albania, Azerbaijan, Kuwait, Saudi Arabia, Yemen, United Arab Emirates) have experienced comparatively low levels of Islamist activism, at least within a framework of Shi'a Islam.

The mystical trend in Islam known as Sufism is also more prominent in some countries of the study than in others. Sufi leaders often preach the primary importance of communion with deity, rejecting intervention in affairs of state.

This generalization has not held true in many contexts, however. Of the twenty-six Muslim countries in which Sufism plays a prominent role in religious organization,[20] about two-thirds have experienced minimal Islamist mobilization. In the others, Islamist political mobilization has occurred within, alongside, or in opposition to Sufi brotherhoods. Sufi brotherhoods have taken active political roles in countries such as the Sudan, Afghanistan, and Pakistan, but these tend to be exceptional. The presence of strong Sufi brotherhoods is more common in low mobilization contexts, but is not a defining factor of them.

In contrast to religious theories, a diverse group of structural theories asserts that large-scale social and political changes are the driving forces behind Islamist mobilization. These changes include colonialism, rapid economic development, exposure to economic and cultural globalization, and proximity to international events such as the Palestine-Israeli conflict, the Soviet invasion of Afghanistan, or the Iranian revolution. Structural perspectives also see authoritarianism or the failure of the secular state as macro-causes of Islamism.

Across the range of cases, there is little support for claims that colonial history, economic development, or globalization are good predictors of Islamist activism. Countries that have been colonized are not more likely to experience Islamist mobilization, but may rather be slightly less prone than countries that were not occupied by a colonial power.[21] This is, in part, because of the extensive European colonial history in sub-Saharan Africa, which has low levels of Islamist mobilization overall. Both GDP per capita and the level of human development are likewise poor linear indicators of mobilization. There does appear to be a non-linear relationship between development and mobilization, however, which is portrayed in Figure 3.4.

Very poor countries, such as those found in West Africa, and rich countries, such as those found in the Arab gulf, both tend to experience considerably

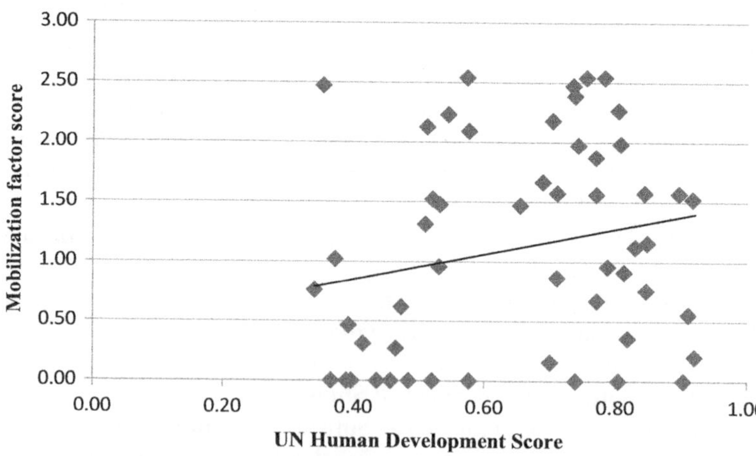


FIGURE 3.4 HDI and Islamist mobilization.

lower levels of mobilization than those in mid-ranges of development. Modernizing countries thus appear to be more prone to Islamist mobilization (and political mobilization in general), but this correlation reverses as countries become increasingly developed. This non-linear relationship is less true when it comes to voting for Islamist parties. Some of the most developed countries in the study, such as Kuwait, Malaysia, or Bahrain, also have significant records of voting Islamist in electoral competition.

Proxy indicators of exposure to global influences, such as number of tourists, level of urbanization, and the number of televisions per capita, are particularly poor predictors of Islamist mobilization and demonstrate little correlation with Islamist activity, linear or otherwise. To the extent that these proxies measure global exposure, this suggests that hypotheses directly linking Islamist mobilization to globalization have little comparative support across the Islamic world.

Levels of state authoritarianism or traditions of state secularism, which some predict should lead to increased Islamist mobilization, do not show this pattern across the population of cases. Average levels of authoritarianism across time[22] are uncorrelated with Islamist mobilization, with the obvious exception that less authoritarian countries are more likely to have experienced Islamist electoral mobilization. Countries in which Islam is the state religion are neither more nor less likely to experience Islamist violence or demonstrations, which suggests that official state secularism is not a good predictor of these mobilization outcomes. Electoral mobilization on behalf of Islamist parties does occur much more frequently in countries where Islam is the state religion, however. Countries in which Islam is not the state religion often have legal restrictions on religious parties, making it difficult for them to compete.

Proximity to defining international conflicts, such as those in Israel–Palestine, Afghanistan, and Iran, may be influential in leading to increased levels of Islamist mobilization, although this is difficult to assess apart from examination of the mobilization process in individual cases. Countries with the most sustained levels of Islamist mobilization tend to be affected by these events, but the response is by no means uniform. Islamist activism in both Tajikistan and Pakistan has been directly influenced by neighboring Afghanistan. Likewise, Islamism in both Lebanon and Egypt has been directly influenced by the Israeli-Palestinian conflict. Other neighbors of Palestine, such as Jordan and Syria, have historically experienced somewhat less Islamist political mobilization despite their proximity to the conflict. The influence of the Islamic revolution in Iran has been rather limited among neighboring Sunni Muslim countries, where the leadership structure of the Shi'ite clerics is not replicated.

Incentive-based theories, which predict that individuals mobilize on behalf of an Islamist cause because of individual economic or political incentives, cannot be tested on a macro level because of the diversity of possible incentives and lack of comparable data. Claims that Islamist mobilization is directly correlated to the distribution of oil revenues likewise cannot be effectively tested with this data set, although countries with oil revenues are not more likely to experience Islamist political mobilization than those without; in fact, oil producers are somewhat less likely to experience mobilization. Nor are countries that neighbor Saudi Arabia, the primary distributor of oil revenues for Islamic causes abroad, more likely to experience mobilization.

What about shifts in domestic policy in which the government supports Islamic activities? These may include constitutional changes that make the state more Islamic, support for Islamic groups against left-wing competitors, or the removal of restrictions on Islamist groups. Such state shifts could provide Islamic groups with increased incentives to mobilize in the political arena. In fact, the evidence on whether these state policy shifts correlate with Islamist mobilization is mixed. State policy changes favorable to Islam show little immediate correlation with Islamist mobilization. However, the data are consistent with the idea that state policy changes supportive of Islamic activities may lead to increased levels of Islamist activism in the long-run. Numerous cases, such as Egypt, Turkey, Libya, Jordan, Syria, and Malaysia, have all shifted state policy in favor of Islam and have seen increased Islamist mobilization in later periods.[23]

Grievance-based theories of Islamist mobilization are often tied to domestic structural changes such as rapid population growth, urbanization, economic stagnation, and impoverishment. These structural changes are then linked to frustration and individual dissatisfaction, which may be channeled in Islamist movements as protest. Political grievances, such as repression, are also hypothesized to lead to Islamist activism against the state.

Overpopulation and rapid urbanization are central elements in many grievance-based stories, which assert that Islamist mobilization is an outcome of rural migrants relocating in urban centers where they find no employment and become socially disoriented. Social anomie in a context of urban overcrowding leads migrant youth to turn to Islamism in an effort to regain their traditional identity and sense of balance. While many converts to Islamist movements may share this background (a background most non-activists would also share), across the population of cases, fertility rates and urbanization rates show no relationship to Islamist political mobilization. Cases where high fertility rates combine with high urbanization rates likewise show no correlation with mobilization outcomes, casting doubt on the strength of this theory.

As indicated earlier, economic development is not well correlated with mobilization, at least linearly. As a measure of economic grievance, GDP per capita also shows no relationship with average levels of mobilization across countries. Poor countries may experience high levels of Islamist mobilization, as is the case with Afghanistan, Pakistan, Somalia, and Yemen, or they may experience no Islamist mobilization, as is the case in much of West Africa. Wealthy countries are unlikely to have high levels of Islamist violence and protest, but may experience moderately high overall levels of Islamist activism, as is the case in Saudi Arabia and Malaysia. Many rich countries also experience very low levels of mobilization, as in the United Arab Emirates or Oman. While poverty may serve as a source of grievance for some Islamist activists, across the range of cases, poverty is not a correlate of mobilization.

Comparable economic growth data are not available for all countries in the study, nor are unemployment data, which are notoriously unreliable in most of the countries under investigation. Initial examination of the available data on these proxies for economic dissatisfaction also yields no correlation with average levels of mobilization across country and (five-year) period. Sudden economic downturns and short-term jumps in the unemployment rate are not measured in the cross-country analysis, however, and may show a dramatically different pattern. The effects of short-term economic changes are considered in individual cases later in the study.

What do the data show regarding the impact of political grievances? Two separate types of political grievances are measured: (a) a shift to authoritarianism from a comparatively more open system within a five-year period and (b) new moves by the state to specifically target Islamist activists or the institutional bases of Islamic movements. Authoritarian shifts are positively correlated with high levels of Islamist violence and street demonstrations, but the correlation is not statistically significant.[24] With exceptions in the cases of Algeria, Tajikistan, and Turkey, these authoritarian shifts are not in response to Islamist activism, but are determined by other causes. The potential positive correlation suggests that in many cases Islamist protest and violence may be a response to political grievances in the form of new restrictions on political liberty. As one might expect, authoritarian shifts are negatively correlated with Islamist electoral mobilization, as electoral mobilization depends on some degree of political openness.

State repression directed principally at Islamic institutions or Islamic movements is correlated with Islamist street demonstrations, with a high degree of statistical confidence, but is somewhat less correlated with Islamist voting or violence. The meaning of this correlation between repression and mobilization is difficult to assess, however, because state action is almost always framed as a response to a perceived Islamist threat, and sometimes occurs after a show of Islamist political force. Often, Islamist activists counter state repression with further protest activity or violence, to which the state subsequently responds. The pattern that results is one in which the state and Islamists respond to one another in an iterative fashion by challenging the most recent activities of the other. Iterative responses to threat and repression have been prominent in Islamist–state conflicts in countries such as Egypt, Algeria, Lebanon, Uzbekistan, Iraq, Libya, Palestine, and Bahrain. In these cycles of repression and response, perceptions of the instigator become blurred and the immediate sources of mobilization are unclear. Nevertheless, cross-national time-series data support the hypothesis that localized repression of Islamists often triggers large-scale protest mobilization from Islamist groups. Extremely high levels of targeted repression, as have occurred in Syria under Hafez al-Assad and in Iraq under Saddam Hussein, may reduce long-term levels of mobilization, but this cannot be effectively assessed from the cross-national data.

What can the cross-national time-series data tell us about the plausibility of the hypotheses outlined in the institutional theory presented in Chapter 2? As is the case with alternative theories, the available cross-national data are at best an imprecise measure of the validity of the hypotheses. Nevertheless, suggestive proxies can be used to evaluate the potential strength of the claims across the range of possible cases. The institutional theory as presented in Chapter 2 examined the role of three types of institutions in affecting mobilization outcomes: diffuse Islamic religious institutions (such as mosques and schools), the nature of Islamic organizations and movements themselves, and the state.

No recognizable measures of the penetration of Islamic institutions across the country set are available. However, three proxies are most likely correlated with the social penetration of Islamic institutions across diverse contexts. These are the amount of time for which a given territory has been converted to Islam, whether or not the state defines itself as an Islamic state, and the extent that the legal institutions are inspired or governed by Islamic law (shari'a). Assumptions are made in using these indicators that time leads to greater institutional and cultural penetration of Islamic ideology and that a legal framework that supports Islamic institutions will facilitate their penetration into local communities. These assumptions may not be empirically accurate in all cases but appear true in most circumstances. Additionally, populations fluent in Arabic have greater accessibility to Islamic (and Islamist) writings, which might serve as a proxy for access to Islamic cultural institutions. Finally, exposure to Communism is useful in assessing the impact of the destruction of Islamic institutions during the Soviet period.

Since Geertz's prominent discussion of Islamic syncretism and heterodoxy on the periphery of the Muslim world in *Islam Observed* (1968), the distance from Mecca has been thought of as an indicator of the regional salience of Muslim institutions. A better general indicator, however, is a historical one, measuring the length of time an area has been converted to Islam. The number of centuries that Muslim areas of a polity have been converted to Islam is, in fact, one of the strongest correlates of average levels of Islamist mobilization in the modern period. The further back in time an area was converted, the more likely the modern polity is to experience mobilization. This is particularly true in the case of Islamist violence and Islamist demonstrations.[25] The correlation between historical exposure to Islam and average mobilization is depicted in Figure 3.5. The length of association with Islamic civilization may be relevant for multiple reasons, but it is hypothesized here that the level of historical exposure corresponds primarily to institutional penetration and exposure to Islamic religious and cultural norms.

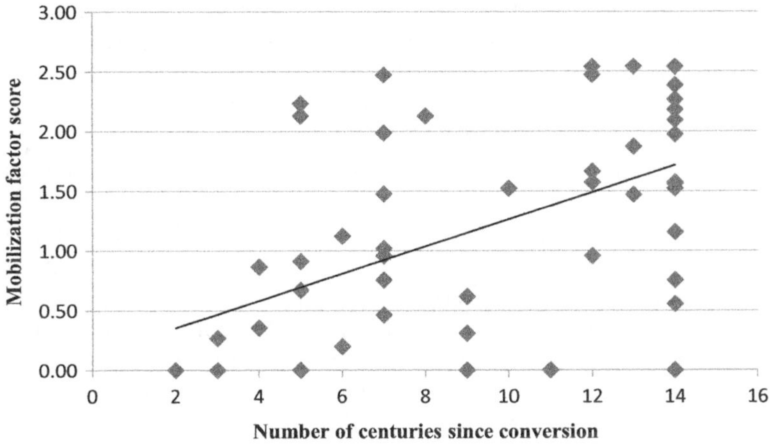


FIGURE 3.5 Islamic history and mobilization.

Of the fifty-seven polities examined in the study, there is considerable diversity regarding the religious definition of the state and the institutionalization of Islamic law. Some states explicitly define themselves as Islamic, others take constitutional inspiration from Islam, while still others are explicitly secular. Likewise, some states make no provision for Islamic law, some use legal systems inspired by Islamic law or have Islamic personal status courts, and others model large portions of their legal system on the basis of shari'a. States that have declared Islam the state religion are more likely to experience Islamist mobilization than others, particularly when it comes to street demonstrations and voting. Similarly, there are some indications that the incorporation of shari'a in the legal system is correlated with mobilization, though not with high confidence. The majority of Islamist mobilization has historically occurred in the thirty polities that at least claim some inspiration under principles of shari'a, although in the last decade Islamist mobilization has spread further afield into countries that have fewer formal Islamic institutions, such as Nigeria or Somalia. States that claim they are fully governed by Islamic law are not necessarily more likely to experience mobilization than those that incorporate it in some form.[26]

Countries that use Arabic as an official language have also historically been more likely (than those in which Arabic is used for religious purposes only) to experience Islamist mobilization, but this relationship has also shifted over the last decade. This lends some support to the argument that the Arabic linguistic tradition provides important resources in the development of Islamist political movements. As Islamist mobilization has spread to more countries in Africa and Asia, however, Arabic becomes a less useful predictor. It must be noted that Arabic-speaking countries also share a similar history of early incorporation into the Islamic empire, and therefore access to Arabic and historical exposure to Islam are highly correlated. When both variables are taken into account, historical exposure to Islam appears to be a more powerful predictor of mobilization than does ready access to Arabic.[27]

It has been hypothesized that countries in which Islamic institutions were largely destroyed by Communist rule would show a lower propensity to experience Islamist political mobilization than countries without a Communist background. This turns out to be the case, with a high degree of statistical significance in most models. Communism was influential in degrading Islamic institutions in the former Yugoslavia, Albania, and in the post-Soviet republics of Central Asia. Communist governments sponsored by the Soviets in Afghanistan were less successful in this regard. Most Muslim countries that experienced Communist rule have not held credible elections, but those that have (Albania, Bosnia-Herzegovina, Kyrgystan, Tajikistan) experienced little electoral mobilization on behalf of Islamist political parties and agendas in the period under investigation. Experience with Communism is also highly correlated with the absence of Islamist street demonstrations, with Tajikistan being the only major exception. A Communist background is somewhat less correlated with the absence of Islamist violence, however. Afghanistan, Tajikistan, and Uzbekistan have all experienced significant levels of violence despite prior governance by Communist institutions. With minor exceptions, Islamist violence has not affected other post-Communist countries in the study, making post-Communist countries less prone to Islamist violence overall than the other countries under investigation.[28]

What about the correlation of structural factors hypothesized to affect the incentives of movement leaders as outlined in Chapter 2? These structural factors may directly affect the incentives of Muslim leaders to politicize or not politicize their religious discourse. Potential factors influencing leadership incentives include regime treatment of Islamist organizations, state rent that can be used to co-opt religious leaders, the structure of competing religious and political institutions, and access to identity markers outside of religion. There are clearly a wide range of potential factors affecting the incentives of Islamist elites to align with the state, but the focus on repression, access to state rent, and identity competition outlined in Chapter 2 are briefly assessed here.

State repression, and particularly repression directed toward Islamist groups, is correlated with Islamist mobilization. Using the blunt instrument of cross-national time series data analysis, it is difficult to tell if this correlation should imply causation. Examination of specific cases, however, does show that Islamist violence and demonstrations often follow targeted state repression, making it likely that repression has causative impact in many circumstances. Because repression raises the potential costs of mobilization, it is striking to note that Islamist demonstrations and the repression of Islamic actors are positively correlated despite the costs.

Although countries with some oil revenue are neither more nor less likely to experience Islamist mobilization than those without, this is not necessarily the case with rentier states. Rentier states, defined here as countries in which at least 30 percent of GDP is generated by petroleum or natural gas, are less likely to have experienced mobilization than other countries in the population.[29] The result is not statistically significant with the inclusion of related control variables, but rentier states show a negative correlation with Islamist activity in all models and across all forms of mobilization measured. While this does not provide a compelling test of the hypothesis that access to rent provides disincentives for Islamist mobilization, it is nevertheless suggestive.

Measures of ethnic fractionalization are used to test whether countries with greater numbers of ethnic identities, and therefore a broader range of identity choices around which to mobilize, are more or less likely to have experienced Islamist mobilization.[30] In fact, there appears to be little evidence that the number of ethnic identities in a given polity affects the potential for religious mobilization. Countries with very high levels of ethnic fractionalization tend to have lower mobilization than those that do not, but almost all of this association can be explained by (ethnically diverse) countries in sub-Saharan Africa having lower average levels of Islamist mobilization. When sub-Saharan African cases are controlled for as being regionally distinct, ethnic diversity appears to have no correlation with average Islamist mobilization outcomes.

Fragmentation of the Islamist movement, as measured by the number of Islamist political groups, is extremely well correlated with mobilization outcomes, however.[31] The average number of Islamist groups in a given polity over time is by far the best predictor of the average extent of Islamist mobilization. This relationship is expected by theories of ethnic radicalization, in which it is argued that competitive challenges from similar groups lead leaders to radicalize in an effort to distinguish themselves from their competitors (Horowitz 1985).

However, much of the relationship is probably the result of additional factors. More groups may be necessary to mobilize large numbers than small numbers, for example. There may be "diseconomies of scale" in which mobilization under one leadership structure becomes more difficult and ineffective as a movement's constituency grows large. Additionally, the more a movement succeeds in mobilizing its constituency, the more incentives potential religious or political competitors may have to inaugurate new movements of their own. Therefore, we may expect that the number of organizations and the level of mobilization are mutually supportive factors. A competitive structure in which there are multiple competing Islamist groups may lead to increased incentives by those groups to actively mobilize against the state in order to distinguish themselves from each other. Likewise, successful mobilization may engender new Islamist organizations that are formed when large groups fail to effectively mobilize at the individual level and which seek to capitalize on an already mobilized constituency.

The third set of institutional drivers of mobilization outlined in Chapter 2 revolves around the role of the state. In particular, it was hypothesized that crises of state order and rapid political liberalization serve as focal points around which Islamist leadership and religious resources can converge to challenge the regime. Crises of order may evolve into crises of confidence in the government or even the state that may persist among certain populations for some time, if those populations are poorly incorporated into state institutions or patronage networks.

One very rough proxy for low state incorporation over time is a geographical one. The presence of mountains often makes incorporation of mountain dwellers into the state quite difficult, and leaves the potential that these groups may have persistently low levels of trust for central state authority. This potential has been realized in many countries around the world, and many guerilla and secessionist actors have emerged in difficult topographies such as mountains and jungle.[32] A similar pattern is found in this study: countries with mountain dwellers are more likely to have experienced high levels of Islamist mobilization than flat countries.[33] The correlation is stronger with levels of Islamist violence and Islamist voting than it is with street demonstrations. This makes sense theoretically if street demonstrations are dominantly an urban phenomenon and mountains make the establishment of large urban centers difficult.[34]

Cross-national proxies for a crisis of state order include the following variables: (a) leadership turnover (as measured by the number of times the chief executive of the government changes in a five-year period), (b) whether early elections are called due to government collapse (in parliamentary systems only), (c) the presence of large-scale civil (non-Islamist) violence, and (d) state collapse (loss of effective control over its territory).

The turnover rate of the chief executive (usually president or prime minister) may be considered a measure of government stability, and ranges from no change to five changes within any individual five-year period measured by the study.[35] Many of the countries that have experienced high leadership instability are located in sub-Saharan Africa, a region that tends to experience low Islamist mobilization. When regional variation is controlled for in panel data models, high levels of leadership instability are positively correlated with mobilization. This is particularly true with electoral mobilization, but also holds true for Islamist violence.[36] The relationship between demonstrations and leadership instability is positive but not statistically significant.

Early elections due to parliamentary breakdown are also correlated with higher levels of Islamist electoral mobilization. Early elections that follow government crisis and breakdown have led to considerable levels of Islamist electoral mobilization in Pakistan, Turkey, Malaysia, Kuwait, Indonesia, and Bangladesh, as well as more recently in Tunisia and in Egypt. By contrast, they have not been followed by Islamist electoral mobilization in countries such as Albania, Bosnia-Herzegovina, Guinea, Kyrgyzstan, Burkina Faso, and Niger.[37]

What about the presence of civil violence or state collapse? Substantial civil violence has occurred among more than two-thirds of the countries of the study at some point between 1970 and 2010. Some degree of state collapse, where the government has lost control over state territory, has also occurred in more than one-third of the study's countries during the same period. Assessed across the range of cases, civil violence is only correlated with Islamist demonstrations at statistically significant levels.[38] This suggests that Islamist violence is not necessarily more common in societies that have greater experience with violence than in more peaceful countries. A significant correlation does exist between violent mobilization and state collapse, however. In a few cases, such as Algeria, Afghanistan, Somalia, Tajikistan, and Yemen, Islamist guerilla activity has been implicated in the collapse of state control. In many other cases, however, state collapse has provided a context in which Islamist violence develops. Islamist electoral mobilization is also high in several contexts of state collapse, including after the partition of Pakistan in the 1970s, in Kuwait after the Iraqi invasion, in Yemen after the civil war, in divided Sudan during the 1980s, and in Iraq in the 2000s.[39]

An alternative focal point that was hypothesized to facilitate Islamic mobilization was political liberalization by authoritarian regimes. Liberalization[40] after a period of authoritarian governance provides new political opportunities for religious leaders, and may give them a mobilizing advantage over new political parties that have not yet developed mobilizing institutions or a common language to coordinate collective action. Controlling for region, political liberalization is significantly correlated with Islamist mobilization in the first three decades of this study. In the 2000s, Islamist electoral mobilization increased, capitalizing on liberal reforms, but these reforms often occurred several years earlier. Political liberalization in sub-Saharan Africa is typically not associated with Islamist mobilization, however. Across other countries, the correlation is the strongest with Islamist electoral mobilization and Islamist violence, but also holds with street demonstrations.[41] While liberalization may open new opportunities to protest and to vote, the correlation between liberalization and mobilization also holds when only countries with comparable levels of political liberty are examined.

In contrast to many countries that have experienced liberalization, countries that maintain a monarch as the head of state[42] are less likely to have experienced Islamist mobilization. This holds true even among countries with similar degrees of political liberty and controlling for region. States ruled by traditional leadership, which is generally more enduring and stable than elected, revolutionary, or military leadership, may appear to provide few alternatives for political mobilization outside of the existing framework. Monarchies may also generate fewer focal points around which to coordinate because of their lack of political dynamism. Likewise, monarchies are often associated with hierarchical family-based social models that make in-group policing easier for religious elites if they have access to the patriarchs of prominent families. It is notable that four monarchies that have experimented with some degree of political liberalization, Jordan, Kuwait, Bahrain, and Morocco, have also experienced considerable Islamist electoral mobilization, however.

Two additional correlates of Islamist mobilization that do not fit into any theoretical perspective discussed to this point are population size and countries of sub-Saharan Africa. They are notable because they appear to be important predictors of mobilization outcomes in statistical tests, but are somewhat difficult to address theoretically. Sub-Saharan Africa appears to be a regional outlier, and is statistically significant in some models. Its significance has faded a bit as Islamist mobilization in Nigeria, Somalia, and Mali increased over the last decade, but countries located in sub-Saharan Africa are less likely than countries in other regions to experience Islamist mobilization, even when all of the quantifiable factors discussed previously have been taken into account.

The statistical evidence thus suggests that regional effects (including shared history and culture) may matter in explaining patterns of low Islamist mobilization, most notably in Africa but also potentially in the Arab Gulf. However, it is also clear from the cross-country analysis that there are important outliers to this observation in each region (such as Sudan, Somalia, and Nigeria in sub-Saharan Africa) and that belonging to a specific cultural, historical, or geographical region is no guarantee that a country will not have high levels of Islamist mobilization. Particularistic political and Islamic institutions within a given country can thus overcome dampening effects of belonging to a region.

Another strong correlate is a country's population. The larger the population of a country, the more likely it is to experience Islamist mobilization across voting, violence, and demonstrations, on average.[43] There may be several combined factors that influence this relationship. Countries with larger populations have more people available to mobilize, and thus more violence or protest may be expected as a result. Small countries may also be able to collect better information on their populations and provide more efficient repression or state police control. A more interesting hypothesis, related to one of the central hypotheses of the study, is that small countries have fewer groups that become alienated from the state because distance from the central state is never very far. Likewise, both in-group policing and state policing of entrepreneurs may be easier in small states because of easier access to information about the entrepreneur. It is not possible to adjudicate between these hypotheses with the cross-national data used in this study, however.

## SUMMARY

What do these observed correlations mean and how confident should we be that they are accurate indicators of underlying relationships? A number of consistent patterns emerge across country and across time that, when combined, suggest that the theoretical relationships outlined in Chapter 2 have some plausibility. Many of the alternative macro-theories reviewed in Chapter 1, by contrast, receive little support in these findings. Nevertheless, a large cross-national study that compares outcomes across very diverse contexts remains limited in its power to sufficiently discriminate between many of the abstract theoretical claims that have been made regarding the sources of Islamist activism. This is particularly true regarding claims about the causal mechanisms (in contrast to structural features) through which mobilization is created. These mechanisms are dealt with to a greater extent in case discussions provided in subsequent chapters.

A broad view of Islamist mobilization across time and space does allow us to make several observations with confidence. Since the early 1970s, and particularly in the late 1990s, the *number of countries* that experienced Islamist violence and Islamist demonstrations dramatically increased. Islamist electoral mobilization has also increased and spread to a greater number of countries from the mid-1980s to the present, with a dramatic spike in the last decade beginning in the 2000s. The total *amount* of Islamist voting and protest has also risen since the 1980s, and greatly increased from 2000 onwards. The overall numbers of people killed in Islamist-related violence has declined since the 1990s, however, with the exception of a few cases such as Iraq, or post-2010 Syria. Islamist mobilization takes place in all regions of the Muslim world, with some geographical variation. Muslim areas of Eastern Europe, post-Soviet Central Asia, and sub-Saharan Africa have had the lowest levels of Islamist activity on average, while the Arab world, core countries of greater Central Asia (Turkey, Iran, Afghanistan), and South/Southeast Asia have had higher levels on average.

Across countries and across time, several structural conditions are generally uncorrelated with Islamist mobilization patterns. These include multiple conditions often held responsible for the rise of Islamism. Strictly religious characteristics, such as the percentage of the population that is Shi'ite Muslim or the presence of institutional Sufism, appear not to be particularly correlated with the emergence of Islamist politics. The percent of the population that is Muslim appears to have some limited correlation, however. Additionally, a history of colonialism, various indicators of globalization, and the level of economic development are poor predictors of mobilization outcomes. While very poor countries are less likely to have experienced mobilization than others, Islamist activism is present across a very broad range of development contexts. These outcomes suggest that theories that locate the source of Islamist activism in a country's historical relationship to "modernity" or to the West are inconsistent with the population of cases.

Other arguments that suggest that Islamist mobilization is primarily an outcome of demographic and social shifts, or a result of general economic stagnation, are not well supported here. Population growth rates, urbanization, and long-term patterns of economic growth are not well correlated with mobilization outcomes across the range of cases. Absolute poverty, which is at times referenced as a major structural factor generating Islamist activism, is a particularly poor indicator of Islamist mobilization across country. Hypotheses that view political Islam as largely tied to oil revenues from conservative Muslim countries are not consistent with the data analysis here either.

The data analysis shows that mobilization outcomes across time and space are much more consistent with the implications of the institutional theory presented in Chapter 2. The strength of Islamic institutions and the penetration of Islamic culture and language, roughly measured by the length of historical exposure to Islam and official state support for Islam and Islamic law, correspond to contemporary levels of Islamist political activism. Countries in which Islamic institutions were significantly damaged or destroyed by Communist regimes have notably lower levels of mobilization, on average, than countries that were not previously Communist.

Institutional factors are also hypothesized to influence the incentives of religious leaders, and the data are generally consistent with the proposed mechanisms in this regard. Rentier states, which have vast financial resources to distribute through networks of political patronage, may create strong economic disincentives for potential Islamist leaders to enter politics. The data reveal that these states have experienced lower Islamist mobilization, on average, than have non-rentier states. States that try to create disincentives for Islamists through repression, however, have mixed results. General repression is inconsistently correlated with increased Islamist activity. Repression specifically targeting Islamist groups is highly correlated with mobilization, however, casting some doubt on the use of repression as an effective strategy for reducing Islamist activism. Evidence suggests that very high levels of targeted repression over time may eliminate overt forms of Islamist mobilization, but the relationship needs much more clarification. Contexts in which there is competition between two or more Islamist movements may create increased incentives both for public mobilization and for radicalization. The data are strongly consistent with the hypothesis that fractionalization of the Islamist movement may lead to increased mobilization, particularly in the form of Islamist violence. The data are not necessarily consistent with the hypothesis that greater numbers of ethnic identities, which could compete against religious identity, would lead to lower levels of Islamist mobilization, however.

Various measures of state crisis and other focal events, which are here hypothesized to coordinate information exchange and protest against the state, demonstrate a strong correlation with patterns of Islamist mobilization. High leadership turnover (due to coups d'état, assassinations, and resignations) and early elections (as a result of parliamentary breakdown), for example, are correlated with high levels of Islamist mobilization. Levels of civil conflict are positively correlated with Islamist demonstrations, and contexts of recent state collapse are correlated both with Islamist violence and with Islamist electoral mobilization. Countries with populations living in mountainous territory, which may have difficulty incorporating these groups into the state, have higher levels of Islamist mobilization on average. All other things equal, the larger a country's population, the more likely it is to experience Islamist mobilization in any of its forms.

TABLE 3.8 *Summary of Variable Correlations with Islamist Mobilization**

| Relationship | + | – | Mixed | None | Relationship | + | – | Mixed | None |
|---|---|---|---|---|---|---|---|---|---|
| Population | + | | | | Islam is religion of state | + | | | |
| % Muslim | | | M | | Shari'a in legal system | | | M | |
| % Shi'i | | | | N | # of Islamist organizations | + | | | |
| Sufi institutions | | | M | | Monarchy | | – | | |
| Arabic language | + | | | | Pro-Islamic policy change | | | M | |
| Centuries since conversion | | | M | | Anti-Islamic policy change | + | | | |
| Sub-Saharan Africa | | – | | | Liberalization | + | | | |
| Ottoman Empire | | | M | | General repression | | | M | |
| Mountainous | + | | | | Early election | + | | | |
| Colonial history | | | | N | Leadership turnover | + | | | |
| Previously communist | | – | | | Islamist participation in government | | | M | |
| Ethnic fractionalization | | | | N | Civil violence | + | | | |
| GDP per capita | | | | N | State collapse | + | | | |
| Fertility rate | | | | N | | | | | |
| Human development index | | | M | | | | | | |
| # of tourists | | | | N | | | | | |
| Urbanization | | | | N | | | | | |
| Televisions per capita | | | | N | | | | | |
| Economic growth (average levels) | | | M | | | | | | |
| Oil revenue | | | | N | | | | | |
| Rentier oil state | | – | | | | | | | |
| Political liberty (average levels) | | | | N | | | | | |

* General direction of correlation across all forms of mobilization as derived from multiple statistical models. Variables that have different relationships to different types of mobilization are classified here as mixed. Supporting statistical models are in the Appendix for reference.

Political liberalization after a period of authoritarian rule is often associated with Islamist mobilization, particularly in the first three decades of this study, and then in the period after 2010. This has sometimes led to Islamists participating in the government, which is strongly correlated with mobilization outcomes. In this case, causation goes both ways, as Islamist mobilization creates opportunities for Islamist parties to participate in government, while Islamists in government can create new opportunities for mobilization. Countries that have not attempted political liberalization, and monarchies in particular, demonstrate lower levels of Islamist activism on average. Proximity to several defining international events, such as the Arab-Israeli conflict, the Soviet invasion of Afghanistan, and the Iranian revolution, may allow these events to serve a greater role in coordinating Islamist mobilization than countries far removed from these events. A visual summary of the relationships described here is provided in Table 3.8.

There is a great deal about the causes of Islamist political activism that is not revealed in the data analysis. Many of the correlations described here are relationships over considerable periods of time,[44] and much deeper evaluation of individual case histories is required to verify the temporal priority of explanatory variables. Additionally, the indicators used in the cross-national analysis are not necessarily representative of the underlying causative factors that drive the hypothesized theoretical relationships. The mechanisms by which structural factors are linked to mobilization outcomes are particularly difficult to assess here, but require detailed discussion of the range of outcomes in individual cases.

The purpose of the discussion in subsequent chapters, which focus on Islamist mobilization in Senegal, Turkey, and Algeria, is to address the variety of contexts in which Islamist actors make decisions about their political participation. In particular, the following chapters address the institutional factors that influence the successes and failures of religious mobilization and the processes by which they do so.

## REFERENCES

El-Affendi, Abdelwahab. 1991. *Turabi's Revolution: Islam and Power in the Sudan*. London: Grey Seal.

Geertz, Clifford. 1968. *Islam Observed: Religious Development in Morocco and Indonesia*. New Haven, CT: Yale University Press.

Horowitz, Donald L. 1985. *Ethnic Groups in Conflict*. Berkeley: University of California Press.

Krain, Matthew. 1978. *Ethnic Fractionalization Dataset*. Published online at http://discover.wooster.edu/mkrain/ethnic-fractionalization-data/.

Saif, Ahmed A. 2001. *A Legislature in Transition: The Yemeni Parliament*. Burlington, VT: Ashgate.

Wiktorowicz, Quintan. 2001. *The Management of Islamic Activism: Salafis, the Muslim Brotherhood, and State Power in Jordan*. Albany: State University of New York Press.

# 4

# Explaining Low Islamist Mobilization

## *Muslims and Politics in Senegal*

As noted in Chapter 3, considerable variation in Islamist political mobilization exists cross-nationally. While statistical analysis provides a number of clues as to the causes of variation in mobilization outcomes across space, more detailed assessment of individual cases is required to understand the historical and institutional foundations of mobilizing Islam. The purpose of this chapter is to assess an important case of low Islamist mobilization, that of modern Senegal. The discussion focuses on both the comparative absence and the periodic emergence of political Islam in Senegalese politics from 1970 to the present, with considerable reference to the patterns and institutions that have influenced its course from earlier periods.

A number of Muslim geographies are notable for having relatively low levels of Islamist mobilization, including parts of Europe, Central Asia, and the Arabian Peninsula, but perhaps the largest concentration of low-mobilizing countries is found in sub-Saharan Africa. Within this area, relatively little explicit political mobilization by Islamists has been apparent outside of the Sudan (which has strong regional ties to the Middle East), Somalia, Northern Nigeria, and, more recently, Mali. This absence of mobilization is in many ways surprising given existing theories of Islamism, however. Many sub-Saharan countries have very high concentrations of Muslims and have significant Islamic "civil societies"; they have significant challenges with poverty and rapid urbanization; their states have often performed poorly and/or been highly repressive; and they have had extensive Western contact as part of colonial empires and are increasingly part of the global economy.

Many of the prominent theories of Islamist mobilization discussed in Chapter 1 appear to be inadequately equipped to explain the relative absence of Islamist mobilization in sub-Saharan Africa, which makes the area potentially helpful in understanding the lower end of the range of mobilization outcomes.[1] An inquiry into a sub-Saharan case of low Islamist mobilization may also help illuminate whether the theory presented in Chapter 2 is useful in explaining why Islamist political mobilization does not occur in some contexts.

Out of all the Muslim countries in sub-Saharan Africa, the absence of sustained Islamist mobilization in Senegal is one of the most puzzling. Senegal has a rich Islamic history, influenced by many Islamic movements over time. It is a dominantly Muslim country, with an extensive network of Islamic organizations comprising the preeminent form of "civil society" in most towns and villages. No other sub-Saharan country (with the exception of the highly mobilized Sudan) has a comparable depth of Islamic institutions or level of participation in some form of Muslim religious activity as Senegal. And yet, Senegal has maintained a decidedly secular state in which Islam has not become actively politicized. As Villalón (1995) notes: "Islam in Senegal has been paradigmatically conformist, capable of accommodating itself to the prevailing political reality of the modern nation-state ... There is little evidence of the social phenomena which might be expected to accompany the politicization of Islam: socio-political cleavages based on religion" (1–2).

Islamic institutions in Senegal have by no means been absent from political calculations, however, and have played, at times, a decisive role in political outcomes. But as Villalón and many others have observed, Islamist mobilization in the political arena for Islamist candidates, causes, or policies has been characteristically low. This is despite considerable political mobilization by an active and divided electorate, as well as large protests and occasional violence in support of a range of other political causes. The few attempts by religious entrepreneurs to politicize Islam, of considerable interest to the question of this study, largely fell flat, either never gaining an audience or else rapidly losing it.

Why then has Islamist political mobilization been largely absent in Senegal? I argue here that the institutional theory as presented in Chapter 2 helps explain low mobilization in the Senegalese case by highlighting structural characteristics of Islamic institutions, religious elites, and the state. Despite the extensive Islamic institutional resources that might be channeled into political mobilization, both the fragmented nature of Senegalese Islamic institutions and the slowly liberalizing trajectory of the Senegalese state create challenges for Islamists looking to mobilize. Even more importantly, I argue that the distance between the incentives of religious elites and the incentives of the state has historically been small. While that distance could potentially widen, Senegal has several economic and structural characteristics that support an alignment of interests between the state and those with the potential to politicize Islam.

This chapter focuses first on a discussion of the nature of Islam and the historical context of Islamic institutions in Senegal. This is followed by a description of the various forms of Islamic activism and several Senegalese attempts at Islamist political mobilization. Attention then shifts from description to an assessment of the reasons for low political mobilization. This is done by examining the Islamic institutional resources for mobilization, the incentives of religious and political elites, and potential focal points around which Islamist mobilization might occur. The discussion is then brought back to the relevance of Senegal for other cases, including neighboring Mali. Prospects for mobilization in Senegal and broader implications of the argument are presented in the Conclusion.

## ISLAM IN THE SENEGALESE CONTEXT

Senegal is a mid-sized African country of about 14 million inhabitants on the Atlantic coast of West Africa. It is positioned between the almost uniformly Muslim country of Mauritania and smaller mixed Muslim/Christian/animist countries to its south. Senegal straddles the Sahel, extending into tropical regions near its southern border. It is dominantly Muslim, with the 1988 census showing a Muslim population of 94 percent, but it is also home to a substantial Christian minority as well as some animists. Like most sub-Saharan countries, it has considerable ethnic diversity. However, it has historically been dominated by the Wolof peoples of the central region, who comprise about 45 percent of the population. Wolof has become the dominant language of the countryside, competing in urban centers with the colonial language of French that is widely spoken among the educated elite.

The forms of Islam in Senegal are intricately tied to the structure of the Senegalese economy. Senegal is a poor country, with a 2010 GDP per capita of around $1700 (in purchasing power parity), although it is not the poorest in the region.[2] It has historically been a major exporter of agricultural goods, primarily peanuts and fish. In the 1960s and 1970s, peanut production accounted for up to 80 percent of the country's export revenue.[3] The economy has slowly diversified into other industries, including the mining of phosphates and refining of petroleum. More than 70 percent of the labor force is involved in agricultural activities, including growing peanuts and millet, herding livestock, and subsistence agriculture.[4]

Islam in Senegal is characterized by an unusually strong tradition of mystical Sufi brotherhoods, which are active throughout the country. The most significant of the Senegalese Sufi orders are the Tijaniyya and Mouridiyya brotherhoods, although the Qadiriyya and the Layenne also claim a number of adherents. The 1988 census revealed that all but about 5 percent of those identifying themselves as Muslims claim allegiance to one of the major Sufi orders in the country – an unusually high percentage of Muslims identifying themselves as Sufi.[5]

Islam first penetrated the Senegambia region early, with an Islamic kingdom established there around the year 1040.[6] Muslim traders developed active routes between North Africa and what is modern Senegal, providing channels for the transmission of knowledge and for conversion. By around 1500, Islam was the dominant religion of the majority of the region's inhabitants.[7] During the seventeenth and eighteenth centuries, a series of Islamic reform movements led by Sufi leaders or Islamic scholars *('ulema)* took place in the region. Some of these movements sponsored military jihads against non-Muslim peoples or colonial forces, but none of them resulted in a Muslim state similar to those built in other areas (e.g., Sokoto). A Muslim state in the broader region emerged from the jihads of a leader in the Tijaniyya brotherhood, al-Hajj 'Umar al-Futi, during the middle of the nineteenth century. Al-Futi was ultimately defeated in a series of engagements by the French in Senegambia, but established a short-lived empire on its eastern borders.[8]

By the time that the French established themselves in the region during the nineteenth century, Islamic movements had demonstrated their potential for militancy.[9] As French rule along the coast became more consolidated, however, relations between the French and Muslim leaders began to evolve from hostility to a tentative coexistence and ultimately to cooperation.[10] The Tijani brotherhood was an important vehicle for Islam in the early colonial period, but a new indigenous brotherhood that developed in Senegal at the close of the nineteenth century was to have an even greater impact. This indigenous brotherhood was known as the Mouridiyya.

The Mouridiyya was founded by Amadu Bamba Mbacké (1853–1927), after his association with several different Sufi orders. Amadu Bamba established a new village for his adherents in 1887, named Touba (meaning "conversion"), and broke away from other orders to found the Mouridiyya in 1904. He had an often-hostile relationship with the colonial authorities, and was exiled from the Senegambia three times by the French.

While the French focused most of their energies on building Dakar and the coastal communes, they realized after some time that Sufi leaders in the countryside (known as *marabouts*) could be useful partners in indirect rule of the hinterland. The French had used the tribal chiefs to collect taxes and provide order in the interior during the late nineteenth century, but became increasingly frustrated with the inability of the chiefs to control their subjects. Despite a previously antagonistic relationship with the founder of the Mourides, by 1907 the French allowed Bamba to return to Senegal. From that point, the Mouride brotherhood and the colonial authority reached a form of mutual accommodation.

The French found that the Sufi *marabouts* were more popular among the peasants than the tribal chiefs because they extracted fewer resources and did not support slavery. They thus proved more reliable in maintaining order in the countryside and in supporting colonial ambitions to increase the production of peanuts as a cash crop for export. By 1910, Amadu Bamba made a public statement regarding the acceptability of French rule, and later encouraged his followers to fight for the allied cause in World War I. In return, the French provided the brotherhood with resources and proactively defended it against its enemies.[11] Bamba maintained the importance of independence from French intervention in most of the brotherhood's affairs, however, resisting French schools, appointing regional officials, and maintaining significant autonomy from the colonial authority for his capital of Touba.[12]

The Mouride order under Bamba rapidly developed a following of peasants, notables, and former slaves in the Wolof hinterland, always demonstrating at least latent hostility to both the system of tribal chiefs and the system of French education and promotion. The more established and numerous Tijani order, on the other hand, was more accommodative to the colonial system. Tijanis developed a considerable social base among the French-educated elite, in the coastal cities, and in rural regions most affected by export agriculture and modern transportation.[13]

In the countryside, the Mouride collaboration with the French had significant economic consequences as the *marabouts* encouraged their disciples to work for the brotherhood in growing both millet and the cash crop of peanuts, which was important for the colony's export income. When Bamba died in 1927, he was succeeded first by his oldest son Mustapha, and then by a younger son Falilou. During this period, the relationship between the *marabouts* and the French authorities grew closer, and the Mourides expanded throughout the peanut agricultural zone, supported by colonial authorities. Millet cultivation began to give way more and more to cultivation of peanuts for export.

The Sufi *marabouts,* both Mouride and Tijani, received significant privileges from the French, including gifts, development assistance, as well as approval and even financial support for mosque construction. The marabouts were useful to the French, in return, as barometers of local opinion, mediators in disputes, and guarantors of a pacified peasant class. In the areas where the Sufi marabouts were most concentrated, including Diourbel, Sine Saloum, and Thies, the marabouts were allowed significant, if informal, administrative power vis-à-vis the colonial administration.[14] In 1937, the French Governor General first appeared at the Mouride religious holiday of *tabaski* (*'aid al-kebir*),[15] a show of support for the brotherhood that served as a prelude to many more official visits to religious ceremonies throughout Senegal's modern history.

By the mid-1900s, it became apparent that Muslim religious leaders would play an increasingly important role in determining the political future of French Senegal. The Mourides had greatly expanded their influence and geographic scope, an international revival of the Tijani brotherhood was being led from the town of Kaolack,[16] and even Islamic reformers influenced by the Arab world were beginning a local dialogue around the role of religion.

The constitutional reforms of the French Fourth Republic in 1946, however, did the most to alter the political equation. Voting rights were extended to Senegalese beyond the traditional four coastal communes of Dakar, Gorée, St. Louis, and Rufisque. While local government was still controlled by the French, this meant that the countryside could now elect representatives to the General Council, forcing the politically minded urban elite to go to the interior to contend for the rural vote.[17] Much of the power to determine Senegal's course on the eve of independence thus rested in the countryside, and much of the power in the countryside rested with the Sufi religious leadership.

This religious leadership was and continues to be institutionally divided among different brotherhoods, but it had significant organizational autonomy and a proven ability to dramatically mobilize the rural population. While Islamic divisions influenced the interaction between religious leaders (foremost the Sufi *marabouts*) and the state, considerable organizational autonomy made Senegalese religious institutions a dominant social force.

Of all Senegalese brotherhoods, the Tijaniyya currently claims the largest portion of the Senegalese population, with around 50 percent of Senegalese as adherents. The Mouridiyya is the second largest, with estimates at around 20 percent of the population.[18] The third largest in size, the Qadiriyya, has between 10 and 20 percent of the population, with the Layenne and other brotherhoods comprising smaller fractions.[19]

Despite its size, the Senegalese Tijani order is fragmented between several notable Tijani *maraboutic* families, including the Niasse family of Kaolack, the Tall family on the Senegal river, and, most importantly, the Sy family at Tivouane. The Tijaniyya has been notable for its open dialogue with political authorities and its dominance of both public and private wage labor. The smaller Mouridiyya, on the other hand, has maintained a greater degree of cohesion and has more organizational capacity than other Senegalese brotherhoods. The Mourides have traditionally dominated organized agriculture and agricultural exports, but have increased their role in urban markets and in international trade over time. The Qadiriyya, while a large brotherhood present in many African countries, is deeply fragmented in Senegal, without a unified organization.[20]

The Sufi brotherhood system is led by a number of *marabouts*, sometimes referred to as *sheikhs*; the most senior in the Mouride order holds the title of *khalife général*, after the "Caliph" of Islamic tradition. The *marabouts* provide spiritual guidance to their disciples, or *talibés*. They dispense blessings and provide the benefits of saintly charisma, or *baraka*, to those with the privilege of associating with them.[21] Additionally, they preside over gatherings for religious chanting, musical worship, and recitiation of the Qur'an or mystical literature.[22]

They also lead the development of the social structure of the brotherhood. The orders are typically built on a model of apprenticeship, in which disciples learn patterns of worship and the mystical teachings of the order from their superiors as they progress through a series of stages toward union with God. In the Mouride order, this often involves lengthy participation in physical labor on behalf of the brotherhood, as members of rural work groups or *daaras*. The Mouride disciple's commitment to labor in work groups has made the brotherhood a formidable economic force over time. Leading *marabouts* often become wealthy landowners and receive a large number of gifts from their disciples. The *sheikh* enjoys the support of disciples both because of his revered status and because he controls resources important to their welfare. While the economic ties to the *marabout* are strongest when the disciple is cultivating the brotherhood's land, urban migrants outside the direct sphere of the *marabout* often continue ties to their sheikh through official brotherhood circles, known as *da'iras*.[23]

While the most revered *marabouts* come into leadership positions in the brotherhoods through descent from the founding *sheikh*, the status of many mid-level *marabouts* within the orders is determined much more by the amount of popular support they command from disciples. Indeed, the status of many *marabouts* is not assured unless the *sheikh* can maintain active support and protection for his disciples, both physical and spiritual. As mid-level *marabouts* bring in more disciples to the order, their statuses within the order are enhanced.[24] Because status is often in flux, each of the Senegalese orders has had many crises over succession in the brotherhood. Central authority has been maintained more effectively in the Mouridiyya than others, but personal positioning for succession or status is constant at mid-levels of leadership in all orders.[25]

Brotherhoods amplify their organizational strength through control of specific geographies and the production of mass ritual events. The principal Tijani families have created areas of sacred space in the cities of Kaolack and Tivouane, while the Mourides have built their own religious mini-state in the city of Touba. These cities serve as places of economic activity and of pilgrimage. Both the Tijani and Mouride orders hold a major yearly pilgrimage event in their respective centers (the Tijani *gammu* takes place in Tivouane, and the Mouride *magal* takes place in Touba). Over the course of the past century, the Mouride capital of Touba has transformed itself through rapid growth from a tiny village to the second-largest city in Senegal, with more than 500,000 inhabitants.[26] The annual Mouride *magal* attracts an enormous number of participants, sometimes up to one out of every eight people in Senegal.[27] These events provide extraordinary opportunities for leaders to communicate with their disciples and have come to be important political moments for the state as well.

Both the Mouridiyya and the Tijaniyya have institutional features that help to construct distinctive common knowledge among those belonging to the brotherhoods. The Mouridiyya has a rigorous discipleship system that involves a ritual of allegiance (*njebbel*) to a chosen marabout. This discipleship is expressed through a pattern of work-related challenges, particularly in rural agricultural communities, and disciples experience a shared work environment and similar difficult rites of passage to progress in the order. Those in rural communities regularly convene in discipleship circles (*daaras*) to strengthen the community and to learn doctrine and the culture of the order. For those in urban areas, this structure is mimicked in an urban *da'ira* in which Mourides consolidate their collective identity and benefit from shared connections and economic patronage. For those disciples of the Tijaniyya, common knowledge is most regularly built through religious (*dhikr*) meetings in which religious phrases are repeated or performed in a call-and-response ritual. The new Tijani disciple is also given a specific set of holy phrases (*wird*) to repeat morning and afternoon, which distinguishes him from those from other traditions. In both of these orders, the common social knowledge built from the major religious pilgrimages, the Grand Magal for the Mouridiyya and the Gammu for the Tijaniyya, would be hard to overstate.

While the Sufi brotherhoods merit by far the most attention among Senegalese Islamic groups due to their size and organization, by the close of the colonial period, Islamic "reformist" leaders had also emerged. Several Muslim intellectuals of the 1920s and 1930s, many of whom had traveled or been educated in the Middle East, became openly critical of brotherhood activities and established their own religious organizations. While denouncing many brotherhood practices as "un-Islamic," they also became adept at forming alliances with members of the brotherhoods as the occasion required. Early reformist groups focused primarily on building institutions for Arabic and Islamic education that would compete with French schools and Sufi *madrasas*. Their schools and cultural organizations had a difficult time rivaling the organizational draw of the urban Sufi *da'iras*, however.[28]

## RELIGIOUS AND POLITICAL MOBILIZATION IN INDEPENDENT SENEGAL

After the constitutional reforms of 1946 extended voting rights to the Senegalese countryside, a political trajectory toward increasing participation and independence from France became apparent. The electorate tripled between 1946 and 1951, with universal sufferage implemented in 1956.[29] Political parties became somewhat more institutionalized in the course of their attempts to reach out to newly enfranchised voters, and debates over Senegal's future relationship with France increased.

Pre-independence elections in the early 1950s brought the Catholic Léopold Senghor into a position of prominence as head of the Bloc Démocratique Sénégalais (BDS), ahead of his primary rival Lamine Guèye.[30] Guèye attempted to turn Senghor's Christianity into a political liability, highlighting the potentially uncomfortable paradox of a Catholic ruling a dominantly Muslim country; this failed to persuade the majority of Muslim voters, who nevertheless cast their ballots for Senghor.[31] Indeed, Senghor's careful attention to the Muslim *marabouts* of the countryside throughout his campaigns paid off in active support from Sufi leaders and many of their disciples, despite religious differences.

By the time Senegalese independence was recognized in 1960 (as part of the Mali Federation), Senghor's progressive politics dominated the political scene, as did his newly renamed Union Progressiste Sénégalaise (UPS) party. Despite the collapse of Senegal's union with Mali, Senghor led an aggressive drive toward economic and social reform, paralleling many of the development ideas of the French Socialist Party. The UPS managed to maintain a pragmatic and often cooperative relationship with France, despite occasionally strong assertions of independence and anti-colonial sentiment.[32] The new constitution of 1959 had many French characteristics and delineated a secular state, to which many individual Islamic leaders were opposed. Despite a push by Sufi leaders to obtain guaranteed representation in the national assembly, independent Senegal emerged with few noticeably Islamic characteristics.[33]

Senghor's party was the dominant one from the early years of independence. The UPS continued to receive the vote of the countryside, and of the Sufi brotherhoods in particular. A serious crisis in 1962 demonstrated the importance of brotherhood support for leaders in the party. During the course of 1962, the Prime Minister, Mamadou Dia, fell out with President Senghor and attempted to assume leadership in the party. Notably, Dia tried to rally support by appealing to various brotherhood leaders, and convinced some important Tijani and other lesser *marabouts* to back his position.[34] Senghor's alliance with the leader of the Mouride brotherhood and his relationships with Sufi leaders throughout the country were too great to overcome, however, and Senghor called upon his brotherhood supporters in a way that successfully consolidated his position.[35] Subsequently, from the mid-1960s until 1974, Senegal was a one-party state. Other parties were either dissolved or strategically absorbed into the UPS.

Some political liberalization began to occur in the mid-1970s with the emergence of official opposition parties. This liberalization continued at a gradual pace, with some reversions to illiberal behavior, throughout the 1980s and 1990s. In 1976, constitutional reforms prescribed a three-party system,[36] with a fourth official party added shortly afterward. The most notable of the opposition parties to emerge in the 1970s was the "liberal" party headed by Abdoulaye Wade, the Parti Démocratique Sénégalaise (PDS). The PDS under Wade's leadership would go on to challenge the ruling party (from 1978, the Parti Socialiste (PS)) for almost two decades.

In 1978, the PDS took 18 of 100 seats in the National Assembly, officially receiving less than 20 percent of the vote. In 1980, long-time president Senghor retired, turning the leadership of the governing party over to his party ally, Abdou Diouf. Political reforms under Diouf further opened the system to a broad range of political parties.[37] Wade remained the primary opponent of the governing party, however, and ran against Abdou Diouf for the Senegalese presidency in subsequent elections of 1983, 1988, and 1993. Despite an increasing sense that the opposition was gaining ground with the electorate, Diouf officially won the 1983 election with more than 83 percent of the vote, and was also re-elected comfortably in 1988. The political opposition in this climate became increasingly hostile and convinced of the state's complicity in electoral fraud.

Economic stress in the late 1970s and early 1980s augmented frustration with the ruling party, boosting the hopes of the liberal opposition. After results were announced in 1983, the opposition refused to take their seats in the National Assembly; after results were announced in 1988, widespread urban rioting and violence took place, with Wade and other opposition leaders arrested for a period. The unprecedented political riots of 1988 were followed by other mass mobilizations, including the widespread killing of ethnic Mauritanians in 1989 and the great urban youth clean-up movement (*set setal*) in 1990. Eventually, the ruling party made concessions to the opposition, bringing Wade into a government position and writing a new electoral code with the consent of the PDS and other opposition parties.[38]

Increased transparency under the new electoral code was in effect for the 1993 presidential and legislative elections, in which the opposition believed that victory was assured. After a long delay in announcing the presidential results, Diouf was once again declared the winner with 58 percent of the vote.[39] Although this was the slimmest margin of victory yet for the governing party, the opposition again asserted that fraud had been committed. The widespread disenchantment with the democratic system that resulted was soon followed by a debilitating devaluation of the CFA franc in 1994 that cut the purchasing power of salaried labor in half and fueled raucous street protests.

Finally, after years of failed attempts, Wade emerged the victor in the presidential election of 2000, and his opposition party secured a majority in the National Assembly the following year. According to official results, Wade and his broad-based opposition coalition essentially reversed the 1993 outcome, winning 59 percent of the vote to the incumbent Diouf's 41 percent.[40] Unlike many of his African contemporaries, Diouf made a graceful exit from power, handing over government power to the opposition without additional contest. President Wade would go on to win relection in 2007 and increasingly dominate Senegalese politics throughout the remainder of the decade. Despite initial pledges not to run for a third term in 2012, the elderly President Wade controversially secured the support of the Constitutional Council to run for a final term. In the presidential runoff elections of 2012, however, Wade lost to his long-time protégé Macky Sall, who was installed as the new President of Senegal. As President Diouf had done in 2000, Wade conceded electoral defeat and stepped aside, confirming earlier patterns of respect for the democratic process.[41]

While President Wade's broad coalition had multiple challenges in maintaining unity and in implementing its policy preferences, the story of democratic transition in Senegal is notable in several respects.

First, a gradual political liberalization occurred, with fairly regular elections that created multiple opportunities to focus public attention on the government's performance. While alternation in power did not occur until 2000, institutions supporting contestation and legal political challenges evolved and expanded over a long period of time. By 2012, power had alternated to a new party, Alliance pour la République (APR), further institutionalizing the democratic process.

Second, episodes of mass mobilization, both electoral and otherwise, increased over the period of the transition. Political protests expanded with each subsequent denial of power to the opposition. Protests occasionally turned violent, and riots left significant physical and social damage. Protests were largely focused on political outcomes, but also addressed major social (e.g., Senegalese-Mauritanian relations, urban environment) and economic (e.g., prices, currency devaluation) issues. Prior to the 2012 elections, protests resumed (in 2010–2011) over plans for constitutional changes as well as over an ostentatious and costly building project spearheaded by President Wade, the African Renaissance Monument. Patterns of political protest have repeatedly demonstrated that Senegalese are not hesitant to mobilize politically on areas of controversy and concern.

Third, the main contestants in the political drama did remarkably little to overtly politicize Islam or dramatize support for an "Islamic" agenda. Islamic leaders and religious entrepreneurs played important, and occasionally political, roles in the Senegalese drama, but they have been far from the kind of open contestants witnessed in many other Islamic countries. Likewise, when religious and political entrepreneurs have attempted to mobilize the Senegalese population around an Islamist agenda, they have not succeeded in changing the principal lines of political cleavage nor in mobilizing significant numbers outside the dominant secular political framework.

This is not to say that the Islamic brotherhoods have not played an important role in determining political outcomes, nor that Senegal has been immune from political Islam. Rather, the manner in which Islamic interests have intersected with Senegalese politics over time provides some clues as to why Senegal has low Islamist political mobilization overall.

Political mobilization by the Sufi brotherhoods has occurred primarily in the form of mass voting for the incumbent political party. Brotherhood leaders, in particular the *khalife général* of the Mouridiyya, have historically issued instructions to their disciples to vote for the governing party in elections. This is done through an official pronouncement known as the *ndigel*. Issuing the *ndigel* prior to national elections was common from the years prior to independence up until the elections of 1988, after which *ndigels* from the highest Sufi authorities were discontinued. Not all of the disciples followed the political instructions of their *khalife*, as many distinguished between the sheikh's authority over religious versus political matters. Often disciples did take the *ndigel* seriously, however, which potentially gave the Sufi brotherhoods the power to directly influence the outcomes of elections. Adherence to the *ndigel* declined in the 1980s as the government became increasingly unpopular. The *ndigel* in favor of incumbent president Abdou Diouf prior to the controversial elections of 1988 was largely ignored among Mouride disciples, and the practice was subsequently discontinued by the new *khalife général*.

While the brotherhoods have often voted as an electoral bloc, it is important to note that they have not voted for Islamist candidates or for specific Islamist policies. Rather, they have voted for secular candidates in the hope that their electoral support will provide material resources for brotherhood ambitions, as well as a significant level of autonomy for brotherhood activities and internal governance. Brotherhood leaders have rarely played a direct role in influencing policy; rather, they have at times attempted to set boundaries that the government cannot cross.[42]

On a few occasions, members of Sufi brotherhoods have politically mobilized around specific policies or events. This type of political mobilization typically did not last long and had little impact on political outcomes. In 1958, just prior to Senegal's independence, a number of *marabouts* attempted to set up a unified opposition that could challenge the government when they formed the Conseil Supérieur de Chefs Religieux to defend the interests of Islam. The council pushed for a constitutional right to appoint half of the deputies to the National Assembly. When the government refused, some council members considered mobilizing their disciples in the streets. The Mouride participants backed out of the Council at these suggestions, and the group disintegrated a year after it was formed without accomplishing its objective.[43] Likewise, brotherhood mobilization in the early 1970s targeted the proposed Senegalese family code, which had European origins and did not reflect Islamic family law. While the brotherhoods maintained relatively united opposition to the proposed code, it was passed into law in 1972. Difficulties of administering the code in areas of brotherhood authority have lessened its impact, but Islamic opposition in this instance again had little impact.[44]

Some mobilization has occurred around inter-brotherhood rivalries, particularly in the 1970s between the Mouridiyya and Tijaniyya. While relations between the brotherhoods are usually not confrontational, they can become strained under provocation. In 1979, a group of Western-educated Mouride intellectuals argued for the special national status of the Mouridiyya and provoked demonstrations against the Tijaniyya as "collaborators." Inter-brotherhood riots followed that required the intervention of senior *marabouts* to bring the situation under control. During the annual pilgrimages of 1980, the chief *marabouts* chose to put additional emphasis on Islamic unity to prevent any recurrence of conflict.[45]

Occasionally, religious leaders have played a direct political role. This ranges from simple activities such as distributing party cards to seeking political office. A few *marabouts* have sought political office at the local or regional level, but the vast majority limit their political ambitions to negotiations with the government through senior brotherhood leadership. Several *marabouts* have associated themselves with opposition parties in a bid to limit their declining influence within the brotherhood itself, or to obtain favors during the campaign that they would not receive from the governing party.[46] Early examples of this include Cheikh Mbacké and Cheikh Anta Diop.

Several marabouts have also formed minor political movements with Islamic overtones. As a reaction to the lack of influence religious leaders had over the new constitution, two marabouts, Cheikh Tidiane Sy and Ibrahima Niasse, organized the Parti de la Solidarité Sénégalaise (PSS) in the late 1950s. The PSS had little coherent political program, however, and the party failed to secure any deputies in the National Assembly elections of 1959.[47]

Inspired by the Iranian revolution, a religious party named Hizboulahi (Party of God) emerged in 1979, led by Ahmad Niasse, who was living in Paris. Niasse was a junior member of the leading Tijani family, but had difficulty generating much interest from Tijanis. Likewise, Mourides had no interest in Niasse's leadership. After a number of bold but failed political moves, the party dissolved in 1981. It spawned a successor party, the Rassemblement pour le Salut National (RNS), which was "inspired in its actions by the principles of Islam," but again had no political success.[48]

By 1996, the first Mouride political party emerged in Senegal. It was founded by the former head of the Mouride student movement in Paris, Cheikh Abdoulaye Dièye, and named the Front pour le Socialisme at la Démocratie – Sewe Sa Dek (save your country) (FSD). Dièye became the deputy-mayor of the town of Saint-Louis after the municipal elections of 1996, and the newly created FSD came third in the municipal elections behind the dominant PS and the PDS.[49] The FSD was a partially successful attempt to channel Mouride identity into the political process, but Dièye's bid for President of Senegal in 2000 yielded only 1 percent of the vote. He subsequently won only 0.5 percent in the 2007 presidential election, and his party won only 1 of 150 seats in the 2007 legislative elections.[50] This very modest success demonstrated that the vast majority of Mourides supported other, more secular candidates rather than voting along lines of religious identity.

During the late 1970s, and early 1980s, many observers noted a renaissance of interest in Islam throughout Senegal.[51] This included an increasing number of personal conversions as well as new interest in Islamic education and religious media. This religious revival affected the brotherhoods, which were gaining new adherents – particularly the Mourides. It also sparked interest in a number of new Islamic student and reform associations. Islamic reform organizations increased in prominence in Senegal throughout the period of interest, but were largely apolitical in their activities.[52]

One of the earliest reform organizations was the Union Culturelle Musulmane (UCM) founded in 1953 by Cheikh Touré. The UCM was initially outspoken in its criticism both of the French and of the Sufi *marabouts* for deviating from what they perceived was the true path of Islam. By the late 1950s, it moderated some of its criticism of the *marabouts*, recognizing that if it was to have influence beyond a narrow urban setting the organization must selectively work with the brotherhoods toward common purposes. The UCM developed a number of *maraboutic* allies and also worked cooperatively with the state after independence. In 1962, a federation of reformist organizations was formed under the leadership of Abdul Aziz Sy, the Fédération Nationale des Associations Culturelles Musulmanes du Sénégal. The Federation pushed actively to increase interest in Arabic and Qur'anic education, but had a difficult time maintaining unity in a context of divided interests among many of the groups.[53] By the 1980s, this group evolved into the Fédération des Associations Islamiques au Sénégal (FAIS), directed by Moustapha Cissé.[54] Reformist intellectuals began to cluster around another organization, the Centre d'Etudes et de Recherches "Islam et Développement" (CERID).[55]

Most of the reformist Islamic activity in Senegal has been based at the university. In the mid-1980s, the Jamatou Ibadou Rahmane grew in prominence and managed to get a mosque constructed on the Dakar campus. In the 1990s, female members of Muslim groups began to wear headscarves for religious reasons, a trend that included about 5 percent female students by the end of the decade. Influenced by reformist groups, brotherhoods also formed associations at the university. An association of Mouride students, the Da'ira des Etudiants et d'Elèves Mourides du Sénégal, was active from 1977 onward. A Tijani association also opened at Dakar University in 1980. Relations between reformists and brotherhood associations have sometimes been strained, but the groups have also cooperated with and imitated each other. Some female Sufi students, for example, began to wear headscarves as a sign of religious commitment.[56]

Two important groups represent a combination of brotherhood ties and reformist impulses, coming out of different brotherhood associations (*tariqas*). Hizbut Tarqiyya emerged from the Mouridiyya, beginning life as an association for Mouride students at the University of Dakar. The association started with the traditional urban *da'ira* model, but attempted to modernize the role of the organization. By the mid-1990s, Hizbut Tarqiyya began to challenge the Mouride idea of hereditary leadership. This led to serious controversy within the brotherhood, and subsequently a decline in the organization's membership. Several Mouride student groups have kept some of Hizbut Tarqiyya's ideology and continue to push for modest reform within the brotherhood.[57]

More important for the purposes of this study is the experience of an organization with Tijani ties, the Moustarchidina wal Moustarchidaty (Movement of Those Who Seek the Straight Path), also known as the Moustarchidine movement. The movement was founded in 1976 and led by Moustapha Sy, a young descendant of the founder of the Tivouane branch of the Tijaniyya. It focused initially on religious instruction and on social activities, placing some reformist emphasis on a brotherhood-based organization.[58] The state supported the development of the Moustarchidine, granting Sy resources and state privileges that enabled him, among other things, to organize the International Conference on Muslim Youth in Dakar in 1989, with 2,000 delegates from twenty countries.[59] By the early 1990s, however, Sy's moderate Islamic position had alienated a number of more radical members, and he was faced with criticism from conservative members of his family as well.

By the presidential election of 1993, Sy made a calculated political move to openly challenge the state in Islamist terms. This was enabled by a falling out between President Diouf and Moustapha's prominent *marabout* father, Cheikh Tidiane Sy, and may also have been based in a belief that Diouf would lose the election. Sy's open challenge to the President's legitimacy was criticized severely by senior leaders of the Tijaniyya and was publicly disavowed by Moustapha's uncle. Although imprisoned shortly after the election, Moustapha's brother rallied the Moustarchidine to action against the state in the wake of controversial election results. This helped drive urban riots that killed several policemen and did significant damage. The Moustarchidine was subsequently declared an illegal organization, and was forced to abandon many of its more radical positions. By 1996, after the intervention of Moustapha's father Cheikh Tidiane, the organization found accommodation with the state and redefined its objectives, focusing on apolitical activities.[60]

What is significant about the rise and reframing of the Moustarchidine movement in the 1990s is both that it showed an increasing willingness to challenge the state in Islamist terms and also that this challenge could not be supported under the current structure of Senegalese religious leadership. By the 2000 elections, in which the incumbent was finally toppled by Abdoulaye Wade, it was clear that the traditional alignment of brotherhood votes toward the governing party had broken down. What the new voting patterns would be remained unknown, but there was moderate concern among secular intellectuals that Islam was increasingly entering the open political sphere. In fact, two minor candidates for the presidency used religious themes in their campaigns (including Dièye, see earlier), but they both received only about 1 percent of the vote. Although the senior brotherhood leaders did not direct support toward any candidate, lesser *marabouts* did continue to instruct their disciples to vote for their chosen parties. The political alliance between political parties and religious leaders became more fragmented, but alliances remained at multiple levels.[61]

After Wade's election, there were some signs that Islamist mobilization would continue and potentially build over time. Wade, himself a Mouride, demonstrated his religious loyalties by going to Touba to be blessed by the *khalife général* on the day of his inauguration. During legislative elections a year later, he led a delegation of his government to Touba again for a blessing. An aborted move by his government to remove the term *état laïque* (secular state) from the constitution was greeted with an uproar. A new law to mandate (pluralistic) religious instruction in schools was passed, however, as a concession to religious groups. [62]

American policies in the Middle East increasingly became a subject of street protests by Islamist organizations. These were led by the Jamatu Ibadou Rahmane, with participation by the Moustarchidine and Hizbut Tarqiyya. A new Islamist organization to push for reforms to the 1972 Family Code was also founded in 2003. The Comité Islamique pour la Reforme du Code de la Famille au Sénégal (CIRCOFS) hoped to bring the code in line with Islamic law but met much resistance.[63]

To summarize, Islamist mobilization in Senegal has been historically low but has occurred intermittently throughout the period under investigation. Brotherhood participation in political activity broadly construed has been significant, but little "Islamist" activity in the sense of political mobilization on behalf of Islamically oriented policies or individuals at the state level has occurred. In the cases where it has been attempted, it has not met much popular success. However, as the broad alliance between the state and the brotherhoods began to fragment from the late 1980s on, more openly Islamist mobilization started to take place. At the same time, the distance between the brotherhoods and Islamic reformers narrowed, as movements from both sides adopted ideologies and tactics from each other. Islam has become increasingly politicized, but remains far from becoming a dominant political cleavage in Senegalese politics, and remains much less politicized than in the other cases discussed in this study.

## PLURAL HIERARCHIES: THE ROLE OF ISLAMIC INSTITUTIONS IN MOBILIZATION OUTCOMES

The institutional theory presented in Chapter 2 highlights the role of Islamic institutions in providing the symbolic repertoire and channels of communication that must be present for Islamist mobilization to succeed. As previously noted, both the extent of Islamic learning and participation in Islamic institutions is relatively high in Senegal. While fewer Senegalese receive Qur'anic instruction or frequent the mosque than Muslims in most countries of the Arab world, the majority does have ties to Islamic institutions and actively participates in Islamic rituals. Despite the success of some secular civil society organizations in urban Senegal, religious brotherhoods provide the most important basis for civil society interactions countrywide.

The development of Islamic common knowledge in Senegal occurs primarily through four channels: Islamic education (e.g., Qur'anic and Arabic schools), participation in Muslim organizations (e.g., work groups (*daara*), community brotherhood associations (*da'iras*), and reformist associations), participation in mass Islamic rituals (e.g., *magal, gammu, tabaski*), and mosque attendance.

Historically, education in Senegal was led by Sufi *marabouts* through a large network of Qur'anic schools. French administrators observed that despite there being a large number of these schools, they provided little real education in matters of importance to the French, and little serious Arabic training either.[64] During the colonial period, French schools were established and heavily promoted, while a few national *madrasas* were built in an unsuccessful attempt to achieve state control over Qur'anic education in Senegal. Despite some native interest in the French schools, they were not heavily funded and grew slowly. The brotherhoods' Qur'anic schools, on the other hand, continued to be the primary form of education despite French attempts to restrict their activities.[65]

In independent Senegal, schooling was divided between students in Francophone schools and those pursuing religious education. Although the majority of children in the early years of independence did not attend school at all, the proportion of students attending school increased over the next decades. French schools were seen as the path to economic success and were always popular, but attendance at French schools was low in the areas dominated by brotherhoods. The Tijaniyya sent their children to French schools more often than Mourides, even though some Mourides received a French education as well. In the early years of independence, more than 40 percent of all young boys in Senegal attended Qur'anic school as their primary form of education.[66]

Over time, as public schooling spread more extensively throughout the country, the French model had considerable influence over more and more students. At the same time, however, the Muslim religious curriculum began to penetrate the public school system, which included compulsory Islamic religious instruction and optional Arabic language instruction.[67] Arabic and Qur'anic schools led by reformist Muslim groups also grew in the late twentieth century as an alternative to the traditional Qur'anic instruction provided by *marabouts*.[68] In 1979, for example, the Institut Islamique de Dakar opened next to the grand mosque. It immediately enrolled more than a thousand students in evening Arabic courses.[69]

Senegal's experience with Islamic education, therefore, has been relatively extensive; however, it has also been highly fragmented. It has historically been dominated by Qur'anic schools led by a wide range of individual marabouts, often teaching very different versions of Islam (or at least focusing on different religious priorities). The young graduate of a local Mouride Qur'anic school may have a very different education from a graduate of a Tijani school or even another local Mouride school. These individuals are likely to have different experiences than their counterparts at reformist-led schools, and very different experiences from the large group attending Francophone schools. This fragmentation has not been particularly conducive to the spread of Islamic common knowledge across Senegal, although the extent of common knowledge within a smaller educational community may be significant. As the educational system gradually becomes more rationalized, the set of knowledge common to the majority of Senegalese is likely to expand, although the extent to which shared conceptions of Islam will form a part of that national common knowledge is open to question.

Participation in religious associations is another important avenue through which Senegalese Muslims develop Islamic knowledge and religious preferences. Even more than in the case of religious education, however, these associations are fragmented across a range of often hierarchical and inward-looking communities. They are potentially powerful channels for communication within those communities, as most of them are based on shared assumptions about appropriate behavior and form a network of mutual trust. For example, Mouride *da'iras* in urban settings provide an immediate network of trusted contacts for the urban migrant. These contacts may enable him or her to obtain rapid employment in the merchant sector, or may serve as an initial welfare network while the individual is seeking employment. *Da'iras* are also a network of communities that can transmit information, religious or political, at rapid speed due to the close contact maintained both among members and between *da'ira* leaders and their religious authorities.[70]

While these associations are potentially agents of rapid mobilization, they are also multiple and diverse. This makes a widespread Islamic mobilization around shared symbols and expectations difficult. Expectations across brotherhood or reformist lines differ and communication channels between organizations of different brotherhoods are usually weak or non-existent.[71] Lines of communication between groups have been increasing in number in recent years, especially when the associations are in close proximity, as at the university. In combination with the gradual erosion of hierarchical leadership in the *da'iras*, this may lead to increased potential for mobilization across Islamic institutions. Muslim protests at the U.S. invasion of Afghanistan in 2002, for example, showed cooperation among several Islamist organizations that subsequently served as a model for what is possible.

Both the opportunities and the challenges of plural Islamic hierarchies are amplified in the organizational spectacle of the great Muslim pilgrimages of Senegal. As described previously, the *grand magal* of the Mouridiyya and the *gammu* of the Tijaniyya together draw more than a million participants in ritual and celebration. The Mouride *magal* is the most impressive; it is a celebration of the life of the Mouride founder Amadu Bamba, but is also an annual reaffirmation of commitment to the brotherhood and opportunity for mass communication to disciples. The *magal* includes a public sermon by the *khalife général* to advise disciples on spiritual topics that may also include political communication regarding the relationship of the brotherhood to the state. The *magal* sermon is distributed throughout the country, and disciples will often read underlying meanings into the sermon regarding the acceptability of the current government.[72] The great pilgrimage sermons are akin to the more frequent Friday sermons at mosques writ large, and have sometimes served as "state of the union" addresses, with the "union" referring to the alliance between the brotherhood and the state.

While the remarkable participation in the key pilgrimages demonstrates the ability of the brotherhoods to mobilize on a grand scale, these pilgrimages are based in distinct religious communities and do not attract large numbers of Muslims outside of that community. They have unique characteristics, symbolism, and meanings that do not resonate well in a broader Muslim audience. So while the political potential of these gatherings is large, that potential does not extend across individual brotherhoods into the national Muslim population.

Greater interaction between members of different *tariqas* does take place in the mosque setting, particularly in urban areas such as Dakar where large mosques attract a diverse crowd of the faithful. In these settings, Friday sermons play a role in creating common religious knowledge. In many small neighborhood mosques, the participants tend to be more affiliated with one *tariqa* or with a particular sheikh. The author's field observations suggest that mosque attendance is less regular in the (urban) Senegalese context than in many other Muslim countries.[73] Islamic communication through the mosque is one option among many, which include communication through educational, associational, and mass ritual channels.

Regardless of the channel, religious symbolism and Islamic common knowledge provide potentially important resources for political mobilization. In the Senegalese case, religious symbolism has been used by Sufi brotherhoods in bargaining with the state over resource allocation or in settling disputes. Religious references have often been used as metaphors for the brotherhoods' relationship with the state.[74] However, the structure of Islamic institutions in Senegal, divided between a few large Sufi brotherhoods as well as between Sufis and non-Sufi reformers, has made the development of widespread Islamic common knowledge difficult. Because most of the Islamic communities are hierarchical and define Islamic knowledge within their own frame of reference, what may be common knowledge within one Muslim group may not be common knowledge for the rest. A typical Mouride's religious references may have limited overlap with the Tijane or the urban reformer. Significant resources for political communication exist within each group (particularly the Mourides), but these are limited across groups.

Note that, as highlighted in Chapter 3, fragmentation of the Islamist movement is correlated with high levels of Islamist mobilization across the total group of cases in this study. I theorize that this is because it creates an environment for greater religious entrepreneurship, including the possibility of defection from one organization to another if in-group policing is attempted. Despite the fragmentation of Islamic organizations in the Senegalese case, this does not have the theorized effect on Islamist entrepreneurship for two reasons. First, the fragmentation is among a few large organizations that have relatively strong hierarchies. Second, the brotherhoods have family or ethnic characteristics, making it difficult to leave one to join another in the event of in-group policing. The Senegalese Islamic organizations are relatively few, rigid, and ethnically based, limiting the potential positive effects of fragmentation on Islamist entrepreneurship.

It is important to recognize that an argument about fragmented common knowledge does not address the issue of the *type* of Islamic common knowledge in Senegal. A common argument used to explain the lack of Islamic mobilization in sub-Saharan Africa is that Sufi Islam is too syncretistic or too "un-Islamic" to mobilize as a political force.[75] While elements of Sufi Islam in Senegal do diverge from conservative Arab notions of Islam, the argument that Sufi Islam is pacifistic or naturally apolitical is rejected here. As a historical overview of sub-Saharan Islam demonstrates, Sufi leaders have often been highly mobilized against ethnic chiefs, colonial authorities, and the modern state. Many brotherhoods, including the Tijanis, have led religious-political jihads to capture territory and establish kingdoms. Some Sufi leaders have attempted to enter politics directly, and have been very successful in countries such as the Sudan.[76]

One important element of Sufi mythology, however, concerns the mystical and often magical nature of brotherhood leaders. Much of a sheikh's authority comes from his ability to dispense blessings in the form of mystical *baraka* to his disciples and from his apparent regular communion with the divine. In practice, many sheikhs choose to remain away from public view except on special occasions, an absence that appears to enhance their reputation for otherworldliness. To maintain this peculiar form of Sufi authority, many sheikhs may have incentives to remain outside of the public sphere, and thus outside of the political arena. However, both Sufis and other religious elites have traditionally also had a broad array of non-religious incentives to refrain from openly challenging the Senegalese state.

## THE SUFI'S "SECRET LOVE": INCENTIVES AND DISINCENTIVES FOR ISLAMIST MOBILIZATION

Cruise O'Brien (2003) has noted that "perhaps the secular state is the Sufi's secret love."[77] Senegal's Sufi brotherhoods emerged in contexts of conflict with the colonial administration and have been at odds with the government of independent Senegal on multiple occasions. Nevertheless, they have also closely aligned themselves with the state for much of the country's modern history. Why have the brotherhoods and other Islamic groups allied themselves with existing state actors and institutions rather than participate in state-building themselves? Why, for the most part, have they refrained from trying to mobilize a devoted population for Islamist political causes? It is not because they have low numbers of devoted followers.

One answer is that the structural incentives of religious elites in Senegal have encouraged rather than discouraged their cooperation with the state; in other words, the distance between the incentives of religious leaders and the incentives of the state has customarily been small. Initially, this may seem an odd claim. After all, the modern Senegalese state is a Western product, historically socialist, secular, and run by French-educated urban politicians and bureaucrats. This is very different from the characteristics and preferences of a historically conservative, rural, and anti-Western religious elite. Nevertheless, structural conditions have supported a long series of cooperative interactions between two very different and powerful groups.

Additionally, the internal organizational structure of religious organizations has given religious elites the capacity to largely control patterns of interaction with the state in the face of internal dissent. In cases where individual religious entrepreneurs have attempted to mobilize in an Islamist framework, religious elites have effectively used organizational resources to provide in-group policing of Islamist activities.

As noted, some Sufi leaders may have incentives to stay away from the public sphere because of the need to maintain mystical legitimacy, which requires a measure of seclusion. The process of competitive politics inherently involves significant criticism of candidates and exposes the candidate's position and potentially his character to public challenge. Senegal's long history of competitive (if flawed) elections, as well as a history of significant freedom of the press, create a credible expectation that politicians will face public personal challenges. This "bad publicity" constraint does not apply to many mid-level Sufi sheikhs or Islamic reformers, however, as they have little personality cult to support through seclusion. Instead, they may expect that entering the political arena could amplify their reputation and thus may have the incentive to mobilize politically. There have been many other incentives for religious elites to refrain from challenging the state, however.

During the course of colonial occupation, the French came to understand that successful administration of the countryside depended on the collaboration of the *marabouts* with the colonial authority. The French, who had limited governing resources, needed the Sufi leaders to maintain order in the countryside and to help develop agricultural crops for export.[78] By the mid-twentieth century, when voting rights were extended to the Senegalese of the interior, native politicians such as Senghor also recognized that the support of Muslim leaders was critical for electoral success. The government's need for support from the *marabouts* has continued throughout modern history. This has been demonstrated by the repeated visits from state authorities, including the president, to Muslim leaders requesting their support for government initiatives.

At the same time, the brotherhoods have recognized the benefits of, if not the need for, state support for their own objectives. This led to a relatively stable pattern of the state providing the *marabouts* with patronage resources in return for the brotherhoods' political support of state goals. In times of tension between the brotherhoods and the state, the patronage cycle has lapsed into mutual threats of withdrawing support. Nevertheless, a sense of mutual dependence between the brotherhoods and the state prevented the relationship from deteriorating into conflict.

The brotherhoods developed an interest in maintaining a constructive relationship with the state because of multiple channels of patronage support that exceeded patronage offered to other groups, such as tribal chiefs. An alliance with the state gave them important economic benefits for their agricultural activities. The Mourides, in particular, received special economic status as *gros producteurs* (large-scale producers) that allowed them to bypass government cooperatives and sell to Dakar at a higher price.[79] They have also received either tax-exempt status (or very low tax rates, depending on the period), lenient treatment under the law, and extraordinary autonomy in governing brotherhood affairs, which includes *de facto* control over some territory.

Additionally, the state has provided resources for mosque construction and access to official channels for Islamic purposes (e.g., Islamic radio programming, Arabic instruction in public schools).

A striking example of both state patronage and brotherhood autonomy is the rapid development of the Mouride city of Touba. Over the course of the past century, Touba has grown from a small village to become the second largest city in Senegal, and it continues to grow. In the decade from 1990 to 2000, its population more than doubled to over a half million inhabitants and since then it has further expanded. This level of growth is heavily dependent on state support in providing scarce resources for infrastructure. The state has provided many unique benefits to Touba that facilitiate its growth, such as maintaining its administrative designation as a *communauté rural* (despite its now clearly urban character), providing superior tax benefits for the area, and giving it a measure of extraterritoriality when it comes to state governance. Touba has maintained many of its own laws in opposition to the Senegalese legal code, such as prohibitions on alcohol, tobacco, gambling, cinema, and even football.[80]

The *grand magal* at Touba is also an occasion for political theater in which the state and the Mouride brotherhood provide affirmation of their political alliance, attempting to make their commitments to one another more credible by proclaiming them in front of a mass audience. During the Official Day ceremonies of the *magal*, the head of state and the *khalife général* offer public speeches, articulating their support for one another. This display can also be an important occasion for issuing implicit threats to the other party as well, if the state–brotherhood alliance is under duress.

The Sufi elite have a range of incentives to cooperate with the state that serve to expand their economic resources, maintain their autonomy, and establish their authority over their disciples. While urban reformist leaders interact with the state in a very different context, they too have come to align themselves with the state both for economic reasons and to improve their inferior position vis-à-vis the brotherhoods. The state has worked pragmatically with the Islamic reformists, authorizing schools for Arabic language instruction, supporting scholarships for Senegalese students to study in Arab countries, and appointing many reformist leaders to bureaucratic posts.[81] Several high-profile reformists have been appointed as ambassadors to countries such as Saudi Arabia or as government ministers. Cheikh Touré, for example, was given charge of Arabic-language programs for Radio Sénégal. As Islamic reformers have been co-opted into the state, they have become even more aligned with state interests than the Sufi elite, because they do not maintain an independent resource base.[82]

Religious entrepreneurs in Senegal may or may not be members of the religious elite, and many of the reformist school do not come from elite Islamic backgrounds. The relationship between the religious elite (largely the Sufi *marabouts*) and the broader class of religious entrepreneurs is often one of tension, particularly if the *marabouts* can make any claim to authority over the entrepreneur by virtue of his family participation in a particular Sufi brotherhood. Many of the Senegalese religious entrepreneurs in fact have some extended ties to Sufi brotherhoods, or at least have an extended relationship in some form to power brokers within those brotherhoods, which allows the religious elite to exercise authority over religious entrepreneurs. Allowing religious entrepreneurs freedom to mix religion with politics is threatening for the religious elite both because it challenges their authority over Islamic symbolism and meaning and because it may have a real effect on the sometimes tenuous tactical alliance between the elite and the state.

In addition to the incentives for cooperating with the state discussed here, there may be a structural disincentive for religious elites to challenge the state. Because Senegal has multiple Islamic hierarchies, if one of them defects from the standard arrangement of cooperation by challenging the state in Islamic terms, this puts the other religious elites in an awkward position. If they join in the challenge, they risk subordination to an alternative religious hierarchy. If they continue cooperation with the state, however, they may benefit from additional patronage resources that are diverted in their direction. As the costs for late challengers under a system of distinctive hierarchies would be high, continued cooperation is a reasonable choice for the other religious elites. Continued cooperation by other groups after an initial challenge by one Islamic group would likely create very poor relations between groups, thus increasing the costs of challenge by the initial challenger. Therefore, an Islamist challenge to the state by one of the major Muslim groups (e.g., the Mouridiyya) could be very costly both because of the loss of patronage resources and because of alienation from other Muslim groups (e.g., the Tijaniyya, Qadiriyya, reformists) that are adversely impacted by the group's decision.

There have been several occasions since 1970 in which the incentives of the *marabouts* do appear to diverge from the incentives of the government. In these cases the marabouts have threatened to withdraw support from the governing party, and some lesser *marabouts* have even offered support to opposition parties. A widespread drought in the early 1970s, for example, put significant strain on the Mouride population that had focused on producing cash crops for the state to sell on the world market. The *khalife général* Abdou Lahatte Mbacké advised his followers to return to subsistence agriculture and refused to help the government collect peasant debts, moves that threatened the government's economic position. These challenges helped pressure the government to effectively double the official producer price for peanuts in return for maintenance of the cash crop economy.[83]

In the elections of 1983, some Mouride disciples began to ignore the *khalife général*'s *ndigel* asking the *talibés* to vote for the incumbent PS. Although the government's legitimacy began to further wane in the late 1980s, the *khalife général* issued a very direct *ndigel* prior to the 1988 elections by saying that "any Mouride who does not vote for [the incumbent] Abdou Diouf will be betraying Serigne Touba (the founder Amadu Bamba)."[84] This was followed by anonymous notes of protest thrown over the sheikh's compound by disciples, and was widely seen as weakening the *khalife général*'s legitimacy.

By the 1993 election, brotherhood leadership decided that issuing an *ndigel* in favor of the ruling PS risked the alienation of more Mouride disciples, and abstained from asking the *talibés* to cast their vote for the government. They did not issue a general *ndigel* in subsequent elections either, although some lesser *marabouts* encouraged their followers to vote for one party or the other. Faced with internal dissention, Mouride leaders removed a pillar of their support for the government, but they also refrained from presenting an open challenge due to continued reliance on the state. As the liberal opposition grew during the 1990s it became more apparent that the government and the state, which were once fused, could now be treated as separate entities. In withdrawing direct support for the president and PS government, the *marabouts* thus retained the option of an alliance with the state, even in the event of an opposition victory.

Although the incentives of the state and of a Muslim organization may be aligned, the incentives of individual members of the organization may not be. Under these circumstances, Muslim elites may attempt to mobilize against the state on their own. In Senegal, this has occurred on several occasions in which *marabouts* are marginalized by their own brotherhoods, and then challenge the state either by joining an opposition party or through their own organization. This is sometimes done to increase the *marabout*'s leverage within the brotherhood, or to build an alternative basis of support outside of the brotherhood.

As hierarchical hereditary organizations, however, brotherhoods have also developed effective methods of in-group policing of those who might destabilize the brotherhood's relationship with the state. In the principal cases of *marabouts* challenging the state in Islamist terms, the forces of the brotherhood have combined either to reorient the *marabout* away from state opposition or to significantly diminish the effectiveness of the attempted mobilization. Despite the presence of several competing Senegalese brotherhoods, the limited fragmentation of the religious elite, combined with their hierarchical and hereditary character, has made these policing efforts largely successful.

In the year before independence, for example, the Mouride *khalife général* stood firmly in support of Senghor, refusing to see any opposition delegations. When the sheikh's eldest son, Modou Bousso Dieng Mbacké, sided with an opposition party in 1959, his father publicly disowned him, cutting off the son's opportunity for future leadership and serving as a warning to all members of the brotherhood.[85]

In the 1993 case of Moustapha Sy discussed previously, the young Tijani *marabout*'s open Islamist challenge to President Diouf was met with rapid condemnation from inside his own brotherhood. The Moustarchidine leader's speech inaugurating an Islamic political challenge was very publicly disavowed by his prominent uncle, and Moustapha's father intervened to reorient the objectives of the movement. Within a short period, the movement had found accommodation with the government of President Diouf. The most influential Tijani sheikhs thus chose to intervene in any attempt to use Islam for political purposes, which might destabilize the relationship between the state and the brotherhood as a whole.[86] Other attempts by brotherhood members to challenge the status quo have been internally quieted, as were the Mouride student leader Atou Diagne's reformist ambitions in 1997, when his association (Hizbut Tarqiyya) was banned by the *khalife général*.[87]

Although the Senegalese state has historically needed the support of Islamic elites, Islamic elites have also repeatedly demonstrated that they need the state. Cruise O'Brien (2003) notes that although Muslim elites in Senegal are very differentiated from each other, they "can come together on at least one very important point. They all need the state: they know that historically, and they keep on finding new ways of projecting that relationship into the future."[88] Through a combination of incentives, including patronage, guarantees of autonomy, and the fear of intra-Muslim conflict, Muslim elites in Senegal have found that their interests are often aligned with the state interests. When that broad alignment is called into question, as it increasingly has been over the last decade, potential Islamist challengers may emerge. To this point, however, reasonably strong internal organization has prevented junior *marabouts* from effective Islamist mobilization that would threaten the privileged relationship between religious elites and the state.

## LOOKING FOR FOCAL POINTS: EXTERNAL CRISES AND LENGTHY DEMOCRATIZATION

Some brief comments are in order regarding the effects of the third major component of the institutional theory described in Chapter 2, state focal points for mobilization. Two types of focal points, specific crises of state legitimacy and rapid political liberalization, were posited as effective focal points around which Islamist leaders could effectively mobilize the population. Although Muslim elites in Senegal have not had strong incentives to mobilize against the state in Islamic terms, it is useful to highlight whether state focal points have been present around which Islamist mobilization could occur if both elite incentives and Islamic common knowledge were present.

Like most developing countries, Senegal has had a number of "crisis" periods during its modern history in which the population was under heightened economic or political stress. In the early 1970s, primarily between 1971 and 1973, the economy performed poorly due to an extended drought. A state economic transformation program during this period appeared out of touch with the day-to-day plight of many Senegalese, increasing anger over the state of the country's economy and leading to a number of strikes and street protests.[89] A number of droughts again appeared in the late 1970s and early

1980s (1977, 1978, 1980, 1981, and 1984), causing temporary recessions due to poor agricultural output. Likewise, from 1975 raw material export prices fell significantly, harming this sector of the economy.

Overall, however, these multiple recessions were short, and somewhat regular. Economic growth in Senegal in the 1970s was low, averaging about 1 percent growth *per annum*. Growth during the 1980s was a bit higher, after a number of liberal economic reforms beginning in 1980. Nevertheless, economic growth was not particularly strong, averaging about 2.5 percent annually from independence until 1990. Looking over multi-year increments, the economy appears relatively steady with low growth rates.[90] Likewise, inflation has not historically been a major challenge, partly due to the stability of membership in the CFA monetary union. A major exception to this was in 1994 with the devaluation of the CFA franc, which put unusual strain on salaried households.[91]

On the whole, Senegal has also enjoyed considerable political stability, with only three different heads of state between independence in 1960 and the year 2012. Additionally, all three presidents left office (Senghor, Diouf, ultimately Wade) willingly, without contesting their successor's position. The National Assembly throughout the twentieth century was dominated by one party (PS), with an opposition coalition led by Wade's PDS providing some measure of political dialogue. Political crisis therefore did not come through governmental instability; rather, it came through a number of short-lived political crises centered around assumptions of electoral fraud in regular elections, and later concern over President Wade's attempt to secure constitutional provisions that would extend his Presidential term.[92]

After the elections of 1983, members of the opposition cried fraud and refused to take their seats in the National Assembly, but many were incorporated into the government shortly thereafter. In 1988, however, high expectations before an electoral loss led the opposition to take to the street. This led to riots and an urban revolt, which led to an extended political crisis affecting the school system and including considerable ethnic violence. After Senegalese were killed in Mauritania in 1989, an uproar in Senegal led to the killing of a large number of ethnic Mauritanians. The comparatively narrow, but unexpected, opposition defeat in 1993 subsequently led to significant disenchantment with the democratic system. This, combined with the assassination of the vice president of the Constitutional Council and the currency devaluation, provided the context in which new political protests took place, including protests by the Islamist Moustarchidine movement. The principal liberal opposition was ultimately persuaded to re-enter the government, however, which it did in 1995.[93]

With the exception of the repeated political crises centered on the opposition's inability to unseat the incumbent government, many of the crises affecting the Senegalese population from 1970 have had external origins. These include multiple droughts, the devaluation of the CFA franc, a drop in export prices, and ethnic violence in Mauritania. A local rebellion in the southern region of Casamance, while very much tied to the state from the perspective of that region, was viewed as more of an "external" crisis for much of Senegal. These crises had little reason to be uniquely resonant with an Islamic audience, but rather served as focal points for mobilization by other types of political actors: by Marxists, unionists, peasants, and ethnic communities.

The theory of this volume suggests, however, that internal state instability and crises of representation may serve as effective focal points for Islamist mobilization. The Senegalese state did face this type of political crisis in 1988 and again in 1993. During these periods Islamist actors failed to mobilize to the extent that other opposition actors did, possibly for the reasons mentioned previously. However, it is interesting to note that new attempts to bring Islamist discourse into politics (e.g., the Moustarchidine challenge) occurred against the backdrop of this broader political alienation and low political support for the government.

While the theory suggests that rapid political liberalization provides another focal point for Islamist mobilization, Senegal's trajectory of political liberalization has been extended and gradual. This long period of liberalization, from the mid 1970s to 2000, was characterized by gradually increasing opportunities for the opposition that culminated in fully free and fair elections. The Freedom House survey of political rights saw Senegal move from "not free" in the 1970s to "partly free" in the 1980s and 1990s, and then to "free" at the turn of the century.[94] In other studies, Senegal has been considered a weakly institutionalized democracy, or even an "anocracy."[95] The level of institutionalization, however, is less relevant than the pace at which political liberalization has occurred. This lengthy period allowed Senegal's multiple opposition parties significant time to build their bases, refine their strategies, and communicate politically.

Although Islamic institutions may have an initial advantage over new political parties in organization and communication channels, over such a long period political parties can build effective mobilizing organizations that rival Islamic ones. This creates additional competition for Islamists in the political arena, as well as denying them an effective focal point for mobilization. Under a period of lengthy democratization, "normal" politics also begins to develop, making the electoral focal points that do occur less attractive to radical groups.

To summarize, in addition to fragmented common knowledge and few political incentives, Islamists in Senegal have had a further challenge in effective mobilization due to a lack of attractive focal points around which religious entrepreneurs can attract political attention. Many of the political and economic crises in Senegal over the past few decades have been external in origin and have little resonance in Islamic frameworks. A state crisis of legitimate governance in the 1980s and early 1990s did create an opportunity for focus on the state's deficiencies, of which a few religious entrepreneurs attempted to take advantage. They did so, however, against a backdrop of multiple, well-organized political competitors that emerged over the course of democratizing reforms. A lengthy period of political liberalization both strengthened political competitors and normalized the focal points of the electoral cycle.

## SENEGALESE EXCEPTIONALISM? A GLANCE AT MALI

Senegal has sometimes been considered exceptional in modern African history for a number of reasons, including its long history of political liberalism, its stable political transitions, its comparatively steady economy, its urban civil society, and its strong Islamic institutions. Do exceptional circumstances in Senegal make it unrepresentative of other countries with low levels of Islamist mobilization?

In one sense Senegal is not representative of other low-mobilizing countries because it has stronger Islamic institutions than many other countries in the study, particularly countries in sub-Saharan Africa. These institutions are what make it a "tough case," rather than simply one in which there is little Islamist mobilization because there is little Islam to mobilize. In many important respects, however, the structural conditions that dampen mobilization outcomes in Senegal are present in other cases of low mobilization. A quick glance at the case of neighboring Mali and the situation of sub-Saharan Africa more broadly shows some resemblance to the situation in Senegal.

What is now the country of Mali straddles the area of the major trade routes between North and West Africa by which Islam was brought south of the Sahara. Because of this location, Islam came to Mali at an early date, and the majority of the population converted to Islam. About 90 percent of the current population identifies as Muslim. Mali also developed a Sufi tradition with multiple brotherhoods, prominent among them the Tijaniyya, familiar in Senegal. The Sufi brotherhoods in Mali developed considerable power in their regions or localities. In contrast to the *marabouts* of Senegal, however, they did not develop a position of national prominence in their relationship with the state. Their presence did create a structural condition similar to that in Senegal, in which the terms of Islamic discourse across brotherhoods and the channels for Islamic communication were quite fragmented. Malian Islamic institutional channels are perhaps even more fragmented than those in Senegal because of the strong presence of an urban "Wahhabi" reformist movement. Malian Islam has been marked by a significant amount of tension between the Wahhabis and the Sufi brotherhoods.[96]

The reformists first came to Mali's capital, Bamako, in the 1920s and 1930s and shared their experiences from both the pilgrimage to Mecca and their education in Arab countries (e.g., at Al-Azhar in Cairo). After World War II, they began to attract a considerable following. After a period of alliance with anti-colonial activists, they began to support the emerging independent state.[97] In the late 1950s, Islamic divisions became publicly prominent. As the wahhabis attempted to establish their own mosques, violent clashes ensued between the reformers and the more established Sufi brotherhoods. Although the colonial authorities had exploited divisions among Islamic groups, the new Malian state began to court Islamic leaders, particularly the urban reformists. Strong clientelistic relationships formed between Muslim activists and the state as the state funneled resources into mosque construction and educational institutions.

Beginning in the 1970s, there was significant growth in both the number of mosques and the number of Islamic educational institutions in Mali.[98] This was aided, in part, by grants from oil-producing Arab countries. Islamic education spread both in the form of Qur'anic schools for religious elites and in the form of more traditional *madrasas*. This growth in Islamic education coincided with a general Islamic revival that took place in the 1970s and 1980s.

The revival included the activists of the 1950s, but also involved new classes of participants, primarily urban businessmen and civil servants.[99] These groups were heavily dependent on their relationship with the state, and therefore their Islamism was tempered by an alignment of personal and state incentives. During this period, the state also attempted to centralize the administration of Islam in Mali and worked to bring the Islamic schools under the umbrella of the Ministry of National Education.[100] The government under authoritarian president Moussa Traoré both allied itself with Islam and politically subjected it to the government's corporatist politics. In 1980, the creation of the Association Malienne pour l'Unité et le Progrès de l'Islam (AMUPI) was a key step in subjecting Islam to official state patronage and control.[101]

One important ethnic group in northern Mali, the Tuaregs, was not well incorporated into the state, however. The nomadic Tuaregs had little interest in being dominated by the South, and sometimes used Islamic language to frame what were essentially ethnic and economic grievances with Bamako. A regional rebellion in the 1990s between Tuaregs and a number of states in the sahel region, including Mali, demonstrated that Islamic frameworks could be used for mobilization within a unified Islamic (and in this case also highly ethnic) hierarchy that had interests strongly opposed to those of the state. As the rebellion became more entrenched in the late 2000s, the Tuaregs began to look around for potential Islamist allies. By early 2012, a new group, Ansar Dine, led by a former leader of the Tuareg rebellion, Iyad Ag Ghaly, began to operate in alliance with Tuareg separatists in launching military incursions. Ansar Dine developed linkages with al-Qa'eda in the Islamic Magreb and has recently sought to impose shari'a law on some towns in northern Mali.

Despite some structural differences with Senegal, Mali also faced a situation of multiple hierarchies of Islamic discourse and communication, which fragment Islamic common knowledge and potential channels for political activation. Additionally, key Muslim elites have been heavily invested in the state, making the use of Islam to contest political power a potentially costly exercise. While Sufi elites in Mali have received less national-level patronage than those in Senegal, the stronger reformist groups have been actively co-opted and integrated into the state, creating little incentive for Islamist mobilization at the center. When religious elites have been poorly incorporated into the state, as with the Tuaregs, Islam has been used for political mobilization within that hierarchical group, but has difficulty spreading beyond it. By far the most active Islamist mobilization has come from the poorly incorporated north of the country.

An important difference separates Mali and Senegal in the potential for focal points around which mobilization may occur. While Senegal experienced a gradual process of political liberalization, Mali experienced a rapid transition from an authoritarian state to a democracy in 1992. How did this period of rapid democratization affect Islamic groups in Mali?

First, a number of Muslim organizations participated in the protests that led the military to remove President Traoré from power. The most active of them was Hizboullah (Party of God), which initially protested, Qur'ans in hand, along with many other non-Islamic groups against the Traoré regime.[102] Many prominent Muslims did not participate in the early demonstrations, however, perhaps because of direct ties to the state. The early protest period therefore divided Muslim groups. Second, as liberalization occurred, a large number of new Muslim organizations emerged as part of the broader trend toward rapid development of urban civil society. These groups were more socially than politically oriented, but they did share Islamic perspectives on the role of the new regime. Third, some Muslim elites became active in a sustained campaign against the publicly avowed secularism of the new democratic regime. The secular mandate handed down from the military continued to be challenged by some prominent Islamic elites throughout the 1990s.[103]

The primary political parties that emerged to contest power through elections in 1992 were not openly Islamic, however. They had generally secular platforms, with an emergent liberal-Marxist political cleavage. It appears that many of the more prominent Islamist activists became subsumed in the broad political coalition for change, an inclusive coalition that was led primarily by secular liberals. Despite a focal opportunity for mobilization, Islamists were divided and either unable or unwilling to compete with the popular liberal movement. It is clear that rapid democratization increased levels of Islamist mobilization, both in the form of protests and through the creation of new interest groups and organizations, but on the whole Islamists were outflanked by groups that were less invested in the old regime.

The case of Mali, therefore, shares some similarities with Senegal, including a pattern of divided Islamic hierarchies and the alignment of Islamic and state interests. These patterns extend beyond Mali to other sub-Saharan states, as well. Many other states have a legacy of multiple, hierarchical Islamic organizations with the capacity of in-group policing through either brotherhood, ethnic, or cell-like organizational mechanisms. When combined with extensive patterns of state patronage throughout the region, Islamist entrepreneurs often have little incentive or ability to politically mobilize. The cases of Senegal and other sub-Saharan countries do diverge, however, in trajectories of liberalization. Rapid liberalization has led to increased Islamist mobilization in Mali, but not enough to change the primary political cleavages there. In other cases, little real political liberalization has taken place to create new focal points around which mobilization may occur.

## CONCLUSION

On the same day in June 1960 that national independence was celebrated throughout Senegal, the first stone was laid for the grand mosque of Dakar.[104] This was far from a symbolic representation of Senegal as an Islamic state – after all, its newly elected president was a Catholic and the constitution was avowedly secular – but it represented an early recognition that the fate of the state and the fate of Islamic interests were intertwined. Over the course of subsequent decades, this shared fate was apparent through multiple demonstrations of mutual support, and also through the effective way that tensions between the state and Islamic leaders were resolved.

I have argued in this chapter that the story of Islamist activism in Senegal is one of overall low mobilization with a number of failed attempts to introduce Islamist political movements. In contrast to some theories that see low mobilization as the result of an inherently apolitical syncretistic Islam, I have argued that low mobilization in this case results from a combination of institutional factors. These include fragmented Islamic common knowledge, an alignment of interests between the Islamic elite and the state, effective Islamic in-group policing, and relatively few focal points of internal state crisis or rapid liberalization around which to mobilize. While Senegal is a unique case in some respects, many of these institutional factors are found in other Islamic countries that also have low Islamist mobilization.

Of all of these factors, perhaps the most critical have been the alignment of Islamic and state interests and the capacity of Islamic groups to provide in-group policing of their members. At present, however, these structural factors appear to be the most vulnerable to change. Certainly the key *marabouts* and other Islamic elites have moved from a position of committed support for the government itself to a position of negotiated support for broader state interests. This has increasingly led to what Villalón has described as "institutionalized uncertainty" in the relationship between the state and the brotherhoods.[105]

While both an alignment with state interests and a capacity for in-group policing are likely to change only slowly, there are indications that both of these attributes are breaking down. The state has fewer resources to dispense as patronage in support of brotherhood activities than it once had; at the same time, the brotherhoods are developing a more independent resource base through remittances and through a growing international trading network. Additionally, increasing urbanization has stretched the traditional ties between Sufi disciples and the *marabouts*, making it considerably more difficult to maintain control over disciples' activities. Reformist activities are likewise becoming less hierarchical and more democratic in organization. The net effect of these changes is that there may be more religious entrepreneurs interested in mobilization attempts if the right focal points for political communication are present.

Currently those focal points are not present, however, and it is too early to predict the demise of a structural equilibrium that has successfully endured several periods of stress throughout its long history. After all, predictions of the breakdown of Senegalese Islamic hierarchies have been around for several decades.[106] Nevertheless, if the causal factors presented here are accurate, there are likely to be more attempts at Islamist mobilization in Senegal in the future than there have been in the past. Given the broad structural challenges in Senegal of developing Islamic common knowledge and collaborating across Muslim communities, however, these attempts are unlikely to fundamentally alter the pattern of political cleavages in Senegal.

The Senegalese experience has a number of implications for other cases, both those with historically little Islamist mobilization and those where Islamist mobilization has been high but is now in decline. In other cases where Islamic institutions are strong, but mobilization has been low – such as in the monarchies of the Arab Gulf – Senegal's experience suggests that heavy patronage and successful in-group policing may be responsible. In situations where Islamist mobilization has destabilized the country (e.g., Algeria or Turkmenistan), Islamist activities could potentially be curtailed through institutions that align the incentives of Islamists with those of the state by helping the parties make credible commitments to one another. Finally, in the violent and uncertain post-2011 regime transitions of countries such as Libya or Yemen, Islamist mobilization may be most effectively contained if the state has the ability to convince Islamist entrepreneurs that they have credible reasons to invest in the state's success.

## REFERENCES

Balzar, John. 1995. "Changing Lifestyles – a Glimpse of Senegal: This Struggling African Nation Practices a More Easy-Going Version of Islam Than Many Societies." *Los Angeles Times*, 17 January.

Behrman, Lucy C. 1970. *Muslim Brotherhoods and Politics in Senegal*. Cambridge, MA: Harvard University Press.

Boye, François. 1990. *A Retrospective Analysis of the Senegalese Economy*. Dakar: Université de Dakar.

Brenner, Louis. 2001. *Controlling Knowledge: Religion, Power and Schooling in a West African Muslim Society*. Bloomington, IN: Indiana University Press.

Charter of the Cercle d'Etudes et de Recherches "Islam et Développement." 1984. *Wal Fadjri*, 3, 17 February: 4–6.

Constantin, François and Christian Coulon. 1997. "Religion et démocratie: Introduction à une problématique africaine." In François Constantin and Christian Coulon, eds. *Religion et transition démocratique en Afrique*, 9–24. Paris: Karthala.

Coulon, Christian. 1983. *Les musulmans et le pouvoir en afrique noire*. Paris: Karthala.
1993. *Le marabout et le prince*. East Lansing, MI: Michigan State University Department of Political Science Working Papers.
Cruise O'Brien, Donal B. 1971. *The Mourides of Senegal: The Political and Economic Organization of an Islamic Brotherhood*. Oxford: Clarendon Press.
1975. *Saints and Politicians: Essays in the Organisation of a Senegalese Peasant Society*. Cambridge: Cambridge University Press.
1988a. "Charisma Comes to Town: Mouride Urbanization 1945–1986." In Donal B. Cruise O'Brien and Christian Coulon, eds. *Charisma and Brotherhood in African Islam*. Oxford: Clarendon.
1988b. "Introduction." In Donal B. Cruise O'Brien and Christian Coulon, eds. *Charisma and Brotherhood in African Islam*. Oxford: Clarendon.
2003. *Symbolic Confrontations: Muslims Imagining the State in Africa*. London: Hurst & Company.
Diagne, Malick. 2000. *Sénégal: Chronique d'une Alternance*. Saint-Louis, Senegal: XAMAL Press.
Dieng, Amady Aly, ed. 2000. *Le Sénégal à la veille du troisième millénaire*. Paris: L'Harmattan.
Ewane, Michel Lobe. 1985. "La montée du discourse fondamentaliste musulman au Sénégal." *Le Monde Diplomatique* (April): 15.
Fearon, James D. and David D. Laitin. 2003. "Ethnicity, Insurgency, and Civil War." *American Political Science Review*, 97: 75–90.
Freedom House. 2004. "Freedom in the World Country Rankings 1972 through 2003." Washington, DC: Freedom House.
Gates, Scott, Havard Hegre, Mark P. Jones, and Havard Strand. 2006. "Institutional Inconsistency and Political Instability: Polity Duration 1800–2000." *American Journal of Political Science* 50/4 (October).
Guèye, Cheikh. 2002. *Touba: La Capitale des mourides*. Paris: Karthala.
Hiksett, Mervyn. 1994. *The Course of Islam in Africa*. Edinburgh: Edinburgh University Press.
Kaba, Lansiné. 2000. "Islam in West Africa: Radicalism and the new Ethic of Disagreement, 1960–1990." In Nehemia Levtzion and Randall L. Pouwels, eds. *The History of Islam in Africa*. Athens: Ohio University Press.
Kane, Momar. 1986. "Entretien avec Serigne Moustapha Sy, President des 'Moustarchidine wal Moustarchidate'." *Etudes Islamiques* 28/29 (March): 11–12.
Laitin, David D. 1986. *Hegemony and Culture: Politics and Religious Change among the Yoruba*. Chicago, IL: University of Chicago Press.
Levtzion, Nehemia and Randall L. Pouwels. 2000. "Introduction." *The History of Islam in Africa*. Athens: Ohio University Press.
Loimeier, Roman. 2001. *Säkularer Staat und Islamishe Gesellschaft*. Hamburg: Lit.
Loum, Mamadou Lamine. 2001. Le Sénégal au 1er Avril 2000. Dakar: EXCAF Editions.
Magassouba, Moriba. 1985. *L'Islam au Senegal: Demain les mollahs?* Paris: Karthala.
Maranz, David E. 1993. *Peace Is Everything: World View of Muslims in the Senegambia*. Dallas, TX: International Museum of Cultures.
Marty, Paul and Jules Salenc. 1914. *Les Ecoles Maraboutiques du Sénégal: La Medersa de Saint-Louis*. Paris: Ernest Leroux.

Mattes, Hanspeter. 1989. *Die islamistische Bewegung des Senegal zwischen Autonomie und Außenorientierung*. Hamburg: Edition Wuquf.

Miles, William F. S. 2004. "Islamism in West Africa: Conclusions." *African Studies Review* 47/2 (September): 109–117.

Ndiaye, Rokhaya. 1986. "L'importance des écoles coraniques." *Wal Fadjri* 66/26 (December): 8–9.

Nour, Salah. 1985. "Manoeuvering Towards an Authentic Islamic Society." *Arabia* (June): 27–28.

Piga, Adriana. 2000. *Dakar e Gli Ordini Sufi: Processi socioculturali e sviluppo urbano nel Senegal contemporaneo*. Rome: Bagatto.

Robinson, David. 2003. *Muslim Societies in African History*. Cambridge: Cambridge University Press.

Salih, Mahdi Sati. 1991. *Ma' al-Islam wa al-thaqafa al-'arabiyya fi al-Sinighal*. Khartoum: African Islamic Center.

Schulz, D. E. 2003. "Charisma and Brotherhood Revisited: Mass-Mediated Forms of Spirituality in Urban Mali." *Journal of Religion in Africa* 33/2 (August): 146–171.

Searing, James F. 2002. *"God Alone Is King": Islam and Emancipation in Senegal*. Portsmouth, NH: Heinemann.

Smith, Gina and Bodil Jorgensen. 1991. *Islamisk mystik i Senegal: En indre jihad*. Cophenhagen: Munksgaard.

Le Soleil. 2003. "Moustarchidina wal Moustarchidaty: Mobilisation exceptionnelle de l'axe de Dakar." 18 August.

SOS Faim. 1996. *Sénégal: Pour une vision politique, économique et sociale*. Brussels: Éditions Action pour le Développement.

Sy, Cheikh Tidiane. 1969. *La Confrérie Sénégalaise des Mourides*. Biarritz: Présence Africaine.

Timéra, Mahamet. 1986. *Jeunesse Urbaine et Renouveau Religieux au Sénégal*. Thesis. University of Dakar.

Triaud, Jean-Louis. 2000. "Islam in Africa Under French Colonial Rule." In Nehemia Levtzion and Randall L. Pouwels, eds. *The History of Islam in Africa*. Athens: Ohio University Press.

Vikor, Knut S. 2000. "Sufi Brotherhoods in Africa." In Nehemia Levtzion and Randall L. Pouwels, eds. *The History of Islam in Africa*. Athens: Ohio University Press.

Villalón, Leonardo A. 1995. *Islamic Society and State Power in Senegal: Disciples and Citizens in Fatick*. Cambridge: Cambridge University Press.

2004. "Islamism in West Africa: Senegal." *African Studies Review* (September): 61–71.

Villalón, Leonardo A. and Ousmane Kane. 1998. "Senegal: The Crisis of Democracy and the Emergence of an Islamic Opposition." In Leonardo A. Villalón and Phillip A. Huxtable, eds. *The African State at a Critical Juncture: Between Disintegration and Reconfiguration*, 143–166. Boulder, CO: Lynne Rienner.

# 5

# Voting for Welfare and Virtue

## *Islamist Electoral Mobilization in Turkey*

### INTRODUCTION

Turkey is a particularly helpful case for assessing a number of hypotheses outlined in Chapter 2. In contrast to the case of Senegal described in Chapter 4, Turkey has experienced considerable levels of Islamist mobilization during most periods of the study. Unlike the case of Algeria, to be described in Chapter 6, Turkey has not experienced dramatically high levels of Islamist activism in any period, and may be thought of as a case that represents moderate levels of mobilization on average (when compared with the population of country cases).

An examination of political Islam in the Turkish context provides a number of theoretical advantages over assessment of other cases. First, Turkey experienced considerable variation in mobilization outcomes both throughout the period of the study and across country regions, variation that can be leveraged in assessing the central hypotheses. Second, data on support for the Islamist movement is better in Turkey than in the vast majority of countries in the Islamic world. This is most explicitly due to accurate electoral results measuring support for Islamist parties across district and across time. Data on possible explanatory variables are also relatively developed and can be tested across region in Turkey. Third, as a case of mid-range outcomes, the Turkish experience may prove relevant to many other cases with both lower and higher levels of mobilization. Turkey has likewise witnessed all forms of mobilization assessed in this study, including Islamist violence, street demonstrations, and electoral mobilization.

Because of the high quality of the electoral data, I focus the majority of this chapter on Islamist electoral mobilization in Turkey, which allows me to control for type of mobilization and thus provide a more careful assessment in the variation in outcomes across space and time. It is important to note that

Turkey is representative of the broader data set in that Turkish electoral mobilization is correlated with the other forms of mobilization. Turkey experienced Islamist violence in two general periods (late 1970s and early 1990s), some street demonstrations, and moderate levels of electoral mobilization. The electoral assessment provided in this chapter may not provide a fully accurate explanation of Islamist protest and violence in Turkey, but it allows me to assess mobilization on behalf of Islamist causes across all regions of the country, whereas Islamist protest and violence have been much more limited in scope. These manifestations have paralleled electoral mobilization, however, in that they have been higher in areas where voting for Islamist parties has been the strongest.

Overall, Turkey is fourteenth place in total levels of mobilization (according to factor score) or ninth place (according to summed ordinal score) out of the fifty-seven polities described in Chapter 3. Turkey is often considered a distinctive case by scholars of political Islam due to its long history of secular nationalist ideology and the Turkish campaign against Islamic institutions early in the twentieth century. In the range of countries examined in the study, however, the presence of a secular nationalist ideology is hardly unique.[1] The religious challenge to secular state ideology that reemerged in the formal political sphere in the 1950s provides useful comparisons with many other states that have witnessed a similar secular-religious cleavage. Political cleavages between a secular-minded state elite and various forms of Islamic civil society emerged in the latter half of the twentieth century in such states as Egypt, Syria, Algeria, Iraq, Indonesia, Yemen, and Uzbekistan.

Perhaps more than the secular orientation of the state, what makes Turkey distinct from these cases is its experience with a democratic tradition in which this cleavage has played out over time. Although Turkey has, at best, modeled a system of interrupted democracy due to several military coups d'état, credible elections have taken place in every decade from the 1950s to the present. On average over time, Turkey has had the most politically open system of any country in the study.[2] Turkey's democratic experience makes it less representative of the average country in the study, but it also allows for much better assessment of real support for Islamically oriented political parties than in all other potential cases.

From the 1970s to the present, a series of political parties with sympathies for an "Islamic" social and political agenda have contested democratic elections in Turkey. These parties have each encountered difficulties maintaining their operational status in the face of political and legal challenges on the part of Turkey's secular establishment. Although multiple political parties in Turkey have, from time to time, expressed solidarity with religious believers, one group of political contestants led by Necmettin Erbakan dominated each of the most identifiable "Islamic" parties from 1970 through the 1990s. These political parties were successively closed by the courts after some time, but closure has inevitably led to the formation of a new party encompassing the same political figures and promoting a similar agenda. In 2001, this united Islamist political movement split for the first time, dividing between two political parties exhibiting generational differences in leadership and modest differences in political platform. In national elections in 2002, the more liberal and centrist of these factions, the Justice and Development Party, took control of the Turkish parliament by winning a majority of seats. The emergence of the Justice and Development Party (Adalet ve Kalkınma Parti, AKP) transformed Islamist politics in Turkey by retreating from traditional Islamist positions in favor of more centrist positions and came to dominate the Turkish government from 2003 to the present. This chapter focuses primarily on voting for Islamist parties prior to the 2002 elections, after which the AKP effectively transformed Islamist politics into what some have described as a "post-Islamist" or "Muslimhood" model in Turkey.[3]

Before the emergence of the AKP in 2002, parties associated with the Islamist movement never captured more than one quarter of the Turkish electorate. However, this series of Islamist political parties had a profound effect on Turkish political culture and society over several decades. Indeed, because of the high fragmentation of the Turkish party system, these parties wielded inordinate influence in parliament on a number of occasions, captured Turkey's two largest municipalities (Istanbul and Ankara) in the 1990s, and even controlled the Turkish government with a coalition partner during 1996–1997. The Welfare Party (Refah Partisi), the Islamist political party that brought the movement to the head of government in 1996, was the most successful in this series of parties prior to the electoral victory of the quasi-Islamist AKP. The rapid rise of Welfare in the 1990s inspired numerous Turkish commentators within the nervous political establishment to question whether the founding secular principles of the Turkish Republic, as embodied in the state ideology of *Kemalism*, were now under attack. Subsequent continued support for Welfare's successors, the Virtue Party (Fazilet Partisi) and the AKP, demonstrated the continued salience of Islamic issues in Turkish politics. The foundations laid by the series of Islamist parties that competed in the three decades from 1970 to 1999 provided the possibility for the ascendancy of the governing AKP in the subsequent decade.

The core arguments presented here are as follows. Significant variation exists in support for Islamist parties in Turkey both across time (denoted by election) and across space (denoted by region and province). This variation can best be accounted for by variable levels of Islamic institutional penetration in society and by the presence of public state focal points that make Islamic common knowledge relevant to electoral behavior. Because of a moderately liberal political climate, a poor alignment of interests between Islamists and the state, and the weak institutional capacity of religious elites, the Turkish structural context has facilitated religious entrepreneurship. Political-religious entrepreneurs have been more successful in some times and regions than in others because of variations in Islamic institutional penetration and the presence of public crises of order and justice. Attempts by the state to set costs on Islamist mobilization have helped to shape the constraints and direction that religious entrepreneurs face. Observed increases in Islamist electoral support over time are driven by increasing opportunities for entrepreneurship (during political liberalization) within a context of increasing Islamic institutional strength. Shorter-term variation can best be accounted for by changes in public state events and by shifts in the alignment of interests between Islamists and the state.

The first part of the chapter provides an overview of political Islam in Turkey, focusing primarily on the series of Islamically oriented political parties that have competed in Turkish elections prior to the development of the governing AKP. Variation in Islamist electoral mobilization across time and space is then discussed. This is followed in the second half of the chapter by an assessment of the theoretical contribution outlined in Chapter 2 as applied to the Turkish case. Structural conditions for religious entrepreneurship, the production of Islamic common knowledge, and state focal points are each discussed. Potential alternative explanations and implications of the argument are presented in the Conclusion.

## POLITICAL ISLAM IN TURKEY

Since 1970, Turkey has witnessed both public protest and political violence on the part of Islamist organizations. Public protest by Islamists was most prominent on university campuses as an alternative to the left in the 1970s and after specific policy reforms by the government that affected religious organizations and movements in the early 1980s and late 1990s. Significant public protests occurred after a state decision to bar the wearing of headscarves on university campuses in 1981, and later with renewed vigor in 1998. Likewise, the state decision to close religious (*İmam Hatip*) junior high schools in 1997 provoked massive public protest in Istanbul where an estimated 500,000-plus individuals turned out to voice unhappiness at the closure decision.

Political violence by Islamist organizations has been on a much smaller scale, with some Islamist groups joining in the violent unrest that plagued Turkish society during the 1970s, and others surviving underground to commit occasional political assassinations. Two of the more prominent radical organizations, Hezbollah and the awkwardly named Great Eastern Islamic Raider's Front (IBDA-C), were accused of multiple assassinations of prominent figures in the secular establishment throughout the 1990s.[4] The victims included some of Turkey's most prominent journalists and civil activists.

Despite the importance of both public protest and violence in the Turkish case, the most extensive, prominent, and continuous form of Islamist mobilization during the past three decades has been through electoral channels. The continual[5] electoral mobilization by Islamists from the early 1970s through the 1990s and then the ascendancy of a party based in Islamic values during the 2000s have few parallels in the rest of the Muslim world. Because electoral mobilization is both the easiest form to measure and effectively controls for mobilization environment over time, Turkish electoral politics presents a unique opportunity to examine the sources of broader Islamist political mobilization. The variable fortunes of Turkish Islamist political parties over time and space provide intriguing variation, which allows us to ask why Islamist parties have achieved notable electoral success in some periods and regions, while they have had more limited popularity in others.

Elections in Turkey provided a competitive context in which Islamic identity emerged as a politically energizing factor. Centrist political parties of the late 1940s and 1950s sought to attract religiously conservative voters by incorporating Islamic language into their appeals. This strategy was initially utilized in the Democrat Party's (Demokrat Partisi, DP) challenge to the secular nationalist tradition of Atatürk's Republican People's Party (Cumhuriyet Halk Partisi, CHP) in Turkey's first multi-party elections in the middle of the century.

In 1970, Turkey's first clearly Islamist-oriented political party, the National Order Party (Milli Nizam Partisi, NOP), was established by a prominent engineer named Necmettin Erbakan. Erbakan had attempted to join the dominant conservative party of the day, the Justice Party (Adalet Partisi), but was denied a position and successfully entered parliament as an independent from the Turkish Islamic center of Konya. The National Order Party articulated an agenda reaffirming the role of Islamic values in public life but was closed down after the Turkish military intervention of 1971 for violating the secular principles of the constitution.

Within a year, Erbakan had established a new party with the name of the National Salvation Party (Milli Selamet Partisi, NSP). Although the NSP heeded the Turkish law requiring that none of the founders of the National Order Party be registered as founders of the new party, this was clearly Erbakan's party and articulated a similar agenda to the NOP. The NSP worked to position itself as a participant in the democratic system and had a great deal of success throughout the 1970s in actively participating in government. In its party platform, the NSP articulated the need for society to achieve a spiritual and moral order (*manevi düzen*) and emphasized state initiative in building heavy industry with the united support of small businessmen (Gülalp 1999). Both the NOP and the NSP benefited from their association with a broader ideological movement led by Erbakan, the National View movement (Milli Görüş), which propogated an indigenous cultural view of Turkey's future.

The NSP competed in the 1973 and 1977 elections at both the national and the local level. In its debut in the 1973 national elections the party won what was considered a surprisingly high percentage of the vote, achieving almost 12 percent. In local elections during the 1970s, and in the subsequent national election of 1977, the party's returns were considerably lower. Despite attracting an overall small percentage of the Turkish electorate, the NSP wielded disproportionate influence at the national level due to the inability of the dominant center-right party (Justice Party) and the dominant center left party (CHP) to form a cooperative relationship in government. As neither of these parties could gain an effective majority, they were dependent on right-wing or Islamist parties such as the NSP to create a governing coalition.[6] Indeed, Erbakan served as deputy prime minister in three governments in the 1970s, first with the Republican People's Party and then twice with the Justice Party. Because the leading government party in each instance was dependent on the NSP's participation, the NSP was able to extract numerous concessions in government appointments in key ministries and had a significant role in influencing the government's budget.

The most significant coup d'état in Turkey's history occurred in 1980, when leading generals comprising the National Security Council dramatically intervened in politics to end the escalating civil violence of the late 1970s. Although it appears that the military had been planning to intervene sometime before the September 12 coup, they did so within the context of an NSP political rally in Konya on September 6. During the NSP rally, Erbakan and party activists protested against Israel's move to make Jerusalem its capital, motivated the crowd using Islamic symbols, and talked of the possibility of Islamic law (*şeriat*) in Turkey (Birand 1987). In the course of the military intervention, the generals suspended the constitution, imposed martial law, removed all politicians from their posts, banned political parties, and devoted attention to detaining and trying Islamist sympathizers. Erbakan was tried, and ultimately acquitted, of attempting to set up an Islamic state in Turkey.

By the time civilian government was restored in 1983, a new constitution was in place that was designed to eliminate the politicians and the parties of the 1970s from Turkey's political future. Erbakan's movement managed to re-emerge in the 1980s, however, redefining itself as a party for radical change as opposed to the "conservative" religious movement of the National Salvation Party. The new party's name, Welfare (Refah), suggested a strong commitment to social justice and became a political competitor with parties of the left.

After legal changes of 1987 allowed pre-1980 politicians the right to return to politics, Erbakan took the helm of the Welfare Party, leading it into a lukewarm showing at the 1987 elections.[7] Welfare differed from the NSP on a number of issues, most prominently in its emphasis on private rather than state initiative in the quest for Turkish economic independence. In general, Welfare was less conservative in both its rhetoric and its constituency than the NSP.[8] Despite some differences, however, the Welfare party was led by NSP politicians and, like the NSP, positioned itself as the Islamist alternative to the other parties beholden to Western norms.

Despite its marginal performance in the provincial and national elections of the 1980s, the party quickly gained support during the 1990s. After failing to enter parliament in 1987, it increased its vote share in each of the four subsequent elections.[9] In the legislative elections of 1991, Welfare entered into a temporary electoral coalition with a right-wing nationalist party[10] in an effort to secure a showing above the 10 percent electoral threshold. Under this arrangement, the party won almost 17 percent of the vote; a considerable increase in support even after the electoral alliance is taken into account.

The real breakthrough for Welfare came after it shed this alliance and astonished the secular establishment in provincial elections of 1994 and in national elections of 1995, where it demonstrated that it was one of the most important political movements in the country. Nationally Welfare received over 19 percent of votes cast in 1994 and over 21 percent of votes a year later, making it the most popular party in Turkey's fragmented system. In 1994 Welfare captured the mayor's post in Turkey's two largest cities (Istanbul and Ankara), penetrating the heart of Atatürk's urban Republicanism, along with numerous other cities and municipalities all across Turkey. In 1995 Welfare captured more seats in the Turkish Grand National Assembly than any other party, but was rebuffed by other parties in its attempts to form a coalition government. Upon the repeated failure of centrist parties to form a viable coalition, President Demirel offered Erbakan a new opportunity to try to create a government. After finding an unlikely coalition partner in the avowedly anti-Islamist True Path Party (Doğru Yol Partisi, DYP), [11] Erbakan became Turkey's first Islamist prime minister in 1996.

Welfare certainly couldn't be described as a militant Islamist organization. Unlike militant Islamist groups in Turkey such as Hizbullah, which was implicated in sporadic assassinations of prominent figures of the secular establishment throughout the 1990s, Welfare was foremost a political party. As such, it commanded the allegiance and sympathies of a much larger number of Turks than the secretive and relatively obscure militant Islamists. Welfare did clearly distinguish itself from mainstream political parties, however. With the Welfare party, Erbakan further extended his national view ideology, describing all of its party competitors as simply mimics of the West.[12] Major themes of Welfare's campaigns included the importance of social justice, Turkey's exploitation by the West, religious freedom, ethnic tolerance, promotion of private enterprise, creation of an interest-free "Islamic" economy, an end to state corruption, and denunciations of an "imperialist Zionist system" that threatened Turkey's national independence.[13] In combination, these themes had the effect of marking Welfare a more anti-system party than its competitors.

Additionally, Welfare was distinctive both in its party organization and in the unconventional policies it pursued in government. As a party organization, Welfare was uncommonly effective at creating a connection between the party and its potential constituency. Unlike mainstream Turkish parties, which were notably elite in their orientation and lacked substantive organic ties with their voting base,[14] Welfare was able to develop substantial support at the grassroots level through an extensive organizational structure. For example, provincial organizational committees[15] were further divided into district committees, which reviewed neighborhood organization through periodic inspections. Neighborhood organizers appointed street representatives that served as

Welfare's presence at ground level even in the poorest neighborhoods. Party representatives were also careful to attend communal events, often distributing municipal welfare services in visible but very local forums.[16]

After Erbakan became Prime Minister in 1996, Welfare initially pursued domestic and foreign policy goals seemingly at odds with those of its coalition partner and the greater Turkish political establishment. For example, Erbakan's early foreign policy activism, which included state visits to Iran and Libya, and efforts to establish an economic bloc of Muslim countries (D-8) were actively questioned by leaders of other political parties and the military establishment. Controversy also erupted when leaders of religious brotherhoods (*tarikatlar*) were invited to participate in a Ramadan dinner at the prime minister's residence, opening Erbakan to accusations that the seat of government had been overrun with clerics. At the municipal level, Welfare mayors who took power in 1994 had demonstrated their ability to provide better municipal services than their predecessors, but also attracted controversy of their own.[17] Popular increases in the provision of local services were accompanied by new restrictions on the sale of alcohol, an upsurge in mosque construction, and changes in local symbols and landmarks to reflect a religious tone. A plan to build an imposing mosque in the heart of modern Istanbul (Taksim square) under Welfare Mayor (and subsequent Prime Minister and President) Tayyip Erdoğan led to considerable controversy among the secular establishment, delaying and undermining the plan.

Despite considerable popular success at the municipal level, Welfare's short tenure at the head of the national government is remembered largely for being ineffectual and compromised by the constraints of governing with a coalition partner and the political boundaries set by the military establishment. Most of Welfare's campaign promises remained unfulfilled because of the political compromises Erbakan found necessary to remain in power. On one side, he had to allow his secular-minded coalition partner, the DYP led by Tansu Çiller, sufficient prerogatives to maintain the partnership. On another, he had to demonstrate sufficient reverence for the principles of the Republican secular constitution, drawn up under the military in the early 1980s, to avoid triggering another military intervention. Within these constraints, Erbakan also had to try to maintain the loyalty of those who voted him into office, many of whom expected Welfare to inaugurate a new era in Turkish politics.

In the end, these conflicting demands proved too much for Welfare's tenuous hold on national power. Coalition partner Çiller, who took on the foreign affairs ministry, appeared to pursue a foreign policy independent from Erbakan's initiatives. Likewise, Erbakan's populist economic policies, which included large wage increases and agricultural subsidies, appeared at odds with Çiller's public promises of fiscal austerity. Erbakan's initiatives to resolve the ethnic Kurdish insurgency in Southeastern Turkey were also not supported by Çiller, who presided over some of the strongest incursions against Kurdish guerillas, nor by the military, which was deeply suspicious of opening peace talks with "terrorists."[18] At the end of 1996, a corruption scandal involving prominent members of Çiller's party tested the limits of the Welfare–DYP alliance.[19] It forced Erbakan to publicly come to his coalition partner's defense in an effort to preserve the fragile union.[20] This served to alienate his constituency, who clearly remembered Welfare's promises to root out corruption, and provoked an anti-corruption movement in civil society.

The initial expansion of Islamic educational and bureaucratic organizations during Welfare's tenure, as well as a new openness to Islamic identity and symbolism in the public sphere, made the military establishment increasingly nervous. The military and parts of secular civil society feared that Islamists would quickly infiltrate state institutions and eventually introduce Islamic law (*şeriat*). Elements within civil society, including the prominent Turkish Industrialists' and Businessmen's Association (TÜSIAD), soon united in opposing the combination of populist economic spending, perceived corruption, and Islamic cultural entrepreneurship by the Welfare government. The National Security Council, composed largely of senior military officers, increasingly tightened their demands on Erbakan in response to perceived threats against the secular character of the state. In order to maintain his position, the traditionally anti-Zionist Erbakan yielded to military pressure to sign a military cooperation agreement with Israel and was forced to dismiss a large number of Islamist sympathizers from the military. In response to these actions and to the increasingly compromised ideological position of the Welfare government, many of Erbakan's natural allies in religious civil society began to vehemently criticize the government's policies and to withdraw their support.

On 28 February 1997, the military establishment issued a set of demands to Erbakan's government that would lead to the government's collapse. Apparently fed up with the continued penetration of the state by Islamist sympathizers and public displays of Islamic mobilization, the military forced Welfare's hand without formally taking power.[21] The essence of the National Security Council's demands was the elimination of Islamic influence and sympathizers within the state, including restrictions on religious civil society. Demands included the closure of hundreds of religious schools, tight controls over religious brotherhoods, and restrictions on Islamic dress. For Erbakan, agreeing to these demands would mean a dramatic alienation from those who voted him into office. After protesting the military interference, Erbakan ultimately signed the recommendations with little apparent interest in enforcing them. For several months the military continued to issue threats toward the government, mobilizing civil society and the media in an anti-Islamic drive.[22] By June 1997 Erbakan was forced to resign, and the President called on opposition parties to form a new government. The new government, led by the center-right but secularist Motherland Party (Anavatan Partisi, ANAP), quickly showed its determination to implement the Security Council's recommendations.

After Erbakan's departure from the premiership, the military maintained its pressure on elements deemed anti-secular. This was done to a large extent by providing the judicial system with incentives and resources to define Islamically oriented political groups and their leaders as anti-system. In May 1997, during Erbakan's last weeks in power, a judicial motion was introduced to ban Welfare for violating the secular principles of the constitution. The judicial process continued until January 1998, when Welfare was formally closed by the Constitutional Court "because of evidence confirming its actions against the principles of the secular republic."[23] Erbakan and five other Welfare deputies were simultaneously banned from political leadership for five years.[24]

As it became apparent that Welfare would be closed by the Constitutional Court, a new party was established to provide an institutional base for parliamentary deputies from the Welfare Party. The Virtue (Fazilet) Party was founded in December 1997 by a number of Islamists close to Necmettin Erbakan.[25] Within Welfare, two separate generations with divergent agendas began to emerge around the choice of who should lead the new party. The younger "reformists" strategically pushed for greater internal democracy within the new party, while Erbakan pressed for the party to be run by personal loyalists.[26] Istanbul mayor Tayyip Erdoğan's subsequent prosecution, however, left the reformists with less leverage in selecting a leader, and a settlement was reached on giving party leadership to a long-time ally of Necmettin Erbakan, Recaï Kutan.[27] Upon the formal closure of the Welfare Party, all Welfare deputies in parliament shifted to the new Virtue Party, making it the largest party in parliament.

At the first convention of the Virtue Party (14 May 1998), Kutan was careful to stress that Virtue was a new party with an essentially democratic agenda. Although this was done, in part, to shield the party from accusations that it was simply a "new Welfare" party that could subsequently be declared illegal, it also reflected a strategic shift by party leadership to reframe their message. Virtue's principal messages, which continued throughout its relatively short life, included the necessity of real democracy in Turkey, the importance of human rights (including Muslim religious rights), and a focus on expanding political liberties.[28]

In December 1998, a new coalition was formed in the Turkish parliament after political defections occurred from Welfare's successor as head of government, the ANAP. Although the Virtue Party was the largest party in parliament, President Süleyman Demirel overlooked Virtue as an unacceptable choice to lead a new government, and eventually agreed to a minority government led by the Democratic Left Party (Demokratik Sol Partisi, DSP). The Democratic Left Party was the fifth-largest party in the National Assembly; its choice as leader of the new coalition violated constitutional norms in an effort to prevent Virtue from participating in government.

As new elections were scheduled for April 1999, splits in the Virtue Party leadership between Erbakan's close associates and a younger generation (modeled by Tayyip Erdoğan and Abdullah Gül) became more apparent. Erbakan's ongoing reputation as the "phantom of the Virtue Party" was criticized both by the secular establishment and by increasing numbers within their party who felt that Erbakan was stifling party democracy.[29]

The outcome of the national elections in 1999 was disappointing for most in the Virtue Party. The party's national vote share fell from over 21 percent in the previous election to about 16 percent, making it the third-largest party in parliament.[30] Virtue's decline in national support was mirrored by a surprise increase in votes for the right-wing National Action Party (Milliyetçi Hareket Partisi, MHP). The divided total electoral returns ultimately resulted in a governing coalition of three parties, but left Virtue in parliamentary opposition.[31]

Virtue did not settle back into its opposition role without controversy. Indeed, the legal demise of the Virtue Party might be traced to the post-election ceremony for the swearing in of new deputies. One of the newly elected deputies, a woman named Merve Kavakçi, had made it clear during the campaign that she would not remove her headscarf in the National Assembly in accordance with law. Virtue Party leaders decided to allow her to follow her conscience during the induction ceremony, and did not mandate that she remove it. Upon entering the Assembly with a headscarf, she was greeted by shouts of "Get out!" and with extended banging on desks by deputies from other parties. After almost an hour of chaos, she left the Assembly unable to take her seat.[32] Virtue thus became a focal point for the ongoing headscarf controversy. The incident led the state prosecutor to inaugurate a closure case against Virtue, accusing the party of serving as a focus of anti-secular activity and for remaining an extension of the banned Welfare party.[33]

While the extended proceedings at the Constitutional Court took place, Virtue worked hard to shore up its moderate image. In November 1999, the party sent a public relations mission to the United States and tried to push forward dramatic proposals in parliament intended to help Turkey fulfill the Copenhagen criteria for entrance into the European Union. Virtue's policy proposals included ending military dominance of the National Security Council, increased provisions for freedom of expression, and changes to electoral and detention laws. Conveniently, all of these proposed changes were also self-serving, reflecting the conclusion that Virtue's survival was dependent on expanded democracy in Turkey.[34] Early in 2000, as new revelations about militant Hizbullah assassinations flooded the media, Kutan worked to completely distance Virtue from the militant group by accusing the military of negligence in not taking forceful action against Hizbullah. Ironically, these accusations provoked the military to make its own statements against Virtue, accusing it of being a mere continuation of Welfare and a threat to the secular republic.

While facing pressure from both the military and the Constitutional Court, the split within the party was ever widening. In protest against Erbakan's personal influence, five key reformists resigned from leadership positions. The reformist challenge came to a head in the Virtue Party congress of

May 2000, when a group of reformers, led by Abdullah Gül, openly challenged Kutan for control of the party. While Kutan managed to retain control of the party, it was clear that his support was severely weakened.[35]

As the Constitutional Court's deliberations over party closure reached their final stages, actors from all sides appeared to want the party closed. For the secularists, Virtue remained a haven for religious zealots that must be closed to reduce the Islamists' influence. Other parties wanted Virtue's closure in the hopes that they could recruit deputies from its ranks. The Virtue Party itself even appeared to be satisfied with closure, as it would allow the divergent tendencies within the party a chance to finally break from each other.[36] In June 2001, the court finally ruled against Virtue. The party was absolved of the charge that it was a continuation of the Welfare Party, but it was still closed because it was deemed a focal point for Islamic militancy. The Court rejected the prosecutor's demand to expel all Virtue deputies from parliament, leaving the vast majority to remain as independents, but banned five Virtue members from political life for five years.

The official closure was all that was needed to formalize the party's split. The reformist grouping under Gül (who would eventually become prime minister and then president) had actually been working for over a year on the outline for a new party. Erbakan loyalists, however, were the first to inaugurate a new party, under a new name chosen by Erbakan himself, the Felicity Party (Saadet Partisi, SP). The new name was meant to signify the state of blissful happiness that comes from spiritual self-realization (and alternatively is translated as "happiness" or "contentment").[37] Although Erbakan remained banned from politics, the party was designed as a vehicle for his re-entry and sought something of a return to the prior successes of Welfare as a social and political movement. One month later, in August 2001, the reformist wing unveiled their new party, the AKP.[38] The AK Party, as it was sometimes known, echoed the meanings of the Turkish word "ak," which signifies both "white" and "clean." The intended implication of such a name was that the AK Party was untainted by the corruption of the past, a clean slate.[39]

Upon the creation of the two new parties, it was not initially clear to observers which one would gain ascendance over time.[40] Many, in fact, thought that the split would destroy the movement as a whole. The Virtue parliamentary deputies divided their allegiance between the two parties. Over time, however, it became apparent that the AKP was building considerable momentum. Although many distrusted the AKP's claims to be a new movement, given that its leadership was composed largely of former Welfare and Virtue politicians, it immediately began to set a distinctive tone. The party emblem symbolized this by departing from variations on the crescent moon logo that was common to Welfare, Virtue, and now the Felicity Party. The AKP's logo was simply a shining light-bulb with the slogan "continual light" (*sürekli aydınlık*).[41]

The AKP emerged with a formidable organization, developed through contact with former Virtue leaders as well as notable politicians from center-right parties. Early defections to AKP from such right-wing parties as the National Action (MHP), True Path (DYP), and Motherland (ANAP) parties served as an indication that politicians in the know were taking it seriously. The organization was built with an extensive grassroots component, modeled after the organizational successes of Welfare, and with a focus on municipalities and neighborhoods. A fundamental tenet of the party was internal party democracy, a legacy of the reformists' reactions to Erbakan's personalistic leadership style. This was to be guaranteed by primary elections for the party list, transparency in decision-making, and extensive debate on policy-formulation issues. As one of the most popular and charismatic politicians in Turkey, Erdoğan took leadership of the party, with checks on his leadership to come from the governing board.

The AKP's agenda was populist in style, with relatively few concrete policy recommendations initially, and a deliberate distancing of the party from its Islamist heritage. Erdoğan described himself as a "man of the middle path" and indicated that the AKP would work to serve as a bridge between traditional and modernizing Turkey. The party was to represent "citizen Osman," the average Turk who was struggling to make it in the modern world. The party did make it clear early on that it would support a market economy and push for Turkey's admission into the European Union. It pledged to respect religious belief and support moral values, but within the context of a secular state (and in between references to Atatürk). For the AKP, true secularism meant no state interference in religious practice, and thus it pledged to resolve the issue of restrictions on headscarves. In the AKP's vision, religion remained the most important human institution, creating a natural moral and social order, but religious institutions could best be maintained in a climate of "religious freedom." The party's role was to fight injustice and inequity exacerbated by the endemic corruption within the Turkish system.

In many respects, the new Felicity Party articulated the same agenda. Over time, however, differences from the AKP in tone and substance became apparent. Recaï Kutan retained leadership of the Felicity Party, leading it to maintain much of the rhetoric of the defunct Virtue Party. Felicity was foremost a party to protect religious and natural human rights, to serve victims of the Turkish economy, and to support nationalistic, emotive, and moral values in society. Although a few progressive members of Virtue stayed on with the Felicity Party because of personal loyalties, the party was marked by its older generation of leadership and retained the more religiously conservative of Virtue's deputies. Members of Felicity felt that they carried the true banner of religious and social change in Turkey, and gradually moved to distinguish themselves from the AKP by using more anti-Western and anti-government rhetoric and by opposing the large-scale structural adjustment reforms supported by the popular economy minister, Kemal Derviş.[42]

As it became apparent in opinion polls that Erdoğan was becoming the most significant threat to the existing political establishment, Felicity attracted less attention from the media, while the AKP was actively followed. Accusations continued to mount that the party was in the pocket of the various Islamic brotherhoods, that it was a gang of religious fundamentalists aiming to create an Islamic state, or that it was intrinsically corrupt. Although constitutional changes were passed that made it more difficult for judiciary to close political parties,[43] the state prosecutor applied to the Constitutional Court to force the AKP to remove Erdoğan from its list of founding members and to bar Erdoğan from running for Parliament. The case against Erdoğan eventually proved successful; the Constitutional Court issued a warning to the AKP, requiring Erdoğan to step down from the Party's list of founding members by October 2002. The issue of whether he could lead a political party without being a founding member was left open.[44] A further court case was filed against Erdoğan, asserting that he had misused public funds as mayor of Istanbul by granting contracts to companies with Islamic ties. He subsequently resigned as a founding member of the AKP, but was determined to lead the party despite the ban on his election to parliament.

The elections of 3 November 2002 dramatically confirmed the AKP's hegemony, proving a bitter defeat for Felicity. Kutan, who had led Virtue to a moderate 15.4 percent showing in 1999, saw his party crushed, with 2.5 percent of the vote. The AKP, on the other hand, dominated the elections by capturing over 34 percent of the vote and almost two-thirds of the seats in parliament. The AKP received substantive returns throughout Turkey, bringing in votes from secular-minded areas in the Western half of the country that had shunned Welfare and Virtue. Felicity, on the other hand, received paltry returns throughout most of the country, demonstrating that the vast majority of Welfare and Virtue supporters nationwide had opted for the AKP. Traditional center-right parties such as True Path (DYP) and Motherland (ANAP) also had poor showings, failing to breach the electoral threshold for seats in parliament.[45] These results demonstrated that AKP had notable success in its stated ambition to become the address for the center-right in Turkey despite its reformist platform.

After taking power, the AKP had several notable policy successes, such as in reducing some measures of corruption, securing the right for Turkish entry discussions within the EU, extending legal conceptions of human rights, and dramatically lowering the perennial economic plague of high inflation. Under the AKP, religious and morality issues have played a relatively minor part in governance, although those that have arisen have resulted in an extended government critique by the secular elite and the liberal media. Proposed legislation in 2004 that addressed adultery, for example, received widespread negative attention, including from the EU, and was dropped from parliamentary consideration. While remaining popular with many, the AKP government was also accused by its own constituency of failing to meet Islamic expectations. The governing party was continuously under attack from secular elites for its inexperience, clumsy foreign relations with allies, and continued patterns of patronage politics.

The AKP subsequently consolidated its position in Turkish politics, increasing its number of supporters over time by appealing directly to the centrist Turkish voter and largely avoiding controversial religious issues. The party's success at courting electoral support after 2002 was astonishing, with the party winning 47 percent of the vote in the 2007 legislative elections and almost 50 percent of the vote in the 2011 elections. Because the AKP substantially modified its ideology, as compared with its predecessors, and because the election of 2002 led to a dramatic shift in voting patterns that continued throughout the subsequent decade, voting for the AKP should be considered a somewhat different phenomenon than voting for previous Islamist parties in Turkey. While many of those who voted for Islamist parties have shifted their loyalties toward the AKP, most votes for the party come from those who do not self-identify as Islamists.

Comparisons of Islamist voting in the two periods before and after the 2002 elections become problematic, and in this chapter I rely primarily on the pre-2002 elections for assessing the correlates of Islamist electoral support. Measuring Islamist electoral support in the AKP era in Turkey has become increasingly difficult over time, in part because the AKP began to entrench itself in the economy and state bureaucracy in ways that made it less the Islamist political choice and more of the establishment political choice. In other words, many of the AKP's voters, particularly after its first election, were drawn from the ranks of those who sought government favors or patronage, making it difficult to measure how much support the AKP commanded because of its mildly Islamist policy preferences. No credible Islamist party has yet emerged as a challenge to the AKP, but if alternate Islamically oriented parties could command attention they would provide some additional leverage in assessing Islamist mobilization in the post-2002 era.

Although each of these Islamically oriented parties had some unique elements in their platforms and agendas, it is important for the present argument to note that, up until the split of 2001, they formed a relatively cohesive movement that presented itself as a distinct choice in elections, regardless of party name. Despite some moderate differences, for the three decades from 1970 to 2000, this series of parties was broadly recognized as the most "Islamist" electoral choice. This characteristic unites the NSP, Welfare, and Virtue parties across time, as a vote for any of these parties may serve as an approximation of the "Islamist" vote. Other parties clearly attracted conservative Muslims throughout this period, but none was distinguished by an "Islamist" platform or identity to the extent that these parties were. The continual (if sometimes shadowy) leadership of Erbakan in each of these parties; similarities in the use of religious symbolic language; continuities in the parties' memberships; the lack of parliamentary defections from Welfare to Virtue; and the grouping of these parties in the Turkish media, political, and academic discussions all suggest that they should be treated as a single movement for the purposes of analysis.

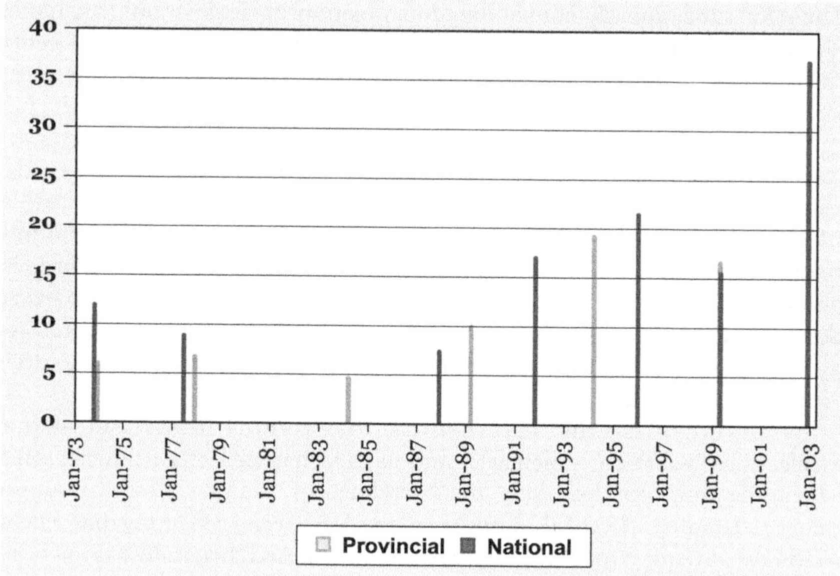


TABLE 5.1 Electoral Returns for Turkish Islamist Parties 1973–2003

Time series electoral results for Turkish Islamic parties are found in Table 5.1. National totals are presented for both parliamentary elections and elections for provincial councils.

## VARIATION IN MOBILIZATION OUTCOMES

Support for the Islamist movement in Turkey has shown considerable variation across time and also across region in Turkey. In national and provincial elections, electoral support over time has varied as illustrated in Table 5.1. The table shows that support for Turkish Islamist parties generally increased over time, and then shot up as centrist AKP transformed the system in 2002. Not all elections saw an increase in average votes for Islamist parties, however. Three exceptions should be noted: a drop in the national vote for the NSP between the 1973 and 1977 parliamentary elections, a drop in the vote upon the Welfare Party's debut in 1984 (after the military coup), and a drop in the vote from 1995 to 1999, after the Virtue Party replaced the Welfare Party. None of these drops in returns was dramatic, although the loss of 6 percent of the electorate between the 1995 and 1999 elections had significant repercussions within the movement.

There has also been variation in support based on the type of election held. In the 1970s, the national electoral returns were higher than the average returns for provincial officials, but the national and provincial returns converged by the

1990s. This initial difference and gradual convergence is likely explained by the importance of local elites in provincial politics, which provides a disadvantage to new political parties. In the 1970s, entrenched local elites were largely affiliated with one of the major centrist political parties, and had established networks of patronage that channeled support to these parties. Political entrepreneurs associated with the NSP needed time to develop a local reputation and resources to effectively compete. At a national level, however, these disadvantages may have actually enhanced the party's reputation as one apart from traditional patronage politics.

What factors best explain the variation in electoral support across time? Commentators on the Turkish Islamist movement have made a number of arguments about the observed growth in Islamist support. With regard to the initial high levels of support for the NSP in the 1973 elections, many argued (in response to modernization theory) that increased education among rural traditionalists and dislocation created by Turkey's rapid industrialization created a state of "anomie," which some voters sought to resolve by supporting an avowedly religious party (Geyikdağı 1984:11–12). Rapid urbanization and politicization of the religiously conservative classes were held responsible for growth in Islamist support during the 1970s, but this was considered to be a passing phenomenon, an intermediary stage on the way to an increasingly modernized secular state (Alkan 1984).

Explanations for the growth in support for Islamists in the late 1980s and 1990s focused, by contrast, on the changing environment of Turkish identity, and on organizational and economic arguments. The "failures of Turkey's extant project of Westernization" and the "postmodern condition" are said to favor radical Islamist discourse (Gülalp 1999:24). Both economic and cultural globalization have also been held responsible, with the argument that globalization has created higher levels of inequality in Turkey, more economic losers, while at the same time eroding the ability of the state to protect the losers. These losers, in turn, respond well to an anti-system (Islamist) argument for social justice. Additionally, cultural globalization is said to create a national identity vacuum to which Islamists can readily appeal (Öniş 1997). One organizational argument focuses on the state's repression of the left after the military coup of 1980 and its attempt to co-opt Islamists by supporting them against the left during the 1980s (Yavuz 1997:67). Another theory is that the effective grassroots party organization of Welfare, in contrast to the dominant "cadre" parties with few societal connections, helps explain the Welfare Party's success at the expense of more mainstream parties (Eligür 2010).

Explanations of drops in electoral support for Islamist parties are fewer in number. These focus largely on the strategies of both the Republican establishment and the parties themselves. For example, the military coup d'état in 1980 and the repression of Islamists that followed are used as the primary explanation for the Welfare Party's poor showing at its debut in 1984. This is paralleled by the "soft" coup of 1997 and the banning of the Welfare Party by the Constitutional Court. Fearing that the Virtue Party may also be banned, the argument goes, voters avoided it. An argument coming from a group of former Virtue Party executives asserts that a strategic error of seeking to postpone the elections in 1999 cost the party some of the public's confidence, which it paid for in the polls.[46] Another argument sometimes posed by leftist intellectuals is that the 1999 drop in votes for the Virtue Party was an indication of a broader anti-Islamic reaction to abuses of personal freedom during Welfare's tenure in office. If this is true, this reaction apparently failed to follow the new AKP into the 2002 elections.

Many of these general explanations for variation in support over time are either difficult to assess with available data or are inconsistent with much of the available data. Some of the more specific strategic claims, on the other hand, may very well be useful in explaining specific moments in the Islamist movement's trajectory, but may not be applicable to explaining patterns of Islamist mobilization over time. By addressing the shifting organizational contexts that underlie the major changes in electoral support, the alternative explanation discussed in Chapter 2 highlights the role of Islamic religious institutions, an increasing number of public state focal points favorable to the Islamist message, and a dynamic context for religious entrepreneurship. Changes in these variables collectively provide an alternative explanation for changes in electoral support over time and are addressed in the following sections.

In addition to variation in support over time, there has been considerable spatial variation in support for the Islamist parties that may provide further help in explaining the Islamists' success. Some of Turkey's provinces averaged close to 30 percent electoral support for Islamist parties across the three decades from 1970 to 2000 (e.g., Bingöl, Bayburt, Erzurum, Kahramanmaraş, Konya, and Sivas), while others averaged less than 5 percent support (e.g., Aydın, Edirne, Izmir, Kırklareli, Muğla, Tekirdağ, and Tünceli).[47] Although sometimes provinces within the same general region may have very different levels of support,[48] in general, provinces within the major geographic regions of Turkey tend to show similar patterns of Islamist voting.

The seven broad geographic regions of Turkey are considerably different from one another both in their general character and in their patterns of electoral behavior. Regional variation in support for Islamists over time is shown in Figure 5.1. The Aegean and Mediterranean coastal regions have shown the lowest levels of support for Islamist parties. The Marmara (Northwestern) region and coastal Black Sea region show more internal variation in support, but generally have not been enthusiastic supporters of the Islamist movement. Within the Marmara region, Istanbul and environs have had the highest electoral returns, which is in contrast to the very low support shown in the rural European provinces West of Istanbul. Within the Black Sea region, provinces farther east and farther inland from the coast show somewhat more electoral support for the Islamists. The highest levels of support for Islamist parties come from three regions, Central Anatolia, Eastern

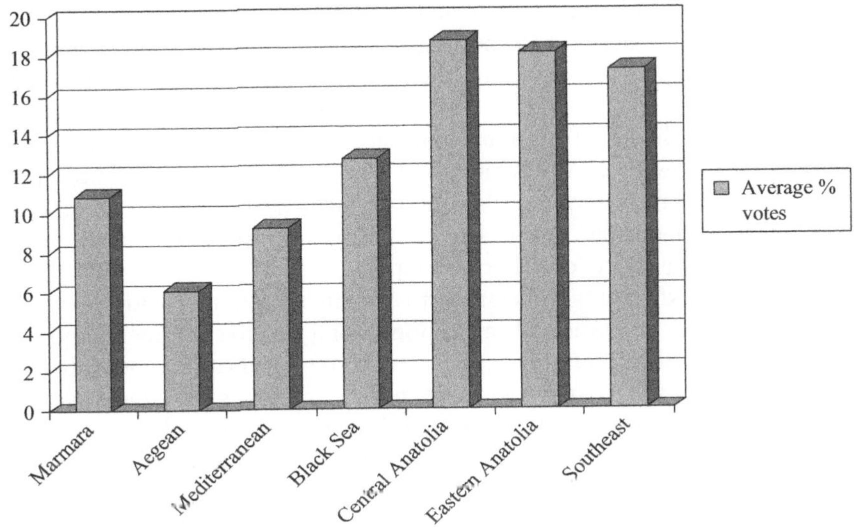


FIGURE 5.1 Average provincial votes for Islamist parties by region, 1970–2000.

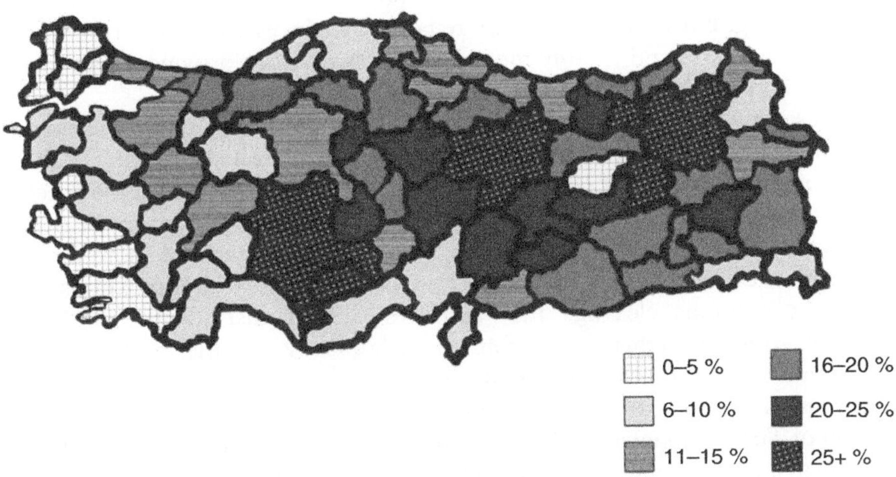


FIGURE 5.2 Average Islamist voting by province in Turkish national elections, 1970–2000.

Anatolia, and the Southeastern (largely Kurdish) provinces. These regions all have some provinces with low support for the Islamist parties, but a dominant majority of the provinces with high levels of support for these parties come from these regions. A map of average support for Islamist parties by province is shown in Figure 5.2. The darker shaded provinces indicate a higher average level of support for Islamist parties.

There have been relatively few formal arguments regarding the geographic variation in Islamist support across Turkey. In interviews I conducted with Turkish political elites and scholars, the observed support for Islamist parties in the Central and Eastern provinces was attributed to one or more of four factors: poverty, the rural (and by extension, unsophisticated) character of these provinces, low levels of literacy, and a traditional culture.[49] Those provinces with significant Alevi populations (an Islamic sect with a tradition of supporting secular parties) and ties to the tourist economy were also thought to have dampening effects on Islamist support.

How do these variables correlate with provincial Islamist voting patterns? Based on a number of statistical regressions using proxies for social and institutional variables, these variables appear not to be significantly correlated with average Islamist voting patterns in the hypothesized ways. Provinces with low levels of Islamist voting tend to have slightly higher levels of human development (from the UN Human Development Index), but the relationship is not statistically significant. This is also the case with literacy rates, when they are included separately from human development. Likewise, neither the level of urban settlement nor the percentage of urban increase in provinces is reliably correlated with Islamist voting patterns. Participation in the tourist economy (as measured by the number of hotel beds) may have some dampening effect on Islamist voting, but is not statistically reliable. Provinces with more traditional family structures[50] tend to vote more Islamist than other provinces, but again the result is not statistically significant.

Interestingly, provinces historically associated with Alevi populations do not show the hypothesized low voting rates for Islamists, but instead many of these provinces show significant support for the Islamists over time. In some specific places, such as Tünceli and the provinces of Thrace, high proportions of Alevis are associated with low Islamist voting rates. In the larger and more diverse provinces of central Anatolia, however, the presence of Alevi populations may provide a religious cleavage that activates the Islamist identity of Sunni Muslims, spurring higher voting rates for Islamically oriented parties despite low Islamist voting on the part of Alevis.

Provinces with a strong Kurdish identity, which dominate the Southeastern portion of Turkey, likewise tend to vote for Islamist parties at a higher rate than other provinces. On the whole, Kurdish provinces also have distinctive socioeconomic qualities, however. When these are included in statistical models, Kurdish identity does not emerge as a statistically significant indicator. Over time, Kurdish provinces have predominantly voted for anti-establishment parties including the Islamists, but the large anti-establishment vote has been shared with parties associated with ethnic Kurdish identity, most notably the Kurdish People's Democratic Party (HADEP) in the period of this study.

Several variables associated with the penetration of Islamic institutions, as well as the historical incorporation of provinces into the state, are significant predictors of Islamist voting outcomes in statistical models. The percentage of a province's population enrolled in Qur'anic educational courses, as well as the growth in the percentage of religious buildings within a province, mirror Islamist voting patterns. Although the percentage of Turks enrolled in Qur'anic courses is not particularly high compared with many Islamic countries, this may be an indicator of a broader institutional commitment to Islamic instruction and association that is not measured by the government. In all statistical models, enrollment in Qur'anic schools was the most reliable predictor of Islamist voting patterns.

Additionally, provinces that saw increases in mosque and other religious building construction over recent decades tend to vote for Islamist parties at a higher rate. Provinces in which religious institutions have expanded tend to be more willing to support religious entrepreneurs at the ballot box, but the causal link behind this relationship is complex. Most mosques are built with the approval of the national bureaucracy, and thus rewarding voters at the provincial level through mosque construction may be difficult; nevertheless, many of these mosques were built during the period of Islamist successes in the provinces at both the national and local levels. Mosque construction appears to be both a precedent and an antecedent to Islamist electoral success.

Provinces in high, mountainous[51] territory are more likely to vote for Islamist parties than other provinces, both before and after socioeconomic and ethnic control variables are taken into account. This geographical variable is used as a proxy for poor regional incorporation into the state. Most of these mountainous provinces are isolated and difficult to reach from Ankara and Istanbul, leading to a historical distance from government centers. The models suggest that mountainous provinces average 5 percent higher electoral returns for Islamist parties (within a provincial average voting range of about 5–30% of the electorate).

Poor incorporation into the economy in the form of unemployment also increases the likelihood of Islamist voting at the rate of close to 2.5 percent additional electoral support for every percentage increase in unemployment. Interestingly, the distance a province is from the historic state center of Istanbul yields mixed results. While provinces farther away from Istanbul tend to vote for Islamists at a greater rate, in the more complete models that include mountainous territory and socioeconomic indicators, there is a slight negative effect for distance, likely because many of the mountainous provinces of the far east have lower Islamist rates than mountainous provinces of East-Central Anatolia.

A summary of statistical models of Islamist provincial voting is provided in Table 5.2. Overall, provincial voting patterns suggest that socioeconomic indicators are unreliably correlated with Islamist voting, with the exception of unemployment rates, which appear to have some impact. On the other hand, variables that highlight religious institutional penetration as well as poor provincial incorporation into the state are more strongly correlated with provincial variation. These results are discussed in their broader context in the following sections.

TABLE 5.2 *Turkish Provincial Correlates of Islamist Voting*

| | Model | | | |
|---|---|---|---|---|
| **Dependent variable:** | | | | |
| Average % voting for Islamist parties by province (1970–2000) | | | | |
| **Independent variables:** | | | | |
| Constant | −11.28 (0.502) | 5.85 (0.005) | 6.38 (0.001) | −0.76 (0.926) |
| HDI | −0.022 (0.129) | | | −0.006 (0.509) |
| Unemployment rate | 2.40 (0.082) | | | 2.37 (0.038) |
| Urbanization | 0.032 (0.639) | | | 0.089 (0.092) |
| % Urban | −8.21 (0.340) | | | 8.07 (0.218) |
| Traditional family | 10.07 (0.156) | | | 6.48 (0.251) |
| Literacy rate | 0.439 (0.087) | | | |
| Hotel beds | −70.40 (0.141) | | | |
| Kurdish | | | 8.37 (0.001) | 3.54 (0.220) |
| Alevi | | | 3.87 (0.028) | 3.48 (0.039) |
| Mosque growth | | 26.17 (0.005) | 17.26 (0.040) | 19.41 (0.025) |
| Qur'anic schools | | 11.58 (0.001) | 16.67 (0.000) | 18.53 (0.000) |
| Mountainous | | 4.63 (0.015) | 4.42 (0.018) | 5.02 (0.008) |
| Distance from Istanbul | | 0.002 (0.273) | −0.002 (0.404) | −0.006 (0.019) |
| Adjusted R-squared | 0.254 | 0.346 | 0.492 | 0.571 |

## INSTITUTIONAL CONTEXTS FOR ENTREPRENEURSHIP

Ever since Atatürk's secularizing reforms in the first half of the twentieth century, there have been considerable opportunities for religious entrepreneurship in Turkey, but within a political system that often posed rigid constraints. Religious entrepreneurship has been supported by periods of instability in state–Islam relations, in which there has been an open cultural market for interpretations of the role of Islam in Turkish society. Although the state has been an active supplier of these interpretations, the dynamism of state–Islam relations and the inability of the state to penetrate many social institutions meant that a number of non-state interpretations of Islam's role also emerged. Religious entrepreneurs benefited from changing patterns of state–society relations because social instability increased demand for public understanding of the role of religion in Turkish politics.

Political competition between Westernist modernizers and religious conservatives was an important feature in the later periods of the Ottoman Empire and continued into the early Turkish Republican period from 1923 onward. The secularizing reforms initiated by the original Kemalist regime targeted a number of symbols of religious piety, including dress, language, religious brotherhoods, and, most notably, the institution of the Islamic

Caliphate. These reforms turned simple traditional acts, such as wearing the fez, into political acts of defiance against the new regime. As Atatürk's reforms were increasingly forced upon unwilling conservative segments of the population, Islamic symbolism and public religious activity became increasingly associated with a political position opposed to the project of "modernization."

The demise of the Islamic caliphate headquartered in Istanbul also had an important impact on the structure of Islamic institutions, as traditional Islamic hierarchies weakened and split off from central control. The clerical class was partly incorporated into the new state and partly dispersed among other roles. A wide variety of mystical brotherhoods, while providing an early challenge to the secular reforms, generally sought to avoid state persecution by going underground and retreating into more isolated and secretive communities after 1925. With the weakening, fragmentation, and dispersion of Islamic hierarchies, the chances of successful in-group policing of religious entrepreneurs diminished considerably.

On the other hand, the republican state increasingly sought control over Islamic institutions and public Islamic practice, primarily through the Directorate of Religious Affairs and other bureaucratic agencies. The state increasingly tried to take control of mosques and programs for advanced religious training. This led to a number of constraints on religious entrepreneurship from outside Islamic groups themselves, as the state sought to raise the costs for any public Islamic activity outside the boundaries of bureaucratic purview.[52]

Initially the distance between the incentives of the state and those of the religious elite was very large, as the state attempted to remove the autonomy of religious leaders and dismantled prominent Islamic institutions such as the Caliphate. Over time, however, as more and more of the *ulema* were incorporated into the state directly as bureaucrats, and as the career path to Islamic service depended on successful relationships with state employees, the incentives of the Islamic elite became increasingly attached to those of the state.

By the second half of the twentieth century, most of what could be considered the religious elite had found some accommodation with the Turkish government, and few challenges to the state from the class of religious elite emerged. However, the pattern of state–society relations and the structure of the religious hierarchy still allowed many opportunities for religious entrepreneurship from outside the religious elite. Experiments in political liberalization in the late 1940s translated into democratic contestation in which the relationship between the state and Islam became an issue with considerable political salience. Religious entrepreneurship, therefore, could be translated into significant political advantage, particularly among the more traditional and religious classes of Turkey that had long felt alienated by the republican regime. In addition, as a result of the bureaucratization of Islamic governance, non-state Islamic hierarchies were weakened and marginalized. They thus had little ability to police religious entrepreneurs in the political arena who were intent on challenging the state. The task of policing religious entrepreneurs fell almost entirely to the state itself, a task that inherently politicized public Islam.

As the one-party Turkish system began to liberalize in the 1940s, political actors opposed to Atatürk's Republican People's Party (Cumhuriyet Halk Partisi, RPP) found it advantageous to tap into conservative discontent with the secularizing modernist project. Initial democratic competition forced both the RPP and its main challenger, the Democratic Party (Democrat Parti), to court the traditional Islamic vote. After the Democratic Party handed the ruling RPP a national electoral defeat in 1950, it offered a number of concessions to its religiously oriented constituency, for which the RPP and military accused it of undermining the secular character of the state. The state's position on religious issues thus became further entwined with political posturing as democratic competition became a reality.

By the late 1960s, political events provided the opportunity for entrepreneurs to politicize Islam from another direction. Left-wing violence triggered a right-wing nationalist reaction, which, despite its secular roots, strategically began to add an Islamic element into the anti-communist agenda. Islam became newly associated with right-wing nationalism and was directly channeled into politics through Erbakan's creation of the National Order Party (1970) and National Salvation Party (1973). Islamists received moral support with the neighboring 1979 revolution in Iran and became increasingly visible in Turkey. A 1980 mass rally by the National Salvation Party in Konya, where participants called for a return to Islamic law (*şeriat*), provided an opportune pretext for the military coup of 1980. That the military coup occurred in this context further politicized Islam, highlighting Islamists as the preeminent anti-system political alternative.

Although the military subsequently tried to co-opt the Islamists by supporting religion as an increasingly important moral force, the onerous restrictions on personal freedom brought about by martial law and the new 1982 constitution created an environment in which religious entrepreneurs could easily utilize Islamic symbols to focus attention around state injustice. One prominent example of how Islam became politicized was the 1980 ban on headscarves in public schools. This immediately provoked public protests declaring that the move was "an act against Islam" (Howe 2000:103). The decision to ban the headscarf turned a religious symbol into an act of political defiance. After gradual liberalization during the 1980s, enforcement of the headscarf law became more ambiguous. By 1990, Parliament passed a law that was interpreted as allowing freedom of dress at universities unless it proved too controversial, which meant different things in different places. By the latter part of the 1990s, however, the military found the increasing proliferation of headscarves a political threat. In 1998, the Ministry of

Education again banned any religious clothing at schools and universities. Mass student demonstrations followed at places such as Istanbul University, whose scarf-wearing medical students were immediately prevented from taking their exams (Howe 2000).

The liberalization of media restrictions in the late 1980s and 1990s also created a new opportunity to use religious symbols in political campaigns. In the early 1980s, the state controlled all radio and television broadcasting in the country, a monopoly that was gradually eroded by Turkish-language broadcasts emanating from places such as Germany and picked up by satellite dish. Satellite receivers proliferated by the late 1980s, allowing a Turkish broadcasting market to proliferate, although without official sanction. This provided an opportunity for the Welfare Party to broadcast electoral campaigns free from direct state interference, using Islamic symbolism in presenting its political platform. In 1993, the broadcasting law was officially changed, allowing private broadcasting in Turkey. This lead to the rapid proliferation of private television and radio stations, allowing the Welfare party further freedom to pursue an Islamically oriented political campaign and to gain greater exposure.

To summarize, religious entrepreneurs in Turkey have had several structural advantages that work to support the introduction of Islam into the political arena. First, as a result of Turkey's state-led modernizing project and secularizing reforms, the relationship between Islam and the state became destabilized and open to reinterpretation. A market for religious entrepreneurship developed in which there was considerable social demand for perspectives on the role of religion in the state. Second, traditional religious hierarchies were dismantled and the religious elite became socially fragmented and marginalized. This effectively destroyed much capacity for in-group policing (in contrast to the Sufi brotherhoods of Senegal), leaving religious entrepreneurs with few obstacles to politicizing Islam apart from constraints imposed by the state itself. Third, early political liberalization (compared with other Muslim countries) introduced formal political opportunities to compete for the support of a conservative segment of the Turkish population long excluded from the state's project of modernizing reform. As a result of this extended (albeit intermittent) forum for electoral competition, religious entrepreneurs had multiple opportunities to politicize Islam and comparatively low personal cost (compared with mobilization through protest or violence).

Additionally, some structural changes over time generated new incentives to politicize Islam in certain periods. The challenge of the radical left in the late 1960s and early 1970s created a context in which Islam could position itself alongside nationalism as a viable political alternative to Marxism. Likewise, the state's tight restrictions on religious freedom imposed in the 1980s (including use of the headscarf) directly politicized manifestations of piety in a way that supported efforts of religious entrepreneurs to make Islam a political issue. Finally, the liberalization of the media in the late 1980s and early 1990s gave religious entrepreneurs new avenues through which Islamic language could be tied to political discourse.

While these changes over time suggest that attempts at religious entrepreneurship should increase,[53] there were also serious institutional challenges for religious entrepreneurs in the form of state-imposed constraints. Most directly, this came in the form of legal restrictions on political organizations taking religious platforms different from the official laicism of the state. Religious entrepreneurship was hampered by the threat of prison and political bans, although in practice this likely shaped the *content* of entrepreneurial attempts more than the *quantity* of attempts. Certainly the history of Islamist parties has shown the ability of religious entrepreneurs to mount multiple attempts to mobilize over time, even though the content of the message is often constrained due to legal limitations.

## GROWTH OF ISLAMIC INSTITUTIONS

The structural context for religious entrepreneurship in Turkey described here explains why we see active attempts by religious entrepreneurs to mobilize others around political Islam. Some of that context has existed for many decades and thus is not particularly effective at explaining changes in electoral behavior toward Islamist parties over time. The second key institutional context under consideration, the social penetration of Islamic religious institutions, may help explain long-term changes in Islamist mobilization. Islamic religious institutions are dynamic in that they grow and contract over time, although the effects of these changes are likely felt only over a period of years.

Looking at the long-term changes in Islamist electoral mobilization in Turkey, it is clear that Islamist electoral returns in Turkey grew significantly from the 1970s through the end of the century (see Table 5.1). This same period saw significant changes in Islamic institutional development in Turkey, demonstrating that growth in the social penetration of Islamic institutions preceded or at least paralleled changes in electoral behavior.

The average electoral returns for Islamists (averaging results for national elections and provincial council elections) were approximately 7–8 percent of the vote during the 1970s and 1980s, but about 18 percent in the 1990s. Although far from a dominant portion of the electorate, this was enough to make both the Welfare and Virtue parties major players either in the government or in opposition during the 1990s. Additionally, growth in electoral returns was steady for five straight elections, from the Welfare Party's national debut in 1987 until a slowdown during Virtue's participation in the 1999 combined national and local elections.

This steady growth appears correlated with an observed Islamic revival in Turkey during the late 1980s and 1990s that is manifest in many areas outside electoral behavior. Traditional religious activity declined in Turkey overall throughout large periods of the past century, as villagers became exposed to

Republican secular ideology through increased state schooling and rapid urbanization. However, a renewed "modern" emphasis on religious fundamentals has been noted in large segments of society since the 1980s (Howe 2000). It is clear that the scope and level of popular exposure to Islamic discourse increased during the late 1980s and 1990s. The 1970s also show signs of increased public exposure to Islamic symbolic language over previous periods, although the parallel growth of the left during the 1970s exposed some segments of the population to increased secularization.

How and why did this increased religious exposure take place? In the late 1960s and 1970s, Islamic activists emerged in an effort to counter the dominant radical ideology of the period, that of Marxism and its communist variations. The propagation of leftist ideology stirred Turkish nationalists and religious leaders to insist on the Islamic character of Turkey. Nationalist discourse often incorporated the Muslim faith as an element of the distinctive Turkish character, a position that continued to find support through the 1980s under the notion of a Turkish-Islamic synthesis (Türk-İslam sentezi). This idea of a synthesis was established in the 1970s as a number of conservative public intellectuals and businessmen founded what were known as "Hearths of the Enlightened" (Aydınlar Ocağı). These discussion groups served as forums for social and political debate and propagated the notion that Islam was an integral part of the Turkish character. This ideology strongly influenced the dominant political party of the 1980s, the ANAP, and military leaders involved in the 1980 coup, including General (and President) Evren (Zürcher 1997:302–303).

After the military coup of 1980, the interim military government supported Islam's role in maintaining public morality and order. A course in religion and ethics was introduced into the basic school curriculum during this period, which essentially taught Sunni Islam and established religion as a source of national duty. Religious activities were further supported by the state under the first post-military government of Turgut Özal, himself a devout Muslim. Throughout this period, influential state figures appeared to have more tolerance for a revival of traditional religious brotherhoods (*tarikats*).[54] New mosques were built and schoolbooks included increasing levels of religious content, as did state-controlled broadcasts (Zürcher 1997:303–304). The increasing popularity of religious brotherhoods had a particularly strong effect on levels of exposure to Islamic symbolic language. Sufi (mystical) Islamic organizations, such as those led by Fethullah Gülen, and the enormous educational networks established as part of his movement created an extensive and deeply symbolic Islamic discourse shared by participants in these educational institutions and *tarikats*.

Three indicators of institutional penetration are useful in assessing changing Islamic institutional trends at the national level: the budget for the state-run Directorate for Religious Affairs, the number of Islamically oriented (*İmam Hatip*) junior high and high schools, and the number of religious publications. Importantly, they all point to increasing public exposure to

Islamic knowledge and institutions during the 1990s. They also show the growth of exposure to Islamic discourse during more limited periods at other times, most notably in the 1970s.

The Religious Affairs budget is an important indicator of government spending on mosques, Islamic clergy, and state-sponsored religious instruction. While this budget is officially intended to propagate the state's vision of Islam's role, the budget helps determine the extent of public exposure to Islamic discourse. For periods during the early and late 1970s, the allocated budget was comparatively high (0.8% and 0.9% of the total national budget). These levels may be attributed to state attempts to temper radical Islamic elements (that had allied with the nationalists in the fight against the left), as well as to the influence of Erbakan's National Salvation Party in making government budgetary decisions. The most significant increase in the budget, however, takes place in the years 1989–1993, in which the Religious Affairs budget remained above 1 percent of Turkey's total budget, reaching as high as 1.4 percent.[55] Some of this budget increase may be attributable to the decision to build increasing numbers of mosques, support proseltyzing activities, and expand state religious services around Turkey, further increasing exposure to Islam. This period of high spending directly preceded the Welfare Party's rise to power in the mid-1990s.

Private religious (*İmam Hatip*) schools also proliferated in spurts since the 1970s. They were designed to provide a conservative religious education to students after the mandatory five-year state education at the elementary level. The enrollment in these schools, as percentage of total school enrollment, dramatically accelerated in the late 1970s, first with junior high schools, and then with further secondary (high school) education. In the 1990s, both the number of religious schools and the percentage enrollment in these schools dramatically increased yet again. Increases in both of these periods may be attributed both to the failure of Turkish state schools to satisfy family expectations for education and to widespread campaigns by religious leaders such as Fethullah Gülen to further the principles of religious and moral instruction. By the late 1990s, the *İmam-Hatip* schools enrolled more than 15 percent of total Turkish high school students, compared with about 2 percent in 1970. The growth of these schools is a principal driver leading to increases in Islamic exposure and the development of Islamic common knowledge in Turkey.[56] See Figure 5.3.

At the provincial level, there is also evidence to suggest that Islamic institutional penetration is highly correlated with voting for Islamist parties. Cross-provincial statistical models (as presented in Table 5.2) suggest that provinces that experienced high levels of growth in mosque construction during the 1980s and 1990s[57] voted for Islamist parties at a higher rate. Additionally, provinces that sent a higher percentage of students to Qur'anic schools also voted much more strongly for Islamist parties than did other provinces. Enrollment in Qur'anic schools, in particular, is highly statistically significant in all models

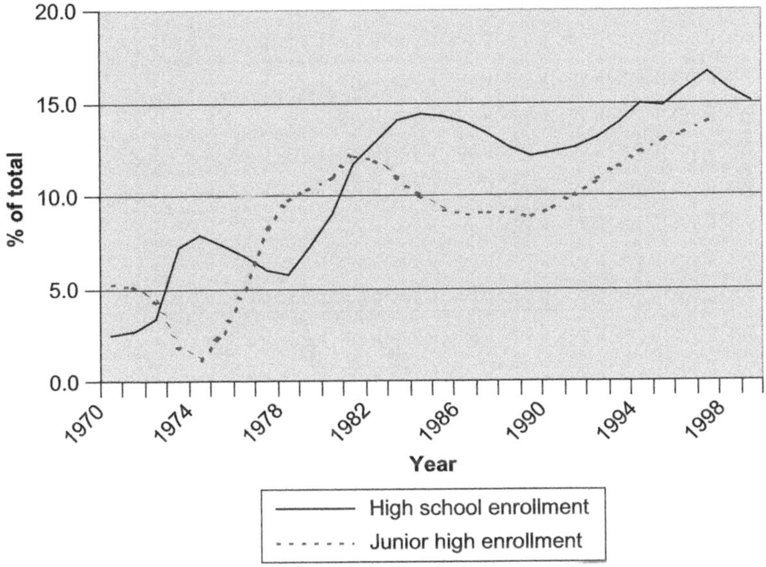


FIGURE 5.3 Percent enrollment in religious secondary schools.

as a correlate of Islamist voting, and the best predictor of Islamist support out of all available cross-provincial data.

Turkey also saw increasing numbers of religious publications during the period of the study. To the extent that their publishers are motivated by profit, this may be an indication of an increasing market for these materials. Yearly publication numbers are highly variable, but publication of religious books and periodicals, as a percentage of the total number of books and periodicals, grew significantly over several periods. The years of unrest preceding the 1980 coup d'état saw growth in religious publications. Religious books (but not periodicals) saw growth in the mid-1980s, while both religious books and periodicals saw rapid growth in their share of the publication market in the 1990s. The comparative number of religious periodicals rose significantly in the 1990s, while a dramatic increase in the number of religious books coincided with the national election victory of the Welfare Party in 1995 and its aftermath. Religious readership increased both during the period of electoral growth and in the period after the Welfare Party's popular success.[58] See Figure 5.4 and Figure 5.5.

Finally, Islamic common knowledge likely increased as a result of the enlarged organizational capacities and expanded mission of Islamist political parties themselves. The religious wings of parties such as the ANAP during the 1980s and the MHP during the 1990s also had some influence. The Welfare (1983–1997) and Virtue (1997–2001) parties were distinctive among Turkish political parties, however, in the extent of grassroots mobilization and

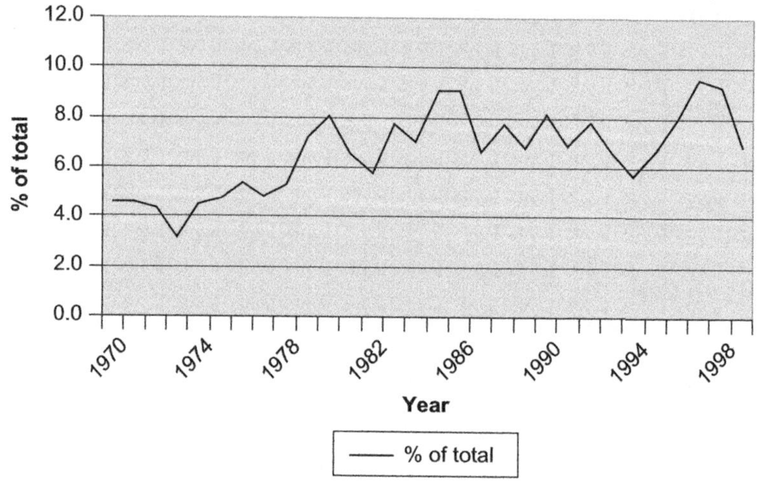


FIGURE 5.4 Religious books as percent of total books.

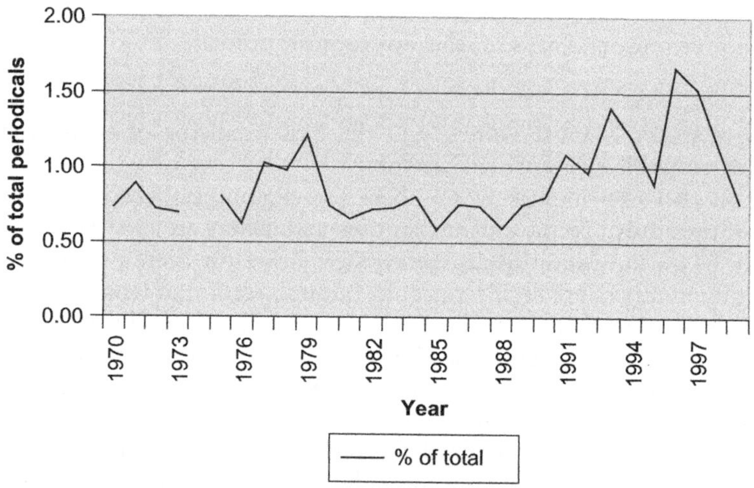


FIGURE 5.5 Religious periodicals as percent of total periodicals.

provision of social support in their constituencies (Özbudun 1999). While I do not argue here that the organizational strength and strategy of Islamist parties were the decisive factors in the growth of the Islamist electorate, the parties' grassroots organization clearly increased the spread of Islamic symbolism and its potential political implications. Financial and institutional support for the spread of Islamic discourse outside the parties were also provided in various forums during the 1980s and 1990s by Iranian and Saudi interests, although it is unclear how successful this was in building Turkish common knowledge about Islam, given divergent Islamic interests of these states.

It is clear from examining the social penetration of Islamic institutions from multiple angles that both provinces and time periods in Turkey with higher levels of institutional penetration show higher levels of voting for Islamically oriented political parties. Additionally, in many cases growth in the social reach of Islamic institutions *precedes* growth in Islamist electoral support, suggesting that explicitly religious institutional growth may be a causal factor in increasing the application of Islam in the political arena.

The theoretical claims presented in Chapter 2 hypothesize that large-scale Islamist mobilization is dependent on religious common knowledge and shared Islamic expectations, which are transmitted directly through Islamic institutions such as mosques, religious schools, and the Islamic media. While religious common knowledge at the individual level cannot be directly tested through the institutional trends presented here, an observable implication of the theory is that areas and time periods with greater social penetration of the institutional vehicles of Islamic common knowledge should be correlated with higher Islamist mobilization. This observation appears to hold in the Turkish case across multiple measures of institutional penetration.

## STATE EVENTS AS FOCAL POINTS

While clearly associated with the growth in Islamist support over a period of time, Islamic institutional variables are less helpful in explaining short-term electoral shifts either toward or away from Islamist parties. These short-term shifts in electoral support can be large, such as the shift to the Welfare Party in 1995, which eventually propelled it to the head of government. What best accounts for short-term increases in electoral support, such as those seen in the 1973 national elections and the series of elections between 1991 and 1995?

I have hypothesized that religious entrepreneurs can channel Islamic common knowledge into the political arena most effectively when public events at the state level unite collective expectations around focal points. These focal points effectively lower the costs of collective action by making coordination easier and by lowering the probability of a wasted effort (such as a "wasted" vote) or of state repression. Public crises of state order and justice are hypothesized to be particularly resonant focal points in a context of Islamic common knowledge. Rapid political liberalization may serve as an alternative type of focal point. Public state focal points can emerge or change quickly and are helpful in explaining short-term variations in Islamist support. The emergence of new focal points can lower the costs of collective action sufficiently such that even individuals without strong Islamic preferences (and thus unwilling to bear high costs) may mobilize around religious entrepreneurs as an act of protest.

While sharing some similarities to street demonstrations or political violence, individuals choosing to mobilize in elections may not directly face some of the hypothesized costs of collective action against the state. Costs of coordination around the timing of the action or anticipated costs from repression are usually lower in electoral mobilization because of the structured nature of the activity, and this has been true in Turkey. Public focal points are therefore less critical in lowering individual costs for mobilization in this context.

Focal points do help resolve one electoral coordination problem, however, which is particularly important in Turkey after 1982. The 1982 constitution established an unusually high electoral threshold (*baraj*) for proportional representation, 10 percent of the national vote. Any party that fails to capture 10 percent of the national vote is denied any seats in parliament, an effort designed to favor larger parties. Voters are thus wary of voting for a marginal party that will fall below the 10 percent threshold, thus denying them representation in parliament. A public political crisis, however, increases the expectation that non-centrist opposition parties may overcome the threshold. The crisis thus serves as a focal point in this case, lowering the expected costs (no representation in parliament) of voting for the Islamist party.

More importantly, however, public crises of political order or justice appear to have given Islamist parties a protest "bounce" in the elections under consideration. The protest vote described here does not indicate a "throw-away" vote, but indicates a vote against the political establishment as defined by the relatively homogenous centrist parties in Turkey. Islamist parties are distinctively able to absorb the votes of those disenchanted with the political system for two reasons. First, Islamic discourse of divine order and governance presents an alternative social vision to the established system, making Islamist parties, on some level, an anti-system choice (prior to 2002 in Turkey). Second, unlike the Marxist alternative, Islamists attempt to transform *existing* communal loyalties and institutional ties into political choice. The social reservoir of common knowledge regarding acceptable moral behavior, divine order, and social justice held through Islamic religious participation is an unparalleled resource for rapid and widespread coordination of protest sentiment.

Although a general lack of confidence in the state plagued Turkey for decades, variations in short-term public experience with state crisis in the study period were considerable. The effects of several manifestations of state crises of order or justice are briefly examined here: civil (left–right) violence, conflict in the Southeast over the Kurdish issue, inflation, government instability, and government corruption scandals.

Political violence in the late 1960s became an important public issue for Turkey. This escalated until clashes between left and right on university campuses, bombings, and kidnappings became common by 1970–1971. The military stepped in during 1971, forcing the government to resign and supporting a technocratic government in an attempt to curb the anarchy. Terrorist attacks after the military's intervention triggered martial law in many areas of Turkey that was to last for two years.

When democracy was restored in 1973, Erbakan's new National Salvation Party, calling for a "spiritual order" (*manevi düzen*), received almost 12 percent of the national parliamentary vote. As a reincarnation of the aborted NOP, it appears that a focus on order (and "national salvation") may have been a particular strength under the chaotic circumstances. As political violence declined during the mid-1970s, the National Salvation Party also lost some of its support and was less successful in the subsequent 1977 parliamentary elections.[59] Political violence once again spiraled out of control in the late 1970s, until the 1980 military coup that precluded further elections. The effects of this renewed political violence on Islamist electoral support thus remain undetermined.

The situation of the Kurdish areas of Southeastern Turkey during the 1970s was one of poverty, underdevelopment, and deep frustration with the state establishment in Ankara. Frustration intensified after new restrictions were placed on the Southeast after the 1980 military coup. Political violence in Kurdish areas began in force with the launching of a guerilla offensive by the Kurdistan Worker's Party (PKK) in 1984. The conflict escalated as the PKK proved to be a surprising match for the Turkish army, turning the region into a zone of military conflict for fifteen years and claiming about 40,000 lives. Throughout the period, Kurdish areas were subjected to long-term conditions of martial law, the use of terror tactics by the PKK, and forced military transfers of civilian populations.

Provinces enduring this extended crisis proved to be some of the strongest supporters of the Islamist parties at the ballot box. This support cannot effectively be attributed to the more traditional religious attitudes prevalent in the region, as traditional religious practices are not strongly correlated with voting for Islamist parties (Çarkoğlu and Toprak 2000). Neither can these votes be attributed directly to supporters of the PKK, who espoused a Marxist ideology and voted for Kurdish parties (e.g., HADEP) when the choice was available. Voting patterns show strong support for the NSP and Welfare parties in the 1977 and 1987 elections, a period of increasing disorder and concern in these provinces. Some dominantly Kurdish provinces (Mardin, Diyarbakır) showed a decline in support for the Welfare Party in 1991 due to Welfare's electoral alliance with the strongly Turkish nationalist MHP, but a large jump in Islamist electoral returns occurs in 1995.

In 1993–1994, an intensified military campaign in the region strongly, and negatively, affected Kurdish citizens. The most dramatic incident was a military bombardment of the town of Lice as revenge for the killing of a gendarme commander. The army also began a "scorched-earth" policy to contain guerillas during these years. Five hundred mountain villages were forcibly evacuated and destroyed in 1993, with nine hundred more to follow in 1994 (Zürcher 1997:327). In the 1995 national elections, the Southeast voted dominantly for the Welfare Party, which had courted the Kurdish vote with promises of equal treatment. Electoral returns in the region reached close to 30 percent, even breaking 50 percent in the province of Bingöl.

Mountainous provinces also have voted for Islamist parties more consistently than have other provinces, even when ethnicity is controlled for in statistical models (See Table 5.2). Mountains may matter to voting patterns because they often represent poor incorporation into the state, either economically, bureaucratically, or in terms of communication networks. While geographic barriers do not effectively change over time, mountainous provinces in Turkey may have developed a lack of confidence in their association with the central state during the long period of state development.[60]

Inflation has been a concern in Turkey throughout recent decades, but sharp increases in inflation rates undermine public confidence in the government's ability to provide stability and are a useful indicator of the public's perception of state crisis. In the early 1970s, inflation rates were comparatively low and stable. This changed at the end of the decade, peaking during the period of military intervention in 1980. Inflation rates started to rise again in the late 1980s, jumping to an unprecedented triple digit inflation rate during 1994. This dramatic rise in inflation rates directly coincides with the jump in votes for the Welfare Party during 1994 and 1995.[61] See Figure 5.6.

Regression analysis of the two-year previous annual average inflation rate for Istanbul on the average percentage vote for Islamist parties during election years yields a statistically significant result.[62] The analysis shows that on average, a 1 percent increase in the inflation rate within the two years prior to the election yields a 0.18 percent increase in Islamist party support (P-value 0.003, R-squared 0.74). Decline in the national economic growth rate and increasing unemployment are weakly correlated with Islamist party support at the national level. However, models of provincial support for Islamists suggest that differences in unemployment across provinces are associated with Islamist voting (See Table 5.2). This may be less an indication of a crisis of state order than an indicator of poor incorporation of these provinces into the national economy. From the data available, it appears that inequality actually decreased in the early 1990s, suggesting that changes in inequality did not determine Welfare's rise as some have suggested (see Öniş 1997). The striking significance of inflation, rather than other economic indicators, suggests that

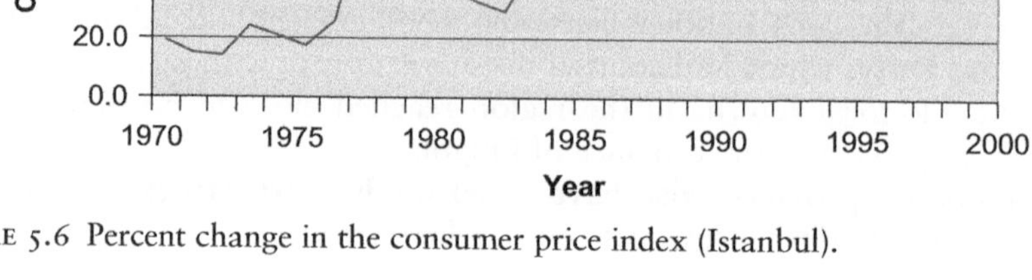


FIGURE 5.6 Percent change in the consumer price index (Istanbul).

short-term perception of state crisis (indicated by rapidly rising prices), rather than the longer-term economic outlook, influences the vote for Islamist parties.

Government instability, as indicated by the fragmentation of government support in parliament, is another useful indicator of a crisis of state confidence. Although politics during the 1960s was dominated by Süleyman Demirel and the Justice Party, by the end of the 1960s the party showed major divisions that paralyzed the government. The right wing of the Justice Party voted with the opposition in February 1970, forcing Demirel to resign as Prime Minister. When he returned to the post shortly thereafter, the right wing discussed leaving the party and a number of members of parliament left the party at the end of the year, founding the new Democratic Party (*Demokratik Parti*). By early 1971, the weakened government was incapable of moving on a constructive agenda in parliament. The paralysis of the government was a major motive for the military intervention of 1971, and was the last civilian government before voters took to the polls in 1973.

The military-sponsored government that took power in the interim itself was somewhat unstable and lacked the ability to pass the proposed reform program. The head of the government (Nihat Erim) resigned after about a year; his successor (Ferit Melen) was succeeded by another (Naim Talu) before the elections of 1973. In the meanwhile, it took fifteen ballots before parliament could agree on a new president. Government instability before the elections of 1973 may therefore help account for the high initial levels of support for the NSP (Zürcher 1997).

Government instability continued throughout the 1970s, but the NSP served as an active partner in three of the coalition governments of this period, a fact that had its own effects on the electoral results of 1977 (more in the following). The post-military 1980s, however, saw comparative governmental stability as parliament was dominated by the new, centrist ANAP. The ANAP was able to control parliament through a majority government, and was popular for a sustained period, until the end of the 1980s.

By the end of the decade, however, a conflict between the right and left wings of the party became clear, government instability increased, and the ANAP lost the elections of 1991 to Demirel's DYP. A coalition of the center-right DYP and the center-left Social Democratic People's Party (Sosyaldemokrat Halkçı Parti, SHP) came to power, finding itself in constant conflict with (now President) Turgut Özal from the ANAP. The coalition was also in constant danger of falling apart. Stability did not improve when Demirel took the Presidency following Özal's sudden death in 1993, as the SHP was constantly threatened by the other leftist parties and the DYP was under pressure to move right from business circles. The rise of the Welfare Party therefore paralleled a period of decreasing governmental stability, a condition to which its own rise eventually came to contribute.

Finally, it must be noted that government corruption took its toll on the public's confidence in the state, and that the electoral growth of the Welfare

Party paralleled a number of important revelations about state corruption. The Welfare Party was particularly able to benefit from the dissatisfaction caused by public revelations of corruption because of its claims to religious piety and its long focus on anti-corruption through establishment of a moral order. In the late 1980s, a series of corruption allegations rocked the Özal government. During the economic privatization process initiated by Özal, much money was to be had by receiving government favors. A series of ANAP party leaders and government ministers were forced to resign as a result of ties to business scandals. Özal's own family made vast amounts of money during the process of economic liberalization, a fact that became increasingly public by 1990.

The True Path government of the early 1990s, likewise, was accused of gross corruption. Accusations targeted Prime Minister Tansu Çiller after taking office in 1993. She was eventually accused of illegally obtaining up to $50 million in personal wealth during her time as head of government. The Motherland Party after Özal's death also had to fend off corruption allegations, including those targeting the new party leader, Mesut Yılmaz. Additionally, corruption in provincial and municipal governments was widely considered endemic to Turkey, a fact that helped catapult Welfare Party mayors to the head of local government in Istanbul and Ankara in 1994. Widespread perception that these mayors effectively worked to combat corruption appears to have provided a further boost to the Welfare Party in the national elections of 1995.

On a number of different levels, therefore, crises of state order and justice have been evident at several moments in recent Turkish history. In the early 1970s, this was largely the result of widespread civil violence and a perception of government deadlock and instability. In the late 1980s and early 1990s, parallel to Welfare's electoral gains, the state crisis was multi-faceted and increasingly severe. It involved the government's demonstrated inability to control the situation in the Kurdish Southeast, increasing political fragmentation and deadlock in the capital, spiraling inflation, and regular revelations of state corruption. These indicators of state crisis are highly correlated with a boost in votes for opposition Islamist parties, through which a significant amount of protest against government action (or government inaction) was channeled.

Up to the point of the Welfare Party taking control of government in 1996, the Turkish state did not significantly respond to increased levels of Islamist electoral mobilization through deliberate attempts to either liberalize or repress the Islamists. The 1980 military coup occurred in the context of increased Islamic radicalism, but was not aimed specifically at Islamists. Limited liberal reforms of 1989–1991 deleted articles from the penal code that banned political parties on the base of class or religion, but in practice, the secular establishment still had considerable leverage to prevent the use of religion in politics. To some extent, however, these liberal reforms may have lowered the costs (the potential lack of representation) of voting for the Welfare Party in the 1990s and may have provided greater political space for Welfare to introduce Islamic discourse into its campaign.

Periods in which a public state crisis of order is present are thus predictive of the relative success of the Islamists at the ballot box in subsequent elections. The emergence of these focal points prior to elections thus helps explain short-term spikes in Islamist success within the overall trend of increasing Islamist support over the past three decades. While it is difficult to directly link one particular focal event to the combined response of the electorate toward Islamist parties, the theory suggests that the public crises of order outlined here should lower the costs of individual coordination around the Islamist alternative and result in the observed increases in Islamist electoral mobilization.

## ISLAMISTS AND THE STATE

The Turkish case demonstrates two important interactions between Islamists and the state that are likely to affect the overall levels of Islamist mobilization. The first is that Islamists in Turkey managed to capture a portion of state power through participation in government on multiple occasions. The second is that the state actively worked to repress the Islamist movement through party closures and political bans, raising the costs of mobilization. Both Islamist participation in the government and state repression are useful in understanding why there was some decline in Islamist electoral support during three periods: 1973–1977, 1977–1984, and 1995–1999.

If political mobilization brings Islamists into government, this may have two opposing effects on future levels of electoral support. First, they can use their power to support state policies and institutions that further the development of Islamic institutions, and thus further build Islamic common knowledge. Second, by associating with government, Islamists may lose a significant portion of whatever protest mobilization they may have previously achieved. As participants in government it is much more difficult for Islamists to use public state crises of order or justice as focal points around which to coordinate expectations of mobilization. Rather, any public state crisis under their watch tends to undermine their credibility and may shift the preferences of their constituency away from the Islamist platform.

A crisis of state order in the early 1970s gave the National Salvation Party an electoral boost in 1973, largely by channeling protest mobilization against the political establishment. After the elections, the NSP participated in coalition with the Republican People's Party throughout most of 1974, a second "National Front" coalition with the Justice Party from 1975 to 1977, and another short-lived coalition after the 1977 elections. In the years and months preceding the 1977 elections, therefore, the NSP was associated with the government. This association prevented them from capitalizing on the increasing political violence and economic difficulties that the government had failed to resolve.

The result was about a 20 percent drop in the NSP's 1977 electoral returns over the previous election. This was despite the NSP's effective penetration of several government ministries during the years of their participation, and their disproportionate influence over government policy when it came to religious issues. The years of NSP participation in the government, for example, were years of rapid growth in the number of *İmam-Hatip* schools. The effects of this policy influence on Islamic mobilization would become more prominent as time went on, but the decline in their support during 1977 suggests that their initial electoral returns were dependent on considerable mobilization of voters dependent on public focal points around which to coordinate expectations of protest against poor governance.

Electoral politics was put on hold by the 1980 military intervention, but when the Welfare Party emerged to compete in their first (local) elections in 1984, they registered a poor showing, with 4.4 percent of the total vote. This is probably due to several factors dependent on the nature of the military intervention. Although the memory of NSP participation in government in the late 1970s and the provocative rally that inspired the coup may have remained to some extent, other factors undoubtedly had a strong influence. The general restrictions on politics still present from the 1982 constitution dealt a strong blow to the new Welfare party. Erbakan was still banned from politics and prevented from campaigning as the party leader, while the introduction of electoral thresholds raised the costs of voting for a new, minor party. Most importantly, however, the new ANAP that competed in the national elections of 1983 had previously absorbed much of the religious vote. It was seen as the most credible anti-establishment party because of its direct challenge to the generals' choice in that election. This also helped it capture the protest mobilization that may have otherwise gone to the Islamists.

Governmental repression of Islamists raises the costs of Islamist mobilization by making political participation difficult. While this risks creating a focal point around the injustice of the repression, it may also limit the spread of Islamic institutions and shift protest mobilization by those with tentative Islamist loyalties to other outlets in which participation is less costly (e.g., alternative anti-establishment parties). The 1980 military coup did not focus repression explicitly on the Islamists, and thus did not generate an Islam-specific focal point nor undermine Islamic religious institutions. By banning Islamist parties while letting other parties compete, however, the intervention shifted much of the previous mobilization away from the Islamists to another outlet, the new ANAP.

The final, and most interesting decline in the Islamist vote occurred between 1995 and 1999. The decline was considerable and somewhat unexpected, for it broke a five-election trend of increasing support for the Islamist party. The national parliamentary returns dropped from 21.4 percent to 16.4 percent, about 20 percent from their high point. Local election returns also declined compared with those in 1994, although to a lesser extent. This drop may be largely explained by the confluence of both previous participation in government and the effects of the anti-Islamist military efforts that began in 1997.

During the year that Erbakan spent as prime minister, it was clear that his leverage to change state policy was limited. The military showed signs of increasing independence, while his coalition partner (DYP) seemed, at times, to be running a separate government. Due to the significant political constraints of keeping both the coalition together and the military at bay, Welfare accomplished little of its campaign agenda and made a number of concessions that contradicted the Welfare Party's earlier positions.[63] The party's early decision not to support a corruption investigation into its coalition partner was upheld after an even larger scandal was revealed in November 1996, when a car crash in the village of Susurluk exposed connections between Welfare's coalition party, the police, and the Turkish mafia. The Welfare-led government seemed to work to obstruct investigation into the affair, protecting the partner that kept it in government.

The Welfare Party's direct association with an ineffectual and scandal-tainted administration is likely the most significant reason for the drop in Islamist electoral support in 1999. While the Islamist cause certainly benefited from a growth in public exposure to Islamic discourse and the support for Islamic institutions under the government, there are reasons to believe that a significant portion of the 1995 vote was protest mobilization, and that the period of Welfare in government deprived the subsequent Virtue party of this mobilization. During the 1996–1997 government, the Islamist movement contradicted its "anti-system" image by participating in some of the unsavory activities common to Turkish politics, and became more of a "normal" Turkish political party in the process.

The public military campaign to weaken the Islamists' political power, which began in 1997, also decreased public exposure to Islamic institutions and discourse. The military's agenda included pressuring the government to change the law on compulsory state schooling, increasing the mandatory number of years in state schools from five years to eight. This had the primary effect of making religious junior high schools illegal, closing down hundreds of these *İmam-Hatip* schools. Subsequently, graduates from *İmam-Hatip* high schools were also prevented from attending any university departments outside of theology, with the determined intention of limiting the attraction of these schools. Dress standards limiting the use of the headscarf in public institutions were increasingly rigid and enforced. Controls on religious brotherhoods were tightened, while new restrictions on Islamically oriented business were instituted in an effort to provide some financial obstacles to the growth of the Islamist movement.

State repression after 1997 also created new focal points around which to coordinate Islamist expectations, however. This was most obvious in turning Islamic expectations about appropriate education into street protests surrounding the closure of religious schools. The new educational policy encouraged many devout but apolitical Muslims who wanted to send their children to these schools to protest against the state. Through all of these policies, the state increasingly framed signs of religious activity as anti-systemic, giving public religious displays in any form greater political connotations.

Government repression in the period after 1997 may have also contributed to lower Islamist support in the subsequent election because many protest voters shifted their votes to alternative anti-system parties. Although repression may increase Islamist mobilization in the absence of other alternatives, in 1999 there were other protest parties available in the election that absorbed some of the Islamist support. Most notably, two significant non-systemic parties in the form of the far right MHP and the pro-Kurdish HADEP captured a large number of voters who cast their votes for Welfare in 1995. They did so because the repression that ousted the Islamists from power raised the costs of voting for the Virtue Party among voters without strong Islamic preferences. The costs were not personal costs of anticipated repression, but the perceived costs of a lack of representation now that it was public knowledge that the state establishment would not allow the Islamic party to participate in government.

The decline in Islamist electoral support between 1995 and 1999 is therefore the result of a number of effects. The association of Erbakan's party with government, and with a deadlocked, ineffectual, and scandal-tainted government at that, had the significant effect of decreasing the protest component of the Islamist electoral mobilization evident in 1995. Repression of the Islamists from 1997 onward also had the combined effect of lowering their electoral support in 1999. While the repression increasingly politicized Islam, it also decreased the level of public exposure to Islamic institutions and further shifted protest mobilization toward alternative parties.

## CONCLUSION

The elections of 1999 were notable elections from the perspective of the Islamist movement in Turkey because they demonstrated an equilibration of Islamist electoral support. After the closure of the Virtue Party in 2001, however, the Islamist movement underwent a transformation. The movement not only split into two parties marked by different generational support and different political strategies, but the more religiously moderate of the two new parties, the AKP, dominated the field during the 2002 elections and captured parliament. By contrast, the Felicity Party performed poorly and did not win sufficient votes to return to parliament. The AKP's success dramatically changed the dynamics of Turkish parliamentary politics as one party won the majority of seats in the Turkish Grand National Assembly for the first time in fifteen years.

Following patterns of Islamist voting in previous elections, the AKP's victory came at a time of acute economic turmoil (the worst recession in Turkey since World War II), parliamentary disorder and deadlock, and new corruption scandals. The early periods of government under the AKP, however, witnessed remarkable economic recovery and governmental stability despite continued policy challenges on a number of fronts. The tenure of the AKP in government was subsequently marked by sustained economic growth, a broad expansion of Turkish diplomatic activity, and ongoing conflict between the governing party and the broader state, in particular the military and national courts. Despite sympathies for Islamic values, the AKP grew inclusive of a wide range of ideologies, significantly transforming itself both ideologically and organizationally beyond the Islamist parties of previous decades. It continued to win government office over a period of more than a decade.

The extensive Turkish experience with political Islam since 1970, and the experience with electoral mobilization in particular, yields several insights in assessing theories of Islamist political mobilization. First, broad socioeconomic arguments about the sources of mobilization do not appear to receive much support in the Turkish case. Provincial variations in human development indicators, urbanization, traditional family structures, and indicators of a tourist economy are not strongly correlated with Islamist electoral mobilization. Likewise, trends in economic equality and national unemployment over time are not predictive of Islamist voting. Two economic indicators do matter at levels of statistical significance, however. These are provincial variations in unemployment rates and national spikes in inflation rates. I interpret these relationships here as indicators of poor regional integration into the national economy (provincial unemployment rates) and of the inability of the state to control economic instability (high and unstable national inflation rates).

Second, the Turkish experience demonstrates the potential for religious entrepreneurship in societies undergoing structural shifts in the relationship between religious elites and the state, when the traditional religious elite are fragmented and dispersed, and when parts of religious society are poorly incorporated into state institutions. Since the bold state-led social reforms of the early twentieth century that sought to redefine the place of Islam in Turkish society, the Turkish state has provided ample (if often unwanted) opportunity for reinterpretation of the state–Islam relationship from many perspectives. At the same time, traditional religious hierarchies were destroyed during the process of modernization, leaving little opportunity for Islamic in-group policing of entrepreneurship outside of the state. Interestingly, religious entrepreneurship through local branches of Islamist parties appears most successful in mountainous areas poorly incorporated into the state, suggesting that areas with fewer state ties may be more open to religious entrepreneurship than those whose interests are better aligned with the state.

Third, growth in the penetration of Islamic religious institutions, particularly Islamic schools, mosques, and media, are associated with long-term growth of Islamist mobilization in the political arena. As Turkish society has become more exposed to Islamic schooling, local religious buildings have been built at an increasing pace, and Islamic media have grown as a portion of total media consumed, Islam has also found a more prominent place in politics. Much of the growth in Islamic institutions precedes developments in the political arena, although as Islamic parties gained a measure of state power they were able to further support the growth of religious institutions. Turkish provinces with larger percentages of students in Qur'anic schools and higher levels of mosque growth also supported Islam in the political arena at a greater rate than other provinces. The growth of religious institutions helped to shape Islammic preferences over time, creating an environment supportive of greater religious entrepreneurship.

Fourth, prominent state crises of order and/or justice are associated with short-term jumps in electoral support for Islamist parties. In Turkey, these crises tend to be in the form of civil (but not Islamist) violence, parliamentary deadlock and collapse, spikes in inflation rates, and public corruption scandals. These public state events are incorporated into the rhetoric and message of Islamically oriented parties, which focused on Islamic visions of order and justice in their campaign messages. Short-term jumps in Islamist electoral success followed these public crises as Islamist parties garnered a significant amount of protest votes. These crises can serve as focal points around which public protest can be channeled through Islamic political entrepreneurs.

Finally, the relationship of the Islamist movement to the state, whether through participation in government institutions or through government repression of Islamists, impacts the level of support for Islamist parties.[64] In the Turkish case these interactions with the state help account for short-term drops in support for the Islamist movement over time. Through participation in government, Islamist parties lose the opportunity to coordinate Islamic common knowledge around public state crises, and voters may retrospectively punish them because of their observed inability to resolve those crises. Likewise, in a political structure in which protest toward the state can be channeled through multiple parties or institutions, repression of the Islamist movement can send voters to less costly and potentially more successful alternatives such as nationalist or ethnic parties.

One of the remarkable successes of the AKP party has been its ability to break out of this cycle that characterized Turkish Islamist parties from the 1970s through the 1990s. The large number of protest voters that initially voted for the AKP as an opposition party in the 2002 elections remained with the party for a significant period of time, supporting it during a decade in which the party helped to stabilize the Turkish economy and political system. The AKP's transformation from a traditional Turkish Islamist party may have been one critical step in maintaining the support of these voters and realigning the political center in Turkish politics. The longer-term future of the AKP is unclear as increasingly authoritarian measures began to trigger increasing levels of protest against the party, including substantive protests against the governing party in 2013.

## REFERENCES


Ahmad, Feroz. 1977. *The Turkish Experiment in Democracy, 1950–1975*. London: Hurst & Co.

1988. "Islamic Reassertion in Turkey." *Third World Quarterly* 10/2: 750–769.

Akarlı, Engin D. and Gabriel Ben Dor. 1975. *Political Participation in Turkey: Historical Background and Present Problems*. Istanbul: Boğaziçi University Press.

Akdoğan, Yalçın. 2000. *Siyasal Islam: Refah Partisi'nin Anatomisi*. Istanbul: Şehir Yayınları.

Akel, Ali. 1998. *Erbakan ve Generaller*. Istanbul: Şura Yayınları.

Akinci, Uğur. 1999. "Municipal Radicalism of Political Islam in Turkey." *Middle East Journal* 53/1: 76–91.

Aktuğ, Emel. 1997. "Welfare Party's Latest Situation." *Turkish Daily News*, 23 May.

Alkan, Türker. 1984. "The National Salvation Party in Turkey." *Islam and Politics in the Modern Middle East*. New York: St. Martin's Press, 79–102.

Arjomand, Said Amir, ed. 1984. *From Nationalism to Revolutionary Islam*. London: Macmillan.

Arslan, Ahmet. 1999. *Islam, Demokrasi ve Türkiye*. Ankara: Vadi Yayınları.

Ayata, Sencer. 1993. "The Rise of Islamic Fundamentalism and Its Institutional Framework." In Eralp, Tünay, and Yeşilada, eds. *The Political and Socioeconomic Transformation of Turkey*. Westport, CT: Praeger.

Aykol, Hüseyin. 1996. Türkiye'de Sağ ve İslamcı Örgütler. Istanbul: Pelikan Yayınları.

Balçi, Kemal. 1999. "FP Unable to Rid Itself of Erbakan's Specter." *Turkish Daily News*, 11 March.

Balım, Ç., E. Kalaycıoğlu, C. Karataş, G. Winrow, F. Yasamee, eds. 1995. *Turkey: Political, Social and Economic Challenges in the 1990s*. Leiden: E.J. Brill.

Bayramoğlu, Ali. 2001. *28 Şubat: Bir Müdahalenin Güncesi*. Istanbul: Birey Yayıncılık.

Belovacikli, Mete. 2001. "New Shape of Opposition." *Turkish Daily News*, 25 June.

Berkes, Niyazi. 1997. *The Development of Secularism in Turkey*. London: Hurst & Co.

Bianchi, Robert. 1984. *Interest Groups and Political Developments in Turkey*. Princeton, NJ: Princeton University Press.

Birand, Mehmet Ali. 1987. *The Generals' Coup in Turkey: An Inside Story of 12 September 1980*. Translated by M.A. Dikerdem. London: Brassey's Defense Publishers.

1991. *Shirts of Steel: An Anatomy of the Turkish Armed Forces. Translated by Saliha Paker and Ruth Christie*. London: I.B. Tauris.

2000. "Everybody Wants the Virtue Party Closed Down!" *Turkish Daily News*, 27 October.

Çakır, Ruşen. 2000. *Direniş ve İtaat: İki İktidar Arasında İslamcı Kadın*. Istanbul: Metis Yayınları.

2001. *Derin Hizbullah: Islamcı Şiddetin Geleceği*. Istanbul: Metis Yayınları.

Çakır, Ruşen and Fehmi Çalmuk. 2001. *Recep Tayyip Erdoğan: Bir Dönüşüm Öyküsü*. Istanbul: Metis Yayınları.

Çalışlar, Oral 1995. *RP Nereden Nereye*. Istanbul: Pencere Yayınları.

Çalışlar, Oral and Tolga Çelik. 2000. *Erbakan-Fethullah Gülen Kavgası: Cemaat ve Tarikatların Siyasetteki 40 Yılı*. Istanbul: Sıfır Noktası Yayınları.

Çalmuk, Fehmi. 2001. *Erbakan'ın Kürtleri: Milli Görüş'ün Güneydoğu Politikası*. Istanbul: Metis Yayınları.

Çarkoğlu, Ali and Binnaz Toprak. 2000. *Türkiye'de Din, Toplum ve Siyaset*. Istanbul: Türkiye Ekonomik ve Sosyal Etüdler Yayınları.

Cemal, Hasan. 1997. *Sabah*, 9 December.

Çevik, Ilnur. 1998. "What Label Should We Put on Our System?" *Turkish Daily News*, 23 December.

1999a. "The New Struggle Within the Virtue Party." *Turkish Daily News*, 27 April.

1999b. "Virtue Party May Face Credibility Problem." *Turkish Daily News*, 23 March.

Cevizoğlu, Hulki. 1998. *28 Şubat: Bir Hükümet Nasıl Devrildi*. Istanbul: Beyaz Yayınları.

Çiçek, Hikmet. 1997. *İrticaya Karşı Genelkurmay Belgeleri*. Istanbul: Kaynak Yayınları.

Dodd, Clement H. 1979. *Democracy and Development in Turkey*. Huntingdon: Eothen.

1990. *The Crisis of Turkish Democracy*. 2nd ed. Huntingdon: Eothen.

Dumont, Paul. 1987. "Islam and a Factor of Change and Revival in Modern Turkey." In Sabri M. Akural, ed. *Turkic Culture: Continuity and Change*. Bloomington: Indiana University Press.

1986. *Radicalismes Islamiques*. Paris: L'Harmattan.

Eligür, Banu. 2010. *The Mobilization of Political Islam in Turkey*. Cambridge: Cambridge University Press.

Eralp, Atila, Muharram Tünay, and Birol Yeşilada, eds. 1993. *The Political and Socioeconomic Transformation of Turkey*. Westport, CT: Praeger.

Erbakan, Necmettin. 1975. *Millî Görüş*. Istanbul: Dergâh Yayınları.

1991a. *Adil Ekonomik Düzen*. Ankara: Aralık Yayınları.

1991b. *Türkiye'nin Temel Meseleleri*. Ankara: Rehber Yayınları.

Ergin, Serdar. 1998. *Hurriyet*, 12 July.

Geyikdağı, Mehmet Yaşar. 1984. *Political Parties in Turkey: The Role of Islam*. New York: Praeger.

Girdner, Eddie J. 1999. "The Twilight of Refah: Turkey and the Islamist Welfare Party." *Scandinavian Journal of Development Alternatives and Area Studies* 18/4: 31.

Gülalp, Haldun. 1999. "Political Islam in Turkey: The Rise and Fall of the Refah Party." *Muslim World* 89/1: 22–41.

2001. "Globalization and Political Islam: The Social Bases of Turkey's Welfare Party." *International Journal of Middle East Studies* 33/3: 433–448.

Güner, Ahmet. 1986. *Tarikatlar*. Istanbul: Milliyet Yayınları

Güneş-Ayata, Ayşe. 1994. "Roots and Trends of Clientelism in Turkey." In Luis Roniger and Ayşe Güneş-Ayata, eds. *Democracy, Clientelism and Civil Society*, 49–64. Boulder, CO: Lynne Rienner.

Gür, Metin. 1997. *Şeriat ve Refah*. Istanbul: Çağdaş Yayınları.

Hale, William. 1976. *Aspects of Modern Turkey*. New York: Bowker.

1984. *Turkish Politics and the Military*. New York: Routledge.

Harris, George S. 1985. *Turkey: Coping with Crisis*. Boulder, CO: Westview.

Hefner, Robert W. 2000. *Civil Islam: Muslims and Democratization in Indonesia*. Princeton, NJ: Princeton University Press.

Heper, Metin. 1985. *The State Tradition in Turkey*. Huntingdon: Eothen.

1997. "Islam and Democracy in Turkey: Toward a Reconciliation?" *Middle East Journal* 51/1: 32.

Heper, Metin and Ahmet Evin, eds. 1988. *State, Democracy, and the Military: Turkey in the 1980s*. New York: Walter de Gruyter.

1994. *Politics in the Third Turkish Republic: The Transition to Democracy*. Boulder, CO: Westview.

Heper, Metin and Jacob M. Landau, eds. 1991. *Political Parties and Democracy in Turkey*. London: I.B. Tauris.

Heper, Metin, Ayşe Öncü, and Heinz Kramer, eds. 1993. *Turkey and the West: Changing Political and Cultural Variables*. London: I.B. Tauris.

Howe, Marvine. 2000. *Turkey Today: A Nation Divided Over Islam's Revival*. Boulder, CO: Westview.

Kalaycıoğlu, Ersin. 1994. "Türkiye'de Köktenci Sağ Partiler ve Seçmen Tercihleri." *Toplum ve Ekonomi* 7/69 (October): 65–84.

Kalyvas, Stathis N. 1996. *The Rise of Christian Democracy in Europe*. Ithaca, NY: Cornell University Press.

Kalyvas, Stathis N. 2000. "Commitment Problems in Emerging Democracies: The Case of Religious Parties." *Comparative Politics* 32/4 (July): 379–398.

Kara, İsmail. 1986. *Türkiye'de İslamcılık Düşüncesi*. Istanbul: Risale Yayınları.

Karpat, Kemal, ed. 1973. *Social Change and Politics in Turkey: A Structural Historical Analysis*. Leiden: E.J. Brill.

Kedourie, Sylvia, ed. 1996. "Turkey: Identity, Democracy, Politics." *Middle Eastern Studies* 32/2.

Kirişçi, Kemal and Gareth M. Winrow. 1997. *The Kurdish Question and Turkey: An Example of Trans-State Ethnic Conflict*. London: Frank Cass.

Köktaş, M. Emin. 1997. *Din ve Siyaset, Siyasal Davranış ve Dindarlık*. Ankara: Vadi Yayınları.

Laçiner, Ömer. 1996. "Seçim Sonuçları Üzerine." *Birikim Dergisi* 81 (January): 3–10.

Landau, Jacob M. 1974. *Radical Politics in Turkey*. Leiden: E.J. Brill.

Langohr, Vickie. 2001. "Of Islamists and Ballot Boxes: Rethinking the Relationship Between Islamisms and Electoral Politics." *International Journal of Middle East Studies* 33: 591–610.

Leder, Arnold. 1976. *Catalysts of Change: Marxist versus Muslim in a Turkish Community*. Austin: University of Texas Center for Middle Eastern Studies.

Mardin, Şerif. 1989. *Religion and Social Change in Modern Turkey: The Case of Bediüzzaman Said Nursi*. Albany: State University of New York Press.

Mason, Whit. 2000. "The Future of Political Islam in Turkey." *World Policy Journal* 17/2: 56.

Mecham, Quinn. 2000. "Political Liberalization and the Future of Islamic Movements in Morocco." In Hunter, Shireen, ed. *CSIS Briefing Notes on Islam, Society, and Politics* 3/2 (September). Washington, DC: Center for Strategic and International Studies.

Middle East Report. 1996. "Turkish Women and the Welfare Party: Interview with Şirin Tekeli." *Middle East Report* 26/2: 28.

*Milliyet*. 2001. 15 August.

Norton, J.D. 1983. "Bektashis in Turkey." In Denis MacEoin and Ahmed al-Shahi, eds. *Islam in the Modern World*, 73–87. London: Croon Helm.

Olsson, Tord, Elisabeth Özdalga, and Catharina Raudvere, eds. 1998. *Alevi Identity: Cultural, Religious, and Social Perspectives*. Richmond: Curzon Press.

Öncu, Ayşe. 1995. "Packaging Islam: Cultural Politics on the Landscape of the Turkish Commercial Television." *Public Culture* 8/1: 51–71.

Öniş, Ziya. 1997. "The Political Economy of Islamic Resurgence in Turkey: The Rise of the Welfare Party in Perspective." *Third World Quarterly* 18/4: 743–66.

Özbudun, Ergun. 1976. *Social Change and Political Participation in Turkey*. Princeton, NJ: Princeton University Press.

1999. *Contemporary Turkish Politics: Challenges to Democratic Consolidation*. Boulder, CO: Lynne Rienner.

Özcan, Ahmet. 1996. *İslami Uyanıştan İslami Harekete*. Istanbul: Bengisu Yayınları.

Özdalga, Elisabeth. 1997. *Official Secularism, Popular Islam and the Veiling Issue in Modern Turkey*. Richmond: Curzon Press.

Pamuk, Muhammed. 2001. *Yasaklı Umut: Recep Tayyip Erdoğan*. Istanbul: Birey Yayıncılık.

Pope, Nicole and Hugh Pope. 1997. *Turkey Unveiled: Atatürk and After*. London: John Murray.

Poulton, Hugh. 1997. *Top Hat, Grey Wolf, and Crescent: Turkish Nationalism and the Turkish Republic*. New York: New York University Press.

Przeworski, Adam and John Sprague. 1986. *Paper Stones: A History of Electoral Socialism*. Chicago, IL: University of Chicago Press.

Robins, Philip K. 2007. "Turkish Foreign Policy Since 2002: Between 'Post-Islamist' Government and a Kemalist State." *International Affairs* 83/2 (March): 289–304.

Saktander, Ayşe. 1998. *Living Islam: Women, Politics and Religion in Turkey*. London: I.B. Tauris.

Sarıbay, Ali Yaşar. 1985. *Türkiye'de Modernleşme Din ve Parti Politikası: Milli Selâmet Partisi Örnekolayı*. Istanbul: Alan Yayınları.

Sayarı, Sabri. 1977. "Political Patronage in Turkey." In Ernest Gellner and John Waterbury, eds. *Patrons and Clients: In Mediterranean Societies*, 103–13. London: Duckworth.

Şaylan, Gencay. 1987. *İslamiyet ve Siyaset: Türkiye Örneği*. Ankara: Vadi Yayınları.

Schedler, Andreas, Larry Diamond, and Marc F. Plattner, eds. 1999. *The Self-Restraining State: Power and Accountability in New Democracies*. Boulder, CO: Lynne Rienner.

Schick, Irvin C. and Ertuğrul Agmet Tonak, eds. 1987. *Turkey in Transition: New Perspectives*. Oxford: Oxford University Press.

Şen, Serdar. 1995. *Refah Partisi'nin Teori ve Pratiği: RP, Adil Düzen ve Kapitalizm*. Istanbul: Sarmal Yayınevi.

Serter, Nur. 1997. *Dinde Siyasal İslam Tekeli*. Istanbul: Sarmal Yayınevi.

Shadid, Anthony. 2001. *Legacy of the Prophet: Despots, Democrats, and the New Politics of Islam*. Boulder, CO: Westview.

Shankland, David. 2000. *Islam and Society in Turkey*. Tallahassee, FL: Eothen Press.

State Institute of Statistics (Turkey). 1928. Statistical Yearbook of Turkey. Ankara: State Institute of Statistics. www.die.gov.tr.

1994. *Census of Population: Social and Economic Characteristics of Population, 1990*. Ankara: State Institute of Statistics.

1996. *Results of General Election of Representatives 24.12.1995*. Ankara: State Institute of Statistics. 2 vols.

1997a. *Provincial and Regional Statistics, 1994*. Ankara: State Institute of Statistics.

1997b. Statistical Indicators 1923–1995. Ankara: State Institute of Statistics.

1998a. *Cultural Statistics, 1996*. Ankara: State Institute of Statistics.

1998b. *National Education Statistics: Formal Education, 1994–1996*. Ankara: State Institute of Statistics.

1998c. *Results of General Election of Representatives 06.11.1983, 29.11.1987, 20.10.1991, 24.12.1995*. Ankara: State Institute of Statistics.

2000. *Results of Elections of Local Administration 18.04.1999*. Ankara: State Institute of Statistics.

2001. *Results of General Election of Representatives 18.04.1999*. Ankara: State Institute of Statistics.

Tapper, Richard, ed. 1991. *Islam in Modern Turkey: Religion, Politics and Literature in a Secular State*. London: I.B. Tauris.

Toprak, Binnaz. 1981. *Islam and Political Development in Turkey*. Leiden: E.J. Brill.

1984. "Politicisation of Islam in a Secular State: The National Salvation Party in Turkey." In Arjomand, *From Nationalism to Revolutionary Islam*.

1992. "Dinci Sağ." In İ. Cemil Schick and E. Ahmet Tonak, eds. *Geçiş Sürecinde Türkiye*. Istanbul: Belge Yayınları

1994. "Women and Fundamentalism." In Valentine Moghadam, ed. *Identity Politics and Women: Cultural Reservations and Feminism in International Perspective*, 292–304. London: Westview.

*Turkish Probe*. 1998. "The Week in Perspective." 25 January.

Ünal, Ismail. 2001. *Fethullah Gülen'le Amerika'da Bir Ay*. Istanbul: Işık Yayınları.

United Nations Development Program. 1997. *Human Development Report Turkey 1996*. Ankara: UNDP Office.

van Bruinessen, M. 1992. *Agha, Sheik, and State*. London: Zed Books.

Vertigans, Stephen. 2003. *Islamic Roots and Resurgence in Turkey: Understanding and Explaining the Muslim Resurgence*. Westport, CT: Praeger.

White, Jenny B. 1997. "Pragmatists or Ideologues? Turkey's Welfare Party in Power." *Current History* 96/606: 25.

2005. "The End of Islamism? Turkey's Muslimhood Model." In Robert Hefner, ed., *Remaking Muslim Politics*, 87–111. Princeton, NJ: Princeton University Press.

Wiktorowicz, Quintan. 2001. *The Management of Islamic Activism: Salafis, the Muslim Brotherhood, and State Power in Jordan*. New York: State University of New York Press.

Yalçın, Soner. 1994. *Hangi Erbakan?* Ankara: Üçüncü Basım.

Yavuz, M. Hakan 1997. "Political Islam and the Welfare (Refah) Party in Turkey." *Comparative Politics* 30/1.

Yıldırım, Ergün. 1995. *Türkiye'nin Modernleşmesi ve İslam*. Istanbul: İnsan Yayınları.

Yılmaz, Turan. 2001. *Tayyip: Kasımpaşa'dan Siyasetin Ön Saflarına*. Ankara: Ümit Yayıncılık.

Yücekök, Ahmet Nuri. 1983. *100 Soruda Türkiye'de Din ve Siyaset*. Istanbul: Gerçek Yayınevi.

Zürcher, Erik J. 1997. *Turkey: A Modern History*. London: I.B. Tauris.

# 6

# When Islam Defines Politics

## *From Voting to Violence in Algeria*

In the late 1970s, the President of the Conseil Supérieur Islamique in Algeria, Cheikh Hamani, argued that Islam is a defining aspect of all things Algerian and that this has political implications for Algeria's future. In a notable journal he stated that "Islam runs through us, as we run through Islam ... It is the religion of liberty – one must obey God only – as well as democracy" (author's translation).[1] At the time, Algeria had little in the way of liberal democracy, and Islam was considerably limited as a political force by the dominant "Arab socialist" state, or at least by the collection of military men and bureaucrats known collectively as "le pouvoir." Nevertheless, Islam had historically been used to mobilize large numbers of people against the French during the drive for independence and remained a core element of Algerian identity. Islam was thus associated with liberty from the French metropole, but was also now conceived of as a potential mechanism to limit the power of an increasingly oppressive one-party state. If Islam was both an essential component of Algerian identity and the religion of political liberty, what did this imply for the state's openness to Islamist actors?

The relationship between Islam and the Algerian state took on increasing significance throughout the 1980s and 1990s, to the point at which it became the dominant political cleavage and the largest source of public political mobilization since the war of independence that ended in 1962. Islamists would lead a diverse cross-section of Algerian society into competitive politics, dominate Algeria's first multi-party elections, direct a massive campaign of civil disobedience and social protest, and play a key role in the development of a brutal Algerian civil war during the 1990s. But at the time that Cheikh Hamani articulated his vision of Algerian Islam in 1979, none of this appeared inevitable. While Islam clearly influenced Algerian identity and political culture, during the 1970s and early 1980s it had a great many competitors for political attention.

Upon independence, the Algerian state embarked upon an official "Arabization" campaign designed to remove the lingering Francophone affections, education, and professional habits left over from France's domination of the country. In a multi-ethnic society that included a large Berber minority, this was often controversial and resulted in the amplification of ethnic tensions lingering beyond the colonial period. Likewise, Arab nationalism had affected Algeria's political world view and Algerian leaders saw the country as one of the pillars of Arabism in the wake of several successive failures of the Arab East against their avowed Zionist enemies. Additionally, Algeria was preoccupied with what it saw as indigenous applications of socialist models of industrialization that placed Algerian politics within a leftist political framework. While remaining somewhat aloof of Cold War rivalries, Algeria nevertheless focused its political and economic development on a model of one-party socialism that included the articulation of an Algerian welfare state, a state-led industrialization program, and an Arab-socialist ideology that owed much to Nasser's Egypt. With right–left, nationalist, and linguistic/ethnic competitors for Algeria's political cleavages, the dramatic rise of political Islam in Algeria during the late 1980s and 1990s requires explanation.

Compared with the experiences of Senegal and Turkey, Algeria saw much higher levels of Islamist political mobilization during the period of the study, and also more significant mobilization levels across each principal manifestation of Islamist mobilization: voting, demonstrations, and political violence. Indeed, as highlighted in Chapter 3, Algeria has one of the highest overall factor scores for Islamist mobilization of any country in the study, comparable with countries such as Pakistan and Afghanistan. While Pakistan's Islamist mobilization has been dominantly electoral and Afghanistan's has been dominantly violent (in the form of attacks by *mujahideen* militias), Algeria has experienced significant Islamist mobilization of all types. This makes it a particularly interesting case to examine in some detail, and also a case that must be addressed effectively by the theoretical predictions of Chapter 2 if they are to hold much explanatory power.

In addition to representing a case of high mobilization outcomes, Algeria shows considerable variation in mobilization outcome over time. Little Islamist mobilization was evident in the 1970s, but there were significantly higher levels in the mid- to late 1980s, with a crescendo of collective action that peaked in the early 1990s. Since 2000, violent Islamist mobilization has remained at comparably low levels, while some limited voting for Islamist parties has taken place.[2] Why did Islamist mobilization levels rise so quickly and then sustain themselves at high levels for a number of years in the 1990s before declining? In addition, why did the type of mobilization shift from protest in the 1980s to electoral mobilization in the early 1990s, back to protest, and then to a sustained campaign of violence throughout the 1990s? In what ways does this shift in Islamists' strategy and methods provide insight into the types of mobilization that can be expected in a given context?

In this chapter I argue that the theoretical predictions of Chapter 2 are directly relevant to explaining mobilization outcomes in the Algerian case. In particular, I assert that the high mobilization outcomes in the Algerian case can be explained by the convergence of three institutional contexts: (a) a rapid development of private Islamic institutions in the 1980s that created higher levels of social exposure to Islamic organizations and built Islamic common knowledge among participants in those organizations; (b) increasing autonomy of Islamic institutions coupled with a decline in state patronage resources and the subsequent unwillingness of the Islamic elite to police an increasingly fragmented field of radicalized "religious entrepreneurs"; and (c) a sequential, highly public series of internal crises of order and justice, coupled with rapid liberalization from an unpopular authoritarian regime. These focal state events activated the Islamic institutional networks in a volatile entrepreneurial religious climate and focused political attention on key mobilization opportunities. Over time, Islamist strategies for many participants migrated from protest and electoral mobilization toward a strategy of political violence as new policies of state repression made the projected individual costs of fighting the state comparable with those of abandoning Islamist demands.

This chapter addresses these arguments by first discussing the history of political mobilization in Algeria, with particular attention to the development of political Islam and manifestations of Islamist political mobilization. This includes a discussion of the key actors and political organizations that sought to mobilize Algerians on behalf of Islamist causes. Second, variations in Islamist mobilization across both time and space are discussed to highlight the variety of mobilization outcomes that resulted within the country. Third, the importance of religious entrepreneurship, the growth of Islamic institutions, and several key public focal points are each discussed in turn. The chapter concludes with a brief discussion of what the Algerian case implies for understanding the conditions under which Islamist mobilization becomes violent.

## ISLAMIST POLITICAL MOBILIZATION IN ALGERIA

The Algerian war for independence was one of the bloodiest and most protracted wars of the twentieth century. Eight years of fighting, from 1954 to 1962, between the Algerian Front de Libération Nationale (FLN) and French military forces and their French settler allies likely left over one million dead and extensively mobilized a wide section of Algerian society.[3] The numbers of dead and the range of participation that the conflict elicited from ordinary citizens during this period have led many to see this as a defining political moment in Algerian history and political culture, creating a repertoire of violence that endures as a conscious reference point in the resolution of political conflict.[4] The vast majority of those participating in this conflict did so in response to personal experience with French domination, making mobilization in the conflict best understood as nationalist in inspiration and objectives.

The nationalism of the FLN explicitly highlighted religious differences with the French as essential to Algerian nationalism, and Islamic symbols and language were used on behalf of the nationalist struggle.[5] Nevertheless, the leaders of the war of independence saw Islam in this period primarily as an identity marker of the Algerian nation rather than as an independent political cleavage with which to mobilize individuals around domestic policy objectives.

Upon independence, political mobilization was channeled through the nascent state organizations, and especially through the FLN as the sole legal political party through which to express popular political aspirations. The FLN-led state began a large-scale program of socialist-oriented industrialization, funded largely through the development of hydrocarbon revenues. In the years after independence, political life was dominated by the party, the new military establishment, and a rapidly developing bureaucracy. This bureaucracy proved an important avenue for the distribution of state patronage and for the development of a socialist welfare state. Despite the socialist inspiration of the FLN's policy objectives, the presence of hydrocarbon rents and the monopoly of political power within the party soon led to high levels of inequality and the consolidation of an elite political class disturbingly reminiscent of the Franco-Algerian elite that it had replaced. Political mobilization in the post-independence period thus largely revolved around jockeying for access to patronage resources and protesting the lack of social justice in patterns of resource distribution.

During the later colonial period some of the Islamic ulema had been active critics of the French, and upon independence a number of them tried to mobilize society to reject continued French influence in favor of Islamic values. One of the most prominent of the colonial era ulema, Abdelhamid Ben Badis, founded the Association of Algerian Ulema in the early 1930s and worked through the Islamic educational system to challenge Sufi orders that had been largely co-opted by the French. The association argued that Islam placed significant demands on the state, such as complying with Islamic principles of consultation with subjects and ruling through their consent, principles that the French state had failed to successfully adhere to in Algeria. These arguments were consistent with Algerian nationalism, and the ulema cooperated with Algerian nationalists to articulate both the collective grievances against the French metropole and Islam's role in the Algerian nation. This incorporation of Islam into nationalist politics continued after independence during the early 1960s with the creation of an Islamic organization known as al-Qiyam (Values), led by al-Hachemi Tijani.

Al-Qiyam initially felt that the FLN's vision of Arab nationalism was consistent with its push to strengthen Islamic values in society, and a number of prominent members were politically allied with Algeria's first president, Ahmed Ben Bella. It did not take long for the Islamic leaders and the state to run into disagreement, however. Ben Bella was overthrown in a coup in 1965, after which Colonel Houari Boumedienne became the chief executive and al-Qiyam lost its connections to the head of state. Al-Qiyam was subsequently closed by the regime in 1966 after the group wrote a letter of protest to Egypt's president, Gamal 'Abd al-Nasser, for executing one of the key figures of Egyptian Islamist political thought, Sayyid Qutb.

Other Islamic groups during the early post-independence period were focused primarily on *da'wa*, or Islamic proselytizing, among less dedicated Muslims. The Jama'at al-Da'wa and other da'wa groups expressed concern with some of the ideological choices of the post-independence governments and were prone to criticizing the secular-minded political elite, but used most of their energies in an effort to stop the deterioration of religious morals in society. Government policies around religious education, language, and land reform did attract the attention of various Islamic groups, however, who recognized the potential impact of these policies on their ultimate vision of a more Islamic society.[6] The independent Algerian state adopted Islam into state policy, mandating religious education in government-run schools and absorbing mosques under state bureaucratic control. While this served to give Islam the official blessing of the state and incorporated it directly into the production of Algerian nationalism, many prominent Islamic leaders were ignored or pushed aside in the process.[7] By the 1970s, this led a number of Islamic leaders to openly criticize the state.

In 1974, a prominent Islamic leader, Cheikh Abdellatif Soltani, published an important argument comparing the state's brand of socialism to that of an early apostate Islamic sect.[8] In the process, he opened the door for further criticism of the state's authoritarian socialist agenda in explicitly Islamic terms. Islamic leaders began to use university campuses as forums for mobilization of young Muslims against state policies. In contrast to the *da'wa* groups most prominent in the previous decade, the university groups were more explicitly political and looked like the beginnings of a potentially radical Islamist movement. This became most evident in the spring of 1975 when Islamists at the University of Letters and Social Sciences in Algiers attempted to force student compliance with conservative Islamic principles. Recognizing that the growing Islamist movement could prove politically useful, some within the state encouraged the presence of Islamists in the ministries of education and religious affairs in an effort to balance a perceived threat from the far left.[9]

The state formally adopted aspects of Islam into state policy with the National Charter of 1976, which articulated a vision of the Algerian state as both industrially sophisticated and religiously conservative. The charter officially recognized Islam as the religion of state and required that the president must be a Muslim. Also that same year, the sale of alcohol was restricted and Friday was made an official day of rest. The charter made some cosmetic changes to the state, but did relatively little to satisfy some Islamist demands for further attention to Islamic law. Upon release of the charter, Mahfoud Nahnah of the Algerian Muslim Brotherhood led violent protests against the state, signaling early Islamist willingness to mobilize for Islamist policy demands.

Within several years, a vigorous debate ensued over the Algerian family code as well. The Iranian revolution of 1979 provided additional inspiration for young Algerian Islamists, particularly the later leader of the Front Islamique du Salut, Ali Belhadj, but it did not have immediate political impact.[10]

Significant changes in state policy were more apparent in the years following Chadli Bendjedid's accession to the presidency in 1978. President Chadli sought to redirect the state away from the most pronounced socialist policies of the 1960s and 1970s and sought Islamist support, portraying Islamists as allies in his agenda for economic reform. The state made significant compromises with Islamist groups on cultural and educational issues, pursued an active Arabization program that strengthened the numbers enrolled in Arabic-language and Islamic instruction, supported the construction of mosques, created a state organization in support of the pilgrimage to Mecca, and facilitated the growth of religious media on television and radio. By 1984, a large new university of Islamic theology had been created in Constantine,[11] led by a prominent member of the Egyptian Muslim Brotherhood. That same year, after years of debate, a new Family Code was adopted that largely reflected the positions of conservative Islamists and enraged secular Algerian feminists.[12] These concessions to the state's newfound Islamist allies were made with the hope that successful co-optation of the Islamists would help provide political balance against the increasing numbers of government opponents from many political perspectives, including labor unions, Berber groups, and liberal democratic groups.[13]

Despite a number of policy concessions to the state's Islamist allies during the early 1980s, radical Islamists were becoming increasingly mobilized and violent. The state pursued the most violent groups and imprisoned many Islamists in the process for protesting against the state. The most violent of the Islamist groups of the early 1980s, the Mouvement Islamique Armé (MIA) led by Mustafa Bouyali, bombed a number of prominent buildings and monuments around the capital and even planned to assassinate the Prime Minister. After several years of eluding the police, Bouyali was killed in a fight in 1987.

One event in late 1982 at Ben Aknoun University in Algiers led to the killing of a leftist student by an Islamist and a subsequent general repression of Islamist activities. After security services closed the University's prayer halls, an Islamist-led protest gathered over 10,000 individuals and led to many arrests. State authorities then targeted a variety of Islamist organizations in subsequent months, which led to several large waves of arrests. Young *arabisants* who had not previously seen themselves as Islamist sympathizers subsequently began to identify with the Islamist cause after such demonstrations of generalized Islamic repression.

The Islamist mobilization of the 1980s must be understood within the context of significant political mobilization in Algeria across many different parts of the political spectrum. Political mobilization in a variety of forms, including industrial strikes, urban riots, women's demonstrations, ethnic demands by Berbers, and protests against the one-party authoritarian regime, was significantly higher than in the previous decade. An increase in Islamist mobilization during this period is therefore not as surprising as it would be if levels of other forms of political mobilization remained low. Nevertheless, by the end of the 1980s, the Islamist groups did appear to have the comparative advantage in mobilizing large numbers and became the dominant force of opposition to the state.

With hydrocarbons accounting for about 60 percent of budget revenues, a drop in world oil and gas prices in 1986 created a significant budget deficit that increased the government's difficulty in maintaining economic subsidies and created economic hardships for much of Algeria's urban population. Likewise, the socialist policies of the 1970s had done relatively little to create internationally competitive industries but had helped to saddle the Algerian economy with high debt levels. President Chadli determined to liberalize the economy due to an increasing realization that there was no viable avenue to maintain high economic subsidies given petrochemical prices. However, there was no obvious way of changing course without amplifying economic discontent and thus taking large political risks.

In 1988, protest against the state for a variety of grievances began to mount and by October, widespread riots occurred to which the state responded with considerable force. About 200 Algerians were killed over the course of the riots by the military and state security forces, an event that marked the first time the Algerian military had used extensive violent repression against Algerian citizens. Despite active participation in the October riots, the now-considerable numbers of Algerian Islamists were only one faction of a diverse collection of groups that led street demonstrations during this period. Shortly after the riots, however, a large group of Islamists took the initiative to openly challenge state institutions, coloring the conflict as one between Islamists and the state. After Friday prayers two days after the riots, several thousand Islamist sympathizers attacked state security forces in the Belcourt quarter of Algiers. The next day, at Kouba, the army opened fire near a mosque, killing dozens. More Islamists were killed at Bab el-Oued later in the week, creating the fear of open warfare between Islamists and the state.

A number of Islamist leaders stepped in to mediate the conflict and to pull the parties back from the initial incidents of violence. Imam Ali Belhadj of Bab el-Oued, and prominent *da'wa* leaders Abassi Madani, Mohamed Sahnoun, and Mahfoud Nahna, were received by President Chadli to help defuse the crisis. The elevation of these leaders to discussion partners with the head of state enabled them to claim leadership of the Islamist movement and make demands on its behalf.

In response to the crisis, and in part to distance himself from the abuses of the state, President Chadli made a bold decision to resolve the tension by initiating extensive political reform. He likely saw this as the best mechanism for ensuring his own popularity and political survival. The first step in political reform was the announcement of a referendum on political change in November 1988, followed by Chadli's reelection as president in December and the adoption of a new constitution in February 1989. The constitutional changes were extensive, including the removal of the privileged constitutional status of the FLN, the affirmation of the right to form political organizations and parties, guarantees of individual rights, and the separation of powers among state institutions. The new constitution anticipated holding competitive elections in the near future.

The Islamist movement gained a great deal from the process of political reform and was well poised to take advantage of new opportunities for political association and competition. The first umbrella structure for Algerian Islamists was the Da'wa League (Rabitat al-Da'wa). It included the newly prominent Islamist leaders but was divided between those who wanted the organization to focus on a social mission and those who wanted to press for an Islamic state that incorporated shari'a. The divisions were resolved in part through the decision of prominent Islamists to form separate political parties under the new organization law. Ali Belhadj and Abassi Madani formed the Front Islamique du Salut[14] (FIS), while Mahfoud Nahnah formed the Mouvement de la Société Islamique (Hamas), and Abdallah Djeballah formed al-Nahda (Renaissance). Of these groups, the FIS quickly became the largest and was soon a mass organization with as many as 3 million members by the early 1990s.[15]

Islamists tested their early political strength through mobilization for street demonstrations in late 1989 and early 1990. In December 1989, over 100,000 responded to the call for counter-demonstrations against feminists who had earlier protested against Islamist restrictions on women.[16] In the spring of 1990, the FIS led a demonstration calling for the dissolution of parliament and holding of new legislative elections that attracted at least 50,000 participants – a clear sign that the FIS both had an explicitly political agenda and had confidence in its ability to challenge the state directly.

The municipal elections of June 1990 clearly demonstrated that the Islamists, and the FIS in particular, had captured the minds of a very large portion of Algerian society. Prior to the elections there were widespread attempts at electoral and protest mobilization from a variety of political parties, especially politically liberal organizations. When the electoral results came in, however, the FIS had captured 55 percent of the overall vote and won control of all of Algeria's big cities and most of the medium-sized cities. Liberal organizations were effectively marginalized across much of the country.

With such stunning success for a new political organization came real challenges in effectively staffing and governing the municipalities that the party won. As an opposition and campaigning organization, the FIS had voiced a great many grievances and made political promises that it had a difficult time fulfilling once in office. Terrified by the municipal results, the National

Assembly decided to write a new electoral law that would institutionally disadvantage the FIS when it came time to vote for a new assembly. The FIS recognized the electoral maneuvering in the assembly and Abbassi Madani chose to respond by calling for a national strike in protest during May 1991. The strike received relatively poor participation, however, and the decision exposed significant divisions within the FIS, as many argued that calling for a strike was a mistake. The strike was followed by large FIS-led street demonstrations against the government, to which the state responded with a change in government, promised revisions to the electoral code, and plans for a presidential election.

Recognizing their influence on state policy, the FIS continued to push for more reforms through demonstrations, which led the military to lose patience with the political disorder. The Algerian military perceived the rapid growth of the FIS as a direct threat to the state and attempted to restrict FIS activities and weaken its organizational structure through active repression. Though previously a military man, President Chadli sought to place himself above the confrontation and portray himself as a source of political order and civil liberty that could effectively mediate between the hardliners in the state and the Islamists on the street. By mid-summer a national conference for dialogue was held, but without the active participation of the FIS, which made a credible resolution of the conflict difficult. Elections for the National Assembly, originally scheduled for the summer of 1991, were re-scheduled to begin in December 1991 under a new electoral law that overrepresented rural areas where the FIS was relatively weak. Many of the FIS leaders were in prison for their role in the disturbances, but decided late in the year that despite the electoral changes and active repression of the party they would field candidates for the elections. The Algerian state appeared to believe that a combination of gerrymandering, repression, and the mixed performance of the FIS in municipalities would cause the FIS to lose much of the support it had received in the municipal elections a year earlier.

Turnout in the December 1991 legislative elections was down from the previous municipal election, with only about 40 percent of the electorate casting ballots. Nevertheless, the FIS received more than double the votes of the ruling FLN, taking 47 percent of the vote and 188 of 231 seats won on the first ballot.[17] As a result, the FIS only needed to win 28 more seats in the second round of elections in order to obtain the two-thirds parliamentary majority required to press for constitutional change.[18] The future of the Algerian experiment with political liberalization was immediately in question as both the state and elements of society openly questioned if the second round of elections should be aborted.

On 2 January 1992, about 300,000 people demonstrated in favor of continuing the electoral process and Chadli equivocated. Within about a week, however, President Chadli resigned under military pressure and the military stepped in to cancel the electoral process midstream, creating a "High Council of State" to govern the country. The then-FIS leader Abdel Kader Hachani rejected calls by FIS members to lead a campaign of violence against the state, but instead worked with other aggrieved political parties to express opposition to the new High Council. During the end of January and early February, however, a number of violent incidents occurred around the arrest of prominent Islamic prayer leaders (*imams*), and the state focused increased attention on repressing the FIS and arresting its leadership. On 9 February a state of emergency was declared and the FIS was declared an illegal organization. Increasing numbers of violent events occurred in February, leading to mass arrests of Islamists and the creation of special desert detention centers to house them. The state condemned several members of Algerian Hezbollah to death, and outlawed the formation of political parties based on religion.

Some resistance against the state continued into the spring of 1992 and President Boudiaf of the High Council of State was assassinated in June. By the end of the year, the FIS was split on whether or not to endorse violence against the state, with Ali Belhadj in favor of armed insurgency and others opposed. Early in 1993, a unified military command under the authority of the FIS abroad united a number of small armed groups, including the Movement Islamique Armé (MIA), veterans of the Afghan conflict, and the Armé Islamique du Salut (AIS) affiliated with the FIS. By late 1993, the more radical Groupe Islamique Armé (GIA) emerged and ultimately became the dominant armed insurgent organization in Algeria, known for brutally violent tactics. With the proliferation of armed groups, by 1994 the conflict had deteriorated into increasing violence on both sides, affecting many parts of Algerian society.[19]

A series of negotiations between the jailed leaders of the FIS and the state took place in 1994, raising the possibility of a negotiated end to the conflict. However, in the process, the militant GIA accused the FIS of playing into the hands of the state and began its own attacks on its Islamist rivals, focusing on the AIS, the militant wing of the FIS. Negotiations between the FIS and the state subeqently collapsed, and new presidential elections were held that gave a dubious mandate to the army's candidate for President, Liamine Zeroual. Intra-Islamist violence continued to escalate, with the GIA using large-scale massacres as a political weapon by 1997. Legislative elections in 1997 gave a new state-backed political party, the Rassemblement National Démocratique (RND) control over the National Assembly; the previously dominant FIS was banned from participating in elections.

At the same time, the AIS felt considerable pressure both from attacks by the Algerian military and from attacks by the GIA and so chose to declare a ceasefire. The GIA, meanwhile, began to fragment around divisions over its brutal attacks against civilians. By 1999, upon the election of a new president, Abdelaziz Bouteflika, new legislation was introduced in an effort to end the civil war. A general amnesty for rebels was offered, which motivated many Islamist guerillas to return to civilian life in a context where victory was increasingly unlikely. The level of Islamist violence subsequently declined in 1999 and the military continued to isolate and remove insurgents in the GIA, ultimately killing the group's leader in 2002. A splinter group that had formed from the GIA in 1998, the Groupe Salafiste pour la Prédication et le Combat (GSPC), continued to fight the state during the 2000s, and eventually allied with al-Qa'eda to form al-Qa'eda in the Islamic Maghreb (AQIM).

AQIM continued to lead violent attacks in Algeria and the Saharan region, but the Islamist insurgency diminished over time and became much smaller compared with the insurgency of the 1990s. While politics continued to be influenced by legacies of military-Islamist violence, Algerian Islamist politics became more and more normalized, as reflected in a 2005 amnesty referendum for remaining guerilla fighters, with moderate Islamic groups with regime ties (Mouvement de la Société pour la Paix, MSP; and al-Nahda) competing against a range of other political parties for seats in the National Assembly in the 2007 legislative elections. Subsequent Algerian politics has remained comparatively muted, if persistently illiberal, as its neighbors have witnessed increasing numbers of political experiments.

## KEY ACTORS IN ALGERIAN ISLAMIST MOBILIZATION

The dramatic story of Islamist mobilization in Algeria demonstrates the potential for Islamist movements to develop very quickly to take advantage of changing political contexts. Before addressing the potential causes for variation in mobilization outcomes, some introduction to the key Algerian Islamist organizations is necessary.

As highlighted previously, the early Algerian Islamic organizations focused primarily on *da'wa* and impacting social morals. Many prominent Islamic intellectuals emerged as leaders in these proselytizing organizations. Da'wa groups were historically very active in Algerian universities and created lasting networks for the distribution of Islamic sermons on cassette, building Qur'anic study groups and mobilizing youth for Islamic solidarity. Some were recipients of Saudi money and had resources for organizing intellectual and social gatherings to discuss Islamic topics. Likewise, a number of members of the Algerian *'ulema* have advocated for key Islamist perspectives such as the incorporation of shari'a into the Algerian legal code and general opposition to the secular socialist state.[20]

Beginning in the 1960s, the Algerian branch of the Egyptian Muslim Brotherhood, led by Mahfoud Nahnah, became an important Islamist voice. In the same decade, the organization known as al-Qiyam (values) was formed around the nationalist Malek Bennabi. Al-Qiyam attempted to restore Islamic values in society through conferences, publications, and other media activities, although it was also implicated in political violence and was forcibly dissolved in 1970.[21] The principal violent Islamist movement of the 1980s, the Mouvement Islamique Armé (MIA) led by Mustafa Bouyali, was formed in 1982 through the unification of several radical groups. Members of the MIA delivered radical Friday sermons at key mosques in Algiers for a number of years, planted bombs at buildings and public monuments, and aspired to assassinate government figures.

These groups, however, failed to remain prominent due to liberalizing constitutional reforms of the late 1980s. These reforms facilitated the creation of new Islamic organizations that sought to openly engage in politics within the existing political system. The most influential organizations to emerge during the reform period were Hamas, al-Nahda, and the FIS, all of which came to play an important role in Algerian politics.

Hamas (not affiliated with Hamas in Palestine) was founded by Mahfoud Nahnah of the Muslim Brotherhood. The group was less politically radical than other Islamist groups, cooperating with the FLN-led government when other Islamists would not. Hamas had a comparably liberal vision of Islam, reflecting a strong commitment to the Islamic principle of *ijtihad*. In the municipal elections of 1990 it chose neither to run candidates for municipal office nor to support the FIS candidates. Nahnah attempted to unite the fragmented Islamist movement in September 1990 under a new association (al-Irshad wa al-Islah), but failed to secure the participation of the FIS, which sharply limited its impact. The organization became a political party in December 1990, known as the Mouvement de la Société Islamique, but only received about 3 percent of the vote and failed to capture any legislative seats.[22] The movement was popularly seen as much more of a personal political vehicle for Nahnah, rather than as the mass movement and umbrella grouping for Islamic interests being developed by the FIS.

To comply with changing party rules prohibiting the religious identification of political parties, Hamas changed its name to the MSP and took 17 percent of the ballots in the 1997 legislative elections, likely capturing some former FIS supporters after the party's political ban. Another branch of the Hamas movement known as al-Islah generated considerable support at the end of the decade and performed comparatively well in the 2002 legislative elections, with 11 percent of the votes. Both of these parties saw their electoral performance drop significantly in the 2007 elections, however, as MSP returns declined to 10 percent and Islah slumped to under 3 percent.

A second influential movement founded by long-time Islamist leader Cheikh Abdallah Djaballah was le Mouvement de la Nahda Islamique, more commonly known as al-Nahda. It was founded in response to the formation of the FIS, after Djaballah refused to join that movement and found himself marginalized.[23] Al-Nahda was legalized in December 1990 and, like Hamas, articulated a more moderate and participatory vision of Islam in politics. Its stated principal purpose was social engagement for the diffusion of Islamic culture. Al-Nahda pushed for greater incorporation of the shari'a, as implemented through pluralist discourse and democratic choice. Al-Nahda joined with Hamas in a failed Islamist alliance early in the 1990s but, in contrast to Hamas, also managed to maintain positive relations with the FIS. Al-Nahda had somewhat weaker electoral returns than Hamas, but secured 9 percent of the vote in the 1997 legislative elections. A precipitous drop in electoral support followed, with al-Nahda winning less than 1 percent of the vote in 2002 and 3 percent of the vote in 2007.

While these new moderate Islamist organizations were politically influential in some respects, they pale in comparison to the political influence of the FIS in the early 1990s, whose success is the primary outcome to be explained. The FIS was considerably more successful than these competitors at mobilizing large numbers of protesters and voters in the initial electoral campaigns before its legal dissolution, in part because it maintained a broader coalition of supporters and avoided becoming the personal vehicle for state patronage fronted by one individual. The Front Islamique du Salut was created by politicized members of the Rabitat al-Da'wa in early 1989 at the al-Sunna mosque in the Bab el-Oued district of Algiers. It was organized around a central governing consultative council (Majlis al-Shura), with local organizations in each quarter of the city and in each province (wilaya). The FIS rapidly became the dominant opposition movement in every region of the country except for the heavily Berber Kabyle region where a Berber-oriented political party, the Front des Forces Socialistes (FFS) played the principal opposition role.

Leadership of the FIS was initially divided between two prominent and distinct personalities, which added to its appeal across a range of Islamically oriented voters, both young and old. The older Abassi Madani, a comparably moderate pragmatist, was the founding president of the organization. The younger, more charismatic and radicalized Ali Belhadj held the position of Vice President. Belhadj, in particular, played a significant role in mobilizing the youth through virulent sermons and in his refusal to compromise with state authorities. He represented what was known as the more rigorously conservative Salafist constituency within the FIS.[24] Both Madani and Belhadj were arrested in 1991, after which Abdelkader Hachani became head of the movement.

In addition to actively utilizing Friday sermons for political purposes, the FIS mobilized many individuals through its development and administration of social service organizations in poor areas, and through its relationships with small traders who saw the FIS as an ally in reducing extensive state control over economic activity. While catering to the socially disadvantaged and merchant class, the FIS appealed to educated intellectuals. About one-quarter of those standing for elections as FIS candidates had post-graduate educations. Their electoral support came dominantly from the Arabophone classes, however, revealing little enthusiasm for the FIS from the Francophone Algerian elite.[25] FIS supporters sported distinctive styles of dress and Islamic-cut beards that provided visible public information about the loyalties of the movement's sympathizers.

## VARIATIONS IN ALGERIAN ISLAMIST MOBILIZATION

The level of Islamist mobilization in Algeria has varied significantly in the period under investigation, raising questions about why Islamist mobilization rose so dramatically in a short period of time. The extent of temporal variation can best be demonstrated by looking at Islamist protest, Islamist violence, and electoral returns for Islamist parties in turn.

Islamist protest in Algeria occurred to some degree throughout the period of this study, but was significantly lower in the 1970s than in subsequent decades. While a few Islamist demonstrations took place in the mid-1970s, major demonstrations started in 1982 when more than 100,000 protested during Friday prayers at a downtown Algiers mosque in response to recent state arrests of large numbers of university Islamists. The scale of protest was unprecedented and represented the largest challenge to state authority since Algeria became independent in 1962.[26] A second massive Islamist protest emerged in the context of the funeral for Cheikh Abdellatif Soltani in 1984. Soltani was incarcerated during the 1982 crackdown and died shortly after he was released to house arrest. In response to the major economic crisis of the mid-1980s, strikes and protests mounted in 1988 from a range of sources, including large numbers of Islamists. During state repression in the wake of political unrest in 1988, many Islamists took over whole neighborhoods of Algiers.

After the municipal elections of 1990 and the crafting of a new electoral law designed to limit FIS success in the 1991 legislative elections, the FIS again organized a strike and street demonstrations. While the workers' strike was not particularly successful, massive demonstrations and FIS occupation of public places at the same time demonstrated once again the ability of the FIS to mobilize large numbers in response to state policy. Shortly after the abrogation of the legislative elections in early 1992, the FIS once again successfully mounted massive, and primarily non-violent, protests against the decision to end the constitutional reforms. Large-scale protests of this type soon faded as political violence escalated through the 1990s and state repression of Islamist activity was widespread. Islamist protests became increasingly associated with violence during the course of the civil conflict.

Similar to the trend in Islamist protest, there was little significant Islamist violence throughout the decade of the 1970s. Tensions between leftists and Islamists mounted on university campuses as the decade progressed, but with few events spilling over into overt violence. This began to change in the early 1980s when clashes between Islamists and leftist students resulted in several deaths. The 1980s also saw the growth of Bouyali's Mouvement Islamique Armé (MIA), which began to stockpile weapons and plan for attacks against official targets and prominent politicians. As the state sought to co-opt Islamists in the mid-1980s and changed state policy to reflect Islamist sentiments, violence remained limited, focusing on armed conflict with Bouyali's small group based around the foothills of the Atlas Mountains.

Violence re-emerged during the riots of 1988, in which Islamists took part. Over the course of the 1988 riots many Islamists lost their lives as a result of clashes with security forces. As political reforms began, however, Islamist violence receded in favor of electoral mobilization. Upon the cancellation of elections in 1992, however, tensions rose dramatically and militants once again began to take the upper hand from the voices of civil disobedience. As the army moved to replace the *imams* of approximately 8,000 mosques controlled by the FIS, violent conflicts began. By mid-1992, assassinations of security forces and members of the judiciary were becoming relatively common, indicating that there were undercurrents both within and outside the FIS in favor of armed insurrection. Attempts to regroup members of Bouyali's former MIA with others in favor of an armed solution led prominent members of the FIS to ultimately endorse armed struggle, and also led to the formation of a new group that played a key role in the rise of Islamist violence, the GIA.

Islamist attacks on the state escalated in 1993, as did state violence against suspected Islamists of many different backgrounds. Attempts to find a negotiated solution to the conflict at first looked like they had potential to diminish the conflict, but as they broke down, the position of many in the FIS hardened and levels of violence increased. While there are few reliable year-to-year numbers of dead, for the purposes of this study it is sufficient to recognize the rapid escalation of violence around 1993, a slight de-escalation in deaths during the period of negotiations during 1994, and then another escalation as talks dissolved in 1995–1996. From 1997 through the end of the decade, Islamist–state violence levels remained high, beginning to decline at a moderate pace at the end of the century. Between 1992 and 2000, most sources recognize that at least 100,000 deaths occurred from violence perpetrated on both sides of the conflict, making the Algerian civil war one of the most violent in the contemporary period.

Electoral mobilization in Algeria was restricted during the 1970s and 1980s because of the institutionalization of the one-party FLN state. The municipal elections of 1990 thus mark the first time that Islamist parties openly competed for state office with a range of other political alternatives. Most observers regard the 1990 municipal elections and the 1991 legislative elections as reasonably transparent, even if the political playing field was not entirely level. Despite the military coup of 1992 that aborted the second round of the legislative elections, restricted competitive elections subsequently took place on several other occasions during the 1990s. Presidential elections took place in 1995, 1999, 2004, and 2009, with new legislative elections in 1997 and again in 2002, 2007, and 2012. The FIS, as the largest opposition party, was banned from participating in each of these elections, calling into question the credibility of these elections in representing popular preferences. Likewise, key parties boycotted several of the elections, further distancing the outcomes from popular preferences. Nevertheless, moderate Islamically oriented parties have continued to compete in the elections, revealing additional information about support for the Islamist movement throughout the decade.

In comparing the two elections in which the FIS participated (1990 municipals and 1991 legislatives), it is apparent both that the Islamists firmly dominated the elections on both occasions and that their support declined somewhat over the course of the year. In the 1990 municipal elections the FIS received about 55 percent of the total vote and 47 pecent of the vote in the 1991 legislatives. The high turnout for the municipal elections (65%) diminished considerably by the legislative elections, as well, with only a little over 40 percent casting votes. On both occasions, the ruling FLN came in second place, with about half of the votes obtained by the FIS.

After the FIS was declared illegal, some former FIS supporters shifted their votes to the legal Islamically minded parties such as Hamas or al-Nahda, but a large percentage refused to support any party and boycotted subsequent elections. This makes tracking Islamist electoral support over time in Algeria a very uncertain business. In the 1995 presidential elections, the army's candidate Liamine Zeroual won with 61 percent of the vote; his principal challenger was the leader of Hamas, Mahfoud Nahnah, who took 26 percent. By the 1999 presidential elections, however, some Islamists supported the government's preferred candidate, Abdelaziz Bouteflika, while others chose to boycott the election all together. Fearing electoral fraud, all candidates except Bouteflika pulled out of the election, making the results of the election meaningless.

Legislative contests after 1991 had a greater degree of competition than the presidential contests, but the 1997 election, in particular, received mixed reports for its freedom and transparency. In 1997, a new government party created to support President Zeroual, the RND, dominated the elections, although two moderately Islamist parties participated (Hamas, renamed the MSP, and al-Nahda) and obtained a combined total of 24 percent of the vote. In the 2002 legislative elections, the Hamas-MSP and a new Islamically oriented al-Islah party jointly polled 22 percent of the electorate. This combined support declined to about 15 percent of the electorate in 2007. The electoral results from 1997, 2002, and 2007 thus seem to imply that other Islamist groups collectively maintained the support of about half of the former FIS supporters (but declining over time), while other FIS supporters abandoned electoral participation or shifted their support to parties affiliated with the state.[27]

How has Islamist mobilization varied across region in Algeria? Importantly, support for the FIS and other Islamist groups collectively has been a nationwide phenomenon. With the partial exception of the heavily Berber Kabyle region of the Atlas mountains, which has preferred to support ethnically based opposition organizations, the Islamists have received support from all major regions of the country.

The FIS was formed in an urban environment and secured a large portion of its support from the population of large cities; however, many Islamists found support in the countryside as well, including Bouyali's MIA. The municipal elections of 1990 were the first real opportunity to map public support for the Islamist movement, and despite the overwhelming success of the FIS in those elections, regional variation highlighted portions of the country that were less enthusiastic Islamist supporters. The predominantly rural south supported the FIS less than the North. The FIS share of the vote in the largest cities was particularly high (64% in Algiers, 71% in Oran, 72% in Constantine), highlighting the party's urban roots. Indeed the FIS won 90 percent of the municipal councils in urban areas with a population of over 20,000.[28] The southern municipalities of the Sahara effectively prevented the ruling FLN from losing everything in the election, where the FLN secured most of its fourteen wilayat (provinces). The south had significantly more entrenched ruling-party control and established patronage networks, which were not under the same threat as they were in the north. The areas of the north that did not vote for the FIS were heavily Berber, including Tizi Ouzou and Bejaia. A similar regional voting pattern, and urban-rural divide, were evident in the 1991 legislative elections despite a slightly less dominant outcome for the FIS.

## SOURCES OF THE ISLAMISTS' SUCCESS

Why did Algerian Islamist groups, and particularly the FIS, succeed at mobilizing such large numbers of individuals so quickly? I argue that several key institutional contexts are critical in explaining the outcome, including the autonomy of Islamic religious institutions that facilitated entrepreneurship, rapid growth of Islamic institutions (particularly urban mosques), sudden political reform that favored established social institutions, major public crises of order, and the blunt repression of Islamist groups through legal and police action. This final factor, and in particular the indiscriminate and reactive repression of the Algerian state, is also a dominant causal factor in Hafez's (2003) explanation of Algerian violence in the 1990s. Before turning to these explanatory factors in the context of the institutional theory presented in Chapter 2, I briefly discuss the impact of two prominent explanatory factors for Islamist mobilization, as applied to the Algerian case: socioeconomic and cultural changes.

Most explanations of the rise of the Islamist opposition in Algeria highlight the importance of socioeconomic factors in explaining mobilization outcomes. In the years before the FIS electoral victories, the Algerian economy was in deep crisis with high debt levels and major budget deficits. Unemployment rates were staggering (between 20 and 30%) and many of the social services Algerians had come to expect from the state were unavailable, as exemplified by a severe housing shortage. The impact of the economic shortfall was compounded by the demography of the Algerian population. With one of the world's highest population growth rates, the number of Algerian youth had tripled in the thirty years since independence, putting severe strains on the state's ability to absorb young men into the workforce.[29]

While it is clear that all of these factors created serious and sustained grievances against the state, by themselves these socioeconomic factors do not effectively explain why mobilization happened when it did and why that mobilization was channeled directly through Islamist movements rather than through alternative opposition channels. General economic grievances help explain the presence of popular sentiments that could be mobilized into collective action but more is required to understand the reasons for the activation of those grievances into a social movement.[30]

A second popular set of explanations for the rise of the Algerian Islamists centers around cultural factors. This set of explanations asserts that the reason discontent was channeled through Islamist movements rather than the alternatives was the acute identity crisis faced by Algeria in its relationship with the West. This identity crisis was manifest in repeated violent encounters with the French colonizer that defined Islam as a characteristic marker of opposition to both the West and the Westernized elite running the Algerian state. The Algerian linguistic battles between Arabophones and Francophones (and to some extent Berber speakers as well) exemplified the tensions between the identity of the masses and that of the elite.[31] While there is no reason to deny that individual Algerians face real issues in identity choice, Algerian identity questions were longstanding and provide little value in explaining variation in mobilization outcomes within the country over time or across region.

Turning to the institutional contexts highlighted in this study, it is apparent that Algeria had a comparably open climate for religious entrepreneurship and that the entrepreneurial climate became even more inviting during the 1980s and early 1990s than it was previously. Compared with many other Muslim countries, Algerian Islamic leaders had significant autonomy from the state prior to the 1990s and were fragmented among a range of competing Islamic organizations that had little hierarchical religious control over potential religious entrepreneurs.

During the 1960s and 1970s, the state often pursued a policy of co-opting important Islamic figures by incorporating them into the bureaucracy. A number of Islamic elites were directly allied with the first Algerian regime under President Ben Bella. For a number of years following independence, prominent Islamists took key state posts, including Malek Bennabi, who became the director of higher education, and future FIS President Abassi Madani, who served as a deputy in the same ministry. During Boumedienne's term as president in the 1970s, however, Islamic elites began to see their interests increasingly threatened by the socialist state and the incentives of Islamists and the state began to diverge. While some in the state saw the Islamists as important allies in balancing a growing threat from the far left, more and more Islamists began to seek allies outside of the state, including among prominent landowners who were threatened by land reform. Together, landowners and Islamists began to build thousands of new mosques outside state control and found numerous religious associations. A loophole in Algerian law allowed these newly constructed mosques to remain outside state control while they remained unfinished. They remained unfinished for many years to maintain their autonomy from the state and thus became centers for the organization of an Islamist opposition.[32]

The contradictions of the Arabization program that was launched upon independence began to further distance the incentives of potential religious entrepreneurs from those of the state. By the early 1980s, large numbers of graduates from Arabic-only schools began to enter the labor force only to discover that most of the good state and private sector jobs required knowledge of French as well.[33] These graduates often found that they were best prepared for employment in Islamic institutions, if they could find employment at all, and thus remained outside the principal economic networks through which state patronage was funneled.

Although the state attempted to control Islam through such institutions as the Islamic High Council and the Ministry of Religious Affairs, by the early 1980s it found its bureaucracy unable to effectively monitor Islamic institutions such as mosques and private religious schools. According to a report by the Ministry of Religious Affairs in 1981, a full 60 percent of prayer leaders at mosques (*imams*) were not considered professionally qualified to comment on religious issues.[34] This demonstrated both that a large portion of mosques remained outside state avenues of religious professionalization and that the demand for religious leadership was substantially unmet by the state. By the time of the state budget crisis in the mid-1980s, existing patronage resources directed toward the religious elite were under severe strain, leading to a decline in the state's ability to effectively control the Algerian Islamic elite. As a result, the loyalty of the *'ulema* and other Islamic leaders to their state patrons inevitably decreased.

Therefore, by the mid-1980s, several institutional changes had taken place that both increased the distance between the incentives of Islamists and the state and limited the possibility that entrepreneurial attempts to challenge the state would be effectively policed by the Islamic elite. The decline in incorporation of prominent Islamists into state bureaucracies, the creation of a tacit alliance between Islamic leaders and landowners threatened by socialist policies, the expansion of autonomous mosques as centers of Islamist organization, the low incorporation of Arabic-only speakers into the state, and a decline in state patronage resources available to the *'ulema* all contributed to the multiplication of Islamic organizations and triggered Islamist entrepreneurship.

During the same period, changes began to take place in the social density of Islamic religious institutions and discourse that facilitated political communication and the development of common Islamic expectations. To start, the state itself began to utilize Islamic language more extensively and to pursue selected policies that created new public expectations about religious behavior. After the state's adoption of Islam as the religion of state in the National Charter of 1976 and, more importantly, after Chadli Bendjedid's accession to the presidency in 1979, references to Islam became more frequent and more systematic in official communications. The Arabization program over time changed the linguistic repertoire of society to incorporate more Islamic terminology in everyday communication. Likewise, an extended debate over the personal status code in the early 1980s, and the formal adoption of a new religiously conservative code in 1984, shifted expectations about social behavior in a decidedly Islamic direction for many parts of society.

More formally, both the extent of education and the type of education in Algeria changed dramatically in the period before widespread Islamist mobilization began. At the beginning of the 1970s, only about 2 million students were enrolled at all levels of instruction, but by the end of the decade the numbers of students had more than doubled.[35] The state facilitated efforts to build Islamic educational institutions by mandating the use of Arabic at many levels of instruction. In an attempt both to support Islamist allies and to control the propagation of Islam, the state also encouraged religious instruction in public schools.

By the early 1980s, Islam had developed a significant role at the university level. Two new universities dedicated to Islamic studies were built by the state, in Constantine and in Laghouat, reflecting the government's willingness to encourage religious study.[36] At the same time, secular universities became forums for significant levels of Islamic discussion and ideological battles between Islamists and the political left. A proliferation of Islamic associations, conferences, and publications in the 1980s, often based at prominent universities, expanded public knowledge of Islam and built networks of Arabic-speaking, religious young men that became increasingly radicalized as they realized that their training had not prepared them for a tight labor market that valued technical skills and French over either Arabic or religious credentials.

Most dramatically of all, the rapid proliferation of independent mosques in the late 1970s and early 1980s served to provide a new institutional base for the Islamist movement to mobilize. The mosques were funded by private benefactors, which allowed them to expand rapidly, unconstrained by the state's looming financial difficulties. While the numbers of new mosques built in the late 1970s was unprecedented, mosque construction accelerated even further after 1980. These mosques were notably independent from the Algerian ulema, which had been both weakened and co-opted by the FLN over time. They served as the home for a wide variety of religious entrepreneurs who could easily maintain independence from the weak religious elite. Their high numbers and diverse perspectives proved exceptionally hard to control for both the traditional ulema and the state.

The independence of the new mosques was crucial to the role they would play in political organization. State mosques with an official *imam* were instructed not to use mosques for unofficial political purposes; the Friday sermon was a bureaucratic tool, delivered to *imams* at the approximately 5,000 state mosques by the Ministry of Religious Affairs.[37] By the end of the 1980s, however, out of the more than 15 thousand mosques in Algeria, relatively few had an official state *imam*. The FIS alone counted 9,000 mosques in its organizational network,[38] almost double the number of official state mosques. Recognizing the impact the independent mosques had on the Islamists' success in municipal elections, the state undertook a series of measures in early 1991 to further regulate the construction and use of prayer halls and explicitly forbade them to serve as arenas for political mobilization. These new regulations led to many confrontations during Friday prayers, the arrest of a number of prominent *imams*, and the further politicization of Islam in the period both before and after the legislative elections of 1991.

Changes in the institutional context that created a fertile climate for religious entrepreneurship, as well as the rapid growth of Islamic educational and religious institutions, facilitated the extension of Islamist mobilization deep into Algerian society. They thus created beneficial conditions for the activation of an Islamic identity in politics. These developments alone are not sufficient, however, to explain the timing and magnitude of the mobilization that took place in the early 1990s. These institutional contexts became particularly relevant only after a series of public events that focused common Islamist expectations around clear crises of state stability and justice, within the broader context of rapid political liberalization from a repressive authoritarian regime.

The Algerian socialist model of industrialization involved the creation of numerous institutions dedicated to social service provision and the distribution of state resources, particularly the rents gained from the exploitation of hydrocarbons. As the Algerian economy grew considerably from a low base during the 1970s and early 1980s, many in the population adjusted their vision of the state's role in their own economic welfare to include expectations of state welfare distribution. This made the state particularly vulnerable to a collapse in oil and gas prices, which occurred in the mid-1980s, and which had a direct impact on the distribution of state benefits to many Algerians. Around the same time, Algeria began a structural adjustment program that included raising interest rates, instituting new public tariffs, and the devaluation of the Algerian dinar, which affected Algerians' ability to buy imported consumables on which the economy had become particularly dependent.[39]

These economic shocks affected the poor and middle-class segments of the population to a much greater degree than the Algerian political elite, who managed to insulate themselves from the worst of it through their positions in state patronage networks. Among the first groups to publicly recognize the new patterns of economic injustice were the recently educated Arabophones, as the large class of new graduates in Islamic literature and legal studies found few avenues for employment in a time of economic crisis. Public comments about the corruption of the regime became widespread and highlighted perceptions that the regime was selfishly pursuing unjust economic policies. Islamist street demonstrations expanded in the mid-1980s at the same time as these economic shocks were felt by the Algerian public, ultimately culminating in the widespread riots of October 1988.

In addition, questions of political justice were acute. Many complaints were raised in the late 1980s against the one-party, authoritarian, bureaucratic state for its political unresponsiveness. Algeria faced serious crises of political justice on two occasions in the early 1990s, the first with changes to the electoral law made prior to the 1991 legislative elections, and the second with the abortion of those elections after the first round. In both cases there was clear public understanding of state interference with the political preferences of its citizens, and both events were occasions for large-scale Islamist street demonstrations in protest.

The FIS and other Islamist organizations attempted to resolve questions of economic and political injustice by designing innovative social solutions to public problems such as sanitation, health care, and the lack of a social safety net. In the process, the FIS asserted the need for high standards of public accountability, the importance of mutual aid, and the Islamic principles of government by consensus and consultation (*shura*). On one specific occasion, the effectiveness of Islamist relief efforts were publicly contrasted with limited state ability to address public needs. After a devastating earthquake in October 1989, the FIS effectively took charge of relief efforts while the state was slow, ineffective, and generally appeared powerless to help. The public nature of the crisis and widespread perceptions of state failure served as a focal point to unite voters around the Islamist opposition in municipal elections the following year.[40]

In addition to the prominent crises of justice discussed, the state faced a crisis of public disorder in 1988 that the Islamists were able to channel into collective action. Widespread grievances coupled with a sharp economic downturn in 1988 led large numbers of Algerians from diverse social and ideological groups into the streets in sustained riots against state policies. As the state began to lose control of the situation it turned in desparation to repressive force, killing many Algerian protesters and calling the state's ability to effectively manage the situation into question. Although the riots were not explicitly Islamist in nature, Islamist groups soon attempted to resolve the chaos by asserting control over whole urban neighborhoods and challenging security services. The state felt threatened by these challenges to its authority and began repressing Islamist actors as a result. As it did so, what was initially a rather spontaneous event led by diverse interests came to be viewed as an Islamist confrontation with the state.

The blunt, public state repression of Islamists triggered many of the most notable episodes of Islamist collective action. These include the early mass demonstrations of 1982 after the closure of university prayer halls and widespread arrests of Islamically oriented students, as well as the 1984 demonstrations at the funeral for Cheikh Soltani, who had been imprisoned by state authorities. In 1992, active military repression of the FIS and a number of prominent *imams* also helped turn many Islamists into proponents of violence against the state. As violent conflict accelerated, state repression affected more and more Islamist sympathizers and helped direct many individuals to Islamist channels of collective action. These acts of state repression became widely known and served as additional focal points for channeling Islamic expectations and common knowledge into political action.

While public focal points of economic crisis, political disorder, and Islam-specific repression helped trigger the large-scale demonstrations and violence of the 1980s and early 1990s, rapid political liberalization did even more to magnify the potential for Islamist collective action in Algeria. It did so for two reasons. First, it institutionalized both a low-cost forum and a specified moment for political mobilization against a highly unpopular authoritarian state. Second, the rapid nature of the political reform process ensured that opposition to the state was likely to be channeled through existing social institutions and discourse rather than through new political party institutions that would take time to develop independent methods of organization and communication.

The enactment of political reform immediately after one of the most severe manifestations of discontent against the state (October 1988 riots) and the public state repression of Islamist activists that followed both enhanced the potential for the electoral expression of opposition to the state and the potential for Islam to become a salient cleavage in the election. As the FIS formed under the new political organizations law, it found ready support in the now-widespread private mosques that had penetrated Algerian cities. By recruiting prominent independent *imams* who used the Friday sermon as a forum for political commentary, the FIS captured a large number of existing Islamic channels that it could use for recruitment and communication. No other opposition party could boast an institutional network even remotely comparable to that of the FIS's mosque network, giving the Islamist movement a significant mobilization advantage over its competitors. Indeed, the electoral returns for the FIS in 1990 and 1991 most certainly overstate the amount of ideological support the party commanded from the Algerian public, and rather reflect an imbalance in mobilization opportunities that favored Islamist organizations over others. The FIS came to be seen as the strategically appropriate choice for the expression of opposition to the state, given public expectations that it was the most likely of the opposition parties to do well.

In subsequent elections after the FIS was banned, some Islamist support migrated to the more accommodative, legal Islamically oriented parties of Hamas-MSP and al-Nahda, but neither could command the high levels of initial support shown for the FIS. This was in part because of the declining legitimacy of the electoral process and in part because the promised Islamic solutions to Algeria's ills had not cured them but, as many admitted, had aggravated them by throwing the country into violent conflict. The somewhat consistent (but slowly declining) voting rates for Islamically oriented parties do reflect a continued willingness to view Islam as a politically salient cleavage, however.

## FROM VOTING TO VIOLENCE

What does the Algerian experience teach us about the conditions under which Islam is mobilized in peaceful or in violent forms? Several patterns from

Algeria should be noted that may be also relevant to other cases. First, both violent and non-violent forms of Islamist mobilization may coexist, offering different political strategies to constituents who may have similar goals. During the 1970s, neither type of mobilization was prominent, but by the early 1980s both a sustained protest movement and a militant Islamist organization (MIA) had emerged. The division in types of state engagement reflected ideological differences between the two groups, but they were able to benefit from each other's activities. Violence by the MIA led to government crackdowns on other Islamists, which amplified Islamist grievances and provided new reasons for protest mobilization. Mass Islamist protests, on the other hand, demonstrated support for Islamist activities and encouraged the MIA to place its militancy within this broader context of public support.

In the 1990s, a variety of violent Islamist organizations such as the GIA led a sustained insurgent campaign against the state at the same time that large numbers of Algerians were voting for Islamists at the polls. It is unlikely that GIA supporters were those at the polls casting ballots for accommodative Islamist candidates, but nevertheless some Islamist supporters were using multiple channels for the expression of preferences simultaneously. A brief comparison with Turkey is instructive here. At the same time that the Welfare Party was most successful with the Turkish electorate in the mid-1990s, violent Islamist activities by organizations such as Hezbollah were also increasing. The scale of violence in the Turkish case was much lower than in Algeria, however, and was clearly overshadowed by electoral mobilization. In the Algerian case both forms of mobilization were prominent.

Second, Islamist violence began with confrontations at the margins of the movement around appropriate state responses to Islamist entrepreneurship. As the Islamist movement grew on university campuses in the late 1970s and early 1980s, Islamist-Leftist clashes occasionally turned violent. State repression of Islamists as a result often served to escalate the violence and focus militants' activities against the state. This pattern was most evident in the period immediately following the disruption of the electoral process and the banning of the FIS in 1992. As the state moved in on the organization to close its offices and interfere with Friday prayers at FIS-affiliated mosques, a number of Islamists at the margins began explicitly targeting the state despite the stated moderation by the movement as a whole. As the state responded to these provocations with even more widespread repression, violence increased and the more moderate leadership of the FIS soon lost control over militant Islamist entrepreneurs.

Third, Islamist violence expanded as options for de-escalation of the conflict narrowed and the perceived individual costs of surrender approached those of continuing to fight the state. As state repression of Islamists became more and more widespread, it became much more difficult to target those implicated in violence individually, and Islamists were punished as a community. A similar collectivization of the target occurred against the state as Islamists indiscriminately targeted state and security organizations and officers. This made it more difficult for individual Islamist sympathizers to disassociate themselves with the violence, constraining opportunities for remaining aloof of the conflict. Leaving the conflict behind thus raised the real possibility of state punishment for previous association with the Islamist insurgency (and potential retribution from the Islamist movement itself), raising perceived individual costs of de-escalation.

Finally, Islamist violence was sustained by the development of its own political economy and declined as that economy became more restricted and opportunities for re-integration into the state polity and economy expanded. Violent Islamist mobilization endured over the course of the 1990s in part because of rugged geography and the growth of informal economic institutions that allowed Islamists to support their activities through participation in a newly developing merchant trade economy outside of state purview. In addition, armed Islamist bands discovered newfound economic freedom in the form of protection rackets that extracted resources from nervous populations, rackets also mirrored by non-Islamist militias.[41]

Beginning in the mid-1990s, however, and continuing into the end of the decade, the state worked to develop innovative solutions to the re-integration of Islamist guerillas into both state and the formal state economy. By the end of the decade and then into the 2000s, Bouteflika's recognition of political amnesty for large groups of Islamist fighters increased the incentives of many to return to participation in the state. Combined with the deteriorating probability of Islamist success in capturing the state, the economic incentives for re-integration led many to abandon armed conflict and dramatically reduced the numbers of armed Islamist combatants over time.

## CONCLUSION

Evidence from the Algerian case broadly supports the predictions of the institutional theory advocated in this study. Compared with the other cases under consideration in previous chapters, Algeria has (a) the most autonomous and fragmented Islamic institutions; (b) the most dramatic misalignment of Islamist and state incentives; (c) the densest social penetration of Islamic institutions of learning and worship; (d) the most public, event-based crises of political order and justice; and (e) the most rapid experiment in political liberalization. The presence of these institutional contexts predicts that Algeria should be the case with the highest levels of Islamist mobilization, which has been empirically demonstrated. Algeria has also had the most varied expressions of Islamist mobilization, with high levels of Islamist voting, protest, and violence.

Additionally, the institutional contexts highlighted earlier have also changed over time in Algeria. While some of these contexts, such as the social density of Islamic institutions, change significantly only over the course of a number of years, others such as public crises of order or political liberalization can occur quite rapidly. The process of the interaction of religious institutional change with dramatic public state focal points determined the overall contours of Algerian Islamist mobilization. Expansion of Islamic institutions in the 1980s, coupled with a shift in the relationship between Islamic leaders and the state, created the institutional environment that Islamist entrepreneurs were well-positioned to take advantage of when appropriate focal points became available at the end of the decade.

## REFERENCES


Bennoune, Mahfoud. 1988. *The Making of Contemporary Algeria, 1830–1987: Colonial Upheavals and Post-Independence Development*. Cambridge: Cambridge University Press.

Fontaine, Jacques. 1990. "Les elections locales Algériennes du 12 Juin 1990: approche statistique et géographique." *Maghreb-Machrek* 129 (July–September): 124–140.

1994. "Quartiers défavorisés et vote Islamiste à Alger." In Pierre Robert Baduel, ed. *L'Algérie Incertain*. Paris: Edisud.

Hafez, Mohammed M. 2003. *Why Muslims Rebel: Repression and Resistance in the Islamic World*. Boulder, CO: Lynne Rienner.

Horne, Alistair. 1978. *A Savage War of Peace*. London: Viking.

Kalyvas, Stathis N. 1999. "Wanton and Senseless? The Logic of Massacres in Algeria." *Rationaliy and Society* 11/3: 243–286.

Lamchichi, Abderrahim. 1992. *L'Islamisme en Algérie*. Paris: L'Harmattan.

Martinez, Luis. 1998. *La Guerre Civile en Algérie*. Paris: Karthala.

2000. *The Algerian Civil War 1990–1998*. Translated by Jonathan Derrick. London: Hurst & Company.

Noyon, Jennifer. 2003. *Islam, Politics, and Pluralism: Theory and Practice in Turkey, Jordan, Tunisia and Algeria*. London: Royal Institute of International Affairs.

Quandt, William B. 1998. *Between Ballots and Bullets: Algeria's Transition from Authoritarianism*. Washington DC: Brookings.

2002. "Algeria's Uneasy Peace." *Journal of Democracy*. 13/4 (October): 15–23.

Ruedy, John. 1992. *Modern Algeria: The Origins and Development of a Nation*. Bloomington: Indiana University Press.

Soltani, Abdellatif. 1974. *Le Mazdaqisme est à l'origine du socialisme*.

Tessler, Mark. 1997. "The Origins of Popular Support for Islamist Movements: A Political Economy Analysis." In John Entelis, ed. *Islam, Democracy, and the State in North Africa*. Bloomington: Indiana University Press.

Tlemcani, Rachid. 1986. *State and Revolution in Algeria*. Boulder, CO: Westview.

Willis, Michael. 1996. *The Islamist Challenge in Algeria: A Political History*. New York: New York University Press.

Yacoubian, Mona. 2002. "*Algeria: The Challenge of Militant Islam and Lessons Learned*." Washington DC: Center for Strategic and International Studies.

7

# Conclusion

## *The Institutional Origins of Islamist Mobilization*

Despite some prominent claims that political Islam has been in decline since the 1980s,[1] Islamists continue to be extremely successful in mobilizing key constituencies across the Islamic world. After 2003, Islamist violence increased significantly in Iraq (although only a small portion of Iraqi violence was clearly Islamist), and Islamist political organizations had notable electoral successes early in the century in Egypt (2005) and Palestine (2006). Islamist electoral mobilization in the Arab world increased after the Arab uprisings of 2011–2012 in Tunisia, Egypt, and Morocco, all of which saw leadership transitions with Islamists taking the helm. Islamist organizations have recently played increasingly major roles in the politics of Nigeria, Saudi Arabia, Yemen, Syria, Kuwait, Comoros, Maldives, and Somalia, among others, and civil wars in Syria, Yemen, Libya, and Somalia became more Islamist over time. The growth and development of the Syria-based "Islamic State" and its affiliates since 2014 is just one of a number of indications that the overall amount of Islamist mobilization around the world continues to be high and is growing in many areas.

Much of today's Islamist mobilization looks different from that which took place a decade ago. Often Islamist groups have made strategic decisions to engage the political system on its own terms, and even compete in elections. This is far from a universal trend, but nevertheless has prominent examples, including the election of a historically radical Islamist movement in Palestine (Hamas) to the dominant position in the Palestinian Authority as well as the decision of multiple Egyptian Islamist groups to compete directly as formal political parties in the Egyptian political system in 2011–2012. Political Islam in the early 2000s thus began to change shape by increasingly working within existing systems.

However, Islamism also evolved in the last decade by becoming increasingly internationalized through networked cells that share radical Islamist ideologies.

The foremost exemplar of this is clearly al-Qa'eda, although sustained pressure on al-Qa'eda after 2001 led to the defeat and fragmentation of a number of international networks. The rise of al-Qa'eda's jihadist competitors, such as the Islamic State group, nevertheless revived the fortunes of violent Islamist groups in recent years. These fragmented networks often play to selected domestic constituencies, but are more international in membership and objectives than most Islamist groups were in much of the period of this study. Despite these substantial changes in the objectives and strategies of Islamist groups, the traditional manifestation of Islamist mobilization as an opposition challenge in the context of domestic politics continues unabated. Islamist violence, Islamist street protests, and Islamist electoral success all continue to shape political outcomes in the Muslim world.

I have argued throughout this study that variation in observed Islamist political mobilization is the result of the interaction of several broad structural factors within a context of interest-based religious entrepreneurship. These structural factors include the following observable patterns of institutional interaction. First, religious-political entrepreneurship can flourish when the interests of religious elites diverge from the interests of the state, and when the hierarchy of Islamic authority is weak. When religious elites and entrepreneurs are at odds with the state, whether because of divergent policy preferences, or simply because of different constituencies and resource bases, religious entrepreneurship within the political arena is more likely.

A common pattern in Muslim countries is one in which the traditional Islamic elite (often the *'ulema* or even leaders of Islamist movements) have been co-opted by the state either through the distribution of state resources, because they have been integrated into bureaucracies, or because they are used as policy advisors. In these contexts, the religious elite are aligned with the state on many issues, and may feel threatened by non-elite religious entrepreneurs who challenge the state and the cooperative relationship between the state and Islamic elites. In these contexts, the level of control the religious elite have over their constituents (and thus the potential pool of religious entrepreneurs) matters. In rigid religious hierarchies, or when family or other organizational hierarchies can be harnessed on behalf of the religious elite, in-group policing is possible and entrepreneurs are often prevented from challenging the state by their own religious organization. In situations where the religious elite are weak, their leadership is in dispute, or when there is little effective Islamic hierarchy, religious entrepreneurship is unlikely to be checked from within Islamic organizations, and thus is more likely to thrive.

The second structural factor that matters in the argument of this book is the degree of social penetration of Islamic religious institutions. I have argued that in institutional contexts where Islamic education, Islamic media, and the mosque have significant social penetration there is more likely to be Islamic common knowledge. Islamic common knowledge is the collective expectation that others hold similar religious values to one's own, that they understand religious meaning or symbolism in a similar way, and that the broader imagined community has similar expectations around appropriate Islamic behavior. Islamic common knowledge may exist only within selected parts of the public sphere, but it is always held by a group broader than one's personal network. It does not by itself trigger collective action, but rather provides for rapid and symbol-laden communication because of embedded shared assumptions. This ability for rapid (and often nonverbal) communication enables collective action when it is triggered.

The level of social penetration by Islamic religious institutions also matters for more straightforward reasons. Islamic institutions build social networks and structures for verbal communication that are flexible enough to incorporate political content into regularized religious discourse. Political arguments can be rapidly integrated into the Islamic media; into weekly Friday sermons at the mosque; and by leveraging networks of Islamic schools, Qur'anic study groups, or charitable associations in which there is routine participation by pious citizens. These institutions exist primarily for non-political reasons and are thus often difficult to suppress by the state. They therefore provide a ready-made social network for communication at politically opportune moments, when no other such communication structures may be in place.

The final structural context that facilitates Islamist mobilization is one in which public state events provide focal points for the coordination of Islamic common knowledge on political issues. These public state events come in two distinct forms, state crises of order and justice or, alternatively, rapid political liberalization. Specific types of state crises, especially those that expose state injustices or the state's incapacity to maintain order, are especially resonant in an Islamic setting. Rapid political liberalization facilitates political mobilization across most political groups, although Islamists are likely to be major beneficiaries of such a state change because alternative social or political institutions are underdeveloped. Islamists are therefore best poised to quickly mobilize large groups through religious communication networks under conditions of rapid liberalization. These types of public state events help religious entrepreneurs in their political efforts by coordinating common expectations around specific state issues at the same time. Focal state events both activate Islamic common knowledge and reward efforts at Islamic entrepreneurship.

These three structural contexts have the most impact on Islamist mobilization when they occur in conjunction one with another. Dense networks of Islamic religious institutions may never become politically activated if there are few incentives for religious entrepreneurship or where public state crises and political change are limited. Likewise, a climate of religious entrepreneurship may facilitate many attempts at Islamist mobilization, but Islamists will have limited appeal if the broader society does not share Islamic expectations or if there are few state events that can coordinate public preferences around defining issues. Finally, large-scale crises of order, justice, or regime change may occur, but if there are either few religious entrepreneurs to take advantage of these events or limited Islamic common knowledge to activate, then political mobilization will likely take non-Islamist forms.

This argument was developed as the result of two processes, the first of which is a deductive process that aimed to isolate the components of religious collective action. This was done in interaction with existing theories of political mobilization. These influential theories largely came from the rational choice and social movement scholarship, as well as scholarship on political Islam. The second process that led to the argument is one of empirical observation. This formally began by building the data set on Islamist mobilization outcomes in fifty-seven polities as discussed in Chapter 3. I then chose focus cases in the remaining chapters that represented mobilization outcomes across the spectrum of the broader data set. Significant portions of the argument were developed in the iterative interaction with my observations of these cases, including ethnographic data collection when possible.

The principal evidence for the accuracy of the argument presented in this study comes in two forms. First, the argument is consistent with the broad historical and geographical data presented on Islamist mobilization outcomes throughout the Muslim world as discussed in Chapter 3. Second, the argument is consistent with the experience of three rather different countries that represent the spectrum of mobilization outcomes around the globe, as presented in the discussions of Senegal, Turkey, and Algeria in Chapters 4–6. Consistency with this empirical data does not directly demonstrate the accuracy of the overall argument, but the argument is consistent with the comparative evidence where other prominent theories are not.

The discussion in Chapter 3 demonstrated several important relationships. First, diverse forms of Islamist political mobilization such as voting for Islamist political parties, participation in Islamist street demonstrations, and Islamist political violence are broadly correlated with one another and usually occur in similar places and in similar periods. Second, there is little relationship between most religious, social, and economic development indicators and actual levels of Islamist mobilization when one compares the population of cases across global region. Variables such as religious sect, colonialism, globalization, level of economic development, population growth rates, and urbanization show little correlation with Islamist mobilization. Third, Islamic and state institutional factors, such as the social penetration of Islamic culture and law, the number of Islamic groups, measures of state disorder, Islamist repression, and rapid political liberalization are all associated with Islamist mobilization outcomes.

The case discussions in Chapters 4–6 reveal much about the mechanisms by which Islamic entrepreneurs can effectively channel religious sentiment into political mobilization. The low-mobilization case of Senegal teaches us that strong alignment between the state and a hierarchically organized religious elite can actively prevent religious entrepreneurship by in-group policing. Likewise, Senegal's religious brotherhoods have divided Islamic common knowledge into competing understandings of Islam, which limits cross-group activation of shared Islamic expectations. Few focal points of internal state crisis or rapid liberalization are available around which religious entrepreneurs could channel the Islamic expectations that do exist.

By contrast, the weak condition of the Islamic elite in Turkey and Algeria has created ample opportunities for religious entrepreneurship. Regional variation in Turkey demonstrates that levels of economic development or traditional culture have little impact on Islamist support there, but also that regions with dense networks of Islamic religious institutions are much more likely to back Islamist politicians. Measures of political and economic instability are also highly correlated with Islamist electoral mobilization in Turkey.

While Islamist mobilization in Turkey has at times been considerable, it was dwarfed by the large-scale Islamist mobilization that Algeria saw in the 1990s, which included widespread Islamist voting, massive public demonstrations, and acute political violence. The Algerian experience of the late 1980s and early 1990s juxtaposed the main causal variables of this study in a short timeframe, creating the perfect storm for Islamist political action. Highly autonomous, socially dense, and fragmented Islamic religious institutions, coupled with a dramatic misalignment of Islamist and state (military) incentives, under conditions of rapid liberalization, public electoral injustices, and a disintegration of social order led to a redefinition of Algerian politics around the Islamist challenge throughout the 1990s.

Although there appears to be considerable evidence to support the principal conceptual and causal arguments outlined in this study, a number of conceptual dilemmas remain that highlight persistent difficulties in the arguments presented here. I will briefly address four of these and speculate on what they imply for our confidence in the argument of this study. The first is the issue of which aspects of this study are particularly Islamic, and whether or not there are true religious entrepreneurs who initiate the mobilization process described in Chapter 2. The second is the presence of an enduring tension between two similar variables that the model predicts should have opposing effects on mobilization outcomes. These are the fragmentation of Islamic common knowledge and the organizational fragmentation of the Islamic movement as a whole. The third issue is the paradoxical role of repression, which appears to suppress mobilization in some contexts while activating it in others. The fourth and broadest issue is the challenge of understanding the direction of causation when some variables may be endogenous to the mobilization process.

I will begin by addressing the issue of whether this is a story about generic political mobilization, a story about generically religious mobilization, or a story that is particular to Islamist political mobilization. The short answer is that we can only have confidence that it is a story about Islamist political mobilization because the research design here employed only looks at variations in Islamist forms of political activity.

That said, Islam has extremely diverse manifestations around the world,[2] and also has many structures, beliefs, and expectations that are similar to those of other religions, especially Judaism and Christianity. The argument here has depended little on Islamic ideology and much more on its institutional forms such as institutions of worship, education, and religious judgements, which are not dramatically different from religious institutions in other traditions. These commonalities lead me to believe that a similar story about religious mobilization could be told for other traditions, although a research design that tested for variations in cross-religious mobilization would be necessary to validate this. Likewise, religious identity should not be dramatically different from other forms of identity, such as ethnic or comprehensive ideological attachments. Therefore, at an abstract level much of the argument here is likely applicable to political mobilization on behalf of identities more generally. Variations in institutional forms, resources, and types of common knowledge would certainly play a differentiating role across context.

Several distinctive features of Islam do play a role in the overall coherence of the argument presented here, however. These include the historical development of Islamic law and its associated public expectations, the historical use of Islam at the state level to legitimize rulers, Qur'anic schools that emphasize memorization and recitation (thus internalizing symbolic references), regularized public prayer at community mosques and associated Friday sermons with their political references, extensive Islamic thought on the importance of just rulers and social order, and the presence of religious scholars and other elites who often play a role in the state. Other religious and identity groups do not have this particular mix of institutional legacies and thus may find some of the variables presented here less relevant in explaining their patterns of mobilization.

The Islamic specificity of this story is related to a problematic issue in conceptualizing both religious entrepreneurs and the religiously mobilized. Because individuals have multiple identities, and can shift the identities that they emphasize depending on how these identities serve their interests, the religious entrepreneur or religiously mobilized individual is an unstable category. One may use religion as the identity of choice in one context where it appears to serve broader ends, and then abandon it when it no longer serves those ends.

Some examples of this include Chechen nationalists, who, despite limited empirical demonstrations of piety, employed Islamist discourse to serve their political ends of mobilizing individuals for an ill-fated conflict with Russia. A prominent opposition leader in the Caucasus, Yuri Shanibov, changed his name to Musa Shanib and began employing Islamist rhetoric because it was an effective mobilization strategy – not because his primary identity was that of an Islamic religious leader.[3] An additional example of identity movement from the other direction comes from Spain, as the Carlist religious entrepreneur Sabino de Arana began to redefine himself as a Basque nationalist, a strategy that proved more successful in mobilizing others around his opposition platform.[4] Political mobilization in the Aceh province of Indonesia has likewise shifted over time from religious mobilization to nationalist mobilization as conditions evolved. Likewise, many of those who vote for an Islamist political party, such as Welfare in Turkey or the FIS in Algeria, have done so not because they are expressing a primary religious identity, but because they are expressing opposition to the current government or regime. Regardless of their religious sentiments, they find that the Islamist party is the most effective vehicle for expressing this opposition.

The instability of religious entrepreneur as a category, however, does not change the observation that religious entrepreneurs as defined in this study exist throughout the Muslim world. Their level of religious piety or devotion does not make them religious entrepreneurs; rather, they are defined by their attempt to mobilize others politically on behalf of an "Islamic" political agenda. The personal journey that they made to reach that decision is in most cases irrelevant to their subsequent success. However, there are two ways in which the instability of this category is sometimes relevant. The first is that opportunistic religious entrepreneurs are less likely to emerge from the ranks of the religious elite, nor do they naturally respond to efforts at in-group policing by those elite. Opportunistic religious entrepreneurs or mobilizers are thus less likely to be quieted by state concessions to Islamic groups. Second, because religious entrepreneurship and mobilization is an unstable category, we should expect to see wide variations in support for Islamist groups as the political context changes. Many political leaders in fact change the amount of emphasis they put on their Islamic identity within short periods of time. Likewise, electoral support for Islamist political parties can vary significantly from one election to the next as the political context changes.

I now turn to a second challenging conceptual issue, which is the issue of Islamic organizational fragmentation and the predicted effect that this has on mobilization outcomes. As noted in the extended discussion around the importance of Islamic institutions in building Islamic common knowledge, Islamic institutions help build Islamic common knowledge when they teach similar topics in a similar way. This creates a canon of symbolic references among a large portion of the population on which the Islamist entrepreneur can draw to communicate with his potential constituency, and around which to coordinate collective action in the context of focal state events.

In theory, a heavily fragmented Islamic movement should build less common knowledge than a unified one. This would be the case if factions within the Islamic movement socialized their constituents in very different ways with different conceptions about the meaning and purpose of Islam. As in the case of Senegal, where different brotherhoods have differentiated conceptions about the responsibilities of the Muslim citizen, Islamic common knowledge is weakened by fragmentation. Likewise, in states with a Sunni–Shi'a split in Islamic organizations, such as in Lebanon, Pakistan,

Saudi Arabia, Bahrain, or Iraq, one should expect common knowledge to be fragmented across these sectarian lines.

How then do we understand the observation noted in Chapter 3 that a high number of Islamic organizations in a given state is correlated with high mobilization outcomes? High levels of fragmentation are theorized to enable a climate of religious entrepreneurship because religious experimentation and defection from one organization to another is supported by such a structure. In-group policing is difficult in a fragmented movement because sanctioned entrepreneurs can defect to alternative Islamist groups. Likewise, high fragmentation increases the pressure on individual groups to differentiate themselves as the most committed Islamist choice, thus radicalizing some groups and leading to more extensive political mobilization.

While in some cases fragmentation does impact mobilization outcomes in opposite directions, in most cases the generic level of fragmentation does not provide enough information to predict which dynamic is in fact dominant. When the Islamist movement is fragmented into groups with clear distinctions in norms, doctrine, or hierarchy, such as Sufi brotherhoods or different Islamic sects, fragmentation should theoretically weaken mass public mobilization across divisions. However, in many cases the distinction between groups is much more superficial and based in personal conflicts between dominant generations or leaders of the different organizations. In these cases the divisions have little relevance to common knowledge, because Islamic common knowledge is developed outside the realm of these organizations, often through religious schooling, Islamic media, and public mosques that serve members of multiple organizations. This type of fragmentation is much more likely to encourage religious entrepreneurship because the rather superficial distinctions between groups make defection from one to another easy, and in-group policing difficult.

A third conceptual challenge is the role of repression in determining mobilization outcomes. In both the case studies and the broader data set, repression appears to have dampening effects on mobilization in some contexts and amplifying effects in others. General shifts toward authoritarianism dampen any Islamist electoral mobilization and are not correlated with other forms of Islamist mobilization at a statistically significant level. On the other hand, repression targeted specifically at Islamist groups is correlated with Islamist mobilization. The direction of causality is difficult to assess with the time-series data employed in this study, but considerable anecdotal evidence from the cases examined here, as well as other cases, suggests that often state repression of Islamists amplifies mobilization outcomes in the immediate aftermath of the repression. This is particularly true regarding violent mobilization outcomes.

This observed correlation appears to contradict an assumption made in Chapter 2, that state repression increases the costs of individual mobilization, as well as its implication that when mobilization is costly there should be less of it. While targeted state repression makes the threat of state sanctions for mobilizing individuals credible, it also has another effect, which is to coordinate common knowledge around repressive activities, thus focusing the attention of mobilizers on perceived state injustice. This coordinating effect on Islamist mobilization should be stronger when the repression is specific to Islamic actors, but weaker under conditions of general state repression when the effect on Islamists is much more diffuse. This prediction is supported by the data, which reveal a much higher correlation between targeted Islamist repression and mobilized Islamist responses than for general political repression as a whole. Indeed, general political repression under authoritarian regimes tends to be associated with low levels of Islamist mobilization, as may be observed in traditionally repressive republican countries such as Syria, Tunisia, Libya, and pre-2003 Iraq.

State decisions to repress Islamists, therefore, appear to have two contradictory effects. Repression both raises the personal costs for individual mobilization and increases the ability of Islamists to coordinate their political activities around a particular issue. Islam-specific repression, in particular, activates common Islamic expectations about the role of the Muslim ruler and his requisite piety and justice. Under conditions of Islam-specific repression, these expectations are bound to be disappointed. The repression further politicizes Islam, and directly implicates the state in anti-Islamic activities. Repression of Islamists is therefore a political gamble, a gamble that the data suggest states often lose.

The final theoretical issue that I address here is the potential problem of endogeneity and missing variable bias in the kind of argument that I have been making in this study. Endogeneity refers to the observation that correlation does not equal causation, and that the causative variables posited may in fact be influenced by those outcomes that they are used to explain. Missing variable bias refers to the problem that two correlated variables may not have a causative relationship, because a third unmentioned variable is impacting both of them in the same direction. These problems are most relevant here regarding the relationship between the growth of Islamic religious institutions and political mobilization. Does Islamist political mobilization affect the growth of Islamic religious institutions, rather than vice versa?

My belief based on case observations and on interviews regarding this subject is that successful Islamist mobilization usually does impact the growth of Islamic institutions in a positive way, thus validating general concerns over endogeneity. When Islamist parties took power in Turkey and Algeria, for example, they encouraged the growth of Islamic religious institutions under areas of their purview. However, this observation that the relationship between institutional development and political mobilization goes both directions does not necessarily weaken the argument that institutional density affects levels of political mobilization. The direction of causation can be tested by careful attention to the chronology of events, demonstrating that institutional growth precedes religious politicization. This is empirically demonstrated in the Algerian case, as the rapid spread of independent mosques in the 1980s preceded the widespread politicization of Islam in the early 1990s. Likewise, in the Turkish case, growth in Islamic educational institutions and the Islamic media preceded the national successes of Welfare in the 1990s. At the provincial level in Turkey, a lagged measure of institutional density is correlated with Islamist voting, suggesting that the prior density of religious institutions matters for future voting patterns.

Can the variables associated with entrepreneurial climate and public state crises also be endogenous to mobilization outcomes? In principle they could be, although I have tried to be careful in distinguishing between both organizational relationships and state crises that result from Islamist mobilization, and those that are clearly distinct from the effects of mobilization outcomes.

Of the variables that represent the structure of entrepreneurship opportunities, Islamist organizational fragmentation is the most likely to be endogenous to Islamist mobilization. This is because in periods of extensive mobilization, Islamist movements often fragment over strategic decisions or personal rivalries, thus multiplying the number of Islamist organizations in the process. Fragmentation can nevertheless be measured prior to periods of mobilization, and earlier fragmentation is associated with later mobilization, suggesting a causal relationship.

One can likewise imagine that extensive Islamist mobilization causes a state crisis of order that is therefore endogenously correlated with mobilization outcomes. Data collection in the course of this study revealed, however, that Islamist-triggered state crises are actually quite rare as a percentage of overall numbers of state crises. The measures of state crisis employed throughout this study dominantly reflect political change that is unrelated to pressures from Islamist mobilization.

While I have tried to pay careful attention to chronology in order to mitigate the risks of endogeneity, missing variable bias remains a concern, particularly with regard to the growth of Islamic religious institutions and mobilization outcomes. It is possible that there are factors that influence both the growth of religious institutions (spurring a religious revival) and the growth of politicized Islam. Why religion becomes more attractive to a population over time remains an unanswered question in this study, which has focused primarily on why religion becomes politicized in some contexts but not in others. It is likely that factors influencing religious revivals also impact religious politicization. Note, however, that there are a significant number of cases in which Islamic revival is not correlated with politicized Islam (including the case of Senegal discussed in this study). This leads me to believe that Islamist mobilization has several triggers distinct from those that trigger the growth of Islam as a religion more generally.

In conclusion, I have not claimed in this study that popular explanatory variables for Islamism, such as long-term trends in demography, urbanization, economic performance, and cultural factors, have no influence on mobilization outcomes. Rather, it seems clear that such factors have had broad impact on the historical trajectory of the cases discussed here, such as the case of Algeria. Nevertheless, I have argued that major mobilization outcomes are best understood by observing the changing institutional contexts highlighted throughout the study, without the need for extensive reference to these alternative contextual factors. Challenges in specifying the precise determinants of mobilization remain because of the complex and diverse processes involved. In particular, unraveling the causes of one mobilization event that is embedded in a broader pattern of state–Islamist interaction (as in a civil war) is often too difficult to do in a convincing manner using large-scale institutional variables. Institutional variables do provide particular leverage when comparing big cases across time, however, and the institutional parallels across diverse contexts of high Islamist mobilization are striking.

The argument made in this study has important implications for the future of political Islam. First, it implies that Islamist mobilization has explicitly political rather than religious or social determinants. While social and religious factors are important in building the type of environment in which Islamic religious entrepreneurs can be successful, these factors alone are unlikely to lead to mass mobilization without the crucial role of political focal points at the state level. Therefore, Islamist mobilization will most likely occur in unstable or rapidly changing political contexts in which religious entrepreneurs can take advantage of key events to focus public attention on perceived violations of Islamic principles of order or justice. This is clearly demonstrated in the political mobilization during elections that occurred in the aftermath of the Arab revolts in 2011–2012.

Second, it implies that mass Islamist mobilization will not occur under conditions of weak Islamic religious institutions, and that the growth of Islamic institutions may in turn facilitate the growth of politicized Islam. Contexts without reasonably dense religious institutions of schools, mosques, and an Islamic media are unlikely to generate the kind of Islamic expectations that can be channeled into political action through symbolic references by religious entrepreneurs. Likewise, a low density of Islamic religious institutions prevents Islamic entrepreneurs from utilizing religious channels for political communication to a mass audience. Ironically, many political leaders concerned about an Islamist threat encourage the growth of Islamic institutions. This is done in part to co-opt a potential religious opposition and in part to assert control over the vision of Islam expressed in these institutions. While Islamic religious institutions are not inherently political, this study demonstrates how they can become so quite quickly as the political context shifts and religious institutions facilitate the political goals of the opposition.

Finally, the results of this study imply that the structural relationship between the state and the Islamic elite, as well as the relationship between the Islamic elite and the class of potential religious entrepreneurs, is crucial to determining the success of attempts at Islamist mobilization. When the religious elite are invested in networks of state patronage as holders of important positions in the state bureaucracy, or as recipients of other forms of state largesse, they are likely to try to police religious entrepreneurs that seek to challenge the state. The contrast between the state–*marabout* alliance in Senegal with the open collapse of state patronage and state–Islamist conflict in Algeria is striking. Likewise, in contexts of hierarchical relationships between the religious elite and their followers, in-group policing is much more likely to be successful than in a context of high fragmentation and autonomy of Islamist groups like that evident in Algeria. As states attempt to limit the impact of Islamist mobilization, finding a successful balance between co-opting Islamic elites through the building of religious institutions and limiting their potential impact in contexts of political disorder or liberalization promises to remain a formidable challenge.

## REFERENCES

Derluguian, Georgi M. 2005. *Bourdieu's Secret Admirer in the Caucasus*. Chicago, IL: University of Chicago Press.

Diez Medrano, Juan. 1995. *Divided Nations: Class, Politics, and Nationalism in the Basque Country and Catalonia*. Ithaca, NY: Cornell University Press.

Geertz, Clifford. 1968. *Islam Observed: Religious Development in Morocco and Indonesia*. New Haven, CT: Yale University Press.

Kepel, Gilles. 2002. *Jihad: The Trail of Political Islam*. Cambridge, MA: Harvard University Press.

Roy, Olivier. 1994. *The Failure of Political Islam*. Cambridge, MA: Harvard University Press.

# Epilogue

## *Islamist Mobilization in the Arab Uprisings*

For a period of multiple years beginning in early 2011,[1] the Arab world experienced significant political upheaval, which led to changes in the political environment of virtually every Arab country, although to different degrees. Dramatic popular mobilization against the ruling governments of Tunisia, Egypt, Yemen, Syria, Morocco, Libya, Iraq, Bahrain, and others created an environment where political mobilization in the Arab world reached much higher levels than it had at the end of the prior decade. Earlier, both Lebanon (2005) and Iran (2009) also experienced very high levels of street protest. This diffuse but intensive period of political mobilization highlights a remarkable period in the contemporary political history of the Middle East. The dramatic increase in popular mobilization has been felt less in the broader set of countries with large Muslim populations, but the growth of the Arab media in the last decade, and the global impact of *al-Jazeera* and its imitators, in particular, make the potential for increased popular mobilization in other parts of the Muslim world a reality.

To what extent do the arguments of this study, which focused on the period until 2010, help to explain the patterns of Islamist mobilization associated with the Arab uprisings? I have argued that Islamist forms of political mobilization are most likely in contexts where religious hierarchies are weak or else religious elites have divergent interests from those of the state, where the social penetration of Islamic religious institutions and networks is high, and where public events at the level of the state provide focal points for coordination. These events may include either state crises of order and justice or rapid political liberalization, both of which can activate Islamic common knowledge and help to solve the coordination challenge associated with mobilization. The political events associated with the Arab uprisings provided very effective (exogenous) state-based focal points, and the extent of these focal points varied across countries, leading to variations in mobilization. The institutional context in which the public responds to these focal points also matters in predicting where mobilization will be most Islamist in orientation and where Islamist political entrepreneurs will be most effective. Under conditions in which Islamist elites have divergent preferences from those of the state, where there are weak elite Islamic hierarchies, and where there is a rich Islamic institutional foundation that provides common knowledge around popular expectations, we should expect substantial amounts of Islamist mobilization. These conditions effectively describe the case for many Arab countries in the wake of the 2011 uprisings. Whether mobilization took the form of voting, protest, or violence largely depended on the opportunities afforded by the state at the moment of heightened mobilization.

All forms of mobilization addressed in this study, including violence, street demonstrations, and voting for Islamist parties, increased in the Middle East during the period after the initial uprisings in 2011. Several countries saw high levels of Islamist violence, including Libya, Yemen, Syria, and Iraq. Major Islamist protests also occurred in a widespread and diverse set of countries, including Egypt, Tunisia, Morocco, Yemen, Bahrain, and others, although Islamist protests sometimes came after the beginning of a broader set of popular protests. Finally, in several countries, including Tunisia, Egypt, and Morocco, Islamist parties demonstrated for the first time through open elections that they could dominate at the polls.

In this epilogue I briefly examine patterns of Islamist mobilization both during and after the early protest cycles of the Arab uprisings, patterns of Islamist militancy during the uprisings, and the results of Islamist electoral mobilization at the end of 2011. I argue that Islamists were increasingly involved in protest in the wake of the Arab uprisings, although in some countries they came late to protest mobilization. The initially muted Islamist responses during popular protests reflect risk management strategies and strategic divisions within Islamist groups, but these groups did ultimately participate and were particularly well-poised to play a large role in shaping the aftermath of protest. I further argue that Islamist electoral mobilization in the Arab world in the three cases that held elections in 2011 (Tunisia, Morocco, and Egypt) suggests that the reasons for high popular mobilization are consistent with the institutional origins of Islamist mobilization in previous periods described in this study. I discuss the low initial levels of Islamist militancy during the early uprisings of 2011, but argue that Islamist violence increased significantly over time for reasons anticipated in this study, including state crises of order and justice, as well as fragmentation of the Islamist movements.

Because the Arab uprisings were initially based in protest mobilization through street demonstrations, I begin with a discussion of the role of Islamist protest. The Arab uprisings raise two important questions in the context of this study. First, why did protest mobilization rise dramatically, including both Islamist and non-Islamist protest? Second, why did Islamists in the initial cases of the uprisings, particularly in Tunisia and Egypt, come late to the street demonstrations? I then turn to a discussion of the mass electoral mobilization by Islamist political parties that occurred in the first two years after the initial protests. I look at reasons for the striking electoral success of Islamist parties in 2011–2012, as well as comparative differences across countries. I then examine the increasing Islamist militancy that characterized the post-2011 period, with a brief discussion of the cases of Libya, Syria, and Yemen. I conclude with an assessment of important emerging trends in intra-Islamist competition and a renewed turn toward repression of Islamists by the state.

## PROTEST

The popular protests that dramatically transformed political expectations in places such as Tunisia, Egypt, and Yemen, as well as the wide-scale popular protests in most other countries throughout the Arab world, were not dominantly Islamist protests. Their origins in the frustrated middle class and youth-driven new media networks left Islamist groups behind in mobilizing their supporters to call for revolutionary change in authoritarian regimes. Prominent Islamist groups such as the Egyptian Muslim Brotherhood engaged the protest movement cautiously and in a way that revealed internal divisions over their position with respect to the popular protests. Islamists in many countries appeared uncharacteristically slow and generationally divided in support of widespread popular protest in those countries where it occurred. There were a number of strategic reasons for this choice, including a desire to allow protesters to highlight the broad, non-ideological character of opposition to government.

Islamist groups did not, however, miss their opportunity to successfully mobilize in key Arab countries undergoing political transformation. Indeed, Islamist groups played major roles as the opposition to authoritarian regimes evolved, both in protest environments and in the electoral arena. In countries such as Egypt and Tunisia, Islamists jumped into the political maelstrom as it became clear that they would not be uniquely repressed and that Islamist leaders would be unable to maintain full control over the mobilization decisions of their supporters.

Islamists were central actors in popular protest in the Middle East during 2011 and beyond, but they generally did not initiate the popular challenge to the state. This requires some explanation given the comparative protest advantages of Islamist groups, as seen in a number of cases in this study. Some of the predictions of the scholarship on Islamism noted in this study suggest that Islamist groups are likely to be uniquely effective in mobilizing protest against political and economic injustice. By the standards of the broader Muslim world, both Egypt and Tunisia have comparatively dense networks of Islamic religious institutions, which create the possibility for the activation of Islamic common knowledge across a large portion of the population. Because of Tunisia's history of limited secularizing reforms under President Habib Bourguiba, these

Islamic religious institutions are less widespread in Tunisia than those in Egypt, but by the standards of many of the countries in this study, they should still create a foundation for Islamist activism under appropriate conditions. However, in the earliest popular uprisings in both Tunisia and Egypt, Islamists either remained on the sidelines or joined the popular protests late. Why?

One answer is that the perceived costs of visibly participating in the popular protests appeared higher than the perceived costs of not participating. This calculation of the relative costs of participation or staying on the sidelines shifted over time in countries such as Egypt, Jordan, and Yemen, and eventually led Islamist groups into the fray but in deliberately secondary positions to other opposition actors. Additionally, leaders of Islamist groups faced important calculations regarding internal group politics (such as the difficulty of maintaining control in the face of challenges from a younger generation of activists), which led to caution in assuming leadership of the protests. Islamists in most of the Arab world were the "usual suspects" in opposition to the state, and it was in their interest that they participate in a broader popular movement.[2]

In each of the countries experiencing mass popular mobilization, including Tunisia, Egypt, Bahrain, and Yemen, the levels of uncertainty regarding the ultimate outcome were very high throughout the early days of the protest, and remained painfully uncertain in many places for some time. While opposition protestors deliberately used non-violent resistance, regime leaders looked for any opportunity to repress in the name of containing a security threat. In most popular protests throughout the Arab world, leaders have been quick to blame Islamists (depicted by the state as religious radicals or terrorists) and to harshly repress them. By blaming religious radicals for popular unrest, leaders try to deflect criticism of state repression both at home and from abroad. This means that Islamist groups face a high risk of repression at the beginning of a new protest cycle, but see few perceptible benefits that would encourage them to claim leadership of the protests. Likewise, non-Islamist protestors also have an interest in keeping Islamists on the sidelines in order to clearly demonstrate the mass popular character of the protests, to reduce the chances of repression, and to expose the fallacy of the security threat narrative that the regimes try to impose upon the protests.

In both Egypt and Libya, for example, state leaders openly (and falsely) accused radical Islamists of leading the protests as a way of justifying state repression. Both Islamists and non-Islamist protestors therefore had similar interests in framing these protests explicitly outside an Islamist framework when a protest cycle began. In contexts of significant Islamist hierarchy, such as within the Egyptian Muslim Brotherhood, movement leaders can provide in-group policing of their followers in order to keep them from creating an Islamist narrative of the popular uprising. In the early days of the Egyptian revolution, the Muslim Brotherhood attempted on numerous occasions to police within the group in order to keep its members from dragging the movement into uncertain political territory. These in-group policing attempts continued even after the Muslim Brotherhood had officially entered the fray, as the movement enforced political allegiances to its new, affiliated political party, the Freedom and Justice Party (FJP).

In Tunisia, Egypt, and Yemen, although members of Islamist groups participated in popular protests reasonably early, they did so within a broader and explicitly non-Islamist narrative, with little attempt to shift that narrative toward an Islamist one. In Bahrain, where most of the traditional opposition actors are Shi'a Islamists, religious and sectarian identities were likewise subordinated early on to a broader non-Islamist narrative of political injustice. This was done, in part, for strategic reasons, as Islamist groups sought to share the potential costs of repression with a broader segment of politicized society and avoid the potential for targeted state repression of Islamist groups.

In countries where Islamists have historically been the backbone of organized opposition, Islamist groups may reasonably see themselves as the natural beneficiaries of democratic regime change, regardless of its source. Islamist groups recognize that they have institutional advantages under contexts of rapid political liberalization and have an incentive for that liberalization to occur, whether or not they are its catalyst. That is, Islamists sense the potential to benefit from the protest behavior of others, receiving the likely benefits of democratic reform but allowing others to pay the high costs. Because they are likely to pay higher costs from repression than other groups who engage in protest, waiting for regime change to fully mobilize can be very attractive. As argued in this study, there is good reason for Islamists to believe that rapid political liberalization will benefit them, and benefit them disproportionately more than other, less institutionalized groups.

There is an additional, organizational reason some Islamist groups were cautious about leading initial protests. From the perspective of the internal politics of Islamist groups, older leaders who sense a potential threat from their younger rivals may be cautious about entering into popular protests that are dominated by a broader youth movement. If they do so, they may unwittingly create new leadership opportunities for their younger internal rivals (who may resonate much more with the youthful protestors), and concede control over the direction of the movement as time goes on. In Egypt, for example, significant divisions across generational lines emerged within the Brotherhood about when to call its members to protest in Tahrir Square and when to refrain, with the youth wing unsuccessfully pushing for more aggressive protest behavior from the broader organization.[3] In these contexts, the potential for in-group policing became increasingly strained, as it was during the period of the Moustarchidine movement in Senegal described in this study.

Despite these pressures for Islamist groups to cede protest leadership to others, there are costs to remaining on the sidelines for too long, and Islamist groups in the Arab world began to feel these pressures within a short period after the uprisings began. As protests in Egypt and Tunisia increasingly looked like they would succeed in meeting their objectives, Islamists became more comfortable and visible in calling for political change. Their ability to provide in-group policing of their members became much more problematic the longer they stayed out of the popular mobilization, and they began to risk internal generational splits unless they joined the protests, as younger members (of the Egyptian Muslim Brotherhood, for example) actively pressured their organizations to participate. In addition, they ran the risk of losing control of the regime change narrative, or of being perceived as out of touch with popular sentiment. Over time, as popular mobilization became more widespread, the anticipated costs of targeted repression declined, while the political costs of remaining on the sidelines increased. Under these circumstances, Islamist groups became more likely to participate in protest. They allowed others to pay the costs of initially challenging the regime, but because of their popularity and institutional resources, they could also anticipate substantial benefits from regime change.

What benefits could Islamist organizations expect to see from political reform? Likewise, under what circumstances would newly empowered publics favor Islamist organizations over their non-Islamist rivals? As the 2011 elections in Tunisia and Egypt demonstrated, Islamist organizations may receive large electoral advantages from democratic transitions to governance through free and fair elections. In contexts of diverse and divided political opposition, Islamist organizations have institutional resources and social networks that allow them to channel popular discontent in politically effective ways; these organizational benefits yielded rich rewards at the ballot box in the first Arab countries to move to free elections.

## ELECTORAL MOBILIZATION

Despite the cautious embrace of 2011's popular protests, Islamists initially emerged as the dominant democratic players in the period following the initial popular mobilization. Prominent Islamist figures returned from exile to countries such as Tunisia and Bahrain, anticipating new opportunities to provide leadership and to help shape the narratives of regime transition. While Islamist groups conceded much of the early protest mobilization to more secular rivals, they were institutionally well-positioned to serve as focal points for voter convergence in the face of highly fragmented, diverse, and untested alternatives. Large-scale Islamist electoral mobilization occurred in several countries during 2011–2012, which provides evidence regarding the correlates of Islamist mobilization discussed in this study.

In the three countries of North Africa where constitutive assembly and legislative elections were held in the wake of the Arab uprisings, Tunisia, Egypt, and Morocco, Islamist political parties scored dramatic successes at the ballot box. Similarly, Islamists scored a surprise electoral victory in Kuwait in early 2012. The popular support for the parties of al-Nahda (Renaissance) in Tunisia, al-Hurriya wa al-'Adala (Freedom and Justice) and al-Nour (Light) in Egypt, and al-'Adala wa al-Tanmiya (Justice and Development Party) in

Morocco was higher than might have been expected simply by looking at the relative levels of Islamist participation in the street protests of these countries. Although the Justice and Development Party in Morocco and the Muslim Brotherhood in Egypt (which formed the Freedom and Justice Party) had a recent track record of competing in elections and mobilizing their constituents to vote, both Tunisia's al-Nahda and Egypt's al-Nour party had to newly form or reconstitute themselves after a long absence in the immediate period prior to the elections. In all cases, the parties performed better in elections than their recent political experience may have suggested.

Why did Islamist parties do so well in the initial transitional polls? There are at least three plausible explanations that are consistent with the arguments of this study. First, in the wake of rapid political reform, Islamists had a clear institutional advantage over their rivals. In most cases, Islamists had a track record of social and political mobilization based in a wide range of institutions that operated under the previous regime, including in the religious, charitable, educational, media, and professional sectors. These organizational foundations provided a ready-made network that could be used for political mobilization and communication, which were not as readily available to their competitors.

A related second explanation is the transitional context in which new opportunities for religious entrepreneurship emerged, coupled with the concurrent breakdown of established Islamist hierarchies and arrangements between the religious elite and the previous governing regime. The Muslim Brotherhood in Egypt and al-Nahda in Tunisia, for example, both had new Salafi-branded Islamist challengers that emerged to help mobilize sympathetic publics and that were completely unmoved by attempts by Islamist elites to police them. This new entrepreneurial context had its parallels among non-Islamist groups, as well, which led to a high degree of fragmentation among the Islamist parties' competitors. However, even as new contexts for political and religious entrepreneurship evolved, the legacy of hierarchy within Islamist organizations benefited highly organized Islamist groups such as the Egyptian Muslim Brotherhood when they decided to explicitly compete for power in a new electoral environment. The impact of internal organizational discipline among Islamist parties such as the Brotherhood, when compared with their liberal and left-wing competitors, proved effective in mobilizing supporters at the polls.

A third explanation that is rooted in perceptions of state crises of order and justice is that the Islamist narrative was particularly compelling to voters in the face of widespread uncertainty and insecurity, both economically and politically. In the wake of political uncertainty, Islamist parties appeared to many to be a known quantity, with a simple, identity-focused message largely untarnished by association with the previous regime. The Islamist narrative in these elections focused both on a return to authenticity and greater social and economic equality, with attention to the most vulnerable. This message was particularly appealing to those worried about their own futures under the new regime, and who sought security in a more extensive moral social order. In all cases, Islamists were long perceived as unjustly treated under the old regimes, making the electorate particularly interested in observing how well they would do without artificial competitive restraints.

As the first Arab country to hold an election for a constitutive assembly in 2011, Tunisia's election was highly anticipated and the results particularly uncertain. Because the mass protests in Tunisia were predominantly led by existing labor and youth groups, Tunisia's revolution was described as explicitly un-Islamist, and the historic opposition party of al-Nahda had long been driven underground, with its leaders in exile. By the time elections were held in October 2011, however, al-Nahda had reconstituted itself as a powerful political force, with an increasingly clear political ideology that articulated a measure of respect for the democratic process and for pluralistic points of view. The veteran Islamist intellectual and al-Nahda's leader, Rachid al-Ghannouchi, returned to Tunisia to help craft the narrative of transition and to carve out a meaningful role of his Islamist group within it. The movement swiftly out flanked its wide range of competitors, winning 37% of the vote and 89 of 217 seats in the assembly elections by appealing to religious identity and articulating a platform of social justice, respect for pluralism, and clean government.

Although Morocco's political reforms during this period were less dramatic, widespread popular protest throughout 2011 led King Mohammed VI to make important changes to the Moroccan constitution in an attempt to pacify demands for regime change. A series of constitutional amendments were passed by a popular referendum prior to elections in November 2011, which required, among other things, the king to appoint a prime minister from the party winning the most seats in parliament. The Justice and Development Party (PJD), an established Islamist competitor committed to working within the monarchical framework, won the elections with 23 percent percent of the vote, leading to 107 out of 395 legislative seats. In a dramatic first for Morocco, the king then invited the PJD's leader Abdeliliah Benkirane to form a government as prime minister. Although significant calls for more meaningful political reform continued, an established Islamist party was able to benefit from the reform environment to expand its voter base and political power within the Moroccan system.

The multi-stage Egyptian elections of 2011–2012 proved particularly interesting from the perspective of Islamist electoral success. Although all observers agreed that the Muslim Brotherhood's newly created Freedom and Justice Party would be very competitive as the most well-known quantity in Egyptian politics, the extent of its success, as well as the level of success of its Islamist (Salafist) competitors, was unknown prior to the elections. At the conclusion of the three-month electoral process for Egypt's constitutive assembly, the Freedom and Justice Party and associated parties dominated the assembly with a large plurality of 37 percent of the vote and 235 of 498 seats, followed by the more conservative Salafist party, al-Nour, and associated parties with 28 percent of the vote and 123 of the 498 seats.[4] This meant that the Islamist groups, which had appeared comparatively marginal throughout the eighteen-day mass uprising that ousted Mubarak in February 2011, were suddenly anything but marginal in determining the future direction of the Egyptian regime, holding the dominant majority of seats in the constitutive assembly. Islamist parties in Egypt were more successful at the polls overall than in similarly free elections in Tunisia, likely because the institutional density of religious organizations is greater in Egypt, leading to greater mobilizational capacity under similar state-based focal points. A dramatic shift had taken place in Egyptian politics, which put comparatively untested Islamist groups in the position of negotiating a transition with an increasingly intransigent and forceful Egyptian military.

Islamists also scored a major success at the polls in the February 2012 Kuwaiti elections, winning 23 of 50 seats, thus becoming newly relevant after a period where Islamist opposition appeared to wane in the face of renewed tribal and family identity politics. Islamist groups were initially well positioned to play a role in uncertain democratic transitions of Yemen and Libya as well, although these transitions devolved into civil war before Islamist electoral mobilization could be fully assessed. The Libyan elections for the General National Congress in 2012 went ahead despite boycotts and some disruptions, and an Islamist party known as the Justice and Construction Party came in a distant second at the polls. Some Islamists and a mix of tribal coalitions asserted that the elections were unrepresentative and ultimately rejected the elected national government in favor of a rival government set up in Tripoli. In Yemen, Islah played a major role in the transitional negotiations, but the Houthi rebellion challenged the state and took over the capital before transitional elections could occur.

The Egyptian elections highlight one of the most interesting developments in Islamist politics in the wake of the Arab uprisings, which is the rise of Salafist groups into the realm of negotiated and electoral politics. Salafism is a broad category based on the Arabic term *salaf* (ancestors of the Islamic community) that is applied to describe very religiously conservative groups that argue for the creation of an Islamic state inspired by the original Islamic community under the leadership of the Prophet Muhammad. Multiple Salafist groups competed in the Egyptian elections, with most Salafi votes going to the al-Nour party. Although observers of Egypt were previously aware of the importance of Salafi movements at the social level, the degree of electoral support that the al-Nour party received was a surprise, despite the party's own predictions of its success. Salafi groups have also risen to heightened prominence in other places, leading violent protests in Tunisia against a broadcast station and increasing their political profile in Yemen, among other countries. Their success in Egypt's first democratic election indicated a strong desire among a minority segment of the population for more dramatic forms of regime and religious policy change than the Muslim Brotherhood pledged to provide.

Not all those who voted for Islamist parties in these elections should be described as Islamists, however, or even as having Islamist political preferences. There are multiple reasons that individuals vote for political parties, including expressive voting to receive an emotional benefit or strategic voting to ensure that the least preferred parties do not win. As previously observed in the chapters on both Turkey and Algeria, protest voting provided a significant bounce to Islamist parties at particular moments, and voting for these parties in the immediate wake of the Arab uprisings should similarly be interpreted as much a vote for change as for an Islamist political agenda. Indeed, popular support for Islamist parties began to waver not long after these parties began to lead governments, and new protest movements appeared in order to challenge their rule.

## POLITICAL VIOLENCE

Although most of the protests associated with the Arab uprisings explicitly sought to challenge existing regimes without resorting to violence, uprisings did become violent in several cases, most notably in Libya and Syria, and to some extent also in Yemen, Egypt, and Bahrain. Protests were actively and violently repressed in many countries, which sometimes led to capitulation on the part of protesters, and in other cases to the transformation of non-violent protest into violent rebellion. In none of these cases was the violence associated with the uprisings initially or exclusively led by Islamist groups, although members of Islamist groups participated in violent rebellion and increasingly came to dominate the rebellion in Syria as time passed. Islamist militancy should be seen within the context of increasing militancy by rebels more broadly, as one of several responses to heightened state repression. The cases of Libya, Syria, and Yemen are most instructive in understanding the role of Islamic militancy in the uprisings.

The context of the initial uprisings provided new opportunities for militants to play a role in consolidating their minority positions within society, and many took advantage of these openings. The subsequent context of the closure of reform experiments in places such as Egypt and Yemen, however, were substantially more important to the rise of Islamist militant groups in those countries. Additionally, severe crises of governance and state weakness in countries such as Syria, Libya, and Yemen allowed Islamist militants to dramatically increase their influence and strength over time. As discussed in this study, contexts of extended state crisis are significantly correlated with both Islamist protest and Islamist violence. The period after 2013 saw state and governance crises throughout much of the Arab world, including in Syria where there was mass regime violence against civilians and in Iraq where the Sunni population was increasingly marginalized by government and the military.

Libya was initially the most fertile ground for the expression of Islamist militancy, in part because former Islamist prisoners of the regime played an important role in the rebel movement that led to the collapse of Qaddafi's regime. Qaddafi's heterodox interpretations of Islamic thought and his aggressive repression of Islamist groups, including the Libyan Muslim Brotherhood, led to long-standing resentment of the regime by Islamist groups, whose members were killed or imprisoned for long periods prior to the beginning of the rebellion. Islamists in Libya thus had an interest in participating in the Libyan rebellion, and provided leadership in key moments, with Abdel Hakim Belhaj, the former emir of the Libyan Islamic Fighting Group, leading a final rebel surge to capture Qaddafi's compound in Tripoli. Despite some concerns from outsiders that the rebellion would be increasingly defined as an Islamist one, the range of actors who participated in the rebellion was very diverse, including a number of defectors from the Libyan army and Qaddafi's government, effectively diluting the number of rebels who defined their rebellion in Islamist terms. As post-Qaddafi Libya transitioned toward state failure with competing militias operating in parallel with electoral politics, however, Islamic identity began to play an increasing role in defining distinctions between competing parties, both in institutionalized government and through militia activities.

The Syrian case has intriguing initial parallels to Libya, including historical militant challenges to the regime by Islamist groups (especially the Muslim Brotherhood), the active repression of those groups, and the reemergence of militancy in the wake of widespread government repression in 2011. As in Libya, the popular uprising in Syria incorporated a wide range of groups, including many that explicitly rejected an Islamist narrative of rebellion in favor of a narrative of democracy and human rights. As unwavering repression tipped the opposition toward militancy and Syria toward civil war, however, opportunities for Islamist militancy grew quickly, particularly in the industrial towns of central Syria (Hama, Homs), which had a history of Islamist organization. By 2013, the dominant rebel groups fighting the Syrian regime used Islamist symbolism and frameworks to mobilize their constituents and effectively began to crowd out militant opposition that was unwilling to use Islamist narratives. Islamist rebel groups also began to fight one another almost as much as they engaged in attacks on the regime, with Jabhat al-Nusra (affiliated with al-Qa'eda) and the Islamic State in Iraq and the Levant (ISIL) battling for supremacy and legitimacy in leading the rebellion and exercising control over conquered territory.

In Yemen, in parallel to the formal Islamist political opposition, represented by the long-standing Islah party, Islamist militancy grew in the waning years of Saleh's presidency and expanded rapidly in the context of ongoing state weakness after the president's departure. Al-Qa'eda in the Arabian Peninsula, a small but explicitly militant group, openly challenged Saleh's regime in the late 2000s and extended its reach in the wake of infighting between state security forces, beginning in 2011. Though marginal to both the formal opposition groups (under the banner of the Joint Meeting Parties) and the mass popular street protests, al-Qa'eda had a history of consolidating its resources in rugged and un-policed parts of the Yemeni countryside and increasingly took advantage of newfound freedom of movement and operations. It eventually took control of substantial portions of Yemeni territory, including the governorate of Hadramaut and its large port city of Mukalla. A further Islamist group with an ideological basis in Zaydi Shi'ism, the Houthi movement, launched successful attacks on the Yemeni state in 2014–2015, taking control of the Yemeni capital Sana'a as well as the southern city of Aden for a period of time and triggering a Yemeni civil war in which both Islamists and non-Islamists fought on both sides of the conflict for control over the Yemeni state. In the process, the poorest country in the Middle East suffered enormous setbacks toward political and economic development.

As this study has illustrated, state weakness by itself does not predict high levels of Islamist mobilization, although the ongoing state crises of order and justice (including perceptions of political injustice) that plagued Libya, Syria, and Yemen after the Arab uprisings provided focal points for higher levels of Islamist activity. This Islamist activity shifted increasingly from protest to violence, as normal political or governmental avenues for mobilization appeared to close. In Egypt, as well, as avenues for Islamist electoral mobilization closed beginning with the coup d'état against President Morsi in July 2013, violent Islamist mobilization began to increase. The harrowing parallels between the Algerian closure of electoral avenues after Islamist electoral victories of 1991 and the Egyptian military closure of competitive elections coupled with determined repression of the Muslim Brotherhood beginning in 2013 are striking. This study has argued that those Algerian political events were critical in making the shift to violent mobilization. After 2013, Islamist violence by small militant groups also began to accelerate in Egypt.

One important trend that accelerated as a result of the rapid and multi-faceted Islamist political mobilization after 2011 was intra-Islamist competition, both in the electoral arena and on the battlefield. The increasing prominence of Salafis in protest movements and in electoral campaigns challenged more mainstream Islamist opposition groups, such as those affiliated with the Muslim Brotherhood. As Islamist groups differ substantively over both their end objective and their strategies in achieving those objectives, the prospect of power (both through elections and through territorial conquest) led to ideological and organizational battles over the direction of Islamist movements. This was particularly notable in the Egyptian national elections, which saw the Muslim Brotherhood face an unexpectedly strong challenge from the new Salafi al-Nour party. Rivalry between Salafis and more mainstream groups also characterized the post-2011 period in Tunisia, leading to significant challenges for the al-Nahda party, and in Yemen, in which the more mainstream Islamist Islah party has had to deal with challenges from rival militants.

Indeed, the future political fault lines of much of the Arab world lie not only across religious-secular lines, but also across the diverse Islamist movements themselves. This was most dramatically highlighted in Iraq and Syria by intra-Islamist fighting that accompanied the rise of the Islamic State group. Cross-sectarian attacks in mixed Sunni–Shi'a communities also became remarkably common in the region beginning in 2013. As this study has highlighted, Islamist fragmentation occurs in a wide variety of countries and is strongly associated with high levels of Islamist mobilization across each of the principal manifestations (electoral mobilization, protest, violence). One of the significant changes in the Arab world since 2011 has been the rapid fragmentation of Islamist groups, fed by divisions over both ideology and political strategy.

Islamist political mobilization in the Middle East after 2011 saw some of its highest levels recorded in this study, as government-affiliated Islamic hierarchies broke down and Islamist opposition groups used their institutional advantages to make use of significant political focal points, including state crises of order and justice, as well as rapid political liberalization. In some countries this mobilization was dominantly electoral (Tunisia, Egypt, Morocco, Kuwait), in some it was dominantly protest-based (Bahrain, Algeria, Saudi Arabia), and in others it descended quickly into Islamist violence (Libya, Syria, Yemen, Iraq). Whether or not popular enthusiasm for Islamist groups can be maintained over time is open to question, however. There is significant evidence to suggest that once Islamists capture state capacity (through elections or otherwise), they lose much of the protest support that they initially received because of popular dissatisfaction with the current system.

In their role as leaders of uncertain and chaotic political transitions, and in their untested governing responsibilities in countries such as Tunisia, Morocco, and Egypt, there are many opportunities for Islamist parties to prove a disappointment to their supporters. This is the case because of their inexperience with governance, because of the enormous structural obstacles to their success, and because of unrealistic popular expectations about the level of ideological purity that can be maintained in coalition politics. As opportunities for militants to challenge the new order increase, and as religious and non-religious minorities begin to fear for their status within a context of shifting power relations, Islamist groups often find that their political honeymoon is shorter than anticipated. This has been true in many cases where Islamists have participated in governing coalitions, and certainly proved to be the case in the Muslim Brotherhood's stunning political reversal after it was deposed in an Egyptian military coup in 2013. Likewise, as the pluralism of Islamist political views puts divisions within the Islamist movements into the political spotlight, multiple contested Islamisms will continue to emerge.

Patterns of Islamist mobilization during the Arab uprisings highlighted how the grassroots potential for successful Islamist mobilization can remain dormant over time until it finds expression in the context of institutional change and new state focal points. Comparing levels of Islamist mobilization in countries such as Tunisia and Egypt before and after the start of the popular uprisings demonstrates the important role played by institutional climates supportive of political and religious entrepreneurship. Perhaps even more importantly, it illustrates the mobilizational potential of clear focal points for coordination at the level of the state. In the months and years following the Arab uprisings, states became increasingly determined to remove those public focal points, most commonly through unambiguous and sustained repression of Islamist movements. Indeed, many of the institutional sources of Islamist mobilization described in this study came under attack by states in an effort to rewind the political changes brought on by the uprisings.

Despite authoritarian governments' best efforts, however, two major shifts in the potential for political mobilization took place as a result of the Arab uprisings: the possibility of expression without repression, and the possibility of public coordination around a particular political narrative and objective. These shifts benefited Islamists and their popular competitors equally. In the end, however, Islamists proved the most successful in mobilizing both Arab electorates and militants around the design of their political future. This was possible because of the comparative strength of Islamic religious institutions in much of the Arab world, which provided opportunities for widespread coordination on social expectations unmatched by their political competitors, because of the rapidity of political liberalization in the context of uncertainty, and because of state crises of order and justice that left many feeling deeply insecure about the future. Islamist groups proved to be the best positioned to take advantage of these multiple political opportunities. Despite Islamists' current inability to successfully navigate a multiplicity of ongoing political challenges, including widespread attempts to restrict their room for political maneuver, the evidence from this study suggests that Islamist mobilization is unlikely to disappear from an increasingly turbulent Middle East in the years to come.

## REFERENCES

Kirkpatrick, David D. 2011. "Muslim Brotherhood Struggles to Find its Balance in Egypt's Whirlwind." *New York Times*, 23 November.

Mecham, Quinn. 2014. "Islamist Movements." In Marc Lynch, ed. *The Arab Uprisings Explained: New Contentious Politics in the Middle East*. New York: Columbia University Press.

# Appendix I

TABLE A.1 *Summed Ordinal Scores of Islamist Mobilization by Country 1970–2010**

| | | | | | | | |
|---|---|---|---|---|---|---|---|
| Algeria | 6.00 | Nigeria | 4.00 | Tanzania | 1.11 | Comoros | 0.00 |
| Iran | 6.00 | Somalia | 4.00 | Eritrea | 0.89 | Cote d'Ivoire | 0.00 |
| Iraq | 6.00 | Sudan | 4.00 | Bosnia | 0.83 | Djibouti | 0.00 |
| Pakistan | 6.00 | Tunisia | 4.00 | Kyrgyzstan | 0.83 | Gambia | 0.00 |
| Afghanistan | 5.67 | Syria | 3.67 | Maldives | 0.67 | Guinea | 0.00 |
| Indonesia | 5.67 | Tajikistan | 3.67 | Niger | 0.67 | Guinea-Bissau | 0.00 |
| Palestine | 5.67 | Jordan | 3.33 | Oman | 0.67 | Kazakhstan | 0.00 |
| Bangladesh | 5.33 | Malaysia | 3.33 | Chad | 0.50 | North Yemen | 0.00 |
| Turkey | 5.00 | Saudi Arabia | 2.50 | Qatar | 0.33 | Sierra Leone | 0.00 |
| Egypt | 4.67 | Uzbekistan | 2.50 | Ethiopia | 0.22 | South Yemen | 0.00 |
| Lebanon | 4.67 | Morocco | 2.22 | Albania | 0.11 | Turkmenistan | 0.00 |
| Yemen | 4.67 | Kenya | 1.94 | Senegal | 0.11 | UAE | 0.00 |
| Bahrain | 4.00 | Libya | 1.67 | Brunei | 0.06 | | |
| Kuwait | 4.00 | Mali | 1.33 | Kosovo | 0.06 | | |
| Mauritania | 4.00 | Azerbaijan | 1.11 | Burkina Faso | 0.00 | | |

* These scores represent the product of the sum of a country's ordinal scores and the highest ordinal mobilization score. A full description is provided in Chapter 3.

# Appendix II

TABLE A.2 *Regression Analyses of Average Levels of Islamist Mobilization 1970–2010*

| | Model 1 | Model 2 | Model 3 |
|---|---|---|---|
| Human development index score | 1.19 (2.62) | | |
| Liberalization | 0.42 (0.67) | | –0.09 (0.07) |
| Political liberty (avg. FH score) | –0.09 (0.11) | | |
| Ethnic fractionalization | | 0.22 (0.19) | |
| Colonial history | –1.01 (0.60) | | |
| Fertility rate | –0.01 (0.22) | | |
| % Urban | –2.18 (1.15) | | |
| TVs per capita | 0.001 (0.001) | | |
| Shari'a in legal system | | | 0.21 (0.27) |
| Monarchy | –0.47 (0.50) | –0.25 (0.26) | –0.67 (0.25)* |
| Centuries since conversion | | 0.09 (0.03)* | 0.12 (0.03)* |
| Mountainous | | 0.63 (0.20)* | 0.72 (0.21)* |
| Population (in 10 millions) | | 0.07 (0.02)* | 0.06 (0.02)* |
| Rentier oil state | | | |
| Sub-Saharan Africa | | –0.19 (0.22) | –0.40 (0.20) |
| Previously communist | –1.11 (0.61) | –0.59 (0.23)* | –0.70 (0.25)* |
| In Ottoman Empire | 0.55 (0.42) | 0.47 (0.21)* | |
| Sufi institutions | 0.14 (0.32) | | |
| Arabic language | 0.72 (0.48) | –0.27 (0.28) | –0.02 (0.26) |
| % Muslim | 0.01 (0.01) | 0.01 (0.001)* | |
| Constant | 1.64 (2.25) | –0.82 (0.43) | 0.36 (0.38) |
| Adjusted R-square | 0.11 | 0.73 | 0.68 |

# Appendix III

TABLE A.3 *Panel Regression Analysis of Islamist Mobilization 1970–2010**

| | Violence | Demonstrations | Voting |
|---|---|---|---|
| Pro-Islamic policy change | −0.08 (0.36) | 0.25 (0.31) | −0.32 (0.17) |
| Anti-Islamic policy change | 0.26 (0.37) | 1.13 (0.32)* | 0.24 (0.17) |
| Liberalization | −0.02 (0.31) | 0.04 (0.27) | 0.13 (0.15) |
| Repression | 0.24 (0.34) | 0.09 (0.29) | −0.39 (0.16)* |
| Early election | −0.35 (0.51) | −0.05 (0.44) | 0.71 (0.23)* |
| Leadership turnover | 0.25 (0.12)* | 0.14 (0.10) | 0.10 (0.05)* |
| Islamist participation in government | 1.31 (0.38)* | 1.07 (0.32)* | 1.21 (0.17)* |
| Civil violence | 0.49 (0.32) | 0.73 (0.27)* | 0.04 (0.14) |
| State collapse | 1.15 (0.40)* | −0.31 (0.34) | 0.14 (0.18) |
| Islam is state religion | −0.22 (0.53) | 0.67 (0.38) | 0.64 (0.21)* |
| Monarchy | −0.88 (0.69) | −0.78 (0.47) | 0.32 (0.26) |
| Centuries since conversion | 0.29 (0.10)* | 0.18 (0.07)* | 0.001 (0.04) |
| Mountainous | 0.42 (0.53) | −0.03 (0.34) | 0.17 (0.19) |
| Population (in 10 millions) | 0.17 (0.06)* | 0.13 (0.04)* | 0.05 (0.02)* |
| Rentier oil state | 0.10 (0.69) | −0.24 (0.42) | −0.59 (0.24)* |
| Sub-Saharan Africa | −0.13 (0.75) | 0.27 (0.48) | 0.01 (0.26) |
| Previously communist | 0.09 (0.83) | −0.60 (0.53) | −0.12 (0.29) |
| Sufi institutions | −0.34 (0.66) | −0.58 (0.43) | −0.25 (0.24) |
| Arabic language | −0.94 (0.70) | −0.28 (0.48) | −0.09 (0.27) |
| Lagged variable | | | |
| Constant | −1.5 (1.06) | −0.94 (0.66) | −0.05 (0.37) |
| Overall R-square | 0.40 | 0.36 | 0.39 |

# Notes

## INTRODUCTION

1 Results of the local elections (12 June 1990) for the Assemblée Populaire Communale (Popular Communal Assembly/PCA) showed 54.3% of the vote cast for the Front Islamique du Salut (FIS) and 28.1% of the vote cast for the Front de Libération Nationale (FLN). In voting for the Assemblée Populaire de Wilaya (Popular Wilaya Assembly/APW), the FIS took 57.4% compared with the FLN's 27.5% (Fontaine 1990, Sutton, Aghrout, Zimche 1992, Willis 1996). Results of the first ballot of National Assembly elections (26 December 1991) are summarized in *Algérie Actualité*, 2 January 1992; Sutton and Aghrout (1992).

2 Morocco experienced occasional radical violence in the 2000s, as well as some voting for an Islamist political party, the Parti de la Justice et de la Développement (PJD). Both the Moroccan PJD and Tunisia's al-Nahda party won a plurality of elections in late 2011.

3 Primary estimates of casualties during the seven-month civil war range from 30,000 to 60,000 (with some estimates going as high as 100,000). Tens of thousands of villages are thought to have been destroyed in the process (Capisani 2000).

4 If the cutoff threshold is lowered to 10%, approximately 20 more countries would be included in the population. The vast majority of these countries have very little or no Islamist political mobilization. Inclusion of these countries would not significantly affect the outcome of the study, but would suggest that incidences of negative outcomes (i.e., no mobilization) are broader among distinct minority Muslim populations. Most of these minority cases are in sub-Saharan Africa: Benin (about 20%), Cameroon (about 20%), Congo (about 10%), Ghana (about 16%), Kenya (about 10%), Liberia (about 20%), Malawi (about 20%), Mauritius (about 17%), Mozambique (about 10%), Swaziland (about 10%), Togo (about 10%), and Uganda (about 10%). Other countries whose Muslim populations fall between 10 and 20% of the total: Bulgaria (about 12%), Cyprus (about 18%), Georgia (about 11%), Guyana (about 10%), India (about 12%), Israel (about 15%), Singapore (about 15%), and Suriname (about 20%). If the cutoff threshold is further lowered, dozens

of other countries would be included, including many countries of Western Europe with immigrant Muslim minorities. The outcome of interest, mobilization to gain a measure of state power, is extremely unlikely in cases where Muslims are clearly a minority. As inclusion of all possible Muslim populations would distort the ability to assess the outcome of interest, the 25% threshold is used. Sources: CIA World Factbook (2002), comparative source material from Adherents.com.

5 Prior to 1990, the country now known as Yemen was divided into two separate polities, North Yemen and South Yemen. All three of these countries are included in the total.

6 Afghanistan is the one country that has experienced considerably more violence by self-defined Islamic actors than Algeria. Much of the violence in Afghanistan took place along tribal lines, however, making the Islamist motivations behind the Afghan violence questionable in many cases. Violence in post-2011 Syria has also risen to extraordinary high levels, but it is not yet clear how many of the deaths can be linked to Islamist violence.

7 With the possible exception of the Sudan, which has had extensive experience with the Muslim Brotherhood due to its proximity to Egypt.

## 1 ISLAM AND POLITICAL MOBILIZATION

1 Fundamentalism was initially used to describe a Protestant Christian movement that focused on a religious understanding of the Bible as the literal word of God. Because the Qur'an is considered the literal word of God in Muslim doctrine, an "Islamic fundamentalism" in this sense is not distinct from Muslim belief more generally. See Beinin and Stork (1997a).

2 Although in some circumstances this may look like a strategic rather than an ideological distinction, it is often driven by ideological claims about the meaning of Islam in society. This arena of ideological concern, however, is prone to shift as the political and social circumstances of Islamic groups also shift.

3 As demonstrated through factor analysis, discussed in Chapter 3. Islamist protest and political violence are particularly highly correlated.

4 A high number of Islamist organizations may be indicative of active Islamist mobilization. In some cases, however, just one organization may be effective at generating mass mobilization. Arrests of large numbers of alleged Islamists may be indicative of active, militant Islamist mobilization involving legal violations, or they may simply indicate widespread state repression or a policy of demonizing religious actors. Arrests of Islamists reveal, most significantly, that the state fears Islamist activists, but is not a reliable indicator of the strength of Islamist mobilization. Pressure on the state by religious elites is also a significant source of Islamist mobilization in some cases, although this is often unreported by the media and difficult to assess in many circumstances.

5 While religious identity has long served as a marker of communal identity in Lebanon, political Islam has been less central to Lebanese political divisions than has class, historical representation, and or ties to external allies. Although Hezbollah is a dominantly Shi'ite organization, the more secular Shiite Amal organization has historically eclipsed Hezbollah prior to the 2006 Israeli attack on Lebanon.

6 Useful summary discussions of some of the works cited here are found in Wiktoriwicz (2003) and Robinson (2004). Literature reviews by these authors were influential in structuring some of the arguments presented here.
7 Prominent theories of the growth of radical parties include party mobilization as a response to economic crisis, demographic changes in society that lead to a multicultural backlash, increasing elite control over the public sphere, structural changes leading to new economic preferences, and opportunities created by the convergence of moderate parties toward the center (Kitschelt 1997). See also Betz and Immerfall (1998).
8 A general overview of recent structural theories of revolution can be found in Wickham-Crowley (1997).
9 For further discussion, see McAdam (1982) and Wiktorowicz (2004a).
10 Examples of arguments found in the political opportunity scholarship include Kitschelt (1986), Tarrow (1998), McAdam, McCarthy, and Zald (1996).
11 See, for example, theories of civil war onset that show a set of opportunities as much more predictive than grievance, Collier, Hoeffler, Sambanis (2005).
12 See, for example, al-Banna's "Toward the Light" and Mawdudi's "The Islamic Law" (Euben and Zaman 2009).
13 Abu Bakr al-Baghdadi, audio broadcast through al-Furqan, 14 May 2015.
14 But note that this social background is extremely common in Egypt, among both Islamists and non-Islamists.

## 2 FROM THE SACRED TO THE STATE

1 These case studies are "critical" in the sense that they allow for important theoretical tests that other country cases do not. For example, given Algeria's exceptionally high mobilization in the 1990s, the theory would fall short if it could not explain the basic dynamics of the Algerian case. Likewise, given the high likelihood of Islamist mobilization in Senegal predicted by some theories of Islamism – despite its comparative absence empirically – Senegal provides an important case for testing. These cases are not strictly critical in the way that Eckstein defines critical cases. Eckstein (1975) describes "critical" cases as those that alone can confirm or disconfirm a theory. By contrast, King, Keohane, and Verba (1994) have argued that single cases (or at least single observations) have little power to confirm or disconfirm because most explanations rely on multiple causal factors. They also assert that most theories are at best probabilistic and should not be expected to hold for all possible cases. I agree with King, Keohane, Verba in their assessment of the limits of single-case observations, but also regard these cases as those collectively providing some of the best possible theoretical tests among the population of cases in the data set.
2 Testing of these assumptions at the individual level is possible, however, through detailed ethnography and social experiments. Empirical testing of hypotheses around individual Islamist decision-making is an important next step in research on this topic.
3 The theory assumes that if individuals decide to mobilize, they will not be prevented from doing so before the mobilization is observed.
4 Note that for the purposes of the theory preferences do not change without an external catalyst.

5 Note that while individual costs are lower, collective costs are likely higher. Successful mobilization within small groups may be easier because of lower coordination costs. See Olson (1965).

6 Because individual costs are lowered when the number of participants increases, mobilization can exhibit rapid growth at certain points in the social process where the costs for many individuals are approximately equal to the expected utility of mobilization. These points are often called "tipping points" and may occur when much of a population has a similar type of preference and similar expectations of individual cost, and where pre-mobilization coordination is difficult. See Kuran (1991), Lohmann (1994), and Laitin (1998).

7 Prominent examples would include Hassan al-Banna and Said Qutb in Egypt, Rashid Ghannouchi in Tunisia, Abbasi Madani in Algeria, Necmettin Erbakan in Turkey, Ayatollah Khomeini in Iran, Muqtada al-Sadr in Iraq, Mullah Omar in Afghanistan, Osama bin Laden in Saudi Arabia, Abu Musab al-Zarqawi in Jordan/Iraq, and Sheikh Yassine in Morocco.

8 Note that new governments may take power and have an interest in changing policy. In practice, a large portion of states within the data set have had only infrequent changes in government.

9 In addition, less prominent entrepreneurs may be able to enhance their reputation through a bold move to mobilize others. More prominent entrepreneurs, on the other hand, may put their established reputation at risk if they attempt to mobilize others and fail.

10 Another possible response to the entrepreneur is to provide active support for the entrepreneur's mobilization attempt. This will increase the likelihood of the attempt's success, but for theoretical purposes it is not distinct from choosing not to police the entrepreneur.

11 An early mobilizer is one with strong Islamist preferences who is willing to bear above-average costs for mobilizing.

12 The total costs that potential mobilizing individuals face are the sum of the coordination costs and the additional costs created by the state.

13 In stating that coordination costs are higher when numbers are low, I assume that prospective mobilizers do not initially know each other. Finding other early mobilizers to coordinate with thus requires more effort because there are fewer of them to be found, and they are found across greater social distances. This is distinct from the claim that mobilizing in small groups is easier because the individuals all know each other and can enforce group activities. See Olson (1965).

14 For a helpful discussion of entrepreneurial efforts in Egypt and their relationship with the state, see Wickham (2002).

15 See James Fearon and David Laitin (1996) for a seminal discussion of ethnic in-group policing. In this model, an in-group policing equilibrium emerges because ethnic groups possess better information about co-ethnics than they do about ethnic rivals. This allows them to target selected individuals within the ethnic group rather than take the punishment for the whole group, which might be meted out by ethnic rivals who have little information about the offending individuals other than their ethnicity. An equilibrium emerges when each group correctly expects that the culprits will be identified and sanctioned by their own ethnic brethren, so that ethnic violence is effectively contained. This in-group policing equilibrium is contrasted

with a "spiral equilibrium" in which interethnic cooperation is sustained from fear that ethnic violence would rapidly spiral out of control.

16 Islamic groups in Afghanistan and neighboring countries, for example, often have a dominant tribal affiliation. Sufi brotherhoods and Muslim nomads in West Africa also often have an ethnic or family character.

17 For a discussion of the importance of Islamic schooling within a state context, including the ways in which Islamic knowledge is generated and controlled, see Brenner (2001).

18 While it is clear that many interpretations of scriptural content are possible, including liberal interpretations, much language of Islamic texts is either explicitly or implicitly theocratic in content. For a discussion, see Lewis (1988).

19 Granovetter (1973) argues that aquaintances or "weak ties" may have more power in creating collective action than networks of friends, or "strong ties," because they bridge social networks and can link them in a way that mobilizes multiple social networks at the same time. Common knowledge can play a similar role, but note that it does so because of shared expectations and not because of actual personal acquaintance across groups as in Granovetter.

20 Lohmann (1994) argues in reference to the fall of the German Democratic Republic that very fragmented information networks were present in East Germany prior to the Monday Demonstratoins in Leipzig (1989–1991). These demonstrations were required for collective action to be successful because they served as an "informational cascade" that finally "made public some of the previously hidden information about the regime" (44). In the process, this new information undermined the viability of the regime. The demonstrations subsequently died out as their informational role declined.

21 An extended discussion of the meaning and utility of common knowledge, along with several common examples of its application, can be found in Chwe (2001).

22 For broad discussion of how symbolic resources can be used to construct meaning around community, and how communities can be defined by an understanding of shared cultural resources, see Anderson (1991); for a theoretical view of the importance of culture as critique, see Ray (2001).

23 Fatah al-Sheik was campaigning with the movement of the prominent young cleric, Muqtada al-Sadr. See Eckholm (2005).

24 On costs of communication and the inherently political nature of communicating durable cultural meaning, see Debray (2000).

25 See Nyang (2002) for examples of how Islam can shape collective expectations of boundaries, both on behavior and otherwise.

26 Cruise O'Brien (2003), p. 25.

27 This process has some similarities to signaling models in game theory, although I am not developing a formal signaling model here. The broader signaling literature often treats state signals as changes in state tactics or levels of repression (as in Lohmann 1994), but I conceptualize focal state events as a much broader class of phenomena. Likewise, focal state events are often unintentional, and not directed to a particular audience or done for purposes of political communication as in many signaling models (Lohmann 1993). The focal state event emphasized in this chapter that appears most like a traditional political signal from the state is that of rapid political liberalization.

28 One can also imagine a situation in which the transition was led by liberal democrats who develop a great deal of status and build a resource base in the fight for political liberalism. This has not been a common pattern in the Muslim world, however.

29 For further discussion of the broad social movement agenda and conceptual perspectives, see McAdam, Tarrow, Tilly (2001).

## 3 A POLITICAL GEOGRAPHY OF THE SACRED

1 In cases where accurate data on religious affiliation are not readily available, previous government census data and scholarly assessments are used to estimate the percentage of the population that would self-identify as Muslim.

2 The polities are all recognized countries, with the exception of Palestine. Prior to 1990, present-day Yemen was composed of two states, here referred to as North Yemen and South Yemen.

3 Based on whether or not the protest resulted in violent clashes with authorities.

4 But note some protests occurred in Tajikistan, which is grouped in the category of low-scale protests.

5 As measured by average Freedom House scores for political liberty.

6 These scores represent only Freedom House scores for political freedom and not the scores for civil liberty. These data are sometimes criticized for failing to capture the variation in political participation in countries of the Middle East and broader Muslim world but remain the most detailed comparative assessment across this broad time period.

7 Positive correlations between the three activities are statistically significant in linear OLS regression as measured in the first three decades of the study (without fixed effects). T-statistics for the correlations are as follows: Violence/Demonstrations (11.98), Demonstrations/Voting (2.68), Violence/Voting (2.47). The R-squared value for Violence/Demonstrations is also notable (0.30).

8 Factor analysis of violence, protest, and voting yield a dominant factor with an eigenvalue of 0.924.

9 Note that countries in which reasonably credible democratic elections have not taken place do not have the same possible total as countries with elections. The sum must therefore be measured against the total possible sum for each country.

10 To the extent reasonable, the ordinal scale follows standard deviations in the data. This is not possible at low ends of the scale because the data are not normally distributed. Country period is a period of five years in one country.

The scale for voting is as follows. The first value is the ordinal score; the second value is the assigned range of average votes for Islamically oriented parties per country period: 0=0; 1=0.1–5.0; 2=5.1–10.0; 3=10.1–20.0 4=20.1–30.0; 5=30.1–40.0; 6=40.1+.

The scale for demonstrations is as follows. The first value is the ordinal score; the second value is a score measuring scale and intensity of Islamist demonstrations based on general size and the presence of violent clashes per country period: 0=0; 1=0.01–0.29; 2=0.3–0.59; 3=0.6–0.89; 4=0.9–1.19; 5=1.2–1.49; 6=1.5+.

The scale for violence is as follows. The first value is the ordinal score; the second value is the number of deaths in incidents involving Islamist violence per country period: 0=0; 1=1–10; 2=11–50; 3=51–100; 4=101–500; 5=501–2500; 6=2501+.

11 The results of the two methods show an R-squared value of .77 when regressed on one another.
12 Note that there is some degree of bias in the data, which were collected through 2010. Events closest to the present are more likely to be captured in the data than events closest to the year 1970 due to increased world reporting of international events and increased data accessibility over the period. The bias was eliminated as much as possible by using sources that recorded events closest to the period when they occurred and is not expected to substantively influence the conclusions of the study. Nevertheless, older data should be considered less complete.
13 The most Islamist of the Sudanese parties, the National Islamic Front (NIF), won about 20% of the seats, but the two largest parties emerging from the election, the Umma Party (NNUP) and the Democratic Unionist Party (DUP), also supported Islamically oriented platforms. See El-Affendi (1991).
14 Including the Islamic Action Front (IAF) and independent Islamists.
15 See Wiktorowicz (2001) for an assessment of these changes.
16 Although Kuwaiti candidates faced considerable restrictions in the electoral process, with Islamists running as independents.
17 The Islamically-oriented party in Yemen, *al-Islah*, competes using both a religious and tribal base. See Saif (2001) for an assessment of *al Islah*.
18 Senegal also saw inconsequential attempts at Islamist electoral mobilization by minor political parties in early 2000.
19 As the combined results of single linear regression models, multiple regression models, and cross-national time series multiple regression models.
20 As coded by the author.
21 But the result is not statistically significant.
22 As measured by the Freedom House score for political liberty.
23 In many of these cases, the state responded to increasing Islamist activism by further changing state policy in order to hinder Islamic groups.
24 Based on multiple random-effects GLS panel regression models. See Appendix A.3 for details.
25 Where the result is statistically significant (0.01) under a range of panel data models.
26 The use of shari'a principles is correlated with a number of other explanatory variables used in the study, and is not a statistically significant indicator of mobilization in all models.
27 In a number of panel data models, Arabic shows little correlation when historical and other control variables are taken into account.
28 Note that considerable "Islamist" violence has taken place in Russia, focused primarily around the conflict over Chechen autonomy. The drive for Chechen independence was framed as a conflict over Islam, however, only as the conflict progressed.
29 The countries of the study that fit into this category include: Algeria, Bahrain, Brunei, Iraq, Kuwait, Libya, Oman, Qatar, Saudi Arabia, Turkmenistan, and the United Arab Emirates.
30 Ethnic fractionalization data is taken from Matthew Krain (1978) and supplemented with the author's estimates for missing cases. Data published online at http://discover.wooster.edu/mkrain/ethnic-fractionalization-data/.

31 The average number of Islamist groups over time statistically accounts for almost two-thirds of the variance in mobilization factor scores. The correlation is strong across all forms of Islamist mobilization. The strength of the correlation suggests that the two variables are not independent from one another, and that the relationship is not solely a causative one.

32 Jungle is only present in a few countries in the study, such as Indonesia and Malaysia. Difficult territories are also often used as the bases for guerilla movements, regardless of where the movement begins, because they are difficult for the state to penetrate militarily.

33 Mountainous countries in the study include: Afghanistan, Albania, Algeria, Azerbaijan, Bosnia, Eritrea, Ethiopia, Indonesia, Iran, Kyrgyzstan, Lebanon, Malaysia, Morocco, Oman, Pakistan, Tajikistan, Turkey, Uzbekistan, and Yemen.

34 While the presence of mountains is not a powerful predictor in all models, it proves statistically significant in several regression models examining averages over time and remains an important (but not statistically significant) indicator in panel data models.

35 Country periods which have seen multiple leadership changes include the following. Five changes: Comoros 95–99, Sierra Leone 95–99, Turkey 70–74. Four changes: Bangladesh 75–79, 05–09, Kosovo 05–09, Lebanon 05–09, Mauritania 05–09, Turkey 95–99. Three changes: Afghanistan 75–79, Azerbaijan 90–94, Bosnia-Hercegovina 05–09, Burkina Faso 80–84, Guinea-Bissau 00–04, Iraq 00–04, Kyrgyzstan 05–09, Mali 90–94, Mauritania 75–79, Nigeria 75–79, Pakistan 90–95, Sudan 85–90, Turkey 75–79, 90–94.

36 The high level of statistical significance in panel data models also reflects the fact that elections are held more often in periods where leadership change occurs. This fails to account for all of the correlation, however. The correlation with Islamist violence is not statistically significant, but nevertheless is notable.

37 High levels of Islamist electoral mobilization have occurred with regularly scheduled elections in countries such as Algeria, Jordan, Kuwait, Malaysia, Sudan, and Yemen.

38 In panel regression models. Results for violence and voting have positive coefficients but are not statistically significant.

39 Islamist demonstrations are not correlated with state collapse, and are likely difficult in many of these contexts.

40 As defined by a movement of two points on the Freedom House scale of political liberty within a period of five years.

41 Countries in which liberalization has paralleled Islamist mobilization include Algeria, Tajikistan, Indonesia, Pakistan, Sudan, Turkey, Yemen, Jordan, Kuwait, and Bangladesh.

42 These include Bahrain, Brunei, Jordan, Kuwait, Morocco, Oman, Qatar, Saudi Arabia, and the United Arab Emirates.

43 In panel models, population is significant at the 0.001 level for demonstrations and the 0.008 level for Islamist violence. Electoral mobilization does not appear to be sensitive to the size of a country's population.

44 The time-series data, for example, are measured in five-year increments.

## 4 EXPLAINING LOW ISLAMIST MOBILIZATION

1 For example, theories that highlight poverty, rapid urbanization, colonial heritage, traditional family cultures, and level of participation in Islamic institutions would all predict higher levels of Islamist mobilization in Senegal than actually occur. Senegal has high levels of poverty, has experienced rapid urbanization, has a strong Francophone colonial heritage, has conservative and traditional large families, and enjoys a high degree of popular participation in Islamic institutions, particularly Sufi brotherhoods and associated pilgrimages. One crucial argument on reasons for low religious mobilization in Nigeria (Laitin 1986) asserts that commonsense political relationships within a cultural subsystem may have broader relevance in providing a model for political action if they are embedded in foundational political moments or are otherwise structurally privileged. While the argument I make here does not explicitly disagree with Laitin's Nigeria evidence, it goes beyond the insights of the Nigeria case to specify the types of structural relationships and incentives within those Senegalese cultural systems that create a pattern of political hegemony excluding explicitly Islamist actors.

2 Neighboring Mali and Guinea-Bissau, for example, have a GDP per capita of $700 and $1,000, respectively.

3 See Cruise O'Brien (1975), p. 137.

4 *The World Factbook*. 2012. Central Intelligence Agency. Washington DC.

5 As described in Villalón and Kane (1998).

6 Given this early conversion date, the theoretical and statistical expectations of Chapters 2 and 3 suggest that Senegal would have high levels of Islamist mobilization. This makes the Senegalese case a more interesting puzzle of low mobilization. The early Islamic kingdom was known as "Takrur," see Hiksett (1994).

7 Robinson (2003), p. 184.

8 By 1862 the empire included important settlements such as Timbuktu, Masina, Hamdallahi, and Segu. The empire fell victim to ethnic divisions, however, with Soninkes rising up against the Tukolor-supported al-Futi. He was killed in 1864, but his empire survived under his son until conquered by the French in 1891. Hiskett (1994).

9 The Qadiriyya jihad in Hausaland is another example from this period.

10 Note that the Tijaniyya brotherhood typically cooperated with French colonials in North Africa, but led some of the resistance to French occupation in West Africa. This resistance turned to cooperation as the French became more entrenched in the area. Levtzion and Pouwels (2000).

11 Another brotherhood, the Hamaliyya, which was founded about 1920 in the French Sudan, argued against the Mouride policy of accommodation. They asserted that rule by the infidel was incompatible with being a Muslim. After a violent quarrel with the Mourides, the Hamaliyya was destroyed by the French. Hiksett (1994).

12 See Robinson (2003).

13 Searing (2002), p. xxix

14 For a fuller discussion, see Behrman (1970).

15 Behrman (1970), pp. 50–53.

16 By the 1940s, Kaolack in French Senegal had become the center of a Tijani movement of mystical evangelism headed by Ibrahim Niasse. The movement spread

the brotherhood's influence throughout Niger, Senegal, Cote d'Ivoire, and parts of Nigeria and the Gold Coast. Hiksett (1994).

17 See Sy (1969), Behrman (1970).

18 Note that many Mourides claim that their numbers are much greater than this, and indeed the Mouride proportion of the population is likely growing.

19 Similar estimates from Cruise O'Brien (2003), pp. 50–51.

20 Cruise O'Brien (2003).

21 They also may provide magical amulets (*gri gri*) for protection or curse. Politicians have often consulted the marabouts for magical intervention in campaigns (Behrman 1970). For a discussion of *baraka*, see Cruise O'Brien (1988a).

22 In the Mouride order, this literature includes much that was written by the founder Amadu Bamba himself.

23 Further discussion in Cruise O'Brien (1971).

24 Vikor (2000) describes the status of the marabouts as determined "from below," because of this characteristic, p. 463.

25 For more on succession crises, see Vikor (2000).

26 Touba has increased in size by about 15% a year for the past thirty years, and its population has more than doubled since 2000. It grew in size from 575 hectares in 1970 to more than 12,000 in the year 2000. However, it is still administratively considered a village and benefits from a measure of extraterritoriality. It has become a significant center for investment by Mourides all over the world (Guèye 2002).

27 The Grand Magal in 1975 attracted half a million, participants, or 1/8 of Senegal's population at the time. Cruise O'Brien (2003).

28 See Coulon (1983), p.121.

29 Cruise O'Brien (1971), p. 266.

30 Guèye was the founder of the earliest Senegalese branch of a French party, the Section Française de l'Internationale Ouvrière (SFIO) (from 1936).

31 Guèye's own questionable devotion to Islam, as well as his marriage to a French Catholic, were highlighted in return by the BDS during the campaigns.

32 For a more detailed assessment of the first year of Senegalese independence, see Behrman (1970), pp. 1–11.

33 A coalition of Sufi leaders had pushed for a constitutional guarantee that they would be represented in forty of the eighty seats of the future National Assembly, a guarantee that they did not receive in the new constitution. See Magassouba (1985), pp. 101–102.

34 Dia himself was a member of the Tijani brotherhood.

35 Dia was also seen as a more progressive reformer than Senghor, who was interested in government control over the rural economy. Many marabouts felt that this would significantly decrease their autonomy and harm their current economic position. Magassouba (1985).

36 A "Socialist," "Liberal," and "Marxist-Leninist" party

37 By 1983, fifteen political parties had been organized, with eight actively competing in the elections. Magassouba (1985).

38 Villalón and Kane (1998).

39 In 1993, the PDS received 32% if the vote, and had 27 deputies in the National Assembly out of 120. SOS Faim (1996).

40 Diagne (2000).

41 President Wade won re-election in 1997 with 56% of the vote. In the 2012 election, he won only 35% of the vote, forcing a runoff with his nearest rival, Macky Sall, who won 27%. During the runoff, the opposition coalesced around Wade's rival, with a runoff result of 66% of the vote going to Sall and only 34% going to the incumbent Wade.

42 Cruise O'Brien (1971), p. 275.

43 Cruise O'Brien (1971), p. 272.

44 Magassouba (1985), SOS Faim (1996).

45 The Mouridiyya views itself as more indigenous and "Senegalese" than the majority Tijaniyya. Tijanis distinguish themselves from Mourides by highlighting their heritage of Muslim reform, as in the pre-colonial jihad movements. They stress their doctrinal purity, Arabic knowledge, and more rigorous devotions compared with the Mourides. Cruise O'Brien (2003).

46 Cruise O'Brien (1971).

47 The party was perceived as an anti-independence and pro-French party because of the circumstances of their opposition; the PSS received 12% of the vote. Magassouba (1985).

48 Hizboulahi sought to increase the religious consciousness of Senegalese Muslims and purify Islam from external influences. The party's program was declared to be simply "the Qur'an." Niasse met with Colonel Qaddafi of Libya to seek his support, and arson at a hotel in Casamance was attributed to the party. Niasse was arrested while in Niger and allowed to return to Senegal on the condition that he give up all political activities. Interestingly, he is the brother of Sidi Lamine Niasse, the founder of the influential Islamic news periodical *Wal Fadjri* (in 1984).

49 The FSD used some of Amadu Bamba's poetry on the campaign trail, but remained much more of a local identity party than one that articulated Islamist positions. Cruise O'Brien (2003), p. 74.

50 Electionworld.org; *Le Soleil.*

51 See Ewane (1985), Timéra (1986), Mattes (1989).

52 A study by Timéra (1986) of the growing Islamic groups at the university found that while youth were seriously unhappy with developments at the state level, religious groups focused almost entirely on religious activities. No relationship existed between political parties and Islamic groups on campus. While young Islamists hoped for an Islamic state, this was considered an ideal model, not a practicality. In the mid-1980s there appeared to be no signs that Islamic groups were interested in rupturing their positive relationship with the state (p. 23).

53 Behrman (1970).

54 Magassouba (1985).

55 Like other associations, CERID made a point of demonstrating that it was an explicitly apolitical organization, see Charter of the Cercle d'Etudes et de Recherches "Islam et Développment" (1984). Other Islamic movements of the period active on the university campus include JAMA, Etudes Islamiques, Mouvement de jeunes de l'UPIS, Mouvement de jeunes de l'UCM. See Timéra (1986), p. 11.

56 Villalón (2004).

57 Villalón (2004). See www.ht.com.sn/ht/index.php for a discussion of the organization's principal activities.

58 In Kane (1986), Sy discusses the purposes of the organization, which include to reject the cultural aggression of the West, help Muslim youth find their true identity,

train students in the Arabic language, help women find their proper role in society, and help Senegal become an Islamic state (through practical measures and patience).

59 See Villalón and Kane (1998).

60 For an extensive discussion of the politics of the Moustarchidine movement, as well as its role in the 1993 presidential election, see Villalón and Kane (1998).

61 This included the surprise last minute announcement of Cheikh Tidiane Sy of the Moustarchidine (father of Moustapha Sy) in support of President Abdou Diouf. Islamic groups lost much of their momentum after the widely celebrated success of Wade's liberal Sopi (change) coalition. See Villalón (2004).

62 This brought Wade into conflict with Tijani Sy family. After a period of high expectations, Mourides gradually became somewhat ambivalent about Wade's presidency (Villalón 2004).

63 During protests against U.S. action in Afghanistan Atou Diagne of the Hizbut Tarqiyya gave a speech in which he suggested the idea of an Islamic state in Senegal under Mouride control, Villalón (2004).

64 See Marty and Salenc (1914).

65 Behrman (1970), pp. 40–56.

66 Behrman (1970), pp. 149–150.

67 Nour (1985).

68 Ndiaye (1986) articulates the push for more Qur'anic schools in Senegal.

69 Coulon (1983), p. 129.

70 Piga (2000) demonstrates the continuing solidarity of these urban religious groups through a study of *da'ira* networks.

71 See Sy (1969), p. 218.

72 Maranz (1993), pp. 216–217.

73 Mosque attendance in key religious cities such as Touba remains very important, but the mosque is dominated by one brotherhood (Mouride).

74 For example, in 1973, the Mouride leader Abdou Lahatte Mbacké gave a speech in which he referred to the workings of the state as similar to those of Satan. Cruise O'Brien (2003), p. 5.

75 Balzar (1995), for example, depicts Senegalese Islam as "fun-loving, pragmatic, devout, and flavoured in African style." While the core belief is intact, the "spiritual energy is progressive and doctrine restrained."

Hiksett (1994) argues that "those areas that were part of the medieval empire of Mali have inherited a tradition of Islam that, while tenacious and sincere at a personal level, has seldom been expansionist or militant" (p. 132).

76 As Vikor (2000) observes, Sufi orders often look militant one day, and otherworldly the next (p. 441). The organization of Sufi orders makes them well-suited to political activity because of committed support and independent internal organization (p.466).

77 Cruise O'Brien (2003), p. 63.

78 See Sy (1969), p. 208.

79 Cruise O'Brien (2003), p. 36.

80 See Guèye (2002).

81 Nour (1985).

82 Coulon (1983) argues that the state incorporates the reformists to increase its legitimacy with the Islamic world, to prevent the emergence of an Islamic opposition, and to use as a counterweight against the influence of the marabouts (pp. 132–133).

83 Cruise O'Brien (2003).
84 Cruise O'Brien (2003).
85 Cruise O'Brien (1971), p. 277.
86 Villalón and Kane (1988).
87 Atou Diagne spurred a riot in Touba when he argued with a member of the Mbacké family over the hereditary structure of the brotherhood. The *khalifa général* banned the Mouride Students' Association, and some members of the Mbacké family reacted violently, injuring several people. Diagne called on the Association's members to all gather in Touba, but then withdrew his opinion against hereditary leadership and received a pardon. After a period the ban on the association was removed, but many of its members did not return. See Cruise O'Brien (2003).
88 He continues: "with a significant element of that cardplayer's standby, the bluff" (p. 50).
89 Magassouba (1985), p. 118.
90 As Boye (1990) asserts, the autonomous dynamism of private consumption in Senegal helped to sustain overall economic activity despite adverse external trade or climactic problems.
91 Boye (1990).
92 Political contestation occurred in 2011–2012 as President Wade sought constitutional provisions to extend his mandate to a third term, although upon defeat, and in conformity with Senegalese norms, President Wade congratulated his successor and stepped aside.
93 Villalón and Kane (1998).
94 Political Rights scores started at "6" from 1972 (when the survey began), then moved to "5" in 1977, moved to "4" in 1978, moved to "3" in 1984, back to "4" in 1989 (during the period of urban riots), back to "3" in 2000, and then ultimately to "2" (free) in 2002. Freedom House (2004).
95 See Fearon and Laitin (2003) and also Gates, Hegre, Jones, and Strand (2006) for arguments that poorly institutionalized regimes (either democracies or autocracies) are associated with political instability. Despite Senegal's designation as an "anocracy" in Fearon and Laitin, the moderate levels of democracy have not increased patterns of Islamist opposition to the state as some recent civil war studies might predict. This suggests that while certain types of state crisis may lead to higher levels of mobilization as noted in this chapter, the particular regime type may have little impact on Islamist mobilization more generally. This conclusion is supported by the lack of correlation between regime type and Islamist mobilization found in the data presented in Chapter 3.
96 Triaud (2000) discusses Muslim divisions in French West Africa, as well as the prominent divisions between tribal chiefs and the Sufi marabouts.
97 Cruise O'Brien (2003), p. 187.
98 See Levitzon and Pouwels (2000), Kaba (2000), Brenner (2001).
99 Kaba (2000).
100 Brenner (2001).
101 Brenner (2001), pp. 200, 293.
102 Brenner (2001).
103 See Schulz (2003) for an example of a prominent Muslim preacher who has been creating public space for the debate.

104 Magassouba (1985), p. 97.
105 Villalón (1995), p. 265.
106 Examples include Behrman (1970), p. 174, and Cruise O'Brien (1988a).

## 5 VOTING FOR WELFARE AND VIRTUE

1 Compare, for example, countries of Central Asia, Eastern Europe, sub-Saharan Africa, South-East Asia, and republican Arab states.
2 Turkey's average Freedom House score for political liberty from 1970 to 2010 is 3.2, which makes it the most free of any country in the study over the same period. This does not include Freedom House scores for civil liberty.
3 See White (2005) or Robins (2007) for prominent examples.
4 An extensive discussion of the Turkish organization Hizbullah is found in Çakır (2001).
5 Military coups d'état and party closures have interrupted some of the continuity.
6 The National Salvation Party won 11.8% of the vote at its debut in the national elections of 1973. The party's national support dropped slightly to 8.7% in the national elections of 1977. It participated in a series of three coalition governments, courted because its seats held the key to a majority coalition. The party's supporters included a considerable segment of small businessmen from Central Anatolia and recent urban immigrants from the countryside (Geyikdağı 1984). See also Toprak (1984), Sarıbay (1985), Ayata (1993).
7 Welfare took 7.2% of the vote, which disqualified it for seats under the 10% electoral threshold rule of the new constitution.
8 Gülalp (1999) argues that the National Salvation Party and Welfare Party shared the distinctive characteristic of articulating the need for a spiritual order (*manevi düzen*) in society that defined both parties as the Islamic choice. However, Welfare was different from the NSP because of its shift in economic policy from state to private initiative, its broader constituency (more middle class professionals and marginal urban workers), and its move to incorporate some of the equality ideology of the left.
9 The subsequent four elections were: 26 March 1989 (local), 20 October 1991 (national), 27 March 1994 (local), 24 December 1995 (national).
10 National Action Party (Milliyetçi Hareket Partisi, MHP).
11 The True Path Party (DYP) was led by a former (female) prime minister, Tansu Çiller.
12 The "national viewpoint" vision was also a component of National Salvation Party ideology and articulated in Erbakan (1975). In the early years of Welfare, the party distinguished itself rhetorically by arguing that there were only two parties in Turkey: Welfare, and all those who unite in "aping" the West.
13 A comparative discussion of many of these themes is found in Gülalp (1999).
14 See Özbudun (1999).
15 These committees were modeled on the Muslim rosary (*tesbih*), with 33 members paralleling the 33 beads of the rosary. Each district likewise had a party committee of 33 members (Yavuz 1997).
16 See Yavuz (1997).

17 In 1994, Welfare captured over 200 municipalities across Turkey. This victory was extended to 325 municipalities by 1998. For an assessment of Welfare's municipal performance, see Akinci (1999).

18 A discussion of these issues is found in Howe (2000).

19 In November 1996, a car crash in the village of Susurluk revealed high-level connections between the True Path Party, organized crime, and senior police officers. Interior Minister Mehmet Ağar's apparent knowledge and approval of the connections with organized crime led to his resignation.

20 In the process of investigating what became known as the "Susuluk affair," Welfare introduced legislation that would limit the media's scrutiny of government affairs, helped maintain Mehmet Ağar's parliamentary immunity, and argued that Çiller did not need to defend her affairs in front of the Supreme Council (Howe 2000).

21 A political rally, led by the Welfare mayor of Sincan (outside of Ankara), particularly disturbed the military. The Iranian ambassador, who served as a prominent speaker at the rally, condemned Turkey's new military alliance with Israel, and encouraged a crowd of radical participants in its denunciation of Israeli policies. The mayor of Sincan also suggested the possible restoration of Islamic law in Turkey as the crowd waved Islamic symbols and chanted religious slogans.

22 Further discussion of what came to be known as the 28 February process can be found in Cevizoğlu (1998), Howe (2000), and Bayramoğlu (2001).

23 Court Chief Justice (and later President) Ahmet Necdet Sezer, as quoted in *Turkish Probe* 25 January 1998. See also Akdoğan (2000), pp. 322 ff.

24 Judicial actions were also taken against other prominent figures in the Welfare party. In December 1997, Erdoğan, the Welfare mayor of Istanbul, came under investigation by a regional state security court for "dividing people by inciting them along the lines of . . . religious . . . differences," a violation of the Turkish Penal Code Article 312. Erdoğan received this charge for reading several lines from Turkish nationalist poet Ziya Gökalp at a political rally in the southeastern town of Siirt: "Minarets are our bayonets, domes are our helmets, mosques are our barracks." By April 1998, the state security court decided against Erdoğan, leading to the end of his mayorship of Istanbul, a short prison sentence, and threatening to remove his eligibility from any future political office. A number of court cases were also prosecuted against "Islamic" businesses and the religiously oriented businessmen's association MÜSIAD (Independent Industrialists' and Businessmen's Association).

25 Speculation ensued as to who might lead such a party given the legal restrictions on Erbakan's political life. Tayyip Erdoğan emerged as a promising candidate due to his popularity in Istanbul and increasingly prominent national presence. Indeed, some saw his provocative statements in Siirt as evidence of his intent to challenge Erbakan for leadership of the party (Cemal 1997).

26 Including the formal founder of the Virtue Party, and long-time Erbakan associate, Ismail Alptekin.

27 Kutan represented the older group of Welfare deputies known to be Erbakan loyalists, although he projected a more moderate and politically careful image than Erbakan.

28 This agenda was supported both by traditionalists and reformists within the new party, but for different reasons. For Kutan, both Welfare's failures and the party closure occurred because of Turkey's democratic deficit. With greater religious and political freedom, the movement would enjoy more room to maneuver and Erbakan

could re-enter the political arena. Virtue's reformists also saw a lack of freedom as their primary obstacle, but they extended this notion to insufficient democracy within the party. Under an increasingly democratic system, they believed, the future was theirs.

29 Virtue's internal rift led to a brief period of political chaos in the month prior to the election, as a number of Erbakan loyalists sided with disgruntled parliamentary mavericks in an effort to postpone the election. They were motivated both by fears of Virtue's standing in political polls and by a belief that an alliance with the parliamentary mavericks could buy time to remove Erbakan's political ban and allow him to lead the party into the next election. Although Kutan was initially against allowing Virtue deputies to support such a move, pressure from Erbakan persuaded him to allow many Virtue deputies to support postponement. Virtue's reformists, most notably Abdullah Gül, vehemently opposed such a move. Although in the end the elections proceeded on schedule, the apparent hypocrisy of the new "democratic" Virtue's anti-democratic move was widely apparent. It appeared to some that Virtue was more interested in saving Erbakan than in maintaining political peace in the country.

30 In municipal elections, however, where Virtue maintained a high 24% share of the vote, the party managed to maintain most of its key municipalities.

31 The new government was led by Bülent Ecevit of the DSP, in coalition with the center-right ANAP and the right-wing nationalist MHP.

32 Kavakçi was later accused of no longer being a Turkish citizen due to a prior marriage to an American, and thus ineligible for her seat. She was also accused of inciting religious hatred; in a prior speech in Chicago she had spoken of a personal "jihad." Kavakçi later remarried a Turkish citizen, receiving her Turkish citizenship again, but was banned from politics for five years in the decision on Virtue's closure.

33 In the indictment by state prosecutor Vural Savaş, members of Virtue were described as "provocateurs" and "blood-sucking vampires."

34 Virtue had recruited a number of center-right conservatives without backgrounds in Welfare in an effort to demonstrate that it was indeed a new party. Additionally, three female intellectuals were invited onto the party's governing board, a move that would have been foreign to the Welfare Party. The presence of women in leadership positions helped to moderate the party's image. Oya Akgönenç, for example, asserted that she never felt pressure from other party leaders to wear a headscarf, and actively sought to portray the party as simply a center-right, conservative party (author's interview, May 2002).

35 Erbakan had argued that the party's electoral disappointment was a result of its increased moderation and compromise with the establishment, but Gül and Erdoğan made the opposite case. They asserted that Erbakan's style of leadership was increasingly out of touch with the Turkish electorate, and argued that Virtue should redefine itself as a contemporary political group with internal party democracy and European-style sensitivities. In the conference's balloting for party leadership, Kutan managed to retain control of the party, but with an unconvincing margin of 633 delegates to Gül's 521. The success of the reformists sent a clear message to Erbakan, who now saw them as a real threat to the party.

36 See Birand (2000).

37 The party's application was submitted on a Friday (the Islamic holy day), echoing its religious roots.

38 A third centrist religious party was also in the works, to be led by former Virtue mayor of Ankara, Melih Gökçek.

39 Having served his prison term and with a recent court ruling allowing him to again participate in party politics, Tayyip Erdoğan took the helm of the new party, hoping to benefit from his reputation as the honest mayor of Istanbul on the national stage. In July 2000, the Constitutional Court ruled that Erdoğan could legally head a political party, although the legality of him holding any subsequent political office because of his prior conviction remained in doubt.

40 For initial reaction, see Belovacikli (2001).

41 Some have claimed that the internal wires in the design resemble a Qur'an stand, thus reflecting the party's religious roots (Milliyet 2001).

42 During the early stages of the American-led attack on the Taliban in Afghanistan, for example, Kutan marked himself as more anti-American than Erdoğan. Although the AKP publicly expressed concerns over Afghan civilian casualties and foreign intervention in the conflict, Felicity openly questioned the legitimacy of the intervention. The party also supported aggressive anti-Israeli rallies in Istanbul in Spring 2002.

43 The court was now required to examine how central any anti-constitutional behavior was to the party organization, rather than closing it because of the actions of a few not directly implicated in party leadership. Provisions were also created that made it possible to give a party a judicial warning and remove government financial assistance without full party closure, if the court deemed it necessary.

44 Author's interview with Chief Justice of the Turkish Constitutional Court, Haşim Kılıç (June 2002).

45 DYP won 9.5% and ANAP won 5% of the vote.

46 Author's interview with Abdullah Gül, former Vice Chairman of the Virtue Party, April 2002.

47 Not including support for the AKP in 2002, which is treated as somewhat distinct from support for the previous Islamically oriented parties.

48 For example, Tünceli, a small mountainous province in Eastern Anatolia, has much lower levels of support for Islamists than its neighbors because of a high concentration of the minority Alevi sect in that province.

49 These attributes of provinces with a high percentage of Islamist votes were highlighted in multiple interviews with Turkish social scientists, bureaucrats, and politicians from a wide variety of parties. Politicians from Islamist parties, by contrast, usually explained high levels of support from these provinces by either their moral culture or frustration with the state.

50 As measured with a variable composed of fertility rates and the percent of marriages ending in divorce. Average number of children per woman is divided by a weighted divorce as percent of marriage variable. (United Nations Development Program 1997).

51 Mountainous in the Turkish context is defined as over approximately 1,500 meters.

52 For more discussion of the impact of republican reform, see Vertigans (2003), pp. 41–49.

53 Indeed, electoral support for Islamist parties is comparatively high during these periods, with the exception of the early 1980s after the military coup, when Erbakan was directly banned from politics and Islamist support largely went to the right-wing ANAP.

54 Feride Acar (1987), as reported in Howe (2000:15)
55 *Statistical Yearbook of Turkey*, selected years 1975–2000.
56 *Statistical Yearbook of Turkey*, selected years 1975–2000.
57 Growth as measured between the years 1984 and 2000.
58 *Statistical Yearbook of Turkey*, selected years 1975–2000.
59 A general disconnect between the NSP vote in the local and national elections during this period appears to be the result of a lack of political institutionalization at the provincial level, which was remedied over time.
60 Note that in the statistical models presented in Table 5.2 distance from Istanbul does not show a positive correlation with Islamist voting when mountainous provinces are included in the model. Rather, a slight negative correlation with distance from Istanbul suggests that some of the far Eastern, but mountainous, provinces are voting for Islamists less than the more centrally located mountainous provinces.
61 *Statistical Yearbook of Turkey*, selected years 1975–2000.
62 Inflation rates do not vary significantly across the country, and the Istanbul rate is used as a representative urban inflation rate.
63 These included signing a military cooperation deal with Israel, postponing negotiation on the civil conflict in the Southeast, and supporting increased cooperation with Europe. An independent foreign policy initiative by Erbakan, in which he visited Iran and Libya, backfired when he was publicly berated by Libya's Colonel Qaddafi for Turkey's Middle East and Kurdish policies.
64 This impact is similar to the one chronicled by Przeworski and Sprague (1986) in their history of electoral socialism. They note in *Paper Stones* that "socialism cannot be achieved without participation in democratic institutions but participation erodes the will for socialism" (p. 2). Likewise, the participation of Christian political parties in European democracy has affected church power, as chronicled by Kalyvas (1996).

## 6 WHEN ISLAM DEFINES POLITICS

1 Original text in *al-Asala*, no. 65–66, January–February 1979, pp. 59–67. Extracts cited by Lamchichi 1992:63.
2 For example, the Islamist parties of MSP and al-Nahda won 10% and 3% of the vote, respectively, in the 2007 legislative elections.
3 Numbers of dead during this period range from French reports of several hundred thousand to 1.5 million in other accounts. See Noyon (2003).
4 See Horne (1978) for an extensive description of the conflict and Quandt (1998) on the violent political culture argument.
5 Islam was included as an essential identifier in the key slogan of Algerian nationalism: "L'Islam est notre religion, l'Arabe est notre langue, l'Algérie est notre patrie."
6 Lamchichi (1992), pp. 67–68.
7 Noyon (2003), pp. 113–114.
8 Soltani (1974).
9 Noyon (2003), p. 117.
10 Lamchichi (1992), pp. 68–69.
11 Université Emir Abd al-Kader des Sciences Islamiques.

12 Tlemcani (1986), p. 205.
13 Lamchichi (1992), p. 66.
14 In Arabic: *al-Jabha al-Wataniyya li al-Inqadh*.
15 Lamchichi (1992), pp. 73–75.
16 Lamchichi (1992), p. 101.
17 The FLN received about 1.6 million votes to the 3.3 million cast for the FIS. Under the electoral system, a majority of votes was required to capture a seat; for seats in which no candidate takes a majority, run-off elections were to be held.
18 For discussion, see Noyon (2003), pp. 126–27.
19 Noyon (2003), pp. 128–129.
20 Examples would be Cheikh Sahnoun and Abdellatif Ben Ali al-Soltani; Soltani's funeral in 1984 was occasion for a large Islamist demonstration. See Lamchichi (1992).
21 Al-Qiyam published the influential Revue de l'éducation musulmane (Majallat al-Tadhib al-Islami).
22 Lamchichi (1992), pp. 104–106.
23 For discussion, see Willis (1996), pp. 164–167, and Lamchichi (1992), pp. 106–108.
24 Yacoubian (2002), p. 12.
25 Noyon (2003), pp. 120–125.
26 Ruedy (1992), p. 242.
27 Although there was some real disillusionment from former FIS voters at the militant tactics used by the Islamist groups throughout the 1990s, given low voter turnouts in these elections it is more likely that most of the decline in support for Islamist parties is due to the withdrawal of former voters from participation in an electoral regime in which the FIS remains banned.
28 Willis (1996), p. 135.
29 Lamchichi (1992), p. 49.
30 See Tessler (1997) for a good example of this type of political economy analysis of the Algerian Islamist movement.
31 See Lamchichi (1992) for an example of this argument.
32 Noyon (2003), p. 116.
33 Tlemcani (1986), p. 196.
34 As cited in Tlemcani (1986), p. 197.
35 Bennoune (1988), pp. 220–229. Cited in Ruedy (1992), p. 227.
36 Tlemcani (1986), p. 206.
37 Tlemcani (1986), pp. 196–197.
38 Noyon (2003), p. 122.
39 Lamchichi (1992), pp. 46–47.
40 Noyon (2003), pp. 122–123.
41 For a discussion of the wartime political economy, see Martinez (1998, 2000).

## 7 CONCLUSION

1 In prominent works such as Olivier Roy's *The Failure of Political Islam* (1994) and Gilles Kepel's magesterial survey *Jihad* (2002).
2 One need look no farther than Geertz (1968) for examples of how Islam is practiced differently in countries separated by extensive geography.

3 The story of Musa Shanib's political development is extensively discussed in Derluguian (2005).
4 As discussed in Juan Diez Medrano (1995).

## EPILOGUE

1 Late 2010 in the case of Tunisia.
2 For further discussion, see Mecham (2014), from which this section borrows some arguments.
3 Kirkpatrick (2011).
4 The Freedom and Justice Party won 213 of the 235 seats won by its broader coalition of parties, the Democratic Alliance for Egypt. Al-Nour won 107 of the 123 seats won by the Islamist Bloc, which it led.

# Index